# DCE/RPC over SMB

## *Samba and Windows NT® Domain Internals*

Luke Kenneth Casson Leighton

MACMILLAN
TECHNICAL
PUBLISHING
U·S·A

# DCE/RPC over SMB

## Samba and Windows NT® Domain Internals

Luke Kenneth Casson Leighton

International Standard Book Number: 1-57870-150-3

Library of Congress Catalog Card Number: 99-63587

Printed in the United States of America

First Printing: December, 1999

03  02  01  00  99        7  6  5  4  3  2  1

Interpretation of the printing code: The rightmost double-
digit number is the year of the book's printing; the rightmost single-digit number is the number of the book's
printing. For example, the printing code 99-1 shows
that the first printing of the book occurred in 1999.

## Trademarks

## Warning and Disclaimer

**Publisher**
*David Dwyer*

**Executive Editor**
*Laurie Petrycki*

**Acquisitions Editor**
*Katie Purdum*

**Product Marketing Manager**
*Stephanie Layton*

**Managing Editor**
*Sarah Kearns*

**Development Editor**
*Allison Beaumont Johnson*

**Project Editor**
*John Rahm*

**Copy Editor**
*Margo Catts*

**Technical Reviewers**
*Matt Chapman*
*Gerald Carter*
*Andre Frech*
*Chris Hertel*
*Jean François Micouleau*
*Michael H. Warfield*

**Indexer**
*Cheryl Lenser*

**Compositors**
*Gina Rexrode*
*Wil Cruz*

## About the Author

**Luke Kenneth Casson Leighton** joined ISS in 1998 as a Senior Network Engineer. He joined the Atlanta team after contracting for ISS Brussels. As a Senior Network Engineer, Luke is involved in the analysis of Windows NT networks. Luke is also a member of the ISS X-Force, a senior research and development team of security experts dedicated to understanding, documenting, and coding new vulnerability checks and tests, attack signatures, and solutions to global security issues.

X-Force regularly incorporates these discoveries in new versions of ISS' SAFEsuite=AE products, enabling them to proactively protect against some vulnerabilities and attacks even before hackers and intruders discover them. X-Force also maintains the industry's most comprehensive online knowledge base for rapid look up of information on hundreds of risks and threats.

Prior to joining ISS, Luke was a Software Engineer for Pi Technology UK Ltd. Pi Technology produces Automotive Software for Diesel Engines. This includes Engine Calibration, Engine and Vehicle Simulation, Diesel truck Data logging, and Fleet Management. Pi Technology's customers include Detroit Diesel; Perkins and Ford.

Luke has been a member of the Samba Team since July, 1996. His work in Network-Reverse-Engineering undocumented Microsoft Network Protocols has assisted Microsoft in documenting their protocols and improving the reliability and security of their flagship operating system, Windows NT.

Luke holds a BEng (honors) degree in Theory of Computing from Imperial College in London.

# About the Technical Reviewers

**Matt Chapman** is no stranger to decoding network protocols. As a member of the Samba Team, working on Samba (a popular Open Source CIFS suite), he has been involved in developing a number of new features including LDAP integration and BDC support. Matt has been involved in computing support at the University of New South Wales, as well as independent consulting. Aside from network reverse-engineering, his interests include security and cryptography.

**Gerald Carter** has been a member of the Samba Team since 1998. However, he has been maintaining Samba servers for the past four years. Currently employed as a network manager by the College of Engineering at Auburn University, Auburn, AL, Gerald maintains over 700 PCs running a melting pot of Microsoft operating systems and 30+ Solaris 2.x servers running Samba. He recently was the lead author of *Teach Yourself Samba in 24 Hours* by Sams Publishing. In addition to teaching tutorials on administering Samba servers, he often writes freelance articles on UNIX and Windows NT integration for various web-based magazines.

**Andre Frech** is a Computer Security Researcher for Internet Security Systems.

**Chris Hertel** is a Network Design Engineer at the University of Minnesota. He is a member of the Samba Team, and is working on the creation of an Open Source SMB implementation in Java as a member of the jCIFS Team. Chris is also a consistently average foil fencer and a consistently above-average husband and father of two.

**Jean François Micouleau** is a network manager currently employed by a French company in the South West of France. He has been using Samba since early 1995 and became an active Samba developer for 2 years. He started writing software in the Sinclair ZX-81 days and networking computers with Novell NetWare 2.2. Jean François can be reached at jfm@samba.org.

**Michael H. Warfield** is a security researcher and applications developer who has been involved with UNIX for over 15 years and used Linux both professionally and personally for over 5 years. He's one of the founders of the Atlanta Linux Enthusiasts and a contributor to several Open Source development projects.

# Overview

# Table of Contents

This book was written using vi and yodl. No Graphical User Interfaces were used or harmed during the writing of this book. There are therefore no pretty pictures in it, so feel free to draw your own.

# Preface

The NT Domains for Unix project started in earnest in July 1997 with some modifications to Samba made by Paul Ashton and the author, Luke K. C. Leighton. There was much celebration when we first successfully logged on to a Samba server from a Windows NT Workstation. In the next few days, we began to realise exactly how much work was going to be needed to complete the task of providing full Windows NT Domain interoperability.

From August 1997 to January 1998, the author carried out an intense study of Windows NT Workstation and Server interaction, identifying the network data and creating code that was capable of fooling one Windows NT host into thinking it was talking to another Windows NT host. Existing documentation, such as the X-Open DCE/RPC specifications, was deliberately avoided at this stage of the project.

Several people joined in to help, as is the way with Open Source projects. Some people, such as Anders Blomdell, simply ran a test every working day for about three months to keep an eye on the author's erratic development style. Jean-Francois Micouleau became interested in what Samba could do and decided to take on a major section of code: Windows NT Printing. Jerry Carter decided to start documenting how to get around some of the problems associated with using early versions of the Samba Domains code. Matthew Chapman became involved with the project later on and started to make significant improvements to its functionality across the board, including Primary / Backup Domain Controller synchronisation. It has been two and a half years so far, and the end is not in sight, even with the addition of new Samba Team members Matthew, Jean-Francois, and Jerry.

Many Samba-based sites have decided to stick with Samba because, despite the difficulties occasionally experienced by some Network Administrators and the amount of effort needed to get round some of the limitations associated with Samba as a Primary Domain Controller, these difficulties are perceived to be infinitely preferable to using Windows NT Server for the same role. Some University Network Administrators rolled out very early versions of the Samba Domains project into production at the start of the 1998 academic year, they needed it that badly.

At the LISA NT August 98 conference, the author was approached by Macmillan Technical Publishing. As there was no detailed, published documentation available on how Windows NT Domains work, this book was asking to be written. There was always the nagging concern that Microsoft may decide to bring out something that reduces the book's role, such as Windows 2000 (to which this book is still significant as MSRPC is heavily entrenched in NT Technology) or their own documentation on the subject.

So, the book was written taking this into account, attempting to widen the audience. For example, cross-referencing the Network traffic with official Microsoft Documentation (MSDN) makes it useful to Win32 programmers.

Adding example IDL function templates makes it useful to DCOM developers. An evaluation of each service makes it useful to people involved with Network Security.

So, there is still much left to do; however, there is enough material to make this book worthwhile. Regarding the style of this book, I have read reference books that refer the reader to sections that refer the reader to other sections, and hated it. I chose instead to repeat information and acronym definitions. I hope that you will use this book as a reference guide instead of reading it end-to-end.

Best Regards,
Luke Kenneth Casson Leighton

## Dedication

*To my father for his intuition and encouragement.*

## Acknowledgments

I'd like to thank the following people for their hard work and dedication on this project:

Samba Team
Internet Security Systems, Inc.
X-Force Research
Sushanth Rai
Seiichi Tatsukawa

John Rahm and Kristy Dawson for their last minute help.

Special thanks goes to Allison Johnson, who worked through a hurricane to meet her final deadline.

## Tell Us What You Think!

As the reader of this book, *you* are our most important critic and commentator. We value your opinion and want to know what we're doing right, what we could do better, what areas you'd like to see us publish in, and any other words of wisdom you're willing to pass our way.

As the Executive Editor for the Open Source team at MTP, I welcome your comments. You can fax, email, or write me directly to let me know what you did or didn't like about this book—as well as what we can do to make our books stronger.

*Please note that I cannot help you with technical problems related to the topic of this book, and that due to the high volume of mail I receive, I might not be able to reply to every message.*

When you write, please be sure to include this book's title and author, as well as your name and phone or fax number. I will carefully review your comments and share them with the author and editors who worked on the book.

| | |
|---|---|
| Fax: | 317-581-4663 |
| Email: | newriders@mcp.com |
| Mail: | Laurie Petrycki |
| | Executive Editor |
| | Linux/Open Source |
| | MTP |
| | 201 West 103rd Street |
| | Indianapolis, IN 46290 USA |

# *Introduction*

Windows NT and Unix. Different systems—often rivals. Samba
brings them together. By providing capabilities normally found only in
Microsoft's proprietary implementation of DCE/RPC (which they call
MSRPC), Samba is being made to look like Windows NT 3.51 and
4.0 Server and Workstation and is merging the Unix and NT worlds.
This book describes the services that have been decoded through the
development of Samba:

- Running User Manager for Domains
- Running Server Manager for Domains
- Providing Primary Domain Controller login services
- Implementing Access Control List (ACL) file permissions from
  Explorer and File Manager
- Administering both Windows NT and Samba Servers from a Unix
  command line through a Samba utility called *rpcclient*

Samba started life as a replacement for DEC's Pathworks Server
because Pathworks was not available for Sun Microsystems Servers. It
turned out that this very early version of Samba was also compatible
with Windows for Workgroups. Since that time, Samba has been
extended to be compatible with Windows 95 and now Windows NT
3.51 and 4.0. Its performance outstrips all competition on equivalent
hardware. Current and development versions are now beginning to
make inroads into NT Domain environments, in businesses and uni-
versities alike, replacing NT Domain Controllers. The users do not
even notice because the reliability is so much better.

DCE/RPC started life with Apollo Inc. as Network Computing
Architecture. The requirement to make NCA work over TCP/IP and
DECNET resulted in a new version, which was submitted to the Open
Systems Foundation as DCE/RPC. This occurred around the time
Apollo was acquired by Hewlett Packard. Paul Leach, one of the

co-founders of Apollo and DCE/RPC, then went to work for
Microsoft. It is, therefore, no coincidence that Microsoft uses
DCE/RPC so comprehensively for Remote Administration of its
Servers.

DCE/RPC over SMB is used in all versions of Windows NT at all
levels. All the administrative programs (such as Performance Monitor,
Server Manager for Domains, and Event Log) that allow remote
configuration or access to Windows NT use DCE/RPC over SMB.
Microsoft's Exchange Server uses DCE/RPC. DCOM (Distributed
Common Object Model) is an extended form of DCE/RPC (see
http://www.microsoft.com/com/dcom.asp). It's everywhere: there are
hundreds of RPC calls being used, and no one knows what they
really look like!

Although it cannot claim to be authoritative, this book describes
how DCE/RPC over SMB has been implemented in Samba, and the
minimum level of services required to allow interoperability with
Windows NT. Without authoritative information from Microsoft
(the designer of these services), there are going to be gaps. If someone
uses a program or feature not normally available (such as KIX32.EXE
or Terminal Server Edition), or if Microsoft issues a new hotfix
or Service Pack, it may use previously unknown DCE/RPC calls or
unknown structures in an existing call. This may reveal that a
previous interpretation was incomplete (hey, who said network-
reverse-engineering was boring).

The reader is advised, for full information on DCF/RPC, to refer
to X-Open DCE/RPC Specifications (http://www.opengroup.org/dce),
and for information on the CIFS (SMB) protocol to Microsoft CIFS
Documentation (ftp://ftp.microsoft.com/developr/drg/CIFS). At the
time of writing, no documentation is known to be published on how
Microsoft has provided DCE/RPC services over SMB, including how
they make secure, encrypted, or authenticated DCE/RPC calls, which
use the NTLM-v1 Secure Service Provider protocol. This book
describes NTLM Secure Service Provider over DCE/RPC at a
minimal level.

It is assumed that the reader is familiar with two things:
NetMonitor on NT (**NETMON.EXE**), which is an almost essential
tool for understanding the links between SMB and DCE/RPC, and the
configuration of Samba itself, particularly on how to set debug log
levels. Throughout this book, illustrations of NetMonitor output are
shown. Where NetMonitor does not provide useful information
(typically because the DCE/RPC call is encrypted, such as for changing User passwords and managing User accounts), Samba internal
debug output will be shown.

Some readers may find that this book reminds them of the "Microsoft Developer Network" documentation (a key phrase to search for: "Net Functions"). This is because some of the functions find their way directly over-the-wire in DCE/RPC calls (for example, **LookupAccountName**). Therefore, you can use the MSDN documentation and its detailed, authoritative (but sometimes incomplete) description of functions and data structures to help build your understanding of their DCE/RPC counterparts, including the use of NTLM-v1 Secure Service Provider. Equally, where MSDN functions are missing, you can deduce what they would look like by examining their DCE/RPC counterparts (which have been empirically verified to work in Samba). A complementary arrangement.

There will also be some information regarding the low-level interaction of the Windows NT security subsystems—the Local Security Authority and one of its incantations (MSV1_0.DLL), along with the SAM database that it accesses (SAMSRV.DLL). This cannot be avoided: anyone wishing to emulate NT Primary Domain Controller functionality must be aware of the workings and effects of these components.

By following the series of DCE/RPC function calls made (by viewing packet traces) when certain User actions are performed (such as logging in to a Domain) and by examining what cursory information is available from MSDN and related sources, the internal workings of Windows NT's security subsystems can be deduced.

So, whether you are a Windows NT or Unix Administrator who would like to know more about those hex bytes on your network that no one wants to explain; a hacker or an anti-hacker, each interested in security issues; a geek like the author, attracted to new information as moths are to light; a Samba devotee looking for clues; an SMB developer looking for clues; or a Microsoft MSDN/Win32 developer also looking for clues, read on!

The chapters in this book break down the subject matter as described here:

- Chapter 1: This chapter discusses DCE/RPC and how it is transferred over SMB. It covers how function calls are converted to network data, as well as how to encrypt DCE/RPC using NTLM Secure Service Provider.

- Chapter 2: This chapter is an overview of how Windows NT's internal security components fit together. Understanding this makes it easier to appreciate what's happening on the wire.

- Chapter 3: This chapter covers the Local Security Authority calls. These calls represent the first necessary steps to providing NT Domain functionality (as either a Domain Controller or a member of a Domain).

- Chapter 4: This chapter covers Windows NT login calls. These calls are the next step in the NT Domain functionality. The Credential Chain attached to each stage is described (as are its weaknesses). The Credential Chain ensures that the User and Workstation cannot be attacked.

- Chapter 5: This chapter covers Windows NT Administration. This is a mixed bag of tricks that includes being able to view files, shares, and sessions that are currently open on a Server, and also how to identify a host's role in a Domain (for example, whether it's a Domain Controller).

- Chapter 6: This chapter covers Windows NT Registry. It describes how the Registry works over-the-wire: how to add, modify, and delete keys and values including Access Control Lists. It's nothing exciting, particularly if you've used the standard MSDN Registry API.

- Chapter 7: This chapter covers Windows NT Service Control Manager. It describes how the Service Control Manager works over-the-wire, such as how to view services running on a remote host. Some of the enumeration functions are a little bit tricky, but other than that, it's standard stuff.

- Chapter 8: This chapter covers Windows NT SAM Database Management. It covers how to add, view, modify, and delete Users and Groups from an NT Domain, as well as some of the security problems associated with this. It discusses how these undocumented functions map to the MSDN API calls. This chapter includes everything about remote SAM database management that Microsoft doesn't want you to know about or use, and why. It's a fascinating (and far too large) chapter.

- Chapter 9: This chapter covers the NT Event Log, including what the Event Viewer does, its own calls, and some Registry access.

- Appendix A: Samba Source Code. The GNU Public License (GPL). Extracts from Samba's source files that contain Really Useful Information. Read the GPL *before* examining these extracts.

- Appendix B: Windows NT Password and Authentication Methods. Formal definitions of some of the algorithms used in Windows NT for authentication verification and authentication token encryption.

# DCE/RPC over SMB

This chapter describes DCE/RPC and how it is transferred over SMB. Normally, connection-less (datagram-based) DCE/RPC is transferred over UDP, and connection-orientated (stream-based) DCE/RPC is transferred over TCP. The DCE/RPC specifications describe how to use other transports such as named pipes, and this is what Microsoft has chosen to do: implement DCE/RPC using SMB named pipes as an additional transport.

This book has been written from the experiences of the Network Reverse Engineering project to develop Windows NT Domains capability in Samba. This project was *not* done with reference to any official DCE/RPC documentation, but from Network Monitor traces. Therefore the viewpoint is going to be a bit strange to people who are familiar with DCE/RPC, and may give a misleading impression to first-time readers.

As Samba is progressing, the developers are learning more about Real DCE/RPC. This book therefore uses some of the official DCE/RPC terminology, but not all of it. The purpose of this chapter is to describe the worlds *in between* DCE/RPC and SMB, and is not intended to be an authority on either. There are, however, brief sections on each of these areas where they have been observed, in Network traffic analysis, to be relevant. These sections are intended to help the reader understand their relationship.

## 1.1: What, Why, and How?

### 1.1.1: What is DCE/RPC?

DCE/RPC stands for "Distributed Computing Environment Remote Procedure Call." A specification was submitted to The Open Systems Foundation as part of the OSF-DCE suite by Hewlett Packard/Apollo and Digital Equipment Corp. DCE/RPC was originally developed as "Network Computing Architecture" (NCA) RPC by Apollo Computer Inc., as part of their Network Computing System (NCS) product. NCA Version 1.x was only supported on connection-less (datagram) transports. There was a demand to run NCS over DECnet, so Apollo started working with DEC on NCA version 2.0, and this became DCE/RPC when it was submitted to the OSF. OSF-DCE is a suite of distributed computing services including security and naming, which uses DCE/RPC for interprocess communication.

DCE/RPC dates back to the times when the phrase "Object-Orientated" was still just a lowly meme associated with well-known languages such as SmallTalk. Unfortunately, the licensing arrangement for DCE/RPC was prohibitive for Microsoft's mass-market usage, so they implemented it themselves. Paul Leach, a founder of Apollo and NCS architect, started work with Microsoft after HP acquired Apollo.

DCE/RPC is different from Sun Microsystems' ONC/RPC. DCE/RPC allows you to:

- Make function calls on a local or a remote computer as if the function call were a local function.

- Associate a set of functions together, and provides revision control of / upgrading of / negotiation for the use of a complete set of functions.

- Authenticate a user prior to use of the set of functions.

- Encrypt the function parameters transparently.

DCE/RPC is sent over named pipes, which are sent over SMB. For those people familiar with DCE/RPC it should be pointed out that these have nothing to do with DCE/RPC IDL pipes. The named pipe names are indicative of the purpose of the function group, as in the following examples:

- \PIPE\NETLOGON provides interactive and pass-through authentication services.

- \PIPE\lsarpc provides access to the *Local Security Authority*.

- \PIPE\samr provides access to and management of the *Security Accounts Manager* database.

- \PIPE\srvsvc provides access to and management of a Workstation's services.

These interfaces also have unique DCE/RPC identifiers (16 bytes) and version numbers (2 bytes), which are informative to hex-crunchers such as computers and geeks, and are known in DCE/RPC terminology as *Abstract Identifiers*. Each interface also has an associated "endpoint," which is a protocol-dependent string specifying how the interface can be contacted. For DCE/RPC over SMB, this is of the form **ncacn_np:***server_name***\\pipe\\***pipe_name*. This book refers, for easy reading, to interfaces by the "named pipe" name rather than the abstract identifier, such as **\PIPE\NETLOGON** rather than UUID 12345678-1234-ABCD-EF00-01234567CFFB version 1. An endpoint mapper is not needed on DCE/RPC over SMB because the endpoint name contains sufficient information to connect directly to the service. By contrast, DCE/RPC over TCP or UDP requires a connection to the endpoint mapper first to find out further information, such as the port number on which the service is running.

The capability to group functions together provides a consistent API, for example in Microsoft's Developer documentation, the **NetServer***, **NetWksta***, and **Lsa*** functions. Also, developers who are used to COM and DCOM will notice that the revision control negotiation available in DCE/RPC makes it a perfect candidate for transferring DCOM calls. COM interfaces can be upgraded but they *must* support previous versions of the interface for backward-compatibility. This is exactly what DCE/RPC provides.

For further inside information on DCOM, a book by Dr. Richard Grimes, *DCOM Programming* (ISBN 1-861000-60-X), describes to experienced C++ Windows programmers how to use DCOM. Chapter 6 of Dr. Grimes' book describes "DCOM Under the Hood." The packet traces in it show DCE/RPC version 5.0 (and it looks like it's connection-less too). This chapter also describes version 5.0, however over SMB only connection-orientated DCE/RPC has been observed, so that is what is described in this book.

Additionally, Microsoft's web site contains information on DCOM. Currently, links can be referenced from `http://www.microsoft.com/com`. The use of DCE/RPC in DCOM has minor extensions that make it incompatible with other implementations of DCE/RPC.

Additionally, the Microsoft Developer Network (MSDN) documentation contains complete documentation on DCE/RPC, including how it works, how it is implemented, annotated example client/server applications, and so on. By contrast, this chapter covers DCE/RPC from the perspective of how it appears over-the-wire.

## 1.1.2: How Is DCE/RPC Implemented?

A full specification can be found at The Open Group (TOG), formerly known as The X-Open Group. In a nutshell, a function call (identified uniquely over-the-wire by an **Opcode** or **Opnum,** a Universally Unique Identifier (UUID), and a revision number), consists of a comma-separated list of data structures. DCE/RPC is a mechanism to:

- Choose an acceptable and common set of functions for both Client and Server to use and a data format for the transfer of the function call arguments. The data format observed to be negotiated is always Network Data Representation (NDR), in DCE/RPC terminology.
- Authenticate the caller, if required.
- Negotiate security, if required.
- Identify function names by associating an Operation Code (Opnum), UUID, and interface revision number with each function.
- "Flatten" data structures in a function call into a continuous data stream. The data stream is passed to a remote computer service, which...
- "Unpacks" this stream, makes the local function call, then...
- "Flattens" the results, and passes them back to the caller. The caller then...
- "Unpacks" this stream, and hands the results to the original function call. The flattening and unpacking described here is known as *marshalling* and *unmarshalling*, in DCE/RPC terminology.

In certain instances, the caller (or the developer using the functions) may not ever be aware that all of this has occurred. Why should they? It's just a function call. They might notice that the function call is a bit slow, but computers are getting faster all the time, right?

### 1.1.3: What Is SMB?

SMB stands for "Common Internet File System." Actually, it stands for "Server Message Block," but in mid-1996 Microsoft decided that it would be better if the protocol had the word "Internet" in it. SMB started life as a DOS Interrupt 21 interface (file/directory services for DOS) over-the-wire. IBM, Xenix, Microsoft, and the Open Group (TOG) have all had a crack at it. IBM introduced the LANMAN 1.0 flavour; Xenix (which used to be Microsoft Unix before Microsoft sold it to the Santa Cruz Operation) introduced the XENIX CORE flavour; Microsoft introduced Windows NT 64-bit file operations and more in LANMAN 0.12.

SMB has expanded like bacteria over the surface of an unwashed, unloved computer from the early 1980s, and it is still in use: all major CIFS vendors are still compatible with MSCLIENT 3.0 (SMB file/print services over TCP/IP, for DOS). SMB is best known for providing File, Print, and Login services for Windows.

As SMB is the original name, it is used in this book to refer to the protocol. Occasionally, CIFS is used. The name change is purely a Cosmetic Marketing Change and there is no actual difference in the protocol as a result of this. Maybe it's that hard-core developers use the name SMB, whilst wimps bottle out and use the word that is pronounced "siffs."

### 1.1.3.1: SMB File Shares
File and Print Services are provided via Shares, and are accessed, from Windows, via the following methods:

- NET.EXE USE <drive_letter>: \\<server_name>\<<share_name>
- Start | Run | \\<server_name>\<share_name>
- Run **EXPLORER.EXE**; select "Network Neighbourhood"; select a server; select a share.
- From the Desktop icon, select "Network Neighbourhood", and so forth.

You can access files and directories remotely over a File Share. Some hidden shares, named **C$** and **ADMIN$**, are accessible to only Administrators. None of these shares is relevant to DCE/RPC: the only reason they are mentioned here is for completeness.

### 1.1.3.2: SMB IPC$ Share
Printers, Login, and other services are provided using *Inter-Process Communication*, which is a special share called **IPC$**. This share provides a means to communicate LanManager functions, some of which are documented on the Microsoft CIFS site. It also serves as a transport for DCE/RPC functions, none of which are documented by Microsoft.

Some functions, whether LanManager or DCE/RPC, require access privileges, which, except for a few specific functions in Windows NT 5, Windows NT grants using internally hard-coded Access Control Lists (Security Descriptors). Windows NT 5 has started to add a system whereby the Security Descriptors for certain functions are read from the Registry. Although a user is not normally expected to know this at a detailed level, an MSDN developer or SMB Client or Server implementor may be expected to cater for such access rights being denied or granted.

Some LanManager functionality is duplicated and also provided by functions that are transferred using DCE/RPC methodology. For example, the MSDN documented API **NetShareEnum** call is provided in both. The LanManager call over-the-wire will be used exclusively by Windows 95, or by Windows NT if it determines that the target system does not support DCE/RPC—a non-trivial task in and of itself. The significant difference in capability between LanManager and DCE/RPC is that LanManager calls cannot be encrypted: the SMB protocol has no capability to support **IPC$** encryption.

### 1.1.4: Why DCE/RPC over SMB?

Why would anyone want to implement DCE/RPC, and specifically, why over SMB? SMB uses NetBIOS, a transport-independent protocol that is available over TCP/IP, IPX/SPX, and NETBEUI. This implies that you can run multiple services and multiple clients, each under or connecting to a different NetBIOS name, on any transport on any machine—including the same machine. Therefore, anything that runs over NetBIOS is going to gain that advantage. As an example, try running "User Manager for Domains" from a Windows NT Administrative Workstation that has only the NETBEUI transport on it. Assuming that the Primary Domain Controller also has NETBEUI, this will work.

Additionally, SMB provides per-user authentication (**SMBsessionsetupX** in user-level security mode). AS DCE/RPC calls can be made over authenticated SMB connections, the DCE/RPC calls also become "authenticated," due to the way that the Windows NT kernel works. Note that this is independent from the authentication mechanism that DCE/RPC itself can use, which overrides authentication provided by its SMB session. MSDN API developers are advised to look up information on the **ImpersonateNamedPipeClient** function. Note also that SMB can provide "anonymous" connections, which in turn implies that any DCE/RPC calls made over such an SMB session will also be unauthenticated.

### 1.1.5: How Is SMB Implemented?

I really don't want to go into this: it's enough of a nightmare for full-time developers to deal with over a period of several months or years, let alone in one sentence. Information on SMB is available from Microsoft's CIFS Documentation, amongst other sources. Usually, and unfortunately, a lot of information on SMB is in developer's heads: developers who, by intuition and by trial and error, are still working out exactly what years of Microsoft programmers haven't needed to tell anyone.

To Microsoft's credit, they have made a significant effort in attempting to document the SMB protocol. In return, a large number of independent vendors have successfully implemented SMB Clients and Servers. The result of this is better documentation and an improvement in the quality, security, and reliability of everyone's products.

## 1.1.6: How Is DCE/RPC Implemented over SMB?

Without going into too much detail at this stage, contrary to appearances:

- An SMB connection is made, starting with **SMBsessionsetupX**, which can either be a NULL session (anonymous) or an authenticated session (which requires a User name, Domain name, and password).

- An **SMBtconX** is sent, which connects to **IPC$**. This is for *Inter-Process Communication*, and is used for data transfer rather than file transfers.

- **SMBopenX** or **NTSMBCreateX** opens a pipe at the SMB level (for example, **\PIPE\wkssvc**).

- An **SMBtrans** call is made, which makes a DCE/RPC *bind request* and receives a DCE/RPC *bind response*; this confirms that the pipe is open at the DCE/RPC level. Part of this stage can involve negotiation for a secure or encrypted data channel whereupon **SMBreadX** and/or **SMBwriteX** calls will be used to finish off this negotiation, if need be.

- Assuming that the bind process succeeds, individual DCE/RPC *requests* and *responses* are made using **SMBwriteX**, **SMBtrans**, and **SMBreadX** to transfer a function's parameters to the server and to return the modified parameters back to the client.

- Finally, after all DCE/RPC transfers have been made, an **SMBclose** is issued, which shuts down both the DCE/RPC channel and closes the SMB pipe (for example, **\PIPE\wkssvc**).

- Sometimes, the SMB session itself will also be closed, with a **SMBtdis** used to disconnect the **IPC$** share and a **SMBulogoff** used to terminate the SMB session. The NetBIOS session (using TCP, SPX, or NETBEUI) will then be dropped.

### 1.1.7: DCE/RPC Pipes: How Many?

There are numerous DCE/RPC pipes, and with each new set of functionality that is introduced, a new pipe will need to be created. Microsoft and third-party developers can introduce new DCOM and DCE/RPC services at any time. Of course, out-of-the-box Windows NT will not normally have third-party RPC services installed on it, so this book describes some of the default Microsoft services that provide at least the minimum Windows NT Domain and administrative capability.

Although this list of default services is definitely incomplete, those that have been observed to date are as follows, with the UUID (Universal Unique Identifier) and interface version number where known:

- **\PIPE\NETLOGON** 8a885d04-1ceb-11c9-9fe8-08002b104860 (02)
- **\PIPE\NETLOGON** 12345678-1234-abcd-ef00-01234567cffb (01)
- **\PIPE\winreg** 338cd001-2244-31f1-aaaa-900038001003 (01)
- **\PIPE\svcctl** 367abb81-9844-35f1-ad32-98f038001003 (02)
- **\PIPE\lsarpc** 12345678-1234-abcd-ef00-0123456789ab (00)
- **\PIPE\srvsvc** 4b324fc8-1670-01d3-1278-5a47bf6ee188 (03)
- **\PIPE\wkssvc** 6bffd098-a112-3610-9833-46c3f87e345a (01)
- **\PIPE\samr** 12345678-1234-abcd-ef00-0123456789ac (01)
- **\PIPE\spoolss** 12345778-1234-abcd-ef00-0123456789ab (01)
- **\PIPE\atsvc** 1ff70682-0a51-30e8-076d-740be8cee98b (01)
- **\PIPE\browsess**
- **\PIPE\winssvc**
- **\PIPE\winsmgr**

Each pipe contains any number of related functions. As many as sixty have been observed. Some of those functions, at Microsoft's design, may have *Info Levels*. For example, **NetServerGetInfo**, implemented on `ncacn_np:server_name\\pipe\\srvsvc`, has seven such Info Levels:

- 100 SERVER_INFO_100
- 101 SERVER_INFO_101
- 102 SERVER_INFO_102
- 402 SERVER_INFO_402

- **403** SERVER_INFO_403
- **502** SERVER_INFO_502
- **503** SERVER_INFO_503

Each of these represents a request for different levels of detailed information. Examining MSDN documentation, Level 100 is shown to request the "platform id" and the Workstation's name. Level 503, shown here, requests a structure containing 34 items, the meaning of which can only be relevant to rabid Windows NT performance fanatics and SMB developers:

```
typedef struct _SERVER_INFO_503
{
    DWORD       sv503_sessopens;
    DWORD       sv503_sessvcs;
    DWORD       sv503_opensearch;
    DWORD       sv503_sizreqbuf;
    DWORD       sv503_initworkitems;
    DWORD       sv503_maxworkitems;
    DWORD       sv503_rawworkitems;
    DWORD       sv503_irpstacksize;
    DWORD       sv503_maxrawbuflen;
    DWORD       sv503_sessusers;
    DWORD       sv503_sessconns;
    DWORD       sv503_maxpagedmemoryusage;
    DWORD       sv503_maxnonpagedmemoryusage;
    BOOL        sv503_enableforcedlogoff;
    BOOL        sv503_timesource;
    BOOL        sv503_acceptdownlevelapis;
    BOOL        sv503_lmannounce;
    LPTSTR      sv503_domain;
    DWORD       sv503_maxkeepsearch;
    DWORD       sv503_scavtimeout;
    DWORD       sv503_minrcvqueue;
    DWORD       sv503_minfreeworkitems;
    DWORD       sv503_xactmemsize;
    DWORD       sv503_threadpriority;
    DWORD       sv503_maxmpxct;
    DWORD       sv503_oplockbreakwait;
    DWORD       sv503_oplockbreakresponsewait;
    BOOL        sv503_enableoplocks;
    BOOL        sv503_enablefcbopens;
    BOOL        sv503_enableraw;
    BOOL        sv503_enablesharednetdrives;
    DWORD       sv503_minfreeconnections;
    DWORD       sv503_maxfreeconnections;
} SERVER_INFO_503, *PSERVER_INFO_503, *LPSERVER_INFO_503;
```

In other words, you have been warned. You can attempt a full implementation of all the DCE/RPC functions available in Windows NT, but to be honest, you'd be better off negotiating with Microsoft for a full or partial source code license. (Don't forget to ask for the right to use it in your products, and also remember to ask for the all-important security updates.) This is a route that several major Unix Operating Systems vendors have taken.

Or, you can even ask Microsoft for the IDL (Interface Definition Language) files, from which all these DCE/RPC remote function calls are generated. However, you would still need to implement the functionality *behind* these calls. This is a route that at least one large CIFS vendor has successfully taken.

Or, you can attempt, by trial and error and with the assistance of this book, to implement a subset of the functionality you require, by running Windows NT, watching what it does over-the-wire, and then doing the same thing.

Remember, however, that these DCE/RPC services are primarily undocumented. As far as I know, Microsoft has no intention of documenting them, and some of their reasons are good ones. For example, if you stick with the MSDN **Net***API then all the code that you write for Windows NT 3.5 and Windows NT 4.0 will work when Microsoft replaces the underlying API with a new one, for Windows NT 5.0 or any other future version.

A disadvantage or possibly even an advantage to leaving this all undocumented is that alternative implementations can show up weaknesses in other vendors' implementations. This has been demonstrated time and time again on Microsoft's client-side and server-side implementation: approximately one bug every ten weeks has been discovered in Windows NT since the development of Samba DCE/RPC code started in July 1997. Then again, there is a *lot* of code to test against, and by the time this development stabilises both Samba and Windows NT will be excellent, robust products.

## 1.2: SMB Calls Used by DCE/RPC

This section introduces the SMBs used to set up and transfer DCE/RPC traffic. There is very little interaction between the two: one *uses* the other as its transport. This is worthwhile bearing in mind, particularly when large numbers of DCE/RPC Protocol Data Unit (PDU) fragments are being transferred: the show gets a little hairy as limits on SMB transaction sizes are hit, and *parts* of DCE/RPC PDU fragments start to be transferred with *multiple* SMBs.

In Microsoft's implementation, there are occasional instances where bugs bring about *some* inter-dependencies that should not be there;

however, those that have been found have been corrected in later
versions, such as in Service Packs 3 and 4 for Windows NT 4.0.

Windows 95 Clients are known to use a slightly different subset of
SMB to transfer DCE/RPC. At the SMB level, for example, they negotiate the use of **SMBreadraw** and **SMBwriteraw** to transfer large numbers of DCE/RPC PDU fragments rather than use **SMBreadX** and
**SMBwriteX**. This book does not deal with Windows 95. The reader
should be aware, however, that due to the capability of SMB Clients
and Servers to negotiate entire sets of sub-functionality to use; a
flavour of SMB; a set of commands; that the observation of one type
of Client with one type of Server will definitely not show up all
variations. The Unix versions of Windows NT (for example, Advanced
Server for Unix) also throw in a new ball to play with: a reduced
DCE/RPC fragment size, resulting in apparently different client and
server behaviour.

## 1.2.1: SMB OpenX

**SMBopenX** can be used to initiate a DCE/RPC connection. The
DCE/RPC endpoint name for the connection being opened in the
following example by the computer named **FERENGI** is
**ncacn_np:**regent**\\pipe\\**lsarpc.

The request is a standard **SMBopenX** request, with the filename
**\\PIPE\lsarpc** to the computer named **regent**.

```
*************************************************************************
Frame   Time    Src MAC Addr   Dst MAC Addr   Protocol  Description
13      2.789   FERENGI        REGENT         SMB       C open & X

  SMB: C open & X, File = \PIPE\lsarpc (RW -Share Deny None)
     SMB: Command = C open & X
          SMB: Word count = 15
          SMB: Word parameters
          SMB: Next offset = 0x0000
          SMB: Open Flags Summary = 0 (0x0)
          SMB: Open mode = 0x0042
          SMB: Search attributes = 0x0006
          SMB: File Attributes = 0 (0x0)
          SMB: File creation time (sec) = Jan 1, 1970 0:0:0.0
          SMB: Open function = 0x0011
          SMB: File size = 0
          SMB: Open timeout = 0
          SMB: Byte count = 13
          SMB: Byte parameters
          SMB: File name = \PIPE\lsarpc

00030:                          FF 53 4D 42 2D 00        .SMB-.
00040:  00 00 00 08 01 00 00 00 00 00 00 00 00 00 00 00   ................
```

```
00050:  00 00 01 C8 8C 0A 01 88 01 00 0F FF 00 00 00 00   ...............
00060:  00 42 00 06 00 00 00 00 00 00 00 11 00 00 00 00   .B.............
00070:  00 00 00 00 00 00 00 00 00 00 0D 00 5C 50 49 50 45   ..........\PIPE
00080:  5C 6C 73 61 72 70 63 00                           \lsarpc.
```

The response contains an acknowledgement of the connection to the
DCE/RPC endpoint and the SMB file handle that represents this endpoint connection (in the following example, the third word parameter
from offset 0x5f to 0x60). If the Server is too busy, then the connection is refused and the error translated into an appropriate SMB error
code.

```
*****************************************************************************
Frame   Time    Src MAC Addr   Dst MAC Addr   Protocol  Description
14      2.790   REGENT         FERENGI        SMB       R open & X

   SMB: R open & X, FID = 0x4805
      SMB: Command = C open & X
         SMB: Word count = 15
         SMB: Word parameters
         SMB: Next offset = 0x0041
         SMB: File ID (FID) = 18437 (0x4805)
         SMB: File name = \PIPE\lsarpc
         SMB: File Attributes = 0 (0x0)
         SMB: Last modify time (sec) = Jan 1, 1970 0:0:0.0
         SMB: File size = 0
         SMB: Open mode = 0x0000
         SMB: File type = Disk file or directory
         SMB: Device state = 0x0000
         SMB: Action taken = 0x0001
         SMB: Unique file ID = 0x00000000
         SMB: Byte count = 0

00030:                          FF 53 4D 42 2D 00           .SMB-.
00040:  00 00 00 88 01 00 00 00 00 00 00 00 00 00 00 00   ................
00050:  00 00 01 C8 8C 0A 01 88 01 00 0F FF 00 41 00 05   .............A..
00060:  48 00 00 00 00 00 00 00 00 00 00 00 00 00 00 00   H...............
00070:  00 01 00 00 00 00 00 00 00 00 00                  ...........
```

## 1.2.2: Windows NT SMB CreateX

**NTSMBCreateX** can be used to initiate a DCE/RPC connection. The
DCE/RPC endpoint name for the connection being opened in the following example by the computer named **brookfields** is
**ncacn_np:**regent\\**pipe\\**netlogon.

The request is a standard **NTSMBCreateX** request, with the pipe
named **NETLOGON** to the computer named **regent**.

```
*****************************************************************
Frame   Time    Src MAC Addr   Dst MAC Addr   Protocol  Description
```

```
18    6.272  brookfields   REGENT        SMB     C NT create & X, File =
➡\NETLOGON
```

```
  SMB: C NT create & X, File = \NETLOGON
      SMB: SMB Status = Error Success
      SMB: Header: PID = 0x26A0 TID = 0x4006 MID = 0x0040 UID = 0x8002
      SMB: Command = R NT create & X
          SMB: Word count = 24
          SMB: Word parameters
          SMB: Next offset = 0x0000
          SMB: Word count = 24
          SMB: Word parameters
          SMB: Name Length (NT) = 18 (0x12)
          SMB: Create Flags DWord = 0x00000006
          SMB: Root Dir FID = 0x00000000
          SMB: Desired Access = 0x0002019F
          SMB: File Allocation Size = 0x0000000000000000
          SMB: NT File Attributes = 0x00000000
          SMB: File Share Access = 0x00000003
          SMB: Create Disposition = Open:  If exist, Open, else fail
          SMB: Create Options = 0 (0x0)
          SMB: Impersonation Level = 0x00000002
          SMB: Security Flags = 0x01
          SMB: Byte count = 21
          SMB: File name = \NETLOGON
```

```
00030:                             FF 53 4D 42 A2 00     .SMB..
00040:  00 00 00 18 03 80 57 80 00 00 00 00 00 00 00 00   ......W.........
00050:  00 00 06 40 A0 26 02 80 40 00 18 FF 00 00 00 00   ...@.&..@.......
00060:  12 00 06 00 00 00 00 00 00 00 9F 01 02 00 00 00   ...............
00070:  00 00 00 00 00 00 00 00 00 00 03 00 00 00 01 00   ...............
00080:  00 00 00 00 00 00 02 00 00 00 01 15 00 00 5C 00   ..............\.
00090:  4E 00 45 00 54 00 4C 00 4F 00 47 00 4F 00 4E 00   N.E.T.L.O.G.O.N.
000A0:  00 00                                             ..
```

The response contains an acknowledgement of the connection to the
DCE/RPC endpoint and the SMB file handle that represents this endpoint connection (in the following example, the third word parameter
from offset 0x60 to 0x61). The SMB response is used to indicate to
the Client that the Server knows that this is a DCE/RPC endpoint, by
setting the FileType field to Message Mode Named Pipe (0x0002). If
the Server was too busy, then the connection would be refused and the
error translated into an appropriate SMB error code.

```
********************************************************************
Frame   Time    Src MAC Addr   Dst MAC Addr   Protocol  Description
19      6.275   REGENT         brookfields    SMB       R NT create & X, FID =
➡0x1007
```

```
  SMB: R NT create & X, FID = 0x1007
      SMB: SMB Status = Error Success
      SMB: Header: PID = 0x26A0 TID = 0x4006 MID = 0x0040 UID = 0x8002
```

```
SMB: Command = R NT create & X
    SMB: Word count = 34
    SMB: Word parameters
    SMB: Next offset = 0x0067
    SMB: Word count = 34
    SMB: Word parameters
    SMB: Oplock Level = NONE
    SMB: File ID (FID) = 4103 (0x1007)
    SMB: File name = \NETLOGON
    SMB: Create Action = File Opened
    SMB: Creation Time = Jan 1, 1601 0:0:0.0
    SMB: NT Last Access Time = Jan 1, 1601 0:0:0.0
    SMB: Last Write Time = Jan 1, 1601 0:0:0.0
    SMB: Change Time = Jan 1, 1601 0:0:0.0
    SMB: NT File Attributes = 0x00000080
    SMB: File Allocation Size = 0x0000000000001000
    SMB: End of File = 0x0000000000000000
    SMB: File type = Message mode named pipe
    SMB: Device state = 0x05FF
    SMB: Boolean Is Directory = 0 (0x0)

00030:                                  FF 53 4D 42 A2 00          .SMB..
00040:  00 00 00 98 03 80 57 80 00 00 00 00 00 00 00 00   ......W.........
00050:  00 00 06 40 A0 26 02 80 40 00 22 FF 00 67 00 00   ...@.&..@.."..g..
00060:  07 10 01 00 00 00 00 00 00 00 00 00 00 00 00 00   ................
00070:  00 00 00 00 00 00 00 00 00 00 00 00 00 00 00 00   ................
00080:  00 00 00 00 00 00 80 00 00 00 00 10 00 00 00 00   ................
00090:  00 00 00 00 00 00 00 00 00 00 02 00 FF 05 00 00   ................
000A0:  00                                                .
```

## 1.2.3: SMB Trans

**SMBtrans** calls are used to communicate with the DCE/RPC Server. At the SMB level, the calls can be made with four sets of information:

- Transaction data
- Transaction parameters
- Setup parameters
- A name

In the example shown here, the number of **transaction data** bytes is 44, which starts at an offset of 84 bytes from the start of the SMB header. The SMB header starts at offset 0x3A, so the **transaction data** starts at offset 0x8E, which contains the DCE/RPC fragment. The number of **transaction parameters** is zero, so the parameter offset is set (unnecessarily) to 84 bytes. The word count, at offset 0x5A, indicates that there are sixteen 16-bit parameters. Word 14 (at offset 0x75 to 0x76) indicates that there are two **setup parameters,** and these follow at offsets 0x77 to 0x7A. The first **setup parameter** with a value of

0x0026 indicates that this is a DCE/RPC pipe function, and the **second parameter** indicates the file handle associated with the DCE/RPC endpoint opened with an **NTSMBCreateX** or **SMBopenX**. The **name** here is **\PIPE\**, in UNICODE format. It starts at offset 0x7e because the **name** is 4-byte aligned with the start of the SMB header, at offset 0x3A. The **transaction data** is also aligned to a 4-byte boundary (at offset 0x8A), which is why bytes at offsets 0x7B to 0x7D and offsets 0x8B to 0x8D are filled with garbage.

```
************************************************************************
Frame   Time     Src MAC Addr    Dst MAC Addr   Protocol  Description
244     6.661    REGENT          brookfields    MSRPC     c/o RPC Request

 SMB: C transact TransactNmPipe, FID = 0x804
     SMB: SMB Status = Error Success
     SMB: Header: PID = 0x2E00 TID = 0x0800 MID = 0x1B40 UID = 0x0800
     SMB: Command = R transact
         SMB: Word count = 16
         SMB: Word parameters
         SMB: Total parm bytes = 0
         SMB: Total data bytes = 44
         SMB: Max parm bytes = 0
         SMB: Max data bytes = 1024
         SMB: Max setup words = 0 (0x0)
         SMB: Transact Flags Summary = 0 (0x0)
         SMB: Transact timeout = 0 (0x0)
         SMB: Parameter bytes = 0 (0x0)
         SMB: Parameter offset = 84 (0x54)
         SMB: Data bytes = 44 (0x2C)
         SMB: Data offset = 84 (0x54)
         SMB: Max setup words = 2
         SMB: Setup words
         SMB: Pipe function = Transact named pipe (TransactNmPipe)
         SMB: File ID (FID) = 2052 (0x804)
         SMB: File name = \svcctl
         SMB: Byte count = 61
         SMB: Byte parameters
         SMB: File name = \PIPE\
         SMB: Transaction data
       SMB: Data: Number of data bytes remaining = 44 (0x002C)
     MSRPC: c/o RPC Request:      call 0x55  opnum 0x0  context 0x0  hint 0x14

00030:                            FF 53 4D 42 25 00          .SMB%.
00040:  00 00 00 18 03 80 6C 80 00 00 00 00 00 00 00 00   ......l.........
00050:  00 00 00 08 00 2E 00 08 40 1B 10
                                   00 00 2C 00 00          ........@....,..
00060:  00 00 04 00 00 00 00 00 00 00 00 00 00 00 00 54   ...............T
00070:  00 2C 00 54 00 02 00 26 00 04 08
                                   3D 00 00 5C 00          .,.T...&...=..\.
00080:  50 00 49 00 50 00 45 00 5C 00 00 00 4D 00          P.I.P.E.\...M.
                                   05 00                   ..
00090:  00 03 10 00 00 00 2C 00 00 00 55 00 00 00 14 00   ......,...U.....
000A0:  00 00 00 00 00 00 00 00 00 00 6B 0F A6 23 AB 8B   ..........k..#..
```

```
000B0:  D2 11 9C 42 00 A0 24 78 7B 3A                    ...B..$x{:
```

The response follows the same pattern as the request. The word count, at offset 0x5a, indicates that there are ten 16-bit parameters, so there are automatically no **setup parameters**. The number of **transaction data** bytes is 48, which starts at an offset of 56 bytes from the start of the SMB header. The SMB header starts at offset 0x3A, so the **transaction data** starts at offset 0x72, which contains the DCE/RPC fragment. The number of **transaction parameters** is zero, so the parameter offset is set (unnecessarily) to 56 bytes. There is no **name**; however, the **transaction data** is aligned to a 4-byte boundary (at offset 0x72), which is why bytes at offsets 0x6F to 0x71 are filled with garbage.

```
****************************************************************************
Frame   Time    Src MAC Addr   Dst MAC Addr   Protocol   Description
245     6.662   brookfields    REGENT         MSRPC      c/o RPC Response

    SMB: R transact TransactNmPipe (response to frame 244)
       SMB: SMB Status = Error Success
       SMB: Header: PID = 0x2E00 TID = 0x0800 MID = 0x1B40 UID = 0x0800
       SMB: Command = R transact
          SMB: Word count = 10
          SMB: Word parameters
          SMB: Total parm bytes = 0
          SMB: Total data bytes = 48
          SMB: Parameter bytes = 0 (0x0)
          SMB: Parameter offset = 56 (0x38)
          SMB: Parameter Displacement = 0 (0x0)
          SMB: Data bytes = 48 (0x30)
          SMB: Data offset = 56 (0x38)
          SMB: Data Displacement = 0 (0x0)
          SMB: Max setup words = 0
          SMB: Byte count = 49
          SMB: Byte parameters
          SMB: Pipe function = Transact named pipe (TransactNmPipe)
             SMB: File name = \svcctl
       SMB: Data: Number of data bytes remaining = 48 (0x0030)
    MSRPC: c/o RPC Response:    call 0x55  context 0x0  hint 0x18  cancels 0x0


00030:                          FF 53 4D 42 25 00           .SMB%.
00040:  00 00 00 98 03 80 6C 80 00 00 00 00 00 00 00 00    ......l.........
00050:  00 00 00 08 00 2E 00 08 40 1B 0A                   ........@..
                                            00 00 30 00 00          ..0..
00060:  00 00 00 38 00 00 00 30 00 38 00 00 00 00 00 31    ...8...0.8.....1
00070:  00 2C                                              .,
                 05 00 02 03 10 00 00 00 30 00 00 00 55 00          .......0...U.
00080:  00 00 18 00 00 00 00 00 00 00 00 00 00 00 00 00    ................
00090:  00 00 00 00 00 00 00 00 00 00 00 00 00 00 00 00    ................
000A0:  00 00                                              ..
```

In this second example, the **SMBtrans** contains a

**SetNamedPipeHandleState** in the **transaction data**. The state is set to 0x4300, a bit field that is interpreted below. The exact meaning of this state is not known.

```
**********************************************************************
Frame   Time    Src MAC Addr   Dst MAC Addr   Protocol  Description
17      2.409   STEELEYE       EMERY          SMB       C transact SNPHS, FID =
➥0x800
```

```
  SMB: C transact SetNmPHandState, FID = 0x800
     SMB: SMB Status = Error Success
     SMB: Header: PID = 0x6645 TID = 0x1807 MID = 0x0001 UID = 0x3003
     SMB: Command = C transact
        SMB: Word count = 16
        SMB: Word parameters
        SMB: Total parm bytes = 2
        SMB: Total data bytes = 0
        SMB: Max parm bytes = 0
        SMB: Max data bytes = 1024
        SMB: Max setup words = 0 (0x0)
        SMB: Transact Flags Summary = 0 (0x0)
           SMB: .............0 = Leave session intact
           SMB: ............0. = Response required
        SMB: Transact timeout = 0 (0x0)
        SMB: Parameter bytes = 2 (0x2)
        SMB: Parameter offset = 76 (0x4C)
        SMB: Data bytes = 0 (0x0)
        SMB: Data offset = 78 (0x4E)
        SMB: Max setup words = 2
        SMB: Setup words
        SMB: Pipe function = Set named pipe handle state (SetNmPHandState)
        SMB: File ID (FID) = 2048 (0x800)
        SMB: File name = \PIPE\lsarpc
        SMB: Byte count = 11
        SMB: Byte parameters
        SMB: Device state = 0x4300
           SMB: Instance count = 0
           SMB: ......11 = Read mode
           SMB: ....00.. = Byte stream pipe
           SMB: .1...... = Server end of pipe
           SMB: 0....... = Reads and writes block if no data available
        SMB: Transaction parameters
```

```
00030:                            FF 53 4D 42 25 00       .SMB%.
00040:  00 00 00 08 01 00 00 00 00 00 00 00 00 00 00 00   ................
00050:  00 00 07 18 45 66 03 30 01 00 10                  ....Ef.0...
                                     02 00 00 00 00           .....
00060:  00 00 04 00 00 00 00 00 00 00 00 00 00 00 02 00 4C  ...............L
00070:  00 00 00 4E 00 02 00 01 00 00 08                  ...N.......
                                     0B 00 5C 50 49          ..\PI
00080:  50 45 5C 00 00 00                                 PE\...
                    00 43                                   .C
```

The response simply contains an acknowledgement of the SMB
request, which contains no data.

```
******************************************************************
Frame   Time    Src MAC Addr   Dst MAC Addr   Protocol  Description
18      2.409   EMERY          STEELEYE       SMB       R transact

  SMB: R transact
     SMB: SMB Status = Error Success
     SMB: Header: PID = 0x6645 TID = 0x1807 MID = 0x0001 UID = 0x3003
     SMB: Command = C transact
        SMB: Word count = 10
        SMB: Word parameters
        SMB: Total parm bytes = 0
        SMB: Total data bytes = 0
        SMB: Parameter bytes = 0 (0x0)
        SMB: Parameter offset = 56 (0x38)
        SMB: Parameter Displacement = 0 (0x0)
        SMB: Data bytes = 0 (0x0)
        SMB: Data offset = 56 (0x38)
        SMB: Data Displacement = 0 (0x0)
        SMB: Max setup words = 0
        SMB: Byte count = 1
        SMB: Byte parameters
        SMB: Pipe function = Set named pipe handle state (SetNmPHandState)
           SMB: File name = \PIPE\lsarpc

00030:                              FF 53 4D 42 25 00    .ta.....8.SMB%.
00040:  00 00 00 88 01 00 00 00 00 00 00 00 00 00 00 00    ...............
00050:  00 00 07 18 45 66 03 30 01 00 0A                   ....Ef.0...
                                    00 00 00 00 00             .....
00060:  00 00 00 38 00 00 00 00 00 38 00 00 00 00 00 01    ...8.....8......
00070:  00 00                                              ..
```

## 1.2.4: SMB ReadX

An **SMBreadX** is used to transparently read DCE/RPC fragment
responses. The fourth SMB word parameter (at offset 0x5F to 0x60 in
the following example) is the SMB file handle (0x80B) associated with
the DCE/RPC endpoint connection. SMB word parameters 7, 8, and
11 specify the amount of SMB data to be read (0x3D0 bytes).

```
******************************************************************
Frame   Time    Src MAC Addr   Dst MAC Addr   Protocol  Description
105     17.874  REGENT         EMERY          SMB       C read & X, FID = 0x80b

  SMB: C read & X, FID = 0x80b, Read 0x3d0 at 0x00000000
     SMB: SMB Status = Error Success
     SMB: Header: PID = 0xCAFE TID = 0x0802 MID = 0x07C0 UID = 0x0802
     SMB: Command = C read & X
        SMB: Word count = 12
        SMB: Word parameters
        SMB: Next offset = 0x0000
```

```
                SMB: File ID (FID) = 2059 (0x80B)
                SMB: File name = \winreg
                SMB: File offset = 0 (0x0)
                SMB: Max count = 976 (0x3D0)
                SMB: Min count = 976 (0x3D0)
                SMB: Open timeout = -1
                SMB: Bytes left = 976
                SMB: File offset, high = 0 (0x0)
                SMB: File Offset (NT) = 0x0000000000000000
                SMB: Byte count = 0
```

```
00030:                               FF 53 4D 42 2E 00           .SMB..
00040:   00 00 00 18 00 80 00 00 00 00 00 00 00 00 00 00   ................
00050:   00 00 02 08 FE CA 02 08 C0                        .........
                                     07 0C FF 00 00 00 0B          .......
00060:   08 00 00 00 00 D0 03 D0 03 FF FF FF FF D0 03 00   ................
00070:   00 00 00 00 00 02                                 ......
```

The **SMBreadX** response contains the DCE/RPC response data
requested. The sixth SMB word parameter shows the actual amount
of data returned (truncated in this example as it's very, very boring).

```
**********************************************************************
Frame   Time    Src MAC Addr   Dst MAC Addr   Protocol  Description
106     17.875  EMERY          REGENT         SMB       R read & X, Read 0x3d0
```

```
    SMB: R read & X, Read 0x3d0
        SMB: SMB Status = Error Success
        SMB: Header: PID = 0xCAFE TID = 0x0802 MID = 0x07C0 UID = 0x0802
        SMB: Command = C read & X
            SMB: Word count = 12
            SMB: Word parameters
            SMB: Next offset = 0x0000
            SMB: File name = \winreg
            SMB: Bytes left = 0
            SMB: Data length = 976 (0x3D0)
            SMB: Data offset = 60 (0x3C)
            SMB: Byte count = 977
            SMB: Byte parameters
```

```
00030:                               FF 53 4D 42 2E 00           .SMB..
00040:   00 00 00 98 00 80 00 00 00 00 00 00 00 00 00 00   ................
00050:   00 00 02 08 FE CA 02 08 C0 07 0C                  ...........
                                     FF 00 00 00 00                .....
00060:   00 00 00 00 00 D0 03 3C 00 00 00 00 00 00 00 00   .......<........
00070:   00 00 00 D1 03 02                                 ......
                        62 00 00 00 6D 00 6F 00 75 00          b...m.o.u.
00080:   63 00 6C 00 61 00 73 00 73 00 00 00 4D 00 6F 00   c.l.a.s.s...M.o.
00090:   64 00 65 00 6D 00 00 00 6D 00 6B 00 65 00 63 00   d.e.m...m.k.e.c.
...
...
00420:   00 00 53 00 79 00 73 00 74 00 65 00 6D 00 00 00   ..S.y.s.t.e.m...
00430:   00 00 6C CD 14 00 8C 07 00 00 74 CD 14 00 8C 07   ..l.......t.....
00440:   00 00 00 00 00 00                                 ......
```

## 1.2.5: SMB WriteX

An **SMBwriteX** is used to transparently write DCE/RPC fragment requests. The third SMB word parameter (at offset 0x5F to 0x60) is the SMB file handle (0x4004) associated with the DCE/RPC endpoint connection. The tenth SMB word (at offset 0x6E to 0x70) indicates the amount of DCE/RPC data being transferred, and the eleventh SMB word (at offset 0x71 to 0x72) indicates where the data starts, relative to the start of the SMB header. The SMB header starts at offset 0x3A, and the data offset is 0x40, so the DCE/RPC data starts at offset 0x7A. The DCE/RPC data in this example happens to be a Bind Request PDU.

```
***********************************************************************
Frame   Time     Src MAC Addr    Dst MAC Addr    Protocol  Description
27      4.583    RDRX861         DOWNDC          MSRPC     c/o RPC Bind

  SMB: C write & X, FID = 0x4004, Write 0x48 at 0x00000000
     SMB: NT status, Code = (0) STATUS_WAIT_0
              SMB: NT Status Severity Code = Success
              SMB: NT Status Customer Code = 0 (0x0)
              SMB: NT Status Reserved Bit = 0 (0x0)
              SMB: NT Status Facility = System
              SMB: NT Status Code System Success = STATUS_WAIT_0
     SMB: Header: PID = 0xFEFF TID = 0x8001 MID = 0x0100 UID = 0xE001
     SMB: Command = C write & X
        SMB: Word count = 14
        SMB: Word parameters
        SMB: Next offset = 0xDEDE
        SMB: File ID (FID) = 16388 (0x4004)
        SMB: File name = \srvsvc
        SMB: File offset = 0 (0x0)
        SMB: Open timeout = -1
        SMB: Write mode = 8 (0x8)
              SMB: ...............0 = Allow write caching
              SMB: ..............0. = Do not return bytes remaining
              SMB: .............0.. = Do not use raw named pipe protocol
              SMB: ............1... = Start of message mode named pipe message
        SMB: Bytes left = 72
        SMB: Data length = 72 (0x48)
        SMB: Data offset = 64 (0x40)
        SMB: File offset, high = 0 (0x0)
        SMB: Byte count = 73
        SMB: Byte parameters
     SMB: Data: Number of data bytes remaining = 72 (0x0048)
   MSRPC: c/o RPC Bind: UUID 4B324FC8-1670-01D3-1278-5A47BF6EE188  call 0x1

00030:                           FF 53 4D 42 2F 00   AP........SMB/.
00040:   00 00 00 18 07 C8 00 00 40 6D 4E F4 8C 6E 13 7B   ........@mN..n.{
00050:   00 00 01 80 FF FE 01 E0 00 01 0E                  ...........
                           FF 00 DE DE 04               .....
```

```
00060:   40 00 00 00 00 FF FF FF FF 08 00 48 00 00 00 48   @.........H...H
00070:   00 40 00 00 00 00 00 00 49 00 EE                  .@.....I..
                               05 00 0B 03 10 00              ......
00080:   00 00 48 00 00 00 01 00 00 00 B8 10 B8 10 00 00   ..H...........
00090:   00 00 01 00 00 00 00 00 01 00 C8 4F 32 4B 70 16   ..........O2Kp.
000A0:   D3 01 12 78 5A 47 BF 6E E1 88 03 00 00 00 04 5D   ...xZG.n.......]
000B0:   88 8A EB 1C C9 11 9F E8 08 00 2B 10 48 60 02 00   ..........+.H`..
000C0:   00 00                                             ..
```

The **SMBwriteX** response simply contains an acknowledgment that
the data was received.

```
***************************************************************
Frame   Time    Src MAC Addr  Dst MAC Addr  Protocol  Description
28      4.585   DOWNDC        RDRX861       SMB       R write & X, Wrote 0x48

  SMB: R write & X, Wrote 0x48
      SMB: NT status, Code = (0) STATUS_WAIT_0
              SMB: NT Status Severity Code = Success
              SMB: NT Status Customer Code = 0 (0x0)
              SMB: NT Status Reserved Bit = 0 (0x0)
              SMB: NT Status Facility = System
              SMB: NT Status Code System Success = STATUS_WAIT_0
      SMB: Header: PID = 0xFEFF TID = 0x8001 MID = 0x0100 UID = 0xE001
      SMB: Command = C write & X
          SMB: Word count = 6
          SMB: Word parameters
          SMB: Next offset = 0x002F
          SMB: Data length = 72 (0x48)
          SMB: Bytes left = 65535
          SMB: Byte count = 0

00030:                             FF 53 4D 42 2F 00   C* }...../.SMB/.
00040:   00 00 00 98 07 C8 00 00 EA 26 80 15 46 DD C3 14   .........&..F...
00050:   00 00 01 80 FF FE 01 E0 00 01 06                  ...........
                               FF 00 2F 00 48              ../.H
00060:   00 FF FF 00 00 00 00 00 00                        .........
```

## 1.2.6: SMB Close

An **SMBclose** is used to terminate the DCE/RPC endpoint connection.
This is done by closing the SMB file handle (0x80A), which is the first
SMB word in this example.

```
***************************************************************
Frame   Time    Src MAC Addr  Dst MAC Addr  Protocol  Description
381     28.772  REGENT        EMERY         SMB       C close file, FID = 0x80a

  SMB: C close file, FID = 0x80a
      SMB: SMB Status = Error Success
      SMB: Header: PID = 0xCAFE TID = 0x0802 MID = 0x1340 UID = 0x0802
      SMB: Command = C close file
          SMB: Word count = 3
          SMB: Word parameters
```

```
                SMB: File ID (FID) = 2058 (0x80A)
                SMB: File name = \EVENTLOG
                SMB: Last modify time (sec) = Feb 7, 2106 6:28:15.0
                SMB: Byte count = 0

00030:                                    FF 53 4D 42 04 00         .SMB..
00040:  00 00 00 18 03 80 00 00 00 00 00 00 00 00 00 00   ................
00050:  00 00 02 08 FE CA 02 08 40 13 03                  ........@..
                                    0A 08 FF FF FF              .....
00060:  FF 00 00 38                                        ...8
```

The **SMBclose** response is just an acknowledgment: there aren't even
any SMB word parameters in SMPclose responses.

```
*********************************************************************
Frame   Time    Src MAC Addr   Dst MAC Addr   Protocol   Description
382     28.773  EMERY          REGENT         SMB        R close file

  SMB: R close file
      SMB: SMB Status = Error Success
      SMB: Header: PID = 0xCAFE TID = 0x0802 MID = 0x1340 UID = 0x0802
      SMB: Command = C close file
          SMB: Word count = 0
          SMB: File name = \EVENTLOG
          SMB: Byte count = 0

00030:                                    FF 53 4D 42 04 00         .SMB..
00040:  00 00 00 98 03 80 00 00 00 00 00 00 00 00 00 00   ................
00050:  00 00 02 08 FE CA 02 08 40 13 00 00 00            ........@....
```

# 1.3: DCE/RPC Initialisation: SMBopenX or NTSMBCreateX

To start a DCE/RPC pipe, assuming that you have a valid **IPC$**
connection open, you must issue a **SMBopenX** with a file named
"**\PIPE\name**" or an **NTSMBCreateX** call with a file named "/name",
each with the DCE/RPC endpoint to be opened. The response will
contain a 16-bit file handle. You may find that even at this stage,
opening a pipe will be refused. Opening **\PIPE\winreg** or **\PIPE\svcctl**
requires an authenticated SMB session rather than a NULL session:
retry with an **SMBsessionsetupX** specifying the User name, Domain,
and user's password in that Domain and another **SMBtconX** to **IPC$**.

If an **SMBopenX** is used, it must be followed up with
**SetNamedPipeHandleState**, using an **SMBtrans**. The combination of
these two calls is equivalent to a single **NTSMBCreateX** call. Note
that the **SMBopenX** *must* be made with the file open mode 0x0042. If
different attributes are requested, then later on when an **SMBreadX** or
**SMBwriteX** is issued, inexplicably an "Access denied" error is

returned. Please don't ask why this happens: it's probably very, very important.

**SMBtrans** calls contain data, parameters, and setup parameters. Most **SMBtrans** calls normally seen in SMB traffic have no setup parameters. However, the **SetNamedPipeHandle SMBtrans** call has two 16-bit setup parameters. The first of the two 16-bit parameters is 0x0001, and the second setup parameter is the SMB file handle obtained from the **SMBopenX** response.

The **SetNamedPipeHandleState** call indicates to the server that the file being opened by the **SMBopenX** call is not a file but is in fact a named pipe. The **NTSMBCreateX** call, however, having several more parameters than an **SMBopenX**, can directly indicate that a named pipe, rather than a file, is being opened.

Samba is quite flexible in what it accepts from **NTSMBCreateX** calls: we really don't care what most of these bits actually do. *However*, Windows NT clearly does care, so it is advisable for implementors to copy these fields verbatim. Even better would be to actually put real functionality behind them, if you understand what they do, which the author does not.

## Decoding, Resource Management, and Net Monitor Issues

At this point, assuming that the target Workstation supports the SMB DCE/RPC calls required, run Server Manager and select the target Workstation. Or, if you have physical access to the target Workstation, run Start | Settings | Control Panel | Server. You will find, in the dialogs available there, that an open file is listed: **\PIPE\name**; also an SMB session will be open (probably an anonymous connection to **IPC$** from the caller's Workstation).

You can terminate the SMB session or forcibly shut down the pipe from these dialogs. A good reason for doing this is to force the client to reconnect. **NetMonitor** will only properly decode a trace if it sees the entire DCE/RPC connection, starting with the **SMBopenX** or **NTSMBCreateX**. As Windows NT clients tend to keep at least one pipe open, you might want to force a disconnection to get a proper **NetMonitor** trace.

Oh, just as a side-note: if you're curious as to why Windows NT keeps **\PIPE\NETLOGON** open, having sent a **NetrSamLogon**, to log the user in to the Domain, it's to keep at least one resource open with the PDC. This resource-hogging mechanism is used to indicate that the user is still logged in.

## 1.4: DCE/RPC Header Fields

DCE/RPC headers consist of two parts. The first part is 16 bytes of information that is common to all requests and responses. An example is shown here:

```
**************************************************************************
Frame   Time    Src MAC Addr   Dst MAC Addr   Protocol  Description
20      6.276   brookfields    REGENT         MSRPC     c/o RPC Bind:
        UUID            12345678-1234-ABCD-EF00-01234567CFFB  brookfields    REGENT

        MSRPC: Version = 5 (0x5)
        MSRPC: Version (Minor) = 0 (0x0)
        MSRPC: Packet Type = Bind
        MSRPC: Flags 1 = 0 (0x0)
            MSRPC: .......0 = Reserved -or- Not the first fragment (AES/DC)
            MSRPC: ......0. = Not a last fragment -or- No cancel pending
            MSRPC: .....0.. = Not a fragment -or- No cancel pending (AES/DC)
            MSRPC: ....0... = Receiver to repond with a fack PDU -or-
                             Reserved (AES/DC)
            MSRPC: ...0.... = Not used -or-
                             Does not support concurrent multiplexing (AES/DC)
            MSRPC: ..0..... = Not for an idempotent request -or-
                             Did not execute guaranteed call (Fault PDU only)
                             (AES/DC)
            MSRPC: .0...... = Not for a broadcast request -or-
                             'Maybe' call semantics not requested (AES/DC)
            MSRPC: 0....... = Reserved -or-
                             No object UUID specified in the optional object field
                             (AES/DC)
        MSRPC: Packed Data Representation
        MSRPC: Fragment Length = 106 (0x6A)
        MSRPC: Authentication Length = 26 (0x1A)
        MSRPC: Call Identifier = 3 (0x3)

00080:                                    05 00   P.I.P.E.\.......
00090:  0B 00 10 00 00 00 6A 00 1A 00 03 00 00 00
```

The fields are as follows:

- **Major and Minor version.** The first and second bytes specify the major and minor version numbers. In this example, version 5.0 is being used.

- **Packet Type.** The third byte specifies the Protocol Data Unit (PDU) packet type.

- **Packed Data Representation.** Bytes five to eight, the Packed Data Representation, specify issues such as the byte order of 2- and 4-byte integers contained in the second part of the header. This can vary on a per-PDU basis: the sender can choose the representation, and it is up to the recipient to sort out the mess.

- **Fragment Length.** The fragment length in bytes 9 and 10 specify the total size of the header, namely 16 bytes plus the following data up to (but not including any part of) the next header.
- **Authentication Length.** The authentication length in bytes 11 and 12 specify the size of the optional authentication verifier (covered in more detail in the following sections).
- **Call ID.** Finally, the last field in bytes 13 to 16 is the Call Identifier, which is an incremental sequence number. It is used to match up requests with responses and also to ensure that sessions are not so easy to attack.

The second part of the header, following the first section that is common to all DCE/RPC transfers, is variable in length. Its interpretation is dependent on information contained in the first part of the header, such as the PDU Packet Type field. The various known PDU types are covered in detail in the following section.

## 1.4.1: DCE/RPC Protocol Data Units

This is a complete list of DCE/RPC *Protocol Data Units*, known as PDUs, used by Samba's DCE/RPC over SMB code:

- **0x00** RPC_REQUEST
- **0x02** RPC_RESPONSE
- **0x03** RPC_FAULT
- **0x0b** RPC_BIND
- **0x0c** RPC_BINDACK
- **0x0e** RPC_ALTCONT
- **0x0f** RPC_AUTH3
- **0x10** RPC_BINDCONT

They are used for the following purposes:

- The Bind, Bind Acknowledge, and Bind Continuation PDUs are used for negotiation.
- The Request PDU is used to make a function call. Any uninitialised function arguments that are expected to be initialised inside the function call are *not* included over-the-wire.
- The Response PDU is used to transfer any function arguments that may have been modified by the function, plus the return result of the function call.

- The Fault PDU is used to indicate an error in the format of the arguments, or an error due to interference by a third party with a Secure Session, and so forth.

When a DCE/RPC Request PDU is sent, there are eight more bytes that follow. The entire DCE/RPC header is shown (a total of 24 bytes) for completeness:

```
**************************************************************************
Frame   Time    Src MAC Addr   Dst MAC Addr   Protocol  Description
22      6.279   brookfields    REGENT         R_LOGON   RPC Client call

  MSRPC: c/o RPC Request:        call 0x1  opnum 0x2  context 0x0  hint 0x156
    MSRPC: Allocation Hint = 342 (0x156)
    MSRPC: Presentation Context Identifier = 0 (0x0)
    MSRPC: Operation Number (c/o Request prop. dg header prop) = 2 (0x2)

00080:                                    05 00   P.I.P.E.\...M...
00090:  00 03 10 00 00 00 A0 01 20 00 01 00 00 00 56 01   ........ .....V.
000A0:  00 00 00 00 02 00
```

When a DCE/RPC Response PDU is sent, again there are eight more bytes that follow, with slightly different meanings. The entire DCE/RPC header is shown (a total of 24 bytes) for completeness.

```
**************************************************************************
Frame   Time    Src MAC Addr   Dst MAC Addr   Protocol  Description
23      6.284   REGENT         brookfields    R_LOGON   RPC Server response

  MSRPC: c/o RPC Response:       call 0x1  context 0x0  hint 0x14C  cancels 0x0
    MSRPC: Allocation Hint = 332 (0x14C)
    MSRPC: Presentation Context Identifier = 0 (0x0)
    MSRPC: Cancel Count = 0 (0x0)
    MSRPC: Reserved = 0 (0x0)

00070:      05 00 02 03 10 00 00 00 90 01 20 00 01 00   ............ ...
00080:  00 00 4C 01 00 00 00 00 00 00
```

The fields are as follows:

- **Allocation Hint.** This *advises* how much DCE/RPC data to expect. Implementations should not rely on this field containing correct data, which makes this field more than useless.

- **Opcode.** The Operation number is a unique identifer that says what function call is being made. Each interface's functions are numbered from zero upwards.

- **Presentation Context Identifier.** It is possible to negotiate different formats for the data (function call arguments) being transferred or presented. The Presentation Context Identifier therefore selects which of the negotiated formats to use.

Normally, only one format is negotiated, the default for
DCE/RPC, known as Network Data Representation (NDR). It is
possible to add, and therefore negotiate and use, data formats
such as Sun Microsystems' ONC/RPC's data representation,
known as Extended Data Representation (XDR).

- **Cancel Count.** DCE/RPC was designed to work in a multi-
  threaded environment. It is possible for a client to indicate that a
  DCE/RPC call that has already been issued (sent over-the-wire)
  should be cancelled. This field indicates the number of cancelled
  PDUs that have been sent.

It is interesting to note that Microsoft's implementation up to
Windows NT 4.0 Service Pack 2 got the calculation of the Allocation
Hint field slightly wrong. UNICODE strings contain two lengths: the
buffer size and the actual string length. The buffer size must be greater
than or equal to the actual string length. As a result, a UNICODE
string need not be NULL-terminated: you can specify that the buffer
size be one greater than the actual string length. This is where the
problems started. Microsoft calculated the Allocation Hint size based
on the sum of the actual string lengths, and calculated the SMB data
size based on the sum of the string buffer sizes. Given that UNICODE
string characters are two bytes, the Allocation Hint was calculated to
be two bytes short per UNICODE string in the Request or response
PDU.

## 1.4.2: DCE/RPC Fragments

How do you know when to expect either one or several DCE/RPC
fragments? Inside the DCE/RPC header is a "flags" field. Each
DCE/RPC fragment is marked in the header with two bits of this field:

- **First Fragment.** First bit of "flags" field. Only the first fragment
  in a stream has this set.
- **Last Fragment.** Second bit of "flags" field. Only the last fragment
  in a stream has this set.

```
*************************************************************************
Frame   Time    Src MAC Addr    Dst MAC Addr    Protocol  Description
71      6.362   REGENT          brookfields     MSRPC     c/o RPC Request

  MSRPC: c/o RPC Request:       call 0x2  opnum 0xE  context 0x0  hint 0x24
      MSRPC: Version = 5 (0x5)
      MSRPC: Version (Minor) = 0 (0x0)
      MSRPC: Packet Type = Request
      MSRPC: Flags 1 = 3 (0x3)
```

```
MSRPC: .......1 = Reserved -or- First fragment (AES/DC)
MSRPC: ......1. = Last fragment -or- Cancel pending
MSRPC: .....0.. = No cancel pending (AES/DC)
MSRPC: ....0... = Reserved (AES/DC)
MSRPC: ...0.... = Not used
MSRPC: ..0..... = Not for an idempotent request
MSRPC: .0...... = Not for a broadcast request
MSRPC: 0....... = Reserved
```

```
00080:                                   05 00   P.I.P.E.\.......
00090: 00 03 10 00 00 00 3C 00 00 00 02 00 00 00 24 00   ......<.......$.
000A0: 00 00 00 00 0E 00
```

When both the first and last fragment fields are set, the DCE/RPC
fragment is alone: no other fragments are expected. If another fragment appears with the same Call Identifier sequence number then
there is a problem, and a "Fault" PDU should be sent on receipt of all
subsequent DCE/RPC requests on the connection.

The only known instance where the "flags" field appears not to be
set properly is in the DCE/RPC "Bind Request" PDU of AT&T's
(www.att.com) Advanced File and Print Sharer for Unix. This was
based on Windows NT 3.5 source code, apparently, so Windows NT
3.5 is also likely to have this bug.

Note that DCE/RPC fragmentation, as part of the DCE/RPC
specification, is completely independent of what may be described to
be "SMB fragmentation." DCE/RPC fragmentation has its own
method for indicating, in the DCE/RPC header, that more fragments
are to follow. The SMB fragmentation is a fragmentation imposed
independently of the data it is transferring, and is due to size limits on
the amount of data that a single SMB call can contain. A DCE/RPC
over SMB implementation's job *appears* to be complex due to the
need to provide two separate fragmentation and de-fragmentation
roles for these two independent protocols.

## 1.5: DCE/RPC Calls: SMBwriteX, SMBtrans, and SMBreadX

DCE/RPC Protocol Data Units (PDUs) are either contained completely
or spread out over several standard **SMBwriteX**, **SMBtrans**, or
**SMBreadX** calls. These three calls are available to the LANMAN 1.0
and above dialects of SMB. Efforts are underway at the time of
writing to get **SMB_COM_TRANSACTION** documented, which,
while similar to **SMB_COM_TRANSACTION2** and correctly
interpreted by **NetMonitor**, is missing from Microsoft CIFS
documentation.

SMBtrans calls must be used in a precise manner to contain DCE/RPC PDUs (or parts thereof). If the PDU is small enough, it will fit inside an SMBtrans request and response: it all depends on what buffer sizes are negotiated on the SMB channel. Typically, Windows NT negotiates a maximum of 1024 bytes for the SMBtrans data size. Any DCE/RPC requests larger than this must use one or more SMBwriteX calls, and any DCE/RPC responses larger than the maximum size must use SMBreadX calls. Remember, however, that any DCE/RPC fragments that are split up by SMB limitations must be reassembled as DCE/RPC fragments independently of the SMB layer.

In theory, just SMBwriteX and SMBreadX calls could be used to transfer DCE/RPC PDUs. However, this is a little inefficient: each SMBwriteX and SMBreadX call requires a reply that serves as purely an acknowledgment. This would increase the transfer time, particularly over high latency networks. The use of the SMBtrans call at least gives you a low latency for small DCE/RPC calls.

## 1.5.1: Small DCE/RPC PDUs—SMBtrans

The number of data bytes, parameters, and setup parameters are set to the size of the DCE/RPC request data, zero, and two, respectively. The two 16-bit setup parameters are used to indicate that the SMBtrans contains a DCE/RPC PDU. The first is set to 0x0026 (for a DCE/RPC data transfer) or 0x0001 (for a SetNamedPipeHandleState call), and the second is set to the 16-bit file handle obtained from the SMBopenX or NTSMBCreateX. The name field (a string) must contain a filename of "\PIPE\." If UNICODE strings have been negotiated on this SMB session, then according to the CIFS documentation, the filename must be in UNICODE. The DCE/RPC PDU itself then follows and is contained in the transaction data portion of the SMBtrans call.

A DCE/RPC response is contained in the SMBtrans reply. The number of data bytes, parameters, and setup parameters are set to the size of the DCE/RPC response data, zero, and zero, respectively. SMBtrans replies do not have and do not need a "name" field. Remember that in both the request and the response, the start of the data must be aligned to a 4-byte boundary (as described in the CIFS documentation). The reason is so that internal buffers in Microsoft's Intel x86 implementations align to x86 4-byte boundaries for increased performance (not a particularly good reason for imposing difficulties at a protocol level if ever there was one). If you fail to align the data you are likely to run into difficulties, depending on which type and revision of SMB Server or Client you are connected to. A number of non-Microsoft SMB Servers do not implement byte alignment correctly: they follow the *exact* packet layout that Windows NT and Windows 95 use. Any deviation, as is perfectly valid as per the SMB specification, and these Servers tend to fall over in a heap.

## 1.5.2: Oversized DCE/RPC PDUs—SMBreadX and SMBwriteX

**SMBtrans** data fields have a maximum size: typically, 1024 bytes. DCE/RPC data streams can be far larger than this (32 bits theoretical maximum), but the data stream is divided into fragments. DCE/RPC has its own independent negotiation for fragments using Bind and Bind Acknowledge PDUs: typically 5680 bytes on Intel Windows NT Workstations and Servers, and 2048 bytes on AT&T's Advanced File and Print Server for UNIX.

So, when making a transfer that is larger than a single **SMBtrans** can handle, a series of **SMBreadX** and/or **SMBwriteX** calls are also used to complete the transfer of the DCE/RPC PDU fragments.

Common sense and simplicity of design dictates that there should be no "interaction" between DCE/RPC data streams and the use of **SMBtrans, SMBreadX** and **SMBwriteX**. However, Microsoft has built additional features into SMB and its use. TCP/IP is a stream protocol that has error-checking and is used to guarantee that a connection is maintained and data is reliably transferred. It is not normally necessary to provide your own error-checking over a TCP connection. However, SMB provides the capability to recover from a lost connection. In theory, and sometimes in practice, a Server can be crashed or switched off (don't do this without permission, kids) and restarted, and access by Windows NT SMB Clients is resumed as if uninterrupted.

When a DCE/RPC request or response is too large for the **SMBtrans** request or response, the packet is marked in the SMB header with a 32-bit status code: **STATUS_BUFFER_OVERFLOW** (0x8000 0005). The highest two bits specify the severity: in this case bit 32 indicates a warning only.

```
************************************************************************
Frame   Time    Src MAC Addr   Dst MAC Addr   Protocol   Description
72      6.364   brookfields    REGENT         MSRPC      c/o RPC Response

  SMB: R transact · NT error, System, Warning, Code = (5) STATUS_BUFFER_OVERFLOW
    SMB: NT status code = 0x80000005
        SMB: NT Status Severity Code = Warning
```

```
SMB: NT Status Customer Code = 0 (0x0)
SMB: NT Status Reserved Bit = 0 (0x0)
SMB: NT Status Facility = System
SMB: NT Status Code System Warning = STATUS_BUFFER_OVERFLOW
```

The equivalent DOS error message to **STATUS_BUFFER_OVER-FLOW** is **ERRmoredata**. The use of DOS error messages is not recommended. Problems with Windows NT Clients and Servers have been known to disappear when SMB Client or Server code is modified to use 32-bit Windows NT error codes rather than the DOS error codes.

Warnings are informational. It is not known whether this warning must be used; it appears to be a redundant mechanism, however, so it is not recommended that any reliance be placed on this error code to deduce that a DCE/RPC response is too large for the **SMBtrans** response data.

How, otherwise, do we detect that a DCE/RPC request is incomplete? Inside the DCE/RPC header is a "fragment length." If the "fragment length" is greater than the **SMBtrans** transaction data, then we know not only that the DCE/RPC request is incomplete but also by how much. This is where the **SMBreadX** calls start rolling in, to complete the transfer of this DCE/RPC fragment and to read any other fragments.

### 1.5.2.1: SMBreadX
SMB negotiation sets a maximum limit (typically in Windows NT this is 4356 (0x1104) bytes) on the size of **SMBreadX** and **SMBwriteX** buffers. The Max Buffer Size is negotiated by the **SMBnegprot** response and **SMBsessionsetupX** request. **SMBreadX** calls will need to be issued by the Client to receive:

- A DCE/RPC PDU fragment that is larger than an **SMBtrans** response can contain.
- Multiple DCE/RPC fragments, regardless of whether they would theoretically all fit in an **SMBtrans** response.

So, keep on sending **SMBreadX** requests for as much of the current DCE/RPC PDU fragment as you can, bearing in mind that your limits are the size of your client-side and server-side buffers and the end of the current DCE/RPC fragment. The SMB Server will acknowledge each **SMBreadX** request. If the end of the current DCE/RPC PDU fragment has not been reached with the current **SMBreadX** call, the SMB error status field will be set to, yes you guessed it: a 32-bit warning **STATUS_BUFFER_OVERFLOW** (0x8000 0005). Again, it is advised that you do not place any particular reliance on this informational warning.

At this point, it is necessary to mention two further points:

- If you attempt to issue an **SMBreadX** call for data beyond the end of the current DCE/RPC PDU fragment, even by one byte, you will confuse the Windows NT DCE/RPC SMB service. Any further attempts to read data will result in errors: you will probably need to close the current DCE/RPC session or better yet, fix your code. So, it is advised that you track exactly how much of the current DCE/RPC PDU fragment you have read so far, and read exactly the correct amount at the end.

- **SMBreadX** calls contain an offset into the file that you wish to read plus the amount. It took several months for the author to realise that the offset is completely ignored (And There Was Much Wailing And Gnashing Of Teeth And The Code Became Simpler Too). However, in Windows NT network traffic, the offset can still be observed to increment when a sequence of **SMBreadX** calls is made. Despite this, the **SMBreadX** offset cannot be relied on; the individual DCE/RPC PDU Fragments can be read correctly only when the amount of data received at the very start in the **SMBtrans** response, and in all subsequent **SMBreadX** calls that are being used to transmit the DCE/RPC response, is added up.

In other words, even if you have one or two bytes left to read of the current DCE/RPC fragment, do not be tempted to have your client code read more than those one or two bytes, or the server *will* fail to answer any further DCE/RPC traffic.

Samba's primitive rpcclient code uses the independence of the SMB and DCE/RPC layers to read the DCE/RPC header first, by requesting 0x18 bytes, and then to read the "Stub Data" into a separate buffer. Each is done with separate **SMBreadX** calls. Although this means that there is an extra round-trip overhead per fragment, it makes for simpler code. A more advanced version that takes into account information about the outstanding amount of the DCE/RPC data stream left is tomorrow's task.

### 1.5.2.2: SMBwriteX

SMB negotiation sets a maximum limit (typically in Windows NT this is 4356 (0x1104) bytes) on the size of **SMBreadX** and **SMBwriteX** buffers (Max Buffer Size negotiated by the **SMBnegprot** response and

SMBsessionsetupX request). A client can issue an **SMBwriteX** call to transfer:

- A DCE/RPC PDU request fragment that is larger than an SMBtrans request can contain.
- Continuation of Bind/Bind Acknowledge Security Negotiation where a response back is not expected, known as an AUTH3 PDU. In three-way Authentication Negotiation, the Client sends a Bind Request PDU; the Server sends a Bind Acknowledge PDU; and the Client sends an AUTH3 PDU.

## 1.5.3: DCE/RPC and SMB Interdependencies

The interdependencies described so far have been the only ones observed to date in Microsoft's use of SMB to transfer DCE/RPC Protocol Data Units (PDUs):

- **SMBreadX** calls ending on a DCE/RPC PDU fragment boundary.
- **STATUS_BUFFER_OVERFLOW** to inform observers that a DCE/RPC PDU fragment boundary has not been reached yet.
- The amount of data being transferred in the DCE/RPC Request or Response being deduced from the SMB data sizes.

This covers as much as the author can deduce from observing network traffic, without a proper specification by the designers of this system. *You have been warned!*

## 1.5.4: DCE/RPC Negotiation PDUs and Security Negotiation

This section describes the DCE/RPC negotiation process, including Security Negotiation. The Protocol Data Units (PDUs) that are used are:

- Bind Request
- Bind Acknowledge
- Three-Way Authentication (AUTH3)

The last of these is not defined in the DCE/RPC specification, however it is documented in:

"Network Computing Architecture Remote Procedure Call RunTime Extensions Specification," version OSF TX1.0.10, by Steven Miller, September 11, 1991, Digital Equipment Corp. and Hewlett Packard Co. (Apollo).

### 1.5.4.1: DCE/RPC Bind Request PDU

This is where DCE/RPC really starts: sending of an **SMBopenX /
NTSMBCreateX** is just making use of SMB to get your act together
by allocating a file handle and getting ready to accept DCE/RPC. The
use of SMB in this way does away with the need to contact a
DCE/RPC endpoint mapper because no additional information is
required. The DCE/RPC Bind PDU transactions start the negotiation
of, amongst other unknown things:

- fragment sizes for the transmission and receipt of data
- the interface to call and its correct version (the "Abstract
  Interface")
- authentication, by setting the Authentication Length to the size of
  an optional Authentication Verifier.

```
**********************************************************************
Frame   Time    Src MAC Addr   Dst MAC Addr   Protocol   Description
27      6.295   REGENT         brookfields    MSRPC      c/o RPC Bind

  MSRPC: c/o RPC Bind:        UUID 4B324FC8-1670-01D3-1278-5A47BF6EE188
        MSRPC: Version = 5 (0x5)
        MSRPC: Version (Minor) = 0 (0x0)
        MSRPC: Packet Type = Bind
        MSRPC: Flags 1 = 0 (0x0)
        MSRPC: Packed Data Representation
        MSRPC: Fragment Length = 72 (0x48)
        MSRPC: Authentication Length = 0 (0x0)
        MSRPC: Call Identifier = 0 (0x0)
        MSRPC: Max Trans Frag Size = 5680 (0x1630)
        MSRPC: Max Recv Frag Size = 5680 (0x1630)
        MSRPC: Assoc Group Identifier = 0 (0x0)
        MSRPC: Presentation Context List
            MSRPC: Number of Context Elements = 1 (0x1)
            MSRPC: Presentation Context Identifier = 0 (0x0)
            MSRPC: Number of Transfer Syntaxs = 1 (0x1)
            MSRPC: Abstract Interface UUID = 4B324FC8-1670-01D3-1278-5A47BF6EE188
            MSRPC: Abstract Interface Version = 3 (0x3)
            MSRPC: Transfer Interface UUID = 8A885D04-1CEB-11C9-9FE8-08002B104860
            MSRPC: Transfer Interface Version = 2 (0x2)

00080:                                        05 00   P.I.P.E.\.......
00090:   0B 00 10 00 00 00 48 00 00 00 00 00 00 00 30 16   ......H.......0.
000A0:   30 16 00 00 00 00 01 00 00 00 00 00 01 00 C8 4F   0..............O
000B0:   32 4B 70 16 D3 01 12 78 5A 47 BF 6E E1 88 03 00   2Kp....xZG.n....
000C0:   00 00 04 5D 88 8A EB 1C C9 11 9F E8 08 00 2B 10   ...].........+.
000D0:   48 60 02 00 00 00                                 H`....
```

If the Authentication Length is non-zero, then the Bind Request PDU also contains, at the end of the request:

- An Authentication Verifier that indicates which Authentication Service the client wishes to use. Only "NTLMSSP" has been observed, although real DCE/RPC caters for much more than just "NTLMSSP."

- Vendor-specific authentication information, identified by the Authentication Verifier.

Microsoft negotiates NTLMSSP (NT LanManager Secure Service Provider), versions 1 and 2. Version 1 is supported in Windows NT 4.0 Service Pack 3 and below; Version 2 is supported in Windows NT 4.0 Service Pack 4 and above. NTLMv1 is partially understood and implemented in Samba, and consequently is documented here.

Getting the Authentication Length field in the DCE/RPC header correct while developing Samba was found to be an absolute nuisance. It turns out that prior to Windows NT 4 Service Pack 4 (beta release r1.44) that there is a bug in the length calculation of this field. Microsoft successfully managed to maintain backward-compatibility whilst also fixing this bug: quite a feat.

### 1.5.4.2: DCE/RPC Bind Acknowledge PDU

The Bind Acknowledge is sent in the reply data of the SMBtrans response. It contains:

- DCE/RPC Header
- Address String
- Results: Acceptance/Rejection status, plus reasons
- Transfer Syntax

```
*************************************************************************
Frame   Time    Src MAC Addr    Dst MAC Addr    Protocol   Description
28      6.296   brookfields     REGENT          MSRPC      c/o RPC Bind Ack

  MSRPC: c/o RPC Bind Ack:
    MSRPC: Version = 5 (0x5)
    MSRPC: Version (Minor) = 0 (0x0)
    MSRPC: Packet Type = Bind Ack
    MSRPC: Flags 1 = 3 (0x3)
    MSRPC: Packed Data Representation
    MSRPC: Fragment Length = 68 (0x44)
    MSRPC: Authentication Length = 0 (0x0)
    MSRPC: Call Identifier = 0 (0x0)
    MSRPC: Max Trans Frag Size = 5680 (0x1630)
```

```
MSRPC: Max Recv Frag Size = 5680 (0x1630)
MSRPC: Assoc Group Identifier = 36576 (0x8EE0)
MSRPC: Secondary Address
    MSRPC: Secondary Address Length = 13 (0xD)
    MSRPC: Secondary Address Port
MSRPC: Padding Byte(s)
MSRPC: Result List
    MSRPC: Number of Results = 1 (0x1)
    MSRPC: Reserved = 0 (0x0)
    MSRPC: Reserved 2
    MSRPC: Presentation Context Results
        MSRPC: Result = Acceptance
        MSRPC: Reason = Reason not specified
        MSRPC: Transfer Syntax
            MSRPC: Transfer Interface UUID = 8A885D04-1CEB-11C9-9FE8-
➡08002B104860
            MSRPC: Transfer Interface Version = 2 (0x2)
```

```
00070:       05 00 0C 03 10 00 00 00 44 00 00 00 00 00    .H........D.....
00080:  00 00 30 16 30 16 E0 8E 00 00 0D 00 5C 50 49 50    ..0.0.......\PIP
00090:  45 5C 6E 74 73 76 63 73 00 00 01 00 00 00 00 00    E\ntsvcs........
000A0:  00 00 04 5D 88 8A EB 1C C9 11 9F E8 08 00 2B 10    ...]..........+.
000B0:  48 60 02 00 00 00                                  H`....
```

The DCE/RPC header will contain acknowledgment of the fragment sizes requested in the Bind Request. Samba simply sends back exactly what the client requested because the only clients currently supported are Intel Windows NT and Samba's own rpcclient program. This has caused problems recently with Sun Microsystems' port of Windows NT to Solaris as they use a different byte ordering from Intel hardware.

Note that the Address string showing the name of the endpoint appears to be for informational purposes only. On Real DCE/RPC systems (which use TCP/IP), the port number (typically port number 135) is put in this field, as an ASCII string.

The Transfer Syntax has always been observed to be the same, as DCE/RPC by default only supports one Transfer Syntax, known as Network Data Representation (NDR). If Sun Microsystems's ONC/RPC data representation, known as XDR, were added to a host, then Samba's behaviour might get a bit unpredictable.

The Results section will tell you whether the Bind Request was accepted or not: Samba does not currently support Bind Acknowledge Rejected, it simply drops the SMB connection, and this seems to be sufficient, although it probably causes resource leaks on Windows NT. If an authenticated Bind Request is received (Authentication Length is non-zero), then the Bind Acknowledge must either be authenticated or a Bind Acknowledge Rejected PDU sent, if the Server does not support the type of authentication requested.

### 1.5.4.3: DCE/RPC Security Negotiation

This section describes the contents of the Security Negotiation used by Microsoft: namely, NTLMSSP. NTLM version 1 uses the Windows NT Challenge / Response system that can be observed in **SMBnegprot** and **SMBsessionsetupX** as its authentication, and goes on from there to generate Session Keys and a Cypher Stream, if this is requested.

#### Bind/Bind Acknowledge Negotiation

The first Authentication Verifier, which is attached to the Bind Request PDU, contains:

- Negotiation Flags (version 1 or 2, Sign, Seal, 40- or 128-bit, and so forth)
- User name
- Domain name

As **NETMON.EXE** does not decode Encrypted RPC calls, the following is an extract from Samba log files. A msg_type of 0x1 indicates an NTLMSSP *Negotiation phase*, similar to that of an **SMBnegprot** request. Also, apparently the auth_type of 0x0a is a documented DCE/RPC Authentication Type:

```
************************************************************************
[050]    0A 06 00 00 70 52 15  00 4E 54 4C 4D 53 53 50   .....pR. .NTLMSSP
[060]  00 01 00 00 00 B7 B2 00  40 04 00 04 00 2B 00 00   ........ @....+..
[070]  00 0B 00 0B 00 20 00 00  00 42 52 4F 4F 4B 46 49   ..... .. .BROOKFI
[080]  45 4C 44 53 54 45 53 54                            ELDSTEST

000048 smb_io_rpc_hdr_auth
    0048 auth_type    : 0a
    0049 auth_level   : 06
    004a stub_type_len: 00
    004b padding      : 00
    004c unknown      : 00155270
000050 smb_io_rpc_auth_verifier: NTLMSSP
    0058 msg_type : 00000001
00005c smb_io_rpc_auth_ntlmssp_neg
    005c neg_flgs : 4000b2b7
    000060 smb_io_strhdr hdr_domain
        0060 str_str_len: 0004
        0062 str_max_len: 0004
        0064 buffer     : 0000002b
    000068 smb_io_strhdr hdr_myname
        0068 str_str_len: 000b
        006a str_max_len: 000b
        006c buffer     : 00000020
    0070 myname: BROOKFIELDS
    007b domain: TEST
```

The Negotiation Flags fields can be any of the following:

- 0x00000001 NEGOTIATE_UNICODE
- 0x00000002 NEGOTIATE_OEM
- 0x00000004 REQUEST_TARGET
- 0x00000010 NEGOTIATE_SIGN
- 0x00000020 NEGOTIATE_SEAL
- 0x00000080 NEGOTIATE_LM_KEY
- 0x00000200 NEGOTIATE_NTLM
- 0x00008000 NEGOTIATE_ALWAYS_SIGN
- 0x00080000 NEGOTIATE_NTLM2
- 0x00800000 NEGOTIATE_TARGET_INFO
- 0x20000000 NEGOTIATE_128
- 0x40000000 NEGOTIATE_KEY_EXCH

The second *Authentication Verifier*, which is attached to the Bind Response PDU, contains:

- Negotiation Flags (what the server has accepted)
- An 8-byte random challenge

As **NETMON.EXE** does not decode encrypted RPC calls, the following is an extract from Samba log files. A msg_type of 0x2 indicates an NTLMSSP *Challenge Response* phase, similar to that of an **SMBnegprot** response.

```
**************************************************************************

api_pipe_bind_req: make response.
000000 smb_io_rpc_hdr_auth
    0000 auth_type    : 0a
    0001 auth_level   : 06
    0002 stub_type_len: 00
    0003 padding      : 00
    0004 unknown      : 00000001
000000 smb_io_rpc_auth_verifier: NTLMSSP
    0008 msg_type : 00000002
000000 smb_io_rpc_auth_ntlmssp_chal
    0000 unknown_1: 00000000
    0004 unknown_2: 00000028
    0008 neg_flags: 000082b1
    000c challenge: 9c 2b 7e ce 62 c2 6f ee
    0014 reserved : 00 00 00 00 00 00 00 00
```

```
[040]                    0A 06 00  00 01 00 00 00 4E 54 4C  `....... .....NTL
[050]  4D 53 53 50 00 02 00 00  00 00 00 00 00 28 00 00  MSSP.... .....(..
[060]  00 B1 82 00 00 9C 2B 7E  CE 62 C2 6F EE 00 00 00  ......+~ .b.o....
[070]  00 00 00 00 00                                    .....
```

The third *Authentication Verifier* is attached to an AUTH3 PDU and is sent using **SMBwriteX** because no response back is expected:

- 24-byte response to challenge, using NT Password Hash
- 24-byte response to challenge, using LM Password Hash
- User name
- Workstation name
- Domain name
- A Session Key (only if Client / Server have negotiated this)
- Negotiation Flags (what the Client has accepted that the Server has accepted!)

As **NETMON.EXE** does not decode encrypted RPC calls, the following is an extract from Samba log files. A msg_type of 0x3 indicates an NTLMSSP *Challenge Response* phase, similar to that of an **SMBsessonsetupX** request.

```
*************************************************************************
write_pipe: 701e name: samr open: Yes len: 172
[010]                    0A 06 00 00  C0 A0 14 00 4E 54 4C 4D  0.0..... ....NTLM
[020]  53 53 50 00 03 00 00 00  18 00 18 00 60 00 00 00  SSP..... ....`...
[030]  18 00 18 00 78 00 00 00  08 00 08 00 40 00 00 00  ....x... ....@...
[040]  08 00 08 00 48 00 00 00  10 00 10 00 50 00 00 00  ....H... ....P...
[050]  00 00 00 00 90 00 00 00  B1 82 00 00 74 00 65 00  ........ ....t.e.
[060]  73 00 74 00 74 00 65 00  73 00 74 00 53 00 54 00  s.t.t.e. s.t.S.T.
[070]  45 00 45 00 4C 00 45 00  59 00 45 00 18 3F 9A AC  E.E.L.E. Y.E..?..
[080]  2E 5F B0 02 77 10 1C 9A  9D C8 9A C6 54 B6 BA AC  ._..w... ....T...
[090]  5F D4 EF 32 69 60 15 E6  A2 84 48 85 DC 60 45 6B  _..2i`.. ..H..`Ek
[0A0]  37 A8 64 1B 07 3F 5F A9  55 85 C6 E5              7.d..?_. U...

00001c smb_io_rpc_auth_verifier: NTLMSSP
   0024 msg_type : 00000003
000028 smb_io_rpc_auth_ntlmssp_resp
   000028 smb_io_strhdr hdr_lm_resp
   000030 smb_io_strhdr hdr_nt_resp
   000038 smb_io_strhdr hdr_domain
   000040 smb_io_strhdr hdr_user
   000048 smb_io_strhdr hdr_wks
   000050 smb_io_strhdr hdr_sess_key
   0058 neg_flags: 000082b1
   005c domain : t.e.s.t.
   0064 user   : t.e.s.t.
   006c wks    : S.T.E.E.L.E.Y.E.
   007c lm_resp : 18 3f 9a ac 2e 5f b0 02 77 10 1c 9a 9d c8 9a c6 54 b6 ba ac 5f d4
```

```
0094 nt_resp : 69 60 15 e6 a2 84 48 85 dc 60 45 6b 37 a8 64 1b 07 3f 5f a9 55 85
➥c6 e5
api_pipe_ntlmssp_verify: checking user details
user: test domain: test wks: STEELEYE
```

At both the Client end and the Server end, each of the two 24-byte responses is generated, and if they match, then there is a high probability that both Client and Server know what the passwords are (without those cleartext equivalent passwords themselves ever being exposed). The generation of a 24-byte response is outlined here:

- expanding the 16-byte clear-text equivalent Password Hash out to 21 bytes, padding it with NULL characters
- splitting the 21 bytes into three 7-byte DES keys
- using each DES key in turn to encrypt three copies of the 8-byte challenge
- concatenating the results of each DES encrypt to produce a 24-byte response

### Encryption Cypher

A well-known encryption cypher, or one that is compatible with the arcfour algorithm, is used to sign or seal the data stream. Only Sign and Seal has been observed to date, so the exact format of Sign-only or Seal-only is not yet known. However, this doesn't really matter because it's never been observed to date, although for completeness it would be nice to know.

The cypher key, in the 40-bit case, is calculated as follows:

- Take the first 7 bytes of the LM cleartext equivalent Password Hash, and use it as a DES key to encrypt the first 8 bytes of the LM 24-byte response seen in the preceding Encryption Bind Negotiation.
- Take the first 5 bytes of the results from the preceding code.
- Concatenate the following 3 bytes: 0xE5 0x38 0xB0, to produce an 8-byte cypher key.

As can be seen, using only the first 5 bytes effectively limits the cypher key to 40 bits. This cypher key is calculated at both Client and Server ends, and is used by the Client to both encrypt requests (which are decrypted by the Server) and decrypt responses (which will have been encrypted by the Server). The cypher stream, once initialised, is never reset no matter how many requests and responses it is used with.

### Secure Signing/Sealing

The purpose of signing a DCE/RPC data stream is to ensure that no unauthorised requests or responses can be made. In the event that an unauthorised intruder sends fake packets that happen to match up with the data stream at a critical point, then any subsequent communication is disrupted, because the real packet will also be received. NTLMSSP verifiers contain an incremental sequence number, which will already have been used by the fake packet.

The purpose of sealing a DCE/RPC data stream is to ensure, for example, that although an unauthorised observer of the network traffic is aware that a user's password has been changed, they do not know the Domain, User name, old password, new password, or whether the password change succeeded or failed. The observer knows that a password change has occurred because the Opnum, which represents the function being carried out, is contained in the DCE/RPC header, and the header is *not* encrypted.

#### 1.5.4.4: NTLMv1 Authentication Verifier

When both Sign and Seal are negotiated, the "Authentication Length" in each DCE/RPC PDU is set to 16 bytes. Attached to each DCE/RPC packet is an Authentication Verifier, which contains:

- a 32-bit version number (only version 1 observed to date)
- a 32-bit reserved field
- a 32-bit CRC32 check-sum
- a 32-bit incrementing Sequence Number

The Authentication Verifier is encrypted with the cypher stream. The version number of the Verifier is left in the clear: only the 12 bytes containing the Reserved field, CRC32, and Sequence Number are encrypted using the cypher stream. Here is a section, initially encrypted, from Samba log files. Following decryption, the Authentication Verifier is easily understood:

```
*********************************************************************

[050]              01 00 00  00 19 9B CB 67 C1 D6 3B   ........ ....g..;
[060] 58 9D D5 93 CC                                    X....

00004c smb_io_rpc_auth_ntlmssp_chk auth_sign
    004c ver     : 00000001
    0050 reserved: 00000000
    0054 crc32   : bde9edb7
    0058 seq_num : 00000000
```

The Sequence Number increments each and every time either a request or a response is sent. The CRC32 Algorithm used is available from Dr. Dobb's Journal (http://www.ddj.com/ftp/1992/1992.05/crcman.zip), and Microsoft based its algorithm on this version. The checksum is calculated from the DCE/RPC fragment's Data Stream, and you can verify that the CRC32 received in the Authentication Verifier (shown in preceding log file section) matches with the one calculated below:

```
**********************************************************************
[000] 01 00 00 00 14 00 14 00  01 00 00 00 0A 00 00 00   ........ ........
[010] 00 00 00 00 0A 00 00 00  5C 00 5C 00 53 00 54 00   ........ \.\.S.T.
[020] 45 00 45 00 4C 00 45 00  59 00 45 00               E.E.L.E. Y.E.
crc32_calc_buffer: bde9edb7
```

## 1.5.5: DCE/RPC Function Calls (Operations)

A DCE/RPC function call is identified by its Operation Code (**Opnum**) and the DCE/RPC pipe name. The third byte in the DCE/RPC header is set to 0x03. A further eight bytes follow, in which the first four bytes indicate how much data is contained in the request (0x24 bytes starting at offset 0xA6 to 0xC9), and bytes seven and eight indicate the **Opnum**.

```
**********************************************************************
Frame   Time    Src MAC Addr   Dst MAC Addr   Protocol   Description
71      6.362   REGENT         brookfields    MSRPC      c/o RPC Request

  MSRPC: c/o RPC Request:      call 0x2  opnum 0xE  context 0x0  hint 0x24
      MSRPC: Version = 5 (0x5)
      MSRPC: Version (Minor) = 0 (0x0)
      MSRPC: Packet Type = Request
      MSRPC: Flags 1 = 3 (0x3)
      MSRPC: Packed Data Representation
      MSRPC: Fragment Length = 60 (0x3C)
      MSRPC: Authentication Length = 0 (0x0)
      MSRPC: Call Identifier = 2 (0x2)
      MSRPC: Bind Frame Number = 67 (0x43)
      MSRPC: Abstract Interface UUID = 367ABB81-9844-35F1-AD32-98F038001003
      MSRPC: Allocation Hint = 36 (0x24)
      MSRPC: Presentation Context Identifier = 0 (0x0)
      MSRPC: Operation Number (c/o Request prop. dg header prop) = 14 (0xE)
      MSRPC: Stub Data

00080:                                        05 00   P.I.P.E.\.......
00090:   00 03 10 00 00 00 3C 00 00 00 00 02 00 00 00    ......<........
                                              24 00                $.
000A0:   00 00 00 00 0E 00                               ......
                         00 00 00 00 6B 0F A6 23 AB 8B     ....k..#..
000B0:   D2 11 9C 42 00 A0 24 78 7B 3A 30 00 00 00 03 00  ...B..$x{:0.....
000C0:   00 00 00 04 00 00 00 00 00 00 00                ..........
```

### 1.5.5.1: Hand-Coded or Auto-Generated DCE/RPC Marshalling

Samba's first implementation of DCE/RPC marshalling and
unmarshalling deals with the data over-the-wire in an almost
unstructured format. Separate functions were used to deal with
DCE/RPC Request PDUs and Response PDUs, because there appeared
to be no connection between the PDUs. As regular patterns became
apparent to the developers, a series of subroutines were developed to
associate C structures with the marshalling or unmarshalling of the
network data. The developers were not aware of what the real C
structures were in the Interface Definition Language (IDL) files created
by the designers of the individual DCE/RPC services that they were
emulating. The only thing that the Samba developers were interested
in was that the responses made to Windows NT Workstations were
sufficient to make Samba look like a Windows NT Primary Domain
Controller. It was only later on that the developers became aware that
they were implementing DCE/RPC's Network Data Representation
(NDR) data format.

DCE/RPC services are *normally* specified in IDL format. Part of the
IDL specification says whether a parameter is an input or output
parameter (or both). To save on network bandwidth, if a parameter is
not to be modified by the remote function call, it is marked as an [in]
parameter, and it is only sent in the DCE/RPC Request PDU. If a
parameter is uninitialised and is to be set by the remote function call,
it is marked as an [out] parameter and is only sent in the DCE/RPC
Response PDU. If a parameter's value is to be used *by* the remote
function call *and* is to be *modified* by the remote function call, then it
is sent in both the DCE/RPC Request *and* Response PDUs.

So the whole reasoning behind Samba's first implementation was to
get up and running as quickly as possible, without having to worry
about any involvement with DCE/RPC specifications or services.
Lately, the developers have gotten to the point where they can look at
the NDR-based network traffic and make a good guess as to what the
IDL definition would be. Each chapter describing individual Windows
NT DCE/RPC-based services has one example that shows the MSDN
function prototype (or an equivalent function prototype if the service
is undocumented), plus the IDL definition from which the function
prototype and associated data structures were likely to have been
generated, followed by the DCE/RPC Request PDU and Response
PDU. This is done to help understand the relationship between the
network data and its actual usage. The intent is to help developers
decide whether to decode the raw DCE/RPC NDR network data or to
attempt to recreate their own IDL files.

### 1.5.5.2: Network Data Representation (NDR) Over-the-Wire

This section describes what Network Data Representation (NDR) data looks like on the wire. It covers formats for the following:

- Integers
- Structures
- Pointers
- References
- Strings
- Arrays
- Unions

*Integers*

1-, 2-, and 4-byte signed and unsigned integers, as individual function parameter arguments, are 4-byte aligned. This is presumably to improve the speed of marshalling and unmarshalling data on processor architectures that either access memory faster on 4-byte or 8-byte boundaries, or require memory to be accessed on such boundaries. The unused bytes following a 1- or 2-byte integer are undefined.

The NDR implementation in Windows NT does not initialise its data buffers to zeros prior to marshalling the function parameters into the buffer. This would seem to lead to confusion until a comparative trace from different times or different servers shows variations in the last bytes of a 4-byte block. From this, it can be deduced that a parameter that appears to be 4 bytes might actually be 2 bytes or even 1 byte. If a future implementation of Windows NT ever clears its network buffers properly prior to use, then a network engineer may incorrectly conclude that the top bytes, containing garbage, are actually important, leading to incompatibilities with other third-party implementations.

It is worth noting here that Windows NT Service Pack 2 and below does not send alignment bytes over-the-wire on the *very* last item in a Request or Response PDU. Therefore, on Service Pack 3 and above the last single byte integer will be followed by three bytes of uninitialised alignment bytes, and on Service Pack 2 and below the alignment bytes will be missing. The reported size of the DCE/RPC fragment in this instance will *not* match with the size of the SMB data being sent over-the-wire. While developing Samba's implementation of DCE/RPC, it was found to be relatively easy to crash DCE/RPC services running on Windows NT Service Pack 2 or below.

### Structures

Signed and unsigned integers in structures, one after the other as part of that structure, are not 4-byte aligned. Two single-byte integers in a structure therefore appear sequentially in the data stream. If those two single byte integers were separate, individual function parameter arguments, then they would be separated by three bytes of uninitialised alignment bytes.

### Pointers

The best way to think of the NDR representation of pointers is as tokens. They "represent" pointers. There must be a monotonic (one-to-one) mapping between the pointer that the token represents and the token itself. Windows NT is primarily implemented on a 32-bit platform, the x86 architecture and the NDR pointer-tokens are also 32-bit. Microsoft therefore puts memory addresses (sometimes actual pointers to kernel memory) over-the-wire, which does the trick and is simple to implement, but not very secure.

The purpose of maintaining a monotonic relationship between pointers and their NDR tokens is in case a structure such as a doubly-linked or circular-linked list is to be sent over-the-wire. In such instances, the NDR tokens must be used to properly reconstruct the back-pointers to the list items.

The usage for pointers over-the-wire is simple enough. If the token is non-zero then the item to which the pointer points will follow at some point in the data over-the-wire. If the token is zero, which represents a NULL pointer, then there is no item to send over-the-wire.

For an individual function parameter argument such as a pointer to a signed/unsigned integer or a pointer to a structure, a non-zero 32-bit token pointer will immediately be followed with the NDR representation of the item being pointed to.

For pointers contained within structures, something slightly different occurs. All pointers within the structure are turned into their 32-bit token representations. The NDR representation of the items being pointed to follows *after* the structure to which the token representations refer. The ordering is very specific, namely that if there is more than one pointer in a structure then the NDR representation of the first item being pointed to is represented first, followed by the second item being pointed to, and so on. If any of the tokens represent the NULL pointer, then of course the item does not follow. In the example shown here, the token pointers are at offsets 0x24 and 0x28, and the two structures to which these tokens refer are at offsets 0x2c and 0x4c, respectively (which are not shown in the following example).

```
0018 num_sids : 00000002
001c ptr: 00000001
0020 num_sids1: 00000002
0024 ptr_sid[00]: 00000001
0028 ptr_sid[01]: 00000001
00002c smb_io_dom_sid2
00004c smb_io_dom_sid2
```

```
[010]              00 00 00  02 00 00 00 01 00 00 00        ........
[020] 02 00 00 00 01 00 00 00  01 00 00 00              ........ ....
```

For pointers contained within lists or arrays of structures, the list or array of structures is treated as a structure. Therefore, any pointers to items in any of the structures are placed in the data stream *after* all the structures themselves. The minimal case for this is if the list or array is a list or array of pointers to items. What then happens is that the data stream is filled with a sequence of tokens and is then followed up with the NDR representation of the items being pointed to.

The implementation for pointers in Samba doesn't bother with monotonic tokens. The token representations are either 0x1 for a non-NULL or 0x0 for a NULL pointer. Windows NT's DCE/RPC unmarshalling code appears not to be bothered by this, which is great because it makes for dramatically simpler marshalling and unmarshalling code.

The following example is a UNICODE_STRING structure. The structure contains a buffer length (in bytes), maximum buffer length (in bytes), and a pointer to a buffer. The buffer itself is shown in the next section.

```
000030 smb_io_unihdr unihdr
    0030 uni_str_len: 0018
    0032 uni_max_len: 0018
    0034 buffer     : 00000001
```

```
[030] 18 00 18 00 01 00 00 00              ........
```

### Strings

Some structures are of variable length, such as strings. Under these circumstances, the actual length and the maximum length are sent over-the-wire in front of the string. The lengths specify the number of characters, where a character can be either one byte for ASCII or two bytes for UNICODE. The structure following the variable-length string will be 4-byte aligned, an issue that has caught the Samba developers out countless times.

The following example is the buffer pointed to in a
UNICODE_STRING structure. The string length and maximum string
length are in UNICODE characters. The fact that there is no NULL-
terminating character in the UNICODE string is normal because this is
the way that UNICODE strings can be specified.

```
000038 smb_io_unistr2
    0038 uni_max_len: 0000000c
    003c undoc     : 00000000
    0040 uni_str_len: 0000000c
    0044 buffer    : N.T.l.o.c.a.l.g.r.o.u.p.

[030]                  0C 00 00 00 00 00 00 00  ........ ........
[040] 0C 00 00 00 4E 00 54 00  6C 00 6F 00 63 00 61 00  ....N.T. l.o.c.a.
[050] 6C 00 67 00 72 00 6F 00  75 00 70 00              l.g.r.o. u.p.
```

Microsoft's use of length and maximum length parsing, for example to
marshall and unmarshall UNICODE strings, has a small bug in
Windows NT Service Pack 2 and below. The length and maximum
length do not have to be the same. The maximum length is specified
as one less character than the string length, and the UNICODE NULL
character is *not* sent in the buffer. The Allocation Hint field in the
DCE/RPC Request and Response PDUs is then two bytes short per
UNICODE string, which is very confusing. Service Pack 3 corrected
this problem.

### Arrays
Arrays, like strings, are of variable length. The number of items in the
array is therefore shown in the data stream before the items in the
array. In the example shown here, the number of items is specified at
offset 0x20. The two items are two pointers, which are at offsets 0x24
and 0x28 respectively.

```
0018 num_sids : 00000002
001c ptr: 00000001
0020 num_sids1: 00000002
0024 ptr_sid[00]: 00000001
0028 ptr_sid[01]: 00000001
00002c smb_io_dom_sid2
00004c smb_io_dom_sid2

[010]            00 00 00  02 00 00 00 01 00 00 00  ........
[020] 02 00 00 00 01 00 00 00  01 00 00 00          ........ ....
```

*References*

References are like pointers, except they can never be NULL. This makes the marshalling and unmarshalling process *much* simpler, but any reference parameters will require checking at run-time to ensure that they are in fact non-NULL. An IDL compiler will generate function prototype stubs that look identical no matter whether a pointer argument is or is not a reference, so examining the function prototype alone is not sufficient. The data over-the-wire must also be examined to look for evidence of pointer tokens preceding an argument.

The use of references is much preferred for simple arguments. Failure to specify that an argument should be a reference will result in a pointer token being sent over-the-wire followed by the argument itself. This can unnecessarily increase the amount of network bandwidth.

# 1.6: Summary

The use of DCE/RPC for Windows NT Services is inspired. DCE/RPC provides authenticated, remote management of those services, and there is no burden placed on users, so they are often not even aware that DCE/RPC is being used. The decision to use SMB as a transport for DCE/RPC is also a very good one. Although the implementation is a little clumsy, using SMB as a transport grants DCE/RPC the benefits of SMB authentication and SMB transport independence. For example, Windows NT 5.0 now has SMB directly over TCP/IP. No modifications will have been necessary at the DCE/RPC layer.

Microsoft's implementation of DCE/RPC on Windows NT 4.0 has a few robustness problems in it, which has been satisfactorily resolved in Windows NT 5.0. These problems are due to lack of checks in the unmarshalling process that can result in Services terminating if they are attacked with deliberately bad MSRPC requests. The author is actively involved in assisting Microsoft to resolve these issues.

# 2

# Windows NT Authentication Internal Architecture

The design of Windows NT is flexible enough to have major components, such as a User Accounts Database, added or replaced. Some of the APIs to implement authentication systems have just recently been published by Microsoft.

Windows NT 4.0 and 5.0 include three well-known Accounts Database systems:

- Security Accounts Manager (SAM)
- NetWare Directory Services (NDS)
- Kerberos 5 and Lightweight Directory Access (LDAP)

Each of these systems is an implementation of a Local Security Authority (LSA), and they must comply to the LSA Server Service (LSASS) API. Default Windows NT 4.0 installations will have the SAM database system enabled, which uses the NETLOGON API to communicate.

## 2.1: Local Security Authority

There are two Local Security Authority (LSA) APIs. One is a client-side API, with documented functions such as **LsaLogonUser** and undocumented functions such as **LsaLogonUserEx**. The other is a server-side API, which is documented on Microsoft's Web site (www.microsoft.com). This is the **LsaAp*** API. Function definitions can be found in **ntsecapi.h**.

The implementation of the client-side API is responsible for enumerating through dynamically installed instances of the server-side API. In this way, it is possible to provide a consistent interface to third-party developers whilst maintaining the capability to replace or update the User Accounts Database *without* the third-party developers needing to rewrite or recompile parts of the Windows NT Operating System. The same goal, namely to provide the same kind of application and operating system independence, is also achieved in the **WNet\*** and **NPNet\*** APIs.

## LSA Servers

Local Security Authority Services are implementations of the **LsaAp** API. The **LsaAp** API contains about four functions, listed here:

- **LsaApInitializePackage**
- **LsaApCallPackage**
- **LsaLogonUser**
- **LsaLogonTerminated**

Of particular note is **LsaApInitialisePackage**, shown here:

```
NTSTATUS LsaApInitializePackage (
            IN ULONG AuthenticationPackageId,
            IN PLSA_DISPATCH_TABLE LsaDispatchTable,
            IN PLSA_STRING Database OPTIONAL,
            IN PLSA_STRING Confidentiality OPTIONAL,
            OUT PLSA_STRING *AuthenticationPackageName
                    );
```

**LsaApInitializePackage** is passed a higher-order function table that contains an array of function pointers, also known in Windows terminology as *callbacks*. The table, known as the **LSA_DISPATCH_TABLE** is listed here:

```
typedef struct _LSA_DISPATCH_TABLE {
    PLSA_CREATE_LOGON_SESSION    CreateLogonSession;
    PLSA_DELETE_LOGON_SESSION    DeleteLogonSession;
    PLSA_ADD_CREDENTIAL          AddCredential;
    PLSA_GET_CREDENTIALS         GetCredentials;
    PLSA_DELETE_CREDENTIAL       DeleteCredential;
    PLSA_ALLOCATE_LSA_HEAP       AllocateLsaHeap;
    PLSA_FREE_LSA_HEAP           FreeLsaHeap;
    PLSA_ALLOCATE_CLIENT_BUFFER  AllocateClientBuffer;
    PLSA_FREE_CLIENT_BUFFER      FreeClientBuffer;
    PLSA_COPY_TO_CLIENT_BUFFER   CopyToClientBuffer;
    PLSA_COPY_FROM_CLIENT_BUFFER CopyFromClientBuffer;
} LSA_DISPATCH_TABLE, *PLSA_DISPATCH_TABLE;
```

This array of functions is responsible, amongst other things, for the management of authenticated users *as represented by the LSA Server instance*. So, when a user is authenticated with the client-side function

**LsaLogonUserEx**, the implementation of **LsaLogonUserEx** is
responsible for calling the **LsaApLogonUser** function of the currently
installed and active LSA Server instance. The function prototype for
**LsaApLogonUser** is shown here:

```
NTSTATUS LsaApLogonUser (
                IN PLSA_CLIENT_REQUEST ClientRequest,
                IN SECURITY_LOGON_TYPE LogonType,
                IN PVOID AuthenticationInformation,
                IN PVOID ClientAuthenticationBase,
                IN ULONG AuthenticationInformationLength,
                OUT PVOID *ProfileBuffer,
                OUT PULONG ProfileBufferLength,
                OUT PLUID LogonId,
                OUT PNTSTATUS SubStatus,
                OUT PLSA_TOKEN_INFORMATION_TYPE TokenInformationType,
                OUT PVOID *TokenInformation,
                OUT PLSA_UNICODE_STRING *AccountName,
                OUT PLSA_UNICODE_STRING *AuthenticatingAuthority
                    );
```

If **LsaApLogonUser** successfully indicates that the user is validated,
then the higher-order function table function **CreateLogonSession** of
the LSA Server instance is called. In this way, the LSA Server instance
can keep track of a list of active, authenticated users.
**CreateLogonSession**, shown below, returns a Local User Identifier
(LUID), which is returned to **LsaApLogonUser** and then to the
client-side implementation of the LSA function, **LsaLogonUserEx**.

```
typedef NTSTATUS
(*PLSA_CREATE_LOGON_SESSION) (
                IN PLUID LogonId
                        );
```

When the user logs out, the client-side LSA implementation calls the
server-side function **LsaApLogonTerminated**, shown here:

```
VOID LsaApLogonTerminated (
                IN PLUID LogonId
                        );
```

The higher-order function table function **DeleteLogonSession**, shown
below, of the LSA Server instance can be called with the LUID of the
user that is logging out, but this should be done only under unusual or
emergency circumstances, as it terminates a logon session with
prejudice.

```
typedef NTSTATUS
(*PLSA_DELETE_LOGON_SESSION) (
                IN PLUID LogonId
```

The LSA Server instance will then remove this LUID from its internal
list of active, authenticated users.

## LSA Applications and GINAs

The default Windows NT 4.0 installation has only one LSA Application installed, which is implemented in **MSV1_0.DLL**. This is the implementation of the Windows NT SAM Database. The installation of the NetWare Client for Windows NT will install a second LSA Application, **NWPROVAU.DLL** plus a replacement Graphical Identification and Authentication (GINA) DLL to allow users to type in their NetWare login information. GINA instances are responsible for *obtaining* identification information such as a password or a retinal scan from a user. GINAs are not to be confused with LSA instances, which are responsible for *validating* the User identification information obtained, for example via a GINA.

As the GINA API is well documented, a number of third parties have implemented GINAs that also combine User validation with obtaining User authentication information. They do this by first obtaining authentication information, validating the information against a third-party database, and then create a dummy user if the validation succeeds. Then the *same* authentication information is passed to the default Windows NT GINA, **MSGINA.DLL**, as a dummy user has been created, **MSGINA.DLL** successfully authenticates the user and initiates a Windows NT interactive session. When the interactive user logs out, the dummy User account is deleted by the third-party GINA. In this way, a user can appear to be successfully logging in to a Windows NT Workstation against, for example, a Unix NIS password database.

The problems with this approach are that only interactive users can be validated in this way. By taking the proper approach, namely to implement an LSA Server Application, non-interactive users can also be validated. In the case where a third party wishes to access files on a Workstation, and the Workstation is a member of a NT Domain, the Workstation will, via the LSA API, contact the Primary Domain Controller. The interactive GINA system is most *definitely* not involved in this particular process in any way.

# 2.2: SAM Database Authentication

Security Accounts Manager (SAM) Database Authentication is implemented in **MSV1_0.DLL**. It is responsible for validating Windows NT Users and providing the user's profile information on request. This is done with the NETLOGON API, specifically the **NetrSamLogon** function.

MSV1_0.DLL's job is to find the server responsible for the Domain that the user has requested to be logged in to and then authenticate the user in that Domain. The Domain can be the local Workstation, the local Primary Domain Controller (PDC), or a Trusted Domain Controller. The responsibility for authenticating a user can therefore be directly against a SAM database on the user's own Workstation, or it can be handed off to a remote, trusted Server. In each instance, the same **NetrSamLogon** call is ultimately used, potentially by different Servers.

The implementation and management of the SAM Database are different issues that do not impact SAM Authentication itself. For completeness, it is worth mentioning that the SAM database itself is stored in the Windows NT Registry, and is managed through the **samr pipe** service. This is in contrast to Windows NT 5.0, which uses Kerberos 5 for authentication and LDAP to store the User Accounts Database.

## 2.2.1: NETLOGON

The **NETLOGON** API provides SAM Database authentication and replication services. It is implemented in **NETLOGON.DLL**. The use of DCE/RPC for the **NETLOGON** API is inspired. It allows users to log in locally to a Workstation, or locally on a PDC, or remotely to a PDC, or remotely to a Trusted Domain.

When a user logs in at the Windows NT interactive login dialog, **NetrSamLogon** is ultimately called, via the LSA API. The use of DCE/RPC ensures that the call is redirected to the local service when the user is logging in locally to the local Workstation or is logging in at the PDC, or to a remote Service when the user is logging in remotely to a PDC or a Trusted Domain.

Sometimes a Domain Controller for the Trusted Domain cannot be found directly, but this does not present a problem. The nearest Domain Controller that has a trust relationship established can be contacted instead. This Domain Controller then contacts the Trusted Domain Controller on behalf of the user. All this activity is *completely* transparent to a user, other than the interactive User login process may take a bit longer than usual.

## 2.3: Kerberos 5 and LDAP

Windows NT 5.0 uses Kerberos 5 for its authentication and LDAP to store User account information. Kerberos authentication can be implemented as just another LSA Service instance, as in fact some third-party developers have already done for Windows NT 4.0.

Details on the exact mechanism implemented by Microsoft are not available at the time of writing and are beyond the scope of this book. There are several white papers on the subject on Microsoft's Web site, and the Massachusetts Institute of Technology is actively being consulted by Microsoft on the development and use of Kerberos.

## 2.4: NIS Authentication

AT&T obtained a source code license for Windows NT, and ported it to Unix as their Advanced File and Print Sharer (AFPS) product. It is rumoured that they also wrote an NIS-based LSA to assist with integration with Unix environments. It is not known how this NIS LSA can be obtained.

## 2.5: Summary

Windows NT User Authentication can be done against any suitable service, with the use of appropriate components. Examples of such services include NT Domains, NDS, Kerberos, and NIS. It is hoped that the publication of the **LsaAp\*** API will result in a more wide-spread adoption of alternative authentication services, which would benefit Administrators and users of mixed computing environments.

# 3

# \PIPE\lsarpc: NT's Local Security Authority Service

The **lsarpc** pipe provides remote access to the Local Security Authority (LSA). All these functions are fully documented in the MSDN documentation. It provides, amongst other things, the resolution of:

- Names in a Domain to Security Identifiers (SIDs).
- SIDs to Domain member names (of the format "DOMAIN\Domain Name").
- The SID of the Domain of which a Server is a member.
- The SID of the SAM database for which a Server is responsible.

The Local Security Authority allows for the resolution of account and other critical information that can be found whilst users are logging in; whilst access is being made to security information on files, registry entries, or other Windows NT objects; whilst User Manager for Domains is providing administration of accounts, and so on.

Fortunately, the functions in this pipe are fully documented, and the MSDN file **ntsecapi.h** lists their prototypes. In fact, the functions listed in **ntsecapi.h** look as if they are generated directly from the original Interface Definition Language (IDL) files. Net Monitor probably also had its LSA parser generated from these IDL files, so it correctly lists these functions. Net Monitor displays these functions as starting with the prefix **Lsar** (and so does this chapter), whilst the functions listed in **ntsecapi.h** start with **Lsa**.

This pipe can be accessed anonymously. It is possible to resolve a considerable amount of information without even a User name, let alone a password.

## 3.1: lsarpc Calls

Samba currently only supports these functions because they provide the minimum level of service required for NT Domain support:

- LsarOpenPolicy2
- LsarQueryInfoPolicy
- LsarLookupNames
- LsarLookupSids
- LsarClose

An **LsarOpenPolicy2** call is made and a policy handle returned. This handle is passed to all function calls, such as **LsarQueryInfoPolicy**, which is used to determine the role of the Server (a Domain Controller or a member of a Domain). Finally, an **LsarClose** call is made to inform the Server that it can free any resources it may have allocated to service the client's requests. It is important to call **LsarClose**: some Servers are known to run out of resources otherwise, and they will eventually require rebooting.

### 3.1.1: LsarOpenPolicy2

**LsarOpenPolicy2** initiates communication with a remote Local Security Authority. The MSDN name for this function is **LsaOpenPolicy**, which is shown here. This function prototype is automatically generated from its IDL file definition.

```
NTSTATUS
LsaOpenPolicy(
    IN PLSA_UNICODE_STRING SystemName OPTIONAL,
    IN PLSA_OBJECT_ATTRIBUTES ObjectAttributes,
    IN ACCESS_MASK DesiredAccess,
    IN OUT PLSA_HANDLE PolicyHandle
    );
```

An attempt to re-create the IDL definition for this function is shown next. It is very similar to the auto-generated MSDN function prototype, above. The [in] and [in out] parameters are sent over-the-wire in the request, and the [in out] and [out] parameters are sent back over-the-wire in the response.

```
typedef struct _OBJECT_ATTRIBUTES {
    DWORD                dwLength;
    HANDLE*              hRootDirectory;
    LPWSTR               pObjectName;
    DWORD                dwAttributes;
    SECURITY_DESCRIPTOR* pSecurityDescriptor;
    SECURITY_QOS*        pSecurityQualityOfService;
} OBJECT_ATTRIBUTES;
```

```
STATUS LsarOpenPolicy2(          /* Function 0x2C */
                [in,unique] LPWSTR              lpServer,
                [in,ref] OBJECT_ATTRIBUTES* pAttr,
                [in] DWORD              dwAccessMask,
                [out] HANDLE*           hPolicy
                    );
```

The request shows all the **[in]** and **[in out]** parameters. It contains the
name of the remote Server plus security context information.

```
**************************************************************************
Frame   Time    Src MAC Addr   Dst MAC Addr   Protocol  Description
151     43.665  REGENT         STEELEYE       R_LSARPC  RPC Client call
  R_LSARPC: RPC Client call lsarpc:LsarOpenPolicy2(..)
      R_LSARPC: PLSAPR_SERVER_NAME SystemName = \\FERENGI
      R_LSARPC: PLSAPR_OBJECT_ATTRIBUTES ObjectAttributes {..}
          R_LSARPC: ULONG Length = 24 (0x18)
          R_LSARPC: PUCHAR RootDirectory = 0 (0x0)
          R_LSARPC: PSTRING ObjectName = 0 (0x0)
          R_LSARPC: ULONG Attributes = 0 (0x0)
          R_LSARPC: PLSAPR_SECURITY_DESCRIPTOR SecurityDescriptor = 0 (0x0)
          R_LSARPC: PSECURITY_QUALITY_OF_SERVICE SecurityQualityOfService = 15857428
➡(0xF1F714)
          R_LSARPC: PSECURITY_QUALITY_OF_SERVICE SecurityQualityOfService {..}
              R_LSARPC: ULONG Length = 12 (0xC)
              R_LSARPC: SECURITY_IMPERSONATION_LEVEL ImpersonationLevel = 2 (0x2)
              R_LSARPC: SECURITY_CONTEXT_TRACKING_MODE ContextTrackingMode = 1 (0x1)
              R_LSARPC: BOOLEAN EffectiveOnly = 0 (0x0)

000A0:                   E0 D6 14 00 0A 00 00 00 00 00    ..........
000B0:  00 00 0A 00 00 00 5C 00 5C 00 46 00 45 00 52 00    ......\.\.F.E.R.
000C0:  45 00 4E 00 47 00 49 00 00 00 18 00 00 00 00 00    E.N.G.I.........
000D0:  00 00 00 00 00 00 00 00 00 00 00 00 00 00 14 F7    ...............
000E0:  F1 00 0C 00 00 00 02 00 01 00 01 00 00 00          ..............
```

The response shows all the **[out]** and **[in out]** parameters. It contains a
Policy Handle and a return status code. If the status code is non-zero,
then the Policy Handle is blank (all zeros).

```
**************************************************************************
Frame   Time    Src MAC Addr   Dst MAC Addr   Protocol  Description
152     43.668  STEELEYE       REGENT         R_LSARPC  RPC Server response

  R_LSARPC: RPC Server response lsarpc:LsarOpenPolicy2(..)
      R_LSARPC: LSAPR_HANDLE PolicyHandle
      R_LSARPC: Return Value = 0 (0x0)

00080:                         00 00 00 00 99 B4    ..............
00090:  37 B5 2A 7A D2 11 80 DD EB AF CB A1 80 CE 00 00    7.*z...........
000A0:  00 00                                              ..
```

## 3.1.2: LsarQueryInfoPolicy

**LsarQueryInfoPolicy** obtains Domain-related information about a remote host. The MSDN name for this function is **LsaQueryInformationPolicy**, which is shown here:

```
NTSTATUS
NTAPI
LsaQueryInformationPolicy(
    IN LSA_HANDLE PolicyHandle,
    IN POLICY_INFORMATION_CLASS InformationClass,
    OUT PVOID *Buffer
    );
```

By making two separate **LsarQueryInfoPolicy** calls, this function is used to determine the status of a remote Server:

- A member of a Workgroup
- A member of a Domain
- A Domain Controller

Samba supports two Policy Information classes: 3 and 5. In the MSDN file **ntsecapi.h,** these are listed as **PolicyPrimaryDomainInformation** and **PolicyAccountDomainInformation,** respectively. Windows NT supports all the Policy Information Classes listed in **ntsecapi.h.**

```
***********************************************************************
Frame   Time    Src MAC Addr   Dst MAC Addr   Protocol   Description
153     43.669  REGENT         STEELEYE       R_LSARPC   RPC Client call

  R_LSARPC: RPC Client call lsarpc:LsarQueryInformationPolicy(..)
      R_LSARPC: LSAPR_HANDLE PolicyHandle
      R_LSARPC: POLICY_INFORMATION_CLASS InformationClass = 5 (0x5)

000A0:                      00 00 00 00 99 B4 37 B5 2A 7A   ............7.*z
000B0:  D2 11 80 DD EB AF CB A1 80 CE 05 00              ............
```

Both the Policy Information responses at Levels 3 and 5 happen to contain a SID, plus a name associated with the SID.

```
***********************************************************************
Frame   Time    Src MAC Addr   Dst MAC Addr   Protocol   Description
156     43.675  STEELEYE       REGENT         R_LSARPC   RPC Server response

  R_LSARPC: RPC Server response lsarpc:LsarQueryInformationPolicy(..)
      R_LSARPC: PLSAPR_POLICY_INFORMATION PolicyInformation {..}
          R_LSARPC: Switch Value = 3 (0x3)
          R_LSARPC: LSAPR_POLICY_PRIMARY_DOM_INFO PolicyPrimaryDomainInfo {..}
              R_LSARPC: LSAPR_UNICODE_STRING Name {..}
              R_LSARPC: PLSAPR_SID Sid = 30946928 (0x1D83670)
              R_LSARPC: PWSTR Buffer [..] = NT5_BORG
              R_LSARPC: PLSAPR_SID Sid {..}
```

```
                 R_LSARPC: UCHAR Revision = 1 (0x1)
                 R_LSARPC: UCHAR SubAuthorityCount = 4 (0x4)
                 R_LSARPC: SID_IDENTIFIER_AUTHORITY IdentifierAuthority {..}
                     R_LSARPC: UCHAR Value [..] = 00 00 00 00 00 05
                 R_LSARPC: ULONG SubAuthority [..] = 00000015 5475B975 2A1F6232
➡65D637A8
     R_LSARPC: Return Value = 0 (0x0)

00080:                            68 15 D8 01 03 00   ..P.......h.....
00090:  37 B5 10 00 12 00 E8 0F D5 01 70 36 D8 01 09 00   7.........p6....
000A0:  00 00 00 00 00 00 08 00 00 00 4E 00 54 00 35 00   ..........N.T.5.
000B0:  5F 00 42 00 4F 00 52 00 47 00 04 00 00 00 01 04   _.B.O.R.G.......
000C0:  00 00 00 00 00 05 15 00 00 00 75 B9 75 54 32 62   ..........u.uT2b
000D0:  1F 2A A8 37 D6 65 00 00 00 00 00                  .*.7.e....
```

Level 3 returns the following structure:

```
typedef struct _POLICY_ACCOUNT_DOMAIN_INFO {

    LSA_UNICODE_STRING DomainName;
    PSID DomainSid;
} POLICY_ACCOUNT_DOMAIN_INFO, *PPOLICY_ACCOUNT_DOMAIN_INFO;
```

Level 5 returns the following structure:

```
typedef struct _POLICY_PRIMARY_DOMAIN_INFO {

    LSA_UNICODE_STRING Name;
    PSID Sid;

} POLICY_PRIMARY_DOMAIN_INFO, *PPOLICY_PRIMARY_DOMAIN_INFO;
```

Information Level 3 (**PolicyPrimaryDomainInformation**) will return
the SID and the Domain name of which the remote Server is a
member. Information Level 5 (**PolicyAccountDomainInformation**) will
return the SID and the SAM database name for which the remote
Server is responsible. When a remote Server is a member of a
workgroup, the SID and the name in the DCE/RPC response are
NULL. This is best illustrated with some examples. In particular, note
the difference between a Domain Member and Domain Controller:

- Member of **Domain**
    - A request for Level 3 returns the Primary Domain SID
      and the Domain name (for example, MYDOMAIN).
    - A request for Level 5 returns the Local Workstation's
      SID and the name of the Workstation (for example,
      \\MYWORKSTATION).
- **Primary Domain Controller**
    - A request for Level 3 returns the Primary Domain SID
      and the Domain name (for example, MYDOMAIN).

- A request for Level 5 returns *exactly* the same information as for Level 3.
  - **Member of Workgroup**
    - A request for Level 3 returns NULL for the SID and an empty UNICODE string buffer for the name.
    - A request for Level 5 returns *exactly* the same information as for Level 3.

In this way, **USRMGR.EXE** can determine whether it is being run on a Workstation (Start | Run | "USRMGR.EXE \\MYWORKSTATION") or a Domain (Start | Run | "USRMGR MYDOMAIN"). User Manager for Domains behaves like **MUSRMGR.EXE**, a program provided with Windows NT Workstation to manage a Workstation's local SAM Database. The exception is if MYWORKSTATION is actually a Domain Controller. In this instance, the **LsarQueryInfoPolicy** call at Level 5 (**PolicyPrimaryDomainInformation**) determines that the Domain isn't a local SAM Database. It therefore shows an informational dialog box onscreen before proceeding to show the Domain Users, as if you had selected the Domain with **USRMGR.EXE** rather than \\MYWORKSTATION. In other words, the local SAM Database on a Domain Controller *is* the Domain SAM Database.

### 3.1.3: LsarLookupNames

**LsarLookupNames** is known in the MSDN as **LsaLookupNames**, shown here:

```
NTSTATUS
LsaLookupNames(
    IN LSA_HANDLE PolicyHandle,
    IN ULONG Count,
    IN PLSA_UNICODE_STRING Names,
    OUT PLSA_REFERENCED_DOMAIN_LIST *ReferencedDomains,
    OUT PLSA_TRANSLATED_SID *Sids
    );
```

**LsarLookupNames** will turn a list of Domain names (of the format DOMAIN\Name) into a list of SIDs. It will also identify whether those names are Users, Groups, Aliases, and so on. A Domain Controller will resolve names from Trusted Domains as well as from its own Domain. A Workstation will only resolve names in its local SAM database.

The data structures returned are optimised. The full SID of each name being looked up is not returned individually. Instead, an additional reference array of Domain SIDs is returned. The structure that contains the reference array is shown here:

```
typedef struct _LSA_REFERENCED_DOMAIN_LIST {

    ULONG Entries;
    PLSA_TRUST_INFORMATION Domains;

} LSA_REFERENCED_DOMAIN_LIST, *PLSA_REFERENCED_DOMAIN_LIST;
```

The actual structure from which the reference array of Domain SIDs is constructed is shown here:

```
typedef struct _LSA_TRUST_INFORMATION {

    LSA_UNICODE_STRING Name;
    PSID Sid;

} LSA_TRUST_INFORMATION, *PLSA_TRUST_INFORMATION;
```

An array of the following structures is also returned:

```
typedef struct _LSA_TRANSLATED_SID {

    SID_NAME_USE Use;
    ULONG RelativeId;
    LONG DomainIndex;

} LSA_TRANSLATED_SID, *PLSA_TRANSLATED_SID;
```

Each name being looked up has an index to this array, plus a Relative Identifier (RID). To reconstruct the full SID, you have to look up the Domain SID by its index in the Referenced Domain array and then append the RID for the name being resolved. In this way, the amount of information going over-the-wire is considerably reduced.

A request contains a valid Policy Handle—the number of names being looked up followed by an array of names, shown here:

```
*****************************************************************************
Frame   Time    Src MAC Addr   Dst MAC Addr   Protocol   Description
7       4.055   FERENGI        REGENT         R_LSARPC   RPC Client call

  MSRPC: c/o RPC Request:       call 0x3  opnum 0xE  context 0x0  hint 0x48
  R_LSARPC: RPC Client call lsarpc:LsarLookupNames(..)
      R_LSARPC: LSAPR_HANDLE PolicyHandle
      R_LSARPC: ULONG Count = 1 (0x1)
      R_LSARPC: PLSAPR_UNICODE_STRING Names [..]
          R_LSARPC: PLSAPR_UNICODE_STRING Names {..}
              R_LSARPC: USHORT Length = 8 (0x8)
              R_LSARPC: USHORT MaximumLength = 8 (0x8)
              R_LSARPC: PWSTR Buffer = 1 (0x1)
          R_LSARPC: PWSTR Buffer [..] = 0074 0065 0073 0074
      R_LSARPC: PLSAPR_TRANSLATED_SIDS TranslatedSids {..}
          R_LSARPC: ULONG Entries = 0 (0x0)
          R_LSARPC: PLSA_TRANSLATED_SID Sids = 0 (0x0)
      R_LSARPC: LSAP_LOOKUP_LEVEL LookupLevel = 1 (0x1)
      R_LSARPC: PULONG MappedCount = 1 (0x1)
```

```
00080:                         05 00 00 03 10 00 00 00 60 00    PE\...........`.
00090:    00 00 03 00 00 00 48 00 00 00 00 00 0E 00 00 00    ......H.........
000A0:    00 00 17 80 C8 BD 21 83 D2 11 8D C7 E0 DF AD 57    ......!........W
000B0:    4E 31 01 00 00 00 01 00 00 00 08 00 08 00 01 00    N1..............
000C0:    00 00 04 00 00 00 00 00 00 00 04 00 00 00 74 00    ..............t.
000D0:    65 00 73 00 74 00 00 00 00 00 00 00 00 00 01 00    e.s.t...........
000E0:    00 00 01 00 00 00                                  ......
```

A response contains an array of Domain SIDs, known as
**ReferencedDomains,** followed by an array of structures that contains
the type, RID, and Referenced Domain index for each successfully or
unsuccessfully resolved name, shown here:

```
*********************************************************************
Frame   Time    Src MAC Addr   Dst MAC Addr   Protocol   Description
8       4.057   REGENT         FERENGI        R_LSARPC   RPC Server response

 MSRPC: c/o RPC Response:    call 0x3  context 0x0  hint 0x74  cancels 0x0
 R_LSARPC: RPC Server response lsarpc:LsarLookupNames(..)
     R_LSARPC: PLSAPR_REFERENCED_DOMAIN_LIST ReferencedDomains {..}
        R_LSARPC: ULONG Entries = 1 (0x1)
        R_LSARPC: PLSAPR_TRUST_INFORMATION Domains = 1475856 (0x168510)
        R_LSARPC: ULONG MaxEntries = 32 (0x20)
        R_LSARPC: PLSAPR_TRUST_INFORMATION Domains [..]
           R_LSARPC: PLSAPR_TRUST_INFORMATION Domains {..}
              R_LSARPC: LSAPR_UNICODE_STRING Name {..}
                 R_LSARPC: USHORT Length = 10 (0xA)
                 R_LSARPC: USHORT MaximumLength = 12 (0xC)
                 R_LSARPC: PWSTR Buffer = 1461880 (0x164E78)
              R_LSARPC: PLSAPR_SID Sid = 1475200 (0x168280)
           R_LSARPC: PWSTR Buffer [..] = 0054 0045 0053 0054 0031
           R_LSARPC: PLSAPR_SID Sid {..}
              R_LSARPC: UCHAR Revision = 1 (0x1)
              R_LSARPC: UCHAR SubAuthorityCount = 4 (0x4)
              R_LSARPC: SID_IDENTIFIER_AUTHORITY IdentifierAuthority {..}
                 R_LSARPC: UCHAR Value [..] = 00 00 00 00 00 05
              R_LSARPC: ULONG SubAuthority [..] = 00000015 23FD786B 71DB117C
➥069E3812
     R_LSARPC: PLSAPR_TRANSLATED_SIDS TranslatedSids {..}
        R_LSARPC: ULONG Entries = 1 (0x1)
        R_LSARPC: PLSA_TRANSLATED_SID Sids = 1473584 (0x167C30)
        R_LSARPC: PLSA_TRANSLATED_SID Sids [..]
           R_LSARPC: PLSA_TRANSLATED_SID Sids {..}
              R_LSARPC: SID_NAME_USE Use = 1 (0x1)
              R_LSARPC: ULONG RelativeId = 1002 (0x3EA)
              R_LSARPC: LONG DomainIndex = 0 (0x0)
     R_LSARPC: PULONG MappedCount = 1 (0x1)
     R_LSARPC: Return Value = 0 (0x0)

00070:          05 00 02 03 10 00 00 00 8C 00 00 00 03 00    .`..............
00080:    00 00 74 00 00 00 00 00 00 00 50 4C 16 00 01 00    ..t.......PL....
00090:    00 00 10 85 16 00 20 00 00 00 01 00 00 00 0A 00    ...... .........
000A0:    0C 00 78 4E 16 00 80 82 16 00 06 00 00 00 00 00    ..xN............
```

```
000B0:   00 00 05 00 00 00 54 00 45 00 53 00 54 00 31 00    ......T.E.S.T.1.
000C0:   00 05 04 00 00 00 01 04 00 00 00 00 00 05 15 00    ................
000D0:   00 00 6B 78 FD 23 7C 11 DB 71 12 38 9E 06 01 00    ..kx.#¦..q.8....
000E0:   00 00 30 7C 16 00 01 00 00 00 01 00 00 00 EA 03    ..0¦............
000F0:   00 00 00 00 00 00 01 00 00 00 00 00 00 00          ..............
```

This function is very similar to **LsarLookupSids**, which instead translates SIDs into names.

## 3.1.4: LsarLookupSids

**LsarLookupSids** is known in the MSDN as **LsaLookupSids**, shown here:

```
NTSTATUS
LsaLookupSids(
    IN LSA_HANDLE PolicyHandle,
    IN ULONG Count,
    IN PSID *Sids,
    OUT PLSA_REFERENCED_DOMAIN_LIST *ReferencedDomains,
    OUT PLSA_TRANSLATED_NAME *Names
    );
```

**LsarLookupNames** will turn a list of SIDs into a list of names. It will also identify whether those names are Users, Groups, Aliases, and so on. Like **LsarLookupNames**, a Domain Controller resolves SIDs from Trusted Domains as well as its own Domain, and a Workstation only resolves SIDs from its local SAM database.

The data structures returned are optimised. The full name of each SID being looked up is not returned individually. Instead, an additional reference array of Domain SIDs is returned. The structure that contains the reference array is shown here:

```
typedef struct _LSA_REFERENCED_DOMAIN_LIST {

    ULONG Entries;
    PLSA_TRUST_INFORMATION Domains;

} LSA_REFERENCED_DOMAIN_LIST, *PLSA_REFERENCED_DOMAIN_LIST;
```

The actual structure from which the reference array of Domain SIDs is constructed is shown here:

```
typedef struct _LSA_TRUST_INFORMATION {

    LSA_UNICODE_STRING Name;
    PSID Sid;

} LSA_TRUST_INFORMATION, *PLSA_TRUST_INFORMATION;
```

An array of the following structures is also returned:

```
typedef struct _LSA_TRANSLATED_NAME {
```

```
        SID_NAME_USE Use;
        LSA_UNICODE_STRING Name;
        LONG DomainIndex;

} LSA_TRANSLATED_NAME, *PLSA_TRANSLATED_NAME;
```

Each SID being looked up has an index to this array, plus a name that is local to the Domain associated with that SID. The amount of information going over-the-wire is considerably reduced by sending the local name separately from the Domain's name.

A request contains a valid Policy Handle—the number of SIDs being looked up followed by an array of SIDs, shown below. Unfortunately, this is one of the few instances where Net Monitor misinterprets data. The mistake has been corrected by editing the frame in Net Monitor so that this request *looks* correct:

```
***************************************************************************
Frame   Time    Src MAC Addr   Dst MAC Addr   Protocol   Description
232     11.464  EMERY          REGENT         R_LSARPC   RPC Client call

 MSRPC: c/o RPC Request:      call 0x13  opnum 0xF  context 0x0  hint 0x54
 R_LSARPC: RPC Client call lsarpc:LsarLookupSids(..)
     R_LSARPC: LSAPR_HANDLE PolicyHandle
     R_LSARPC: PLSAPR_SID_ENUM_BUFFER SidEnumBuffer {..}
         R_LSARPC: ULONG Entries = 1 (0x1)
         R_LSARPC: PLSAPR_SID_INFORMATION SidInfo = 1241088 (0x12F000)
         R_LSARPC: PLSAPR_SID_INFORMATION SidInfo [..]
             R_LSARPC: PLSAPR_SID_INFORMATION SidInfo {..}
                 R_LSARPC: PLSAPR_SID Sid = 1342496 (0x147C20)
             R_LSARPC: PLSAPR_SID_INFORMATION SidInfo {..}
                 R_LSARPC: PLSAPR_SID Sid {..}
                     R_LSARPC: UCHAR Revision = 1 (0x1)
                     R_LSARPC: UCHAR SubAuthorityCount = 5 (0x5)
                     R_LSARPC: SID_IDENTIFIER_AUTHORITY IdentifierAuthority {..}
                         R_LSARPC: ULONG SubAuthority [..] = 00000015 23FD786B 71DB117C
➤069E3812 00000102
                         R_LSARPC: UCHAR Value [..] = 00 00 00 00 00 05
         R_LSARPC: PLSAPR_TRANSLATED_NAMES TranslatedNames {..}
             R_LSARPC: ULONG Entries = 0 (0x0)
             R_LSARPC: PLSAPR_TRANSLATED_NAME Names = 0 (0x0)
         R_LSARPC: LSAP_LOOKUP_LEVEL LookupLevel = 1 (0x1)
         R_LSARPC: PULONG MappedCount = 0 (0x0)

00080:  50 00 49 00 50 00 45 00 5C 00 00 00 00 0D 05 00    P.I.P.E.\.......
00090:  00 03 10 00 00 00 6C 00 00 00 13 00 00 00 54 00    ......l.......T.
000A0:  00 00 00 00 0F 00 00 00 00 00 74 18 B8 F1 C4 53    ..........t....S
000B0:  D2 11 8D B8 E3 E1 85 20 1B 22 01 00 00 00 00 F0    ....... ."......
000C0:  12 00 01 00 00 00 20 7C 14 00 05 00 00 00 01 05    ...... |........
000D0:  00 00 00 00 00 05 15 00 00 00 6B 78 FD 23 7C 11    ..........kx.#|.
000E0:  DB 71 12 38 9E 06 01 02 00 00 00 00 00 00 00 00    .q.8............
000F0:  00 00 01 00 02 00 00 00 00 00                      ..........
```

A response contains an array of Domain SIDs plus the Domain name, known as **TranslatedNames** array, followed by an array of structures that contain the type, name, and Referenced Domain index for each successfully or unsuccessfully resolved SID, shown here:

```
****************************************************************************
Frame   Time    Src MAC Addr   Dst MAC Addr   Protocol  Description
233     11.465  REGENT         EMERY          R_LSARPC  RPC Server response

  MSRPC: c/o RPC Response:     call 0x13  context 0x0  hint 0x9C  cancels 0x0
  R_LSARPC: RPC Server response lsarpc:LsarLookupSids(..)
      R_LSARPC: PLSAPR_REFERENCED_DOMAIN_LIST ReferencedDomains {..}
          R_LSARPC: ULONG Entries = 1 (0x1)
          R_LSARPC: PLSAPR_TRUST_INFORMATION Domains = 1512896 (0x1715C0)
          R_LSARPC: ULONG MaxEntries = 32 (0x20)
          R_LSARPC: PLSAPR_TRUST_INFORMATION Domains [..]
              R_LSARPC: PLSAPR_TRUST_INFORMATION Domains {..}
                  R_LSARPC: LSAPR_UNICODE_STRING Name {..}
                      R_LSARPC: USHORT Length = 10 (0xA)
                      R_LSARPC: USHORT MaximumLength = 12 (0xC)
                      R_LSARPC: PWSTR Buffer = 1468888 (0x1669D8)
                  R_LSARPC: PLSAPR_SID Sid = 1471712 (0x1674E0)
              R_LSARPC: PWSTR Buffer [..] = "TEST1"
              R_LSARPC: PLSAPR_SID Sid {..}
                  R_LSARPC: UCHAR Revision = 1 (0x1)
                  R_LSARPC: UCHAR SubAuthorityCount = 4 (0x4)
                  R_LSARPC: SID_IDENTIFIER_AUTHORITY IdentifierAuthority {..}
                      R_LSARPC: UCHAR Value [..] = 00 00 00 00 00 05
                  R_LSARPC: ULONG SubAuthority [..] = 00000015 23FD786B 71DB117C
➡069E3812
      R_LSARPC: PLSAPR_TRANSLATED_NAMES TranslatedNames {..}
          R_LSARPC: ULONG Entries = 1 (0x1)
          R_LSARPC: PLSAPR_TRANSLATED_NAME Names = 1468952 (0x166A18)
          R_LSARPC: PLSAPR_TRANSLATED_NAME Names [..]
              R_LSARPC: PLSAPR_TRANSLATED_NAME Names {..}
                  R_LSARPC: SID_NAME_USE Use = 2 (0x2)
                  R_LSARPC: LSAPR_UNICODE_STRING Name {..}
                      R_LSARPC: USHORT Length = 24 (0x18)
                      R_LSARPC: USHORT MaximumLength = 24 (0x18)
                      R_LSARPC: PWSTR Buffer = 1470128 (0x166EB0)
                  R_LSARPC: LONG DomainIndex = 0 (0x0)
                  R_LSARPC: PWSTR Buffer [..] = "Domain Users"
      R_LSARPC: PULONG MappedCount = 1 (0x1)
      R_LSARPC: Return Value = 0 (0x0)

00070:       05 00 02 03 10 00 00 00 B4 00 00 00 13 00   .l............
00080:  00 00 9C 00 00 00 00 00 00 00 D8 70 16 00 01 00   ...........p....
00090:  00 00 C0 15 17 00 20 00 00 00 01 00 00 00 0A 00   ...... .........
000A0:  0C 00 D8 69 16 00 E0 74 16 00 06 00 00 00 00 00   ...i...t........
000B0:  00 00 05 00 00 00 54 00 45 00 53 00 54 00 31 00   ......T.E.S.T.1.
000C0:  00 05 04 00 00 00 01 04 00 00 00 00 00 05 15 00   ................
000D0:  00 00 6B 78 FD 23 7C 11 DB 71 12 38 9E 06 01 00   ..kx.#¦..q.8....
000E0:  00 00 18 6A 16 00 01 00 00 00 02 00 14 00 18 00   ...j............
```

```
000F0:  18 00 B0 6E 16 00 00 00 00 00 0C 00 00 00 00 00    ...n..........
00100:  00 00 0C 00 00 00 44 00 6F 00 6D 00 61 00 69 00    ......D.o.m.a.i.
00110:  6E 00 20 00 55 00 73 00 65 00 72 00 73 00 01 00    n. .U.s.e.r.s...
00120:  00 00 00 00 00 00                                  ......
```

This function is very similar to **LsarLookupNames,** which instead translates names into SIDs.

### 3.1.5: LsarClose

**LsarClose** frees a Policy Handle. Its MSDN name is **LsaClose,** shown here:

```
NTSTATUS
LsaClose(
    IN LSA_HANDLE ObjectHandle
    );
```

The Server deduces that any resources allocated to service the client's requests using that handle are no longer needed. The **LsarClose** request simply contains the Policy Handle:

```
**********************************************************************
Frame   Time    Src MAC Addr   Dst MAC Addr   Protocol   Description
157     43.675  REGENT         STEELEYE       R_LSARPC   RPC Client call

  R_LSARPC: RPC Client call lsarpc:LsarClose(..)
      R_LSARPC: LSAPR_HANDLE ObjectHandle

00090:                              00 00 00 14 00    .....,........
000A0:  00 00 00 00 00 00 00 00 00 00 99 B4 37 B5 2A 7A    ............7.*z
000B0:  D2 11 80 DD EB AF CB A1 80 CE                      ..........
```

The response contains a blank Policy Handle and a status code. An error code is likely to be returned only when an **Lsar** policy handle that is not outstanding is passed to this call.

```
**********************************************************************
Frame   Time    Src MAC Addr   Dst MAC Addr   Protocol   Description
158     43.690  STEELEYE       REGENT         R_LSARPC   RPC Server response

  R_LSARPC: RPC Server response lsarpc:LsarClose(..)
      R_LSARPC: LSAPR_HANDLE PolicyHandle
      R_LSARPC: Return Value = 0 (0x0)

00080:                              00 00 00 00 00 00    ..............
00090:  00 00 00 00 00 00 00 00 00 00 00 00 00 00 00 00    ..............
000A0:  00 00                                              ..
```

## 3.2: lsarpc Security Issues

Anonymous access to this pipe, a risk in and of itself, allows too much information to be obtained, such as:

- The SID and the role of a Server
- Enumeration of a list of Domain names and their types
- A list of Trusted Domains

Each of these examples is discussed in the following sections.

### 3.2.1: SID and Server Role

Allowing an anonymous user to query whether a server is a Domain Controller, Domain Member, or Workstation is not good, particularly because the SID is also returned. Such a query is the first step in an attack using this pipe, as the SID needs to be known in order to resolve names in the Domain.

### 3.2.2: Enumerating Domain Names

After an attacker knows the SID for the target machine, he can begin to guess the SIDs for accounts in that Domain. This would be done by making multiple **LsarLookupSids** calls with arrays of SIDs, starting at the lowest well-known RID and going up. In this way, successful responses will tell the attacker not only whether a SID is in use, but the name and its type: User, Group, or Alias. A Workstation or other Trust Account can be identified by the $ on the end of the name. See Section 4.2, "NETLOGON Security Issues," for an analysis of Workstation Trust Account vulnerabilities.

Some sites advocate that the name of the well-known administrative accounts should be changed for security reasons. This attack makes a mockery of this good advice. It should be pointed out that if access to the LSA service and all other DCE/RPC services is blocked by a firewall and your only concern is external attacks (from outside the firewall), changing the names of all well-known accounts is still a good idea.

### 3.2.3: Enumerating Trusted Domains

An attacker can anonymously obtain a list of *other* Domains that are potential targets using a function call called **LsarEnumerateTrustedDomains**. This call is made at the Windows NT Login screen prior to the user having logged on, which is probably why this information is available anonymously.

Even if the attacker cannot resolve the location of the Domain Controllers they obtain in this list, they can ask the original Domain Controller that answered the **LsarEnumerateTrustedDomains** call to enumerate a list of users, using **LsarLookupSids**.

## 3.3: Summary

The Local Security Authority is a critical component of the Windows
NT Security model. The LSA *has* to provide Domain-related
information over a network, and using DCE/RPC is a very good way
to do this. The functions described here for this pipe are sufficient to
provide full NT Domain Controller or membership.

The decisions made by the LSA designers on what is considered to
be Too Much Information unfortunately conflicts with most security
experts' opinions. The Referenced Domains array in the LSA lookup
calls is very efficient in terms of network bandwidth and also in
memory efficiency; these lookup routines, however, are a bit of a pain
for developers to actually use. Other than these things, the LSA API
is very well designed, in terms of its usability, functionality, and
efficiency.

# 4

# \PIPE\NETLOGON: NT
# *Login and Authentication*
# *Services*

The **NETLOGON pipe** provides NT-style authentication to NT
interactive users, Backup Domain Controllers, and Trusted Domain
Controllers, and is also used by a Workstation to verify a third party
that contacts that Workstation. This last catagory is known as
*Pass Through* authentication, whereby the Workstation passes the
responsibility for authentication through to the Domain Controller.

Connections to the **NETLOGON pipe** are over anonymous IPC$.
A Credential Chain is established between the Workstation and the
Domain Controller by using a well-known secret known as a *Trust
Account password*. A Trust Account password is a 16-byte cleartext
equivalent LM hash. On an NT 4.0 Domain Controller, this is stored
in the SAM database as just another user account. On an NT 5.0 box,
Trust Accounts and User Accounts are kept in different parts of the
LDAP database.

The NETLOGON API is not documented. The reason for this is
that it is simply an instance of an internal API that is called by the
Local Security Authority API. The LSA has two login functions:
**LsaLogonUser**, which is documented, and **LsaLogonUserEx**, which is
not. Microsoft uses the latter. Inside the LSA Service, it calls each LSA
instance. On NT 3.5 and 4.0, by default this is MSV1_0.DLL. This
particular LSA instance will, on request, either verify a user against
the local SAM database or call NETLOGON functions to verify the
user against the Domain Controller's SAM database. On a Workstation on which the NetWare Login system has been installed, the

LSA Service will call the NetWare LSA instance. The order and number of LSA instances is specified in this Registry key:

REGEDIT4

```
[HKEY_LOCAL_MACHINE\SYSTEM\CurrentControlSet\Control\Lsa]
"Authentication Packages"=hex(7):6d,73,76,31,5f,30,00,00 "msv1_0"
```

Throughout all of this, MSDN users of the LSA API need not know what is going on underneath and need not change any of their code if an LSA instance is modified or even replaced. However, potential implementers emulating an LSA instance should be aware that Microsoft can update or replace an LSA at any time. For example, with the introduction of NT 4.0 Service Pack 4, an undocumented modification of the undocumented NETLOGON API has been added that is purported to have fixed a security problem. To date, information regarding this modification (called NETLOGON Secure Channel negotiation) has been withheld, in strict accordance with current Microsoft Business Policy.

# 4.1: NETLOGON Calls

The **NETLOGON pipe** calls that have been observed to date are listed here. Each of these calls is discussed in detail in the following sections.

- NetrServerRequestChallenge
- NetrServerAuthenticate2
- NetrServerPasswordSet
- NetrSamLogon
- NetrSamLogoff

These calls are used to authenticate users. **NetrServerRequest Challenge** and **NetrServerAuthenticate2** are used to establish a Credential Chain. All subsequent **NetrServerPasswordSet, NetrSamLogon,** and **NetrSamLogoff** calls will have Credential Challenges attached to them. The intention of these Challenges is to ensure that no malicious user can interfere with the logon process.

When a user logs on from a Workstation, a **NetrSamLogon** call is made. To indicate that the user is still logged on, at least one resource (a file or a pipe) is kept open on the Domain Controller. Usually this is the **NETLOGON pipe**. To indicate that a user is logging off, either a **NetrSamLogoff** call is made, or the last resource used by the user is disconnected. However, a bug in NT Workstation is under investigation by Microsoft at the time of writing: when the last resource is not disconnected, the Domain Controller effectively thinks the user is still logged on.

## 4.1.1: NETLOGON Credential Chain

The purpose of the Credential Chain is to ensure that a NETLOGON session cannot be hijacked (man-in-the-middle attacks). In NT 4.0 Service Pack 3 and below, no other forms of security are provided. Introduced in Service Pack 4 was a new Secured Channel. At the time of writing, no further information is available on this. No information has been provided as to what kinds of attacks this modification prevents.

The Credential Chain is generated from a shared secret, known as the Workstation Trust Account Password. When a Workstation is added to a Domain, a special account must be created in the Domain Controller's SAM database. Either Server Manager for Domains or the Network Control Panel, when an Administrator's User name and password are specified, can be used to do this. Without a Workstation Trust Account and the correct password, a user cannot log in to a Domain from a Workstation, for security reasons.

The Workstation Trust Account Password is initialised to the name of the Workstation in lowercase. This solves the problem of joining a Workstation to a Domain while the Workstation is not connected to the network; however, it presents a security risk that Microsoft is in the process of fixing, at the time of writing. Leaving this problem aside, there follows a verbose description on how the Credential Chain is generated and references to more detailed information.

The Client and Server generate and exchange two random 8-byte challenges using **NetrServerRequestChallenge**. Using **NetrAuthenticate2**, they then each generate and exchange Credentials created from a shared secret, known as the Workstation Trust Account Password. This proves to both the Client and the Server that they both know this shared secret. All subsequent calls (such as **NetrSamLogon**) will then have a Credential exchange attached.

Each time a Credential is generated, the recipient calculates the same credential and verifies that it is the same as the one it receives. At any time, if the Credentials do not match, the recipient assumes the channel is being hijacked. The Server will always return an error message to that and any other subsequent calls on that channel, and the Client will drop the connection. For more detailed information, refer to Appendix B, Section B.3.3, and to Samba Source code file credentials.c in Appendix A.

## 4.1.2: NetrServerRequestChallenge

This is the first call that is sent after a NETLOGON pipe is
established. The Credential Chain starts with a
**NetrServerRequestChallenge** call. A Workstation named
BROOKFIELDS is contacting the Domain Controller EMERY. The
Client (BROOKFIELDS) sends an 8-byte random challenge and
identifies itself to the Server (EMERY), as follows:

```
****************************************************************************
Frame   Time     Src MAC Addr   Dst MAC Addr   Protocol   Description
471     177.924 brookfields    EMERY          R_LOGON    RPC Client call
  MSRPC: c/o RPC Request:       call 0x1  opnum 0x4  context 0x0  hint 0x4C
  R_LOGON: RPC Client call logon:NetrServerReqChallenge(..)
     R_LOGON: LOGONSRV_HANDLE PrimaryName = \\EMERY
     R_LOGON: wchar_t ComputerName = BROOKFIELDS
     R_LOGON: PNETLOGON_CREDENTIAL ClientChallenge {..}
        R_LOGON: CHAR data [..] = 55 A6 B9 56 58 FF AE 01
000A0:                     60 D2 14 00 08 00 00 00 00 00   ......`.........
000B0:   00 00 08 00 00 00 5C 00 5C 00 45 00 4D 00 45 00   ......\.\.E.M.E.
000C0:   52 00 59 00 00 00 0C 00 00 00 00 00 00 00 0C 00   R.Y.............
000D0:   00 00 42 00 52 00 4F 00 4F 00 4B 00 46 00 49 00   ..B.R.O.O.K.F.I.
000E0:   45 00 4C 00 44 00 53 00 00 00 55 A6 B9 56 58 FF   E.L.D.S...U..VX.
000F0:   AE 01                                             ..
```

If the Client is not known to the Server, the Server will respond with a
non-zero error status and return a challenge consisting of all zeros.
Otherwise, the Server responds with its own random 8-byte challenge:

```
****************************************************************************
Frame   Time     Src MAC Addr   Dst MAC Addr   Protocol   Description
472     177.924 EMERY          brookfields    R_LOGON    RPC Server response

  MSRPC: c/o RPC Response:      call 0x1  context 0x0  hint 0xC  cancels 0x0
  R_LOGON: RPC Server response logon:NetrServerReqChallenge(..)
     R_LOGON: PNETLOGON_CREDENTIAL ServerChallenge {..}
        R_LOGON: CHAR data [..] = C9 4B A4 42 30 00 00 00
     R_LOGON: Return Value = 0 (0x0)

00080:                             C9 4B A4 42 30 00         ..........K.B0.
00090:   00 00 00 00 00 00                                   ......
```

In exchanging random credentials, the Client and Server ensure a high
probability that the session will not be hijacked. Both the Client and
the Server calculate an 8-byte Session Key from the two random
challenges and encrypt this key using the first eight bytes of a
well-known secret: the Workstation Trust Account Password.

The *Session Key* is associated with the NETLOGON session and
must be stored. It is used by both Client and Server to calculate
challenges, and it is also used to encrypt the user's password in
Interactive **NetrSamLogon** responses.

## 4.1.3: NetrServerAuthenticate2

The Client will have calculated an 8-byte *Session Key* based on the two challenges received in the **NetrRequestChallenge** exchange and the Workstation Trust Account Password. The Session Key is then used to generate a verification challenge that is sent to the Server; the Server calculates the same. If the Server matches what it calculates with what it receives, it calculates a verification challenge and sends it back to the Client. The Client can then, in the same way, verify the Server. If the verification fails, the NETLOGON session will not proceed.

In this way, both the Client and the Server can establish that, to a high degree of probability, there has not been a man-in-the-middle attack on the session. This of course assumes that the man-in-the-middle does not know the Workstation Trust Account Password (which, of course, starts out as a well-known value).

The Client **NetrServerAuthenticate2** call also contains negotiation flags. NT 3.51 has been known to send 0x000 000ff; NT 4.0 to NT 4.0 SP3 has been known to send 0x0000 01ff; and NT 4.0 SP4 to NT 4.0 SP4 has been known to send 0x4000 01ff. The meaning of these flags is not known, except that Microsoft added the 0x4000 0000 bit to Service Pack 4 due to a security problem found by Paul Ashton, of the Samba Team.

The Client **NetrServerAuthenticate2** call also contains an AccountType. For a Workstation Trust Account, this is set to 2. For an Inter Domain Trust Account, this is set to 4.

```
**************************************************************************
Frame   Time    Src MAC Addr   Dst MAC Addr   Protocol  Description
473     177.927 brookfields    EMERY          R_LOGON   RPC Client call

 MSRPC: c/o RPC Request:      call 0x2  opnum 0xF   context 0x0  hint 0x78
 R_LOGON: RPC Client call logon:NetrServerAuthenticate2(..)
     R_LOGON: LOGONSRV_HANDLE PrimaryName = \\EMERY
     R_LOGON: wchar_t AccountName = BROOKFIELDS$
     R_LOGON: NETLOGON_SECURE_CHANNEL_TYPE AccountType = 2 (0x2)
     R_LOGON: wchar_t ComputerName = BROOKFIELDS
     R_LOGON: PNETLOGON_CREDENTIAL ClientCredential {..}
         R_LOGON: CHAR data [..] = 0B 93 F0 16 35 CC 09 3B
     R_LOGON: PULONG NegotiateFlags = 1073742335 (0x400001FF)


000A0:            60 D2 14 00 08 00 00 00 00 00   ......`.........
000B0:   00 00 08 00 00 00 5C 00 5C 00 45 00 4D 00 45 00   ......\.\.E.M.E.
000C0:   52 00 59 00 00 00 0D 00 00 00 00 00 00 00 0D 00   R.Y.............
000D0:   00 00 42 00 52 00 4F 00 4F 00 4B 00 46 00 49 00   ..B.R.O.O.K.F.I.
000E0:   45 00 4C 00 44 00 53 00 24 00 00 00 02 00 0C 00   E.L.D.S.$.......
000F0:   00 00 00 00 00 00 0C 00 00 00 42 00 52 00 4F 00   ..........B.R.O.
00100:   4F 00 4B 00 46 00 49 00 45 00 4C 00 44 00 53 00   O.K.F.I.E.L.D.S.
00110:   00 00 0B 93 F0 16 35 CC 09 3B FF 01 00 40         ......5..;...@
```

The Server response contains the Server Credential from which the Client is able to verify the Server, plus the Server Negotiation flags. In this example, an NT 4.0 Domain Controller has responded by indicating that it does not support the new NT 4.0 SP4 NETLOGON flag 0x4000 0000:

```
*****************************************************************************
Frame   Time     Src MAC Addr   Dst MAC Addr   Protocol   Description
474     177.934  EMERY          brookfields    R_LOGON    RPC Server response

  MSRPC: c/o RPC Response:     call 0x2  context 0x0  hint 0x10  cancels 0x0
  R_LOGON: RPC Server response logon:NetrServerAuthenticate2(..)
      R_LOGON: PNETLOGON_CREDENTIAL ServerCredential {..}
          R_LOGON: CHAR data [..] = 4E 2D 95 09 82 66 1E 1B
      R_LOGON: PULONG NegotiateFlags = 511 (0x1FF)
      R_LOGON: Return Value = 0 (0x0)

00080:                       4E 2D 95 09 82 66    ..........N-...f
00090:  1E 1B FF 01 00 00 00 00 00 00             ..........
```

## 4.1.4: NetrServerPasswordSet

The **NetrServerPasswordSet** call is sent once per week. It is first sent when a user first logs in from a new Workstation that has just been made a member of the Domain. It uses the old Trust Account Password as a cypher stream key to encrypt the new Trust Account Password. A validation credential is also attached to the call.

```
*****************************************************************************
Frame   Time     Src MAC Addr   Dst MAC Addr   Protocol   Description
476     178.312  brookfields    EMERY          R_LOGON    RPC Client call

  MSRPC: c/o RPC Request:      call 0x3  opnum 0x6  context 0x0  hint 0x88
  R_LOGON: RPC Client call logon:NetrServerPasswordSet(..)
      R_LOGON: LOGONSRV_HANDLE PrimaryName = \\EMERY
      R_LOGON: wchar_t AccountName = BROOKFIELDS$
      R_LOGON: NETLOGON_SECURE_CHANNEL_TYPE AccountType = 2 (0x2)
      R_LOGON: wchar_t ComputerName = BROOKFIELDS
      R_LOGON: PNETLOGON_AUTHENTICATOR Authenticator {..}
          R_LOGON: NETLOGON_CREDENTIAL Credential {..}
              R_LOGON: CHAR data [..] = 0C F0 18 63 7D 93 7C D0
          R_LOGON: DWORD timestamp = 913409917 (0x3671877D)
      R_LOGON: PENCRYPTED_LM_OWF_PASSWORD UasNewPassword {..}
          R_LOGON: CYPHER_BLOCK data [..]
              R_LOGON: CYPHER_BLOCK data {..}
                  R_LOGON: CHAR data [..] = E6 21 3A A5 AB CE 74 68
              R_LOGON: CYPHER_BLOCK data {..}
                  R_LOGON: CHAR data [..] = F9 26 AD 75 22 55 E3 0A

000A0:                    60 D2 14 00 08 00 00 00 00 00    ......`.........
000B0:  00 00 08 00 00 00 5C 00 5C 00 45 00 4D 00 45 00    ......\.\.E.M.E.
000C0:  52 00 59 00 00 00 0D 00 00 00 00 00 00 00 0D 00    R.Y.............
```

```
000D0:   00 00 42 00 52 00 4F 00 4F 00 4B 00 46 00 49 00     ..B.R.O.O.K.F.I.
000E0:   45 00 4C 00 44 00 53 00 24 00 00 00 02 00 0C 00     E.L.D.S.$.......
000F0:   00 00 00 00 00 00 0C 00 00 00 42 00 52 00 4F 00     ..........B.R.O.
00100:   4F 00 4B 00 46 00 49 00 45 00 4C 00 44 00 53 00     O.K.F.I.E.L.D.S.
00110:   00 00 0C F0 18 63 7D 93 7C D0 7D 87 71 36 E6 21     .....c}.|.}.q6.!
00120:   3A A5 AB CE 74 68 F9 26 AD 75 22 55 E3 0A           :...th.&.u"U..
```

If the next step in the Credential Chain (received from the Client) is valid, the response from the Server contains another next step in the Credential Chain. In this way, both the Client and the Server assume that no interruptions in their communications have been attempted.

```
*************************************************************************
Frame   Time     Src MAC Addr   Dst MAC Addr   Protocol   Description
477     178.371  EMERY          brookfields    R_LOGON    RPC Server response

  MSRPC: c/o RPC Response:    call 0x3  context 0x0  hint 0x10  cancels 0x0
  R_LOGON: RPC Server response logon:NetrServerPasswordSet(..)
       R_LOGON: PNETLOGON_AUTHENTICATOR ReturnAuthenticator {..}
            R_LOGON: NETLOGON_CREDENTIAL Credential {..}
                 R_LOGON: CHAR data [..] = F3 FA C8 04 1E 2B 88 98
            R_LOGON: DWORD timestamp = 1453300 (0x162CF4)
       R_LOGON: Return Value = 0 (0x0)

00080:                           F3 FA C8 04 1E 2B     ..............+
00090:   88 98 F4 2C 16 00 00 00 00 00                  ...,......
```

Note that there is no way for the Server to validate that the Client is changing the Trust Account Password to a valid one. It is assumed that because the Credential Chain uses the Trust Account Password to set up a Session Key, the Client knows the Trust Account Password.

It is assumed that the Client knows the encryption mechanism and can, therefore, use the old Trust Account Password to encrypt the new one. This was the cause of problems with implementing Samba: we did not know the exact encryption mechanism, therefore we decoded or set the new Trust Account Password incorrectly. Subsequent logins from that Workstation failed because the Credential Chain could not be established due to inconsistent Trust Account Passwords.

## 4.1.5: NetrSamLogon

The **NetrSamLogon** call authenticates a user, and in response, the user's profile is returned. There are four versions of the SAM logon request. The two known versions are the *Interactive Logon* and the *Network Logon,* discussed in the following sections.

**Interactive Logon**

An Interactive Logon contains the following information:

- Domain Name
- Logon Identity (purpose unknown)
- User Name
- Workstation Name
- Obfuscated LM Password hash
- Obfuscated NT Password hash

The actual LM and NT 16-byte cleartext equivalent password hashes are sent over-the-wire, and they are encrypted with a well-known Cypher Stream using the Session Key calculated in the setup of the NETLOGON Credential Chain. A **NetrSamLogon** request follows:

```
************************************************************************
Frame   Time    Src MAC Addr   Dst MAC Addr   Protocol   Description
560     261.744 brookfields    EMERY          R_LOGON    RPC Client call

MSRPC: c/o RPC Request:      call 0x4  opnum 0x2  context 0x0  hint 0x10C
R_LOGON: RPC Client call logon:NetrLogonSamLogon(..)
    R_LOGON: LOGONSRV_HANDLE LogonServer = \\EMERY
    R_LOGON: wchar_t ComputerName = BROOKFIELDS
    R_LOGON: PNETLOGON_AUTHENTICATOR Authenticator {..}
        R_LOGON: NETLOGON_CREDENTIAL Credential {..}
            R_LOGON: CHAR data [..] = 64 89 5E CD 13 79 BE 8B
        R_LOGON: DWORD timestamp = 913410000 (0x367187D0)
    R_LOGON: PNETLOGON_AUTHENTICATOR ReturnAuthenticator {..}
        R_LOGON: NETLOGON_CREDENTIAL Credential {..}
            R_LOGON: CHAR data [..] = 6D 6F F6 77 00 00 14 00
        R_LOGON: DWORD timestamp = 0 (0x0)
    R_LOGON: NETLOGON_LOGON_INFO_CLASS LogonLevel = 1 (0x1)
    R_LOGON: PNETLOGON_LEVEL LogonInformation {..}
        R_LOGON: Switch Value = 1 (0x1)
        R_LOGON: PNETLOGON_INTERACTIVE_INFO LogonInteractive {..}
            R_LOGON: NETLOGON_LOGON_IDENTITY_INFO Identity {..}
                R_LOGON: UNICODE_STRING LogonDomainName {..}
                R_LOGON: ULONG ParameterControl = 0 (0x0)
                R_LOGON: OLD_LARGE_INTEGER LogonId {..}
                    R_LOGON: ULONG LowPart = 8304 (0x2070)
                    R_LOGON: LONG HighPart = 0 (0x0)
                R_LOGON: UNICODE_STRING UserName {..}
                R_LOGON: UNICODE_STRING Workstation {..}
            R_LOGON: LM_OWF_PASSWORD LmOwfPassword {..}
                R_LOGON: CYPHER_BLOCK data [..]
                    R_LOGON: CYPHER_BLOCK data {..}
                        R_LOGON: CHAR data [..] = 5C C8 6B 09 B3 DE C9 DD
                    R_LOGON: CYPHER_BLOCK data {..}
                        R_LOGON: CHAR data [..] = 67 F6 0C 17 60 0C 51 5B
            R_LOGON: NT_OWF_PASSWORD NtOwfPassword {..}
                R_LOGON: CYPHER_BLOCK data [..]
```

```
            R_LOGON: CYPHER_BLOCK data {..}
                R_LOGON: CHAR data [..] = 51 82 A5 EA 51 95 37 4B
            R_LOGON: CYPHER_BLOCK data {..}
                R_LOGON: CHAR data [..] = E7 A7 38 5B A6 A0 C0 82
        R_LOGON: USHORT * Buffer [..] = ROCKNROLL
        R_LOGON: USHORT * Buffer [..] = lkcl
        R_LOGON: USHORT * Buffer [..] = BROOKFIELDS

000A0:                   60 D2 14 00 08 00 00 00 00 00    ......`.........
000B0:  00 00 08 00 00 00 5C 00 5C 00 45 00 4D 00 45 00   ......\.\.E.M.E.
000C0:  52 00 59 00 00 00 E4 B7 1A 50 0C 00 00 00 00 00   R.Y......P......
000D0:  00 00 0C 00 00 00 42 00 52 00 4F 00 4F 00 4B 00   ......B.R.O.O.K.
000E0:  46 00 49 00 45 00 4C 00 44 00 53 00 00 00 E0 F9   F.I.E.L.D.S.....
000F0:  39 01 64 89 5E CD 13 79 BE 8B D0 87 71 36 EC F9   9.d.^..y....q6..
00100:  39 01 6D 6F F6 77 00 00 14 00 00 00 00 00 01 00   9.mo.w..........
00110:  01 00 CC FC 39 01 12 00 12 00 9E D3 14 00 00 00   ....9...........
00120:  00 00 70 20 00 00 00 00 00 00 08 00 08 00 94 D3   ..p ............
00130:  14 00 16 00 18 00 E0 67 14 00 5C C8 6B 09 B3 DE   .......g..\.k...
00140:  C9 DD 67 F6 0C 17 60 0C 51 5B 51 82 A5 EA 51 95   ..g...`.Q[Q...Q.
00150:  37 4B E7 A7 38 5B A6 A0 C0 82 09 00 00 00 00 00   7K..8[..........
00160:  00 00 09 00 00 00 52 00 4F 00 43 00 4B 00 4E 00   ......R.O.C.K.N.
00170:  52 00 4F 00 4C 00 4C 00 00 00 04 00 00 00 00 00   R.O.L.L.........
00180:  00 00 04 00 00 00 6C 00 6B 00 63 00 6C 00 0C 00   ......l.k.c.l...
00190:  00 00 00 00 00 00 0B 00 00 00 42 00 52 00 4F 00   ..........B.R.O.
001A0:  4F 00 4B 00 46 00 49 00 45 00 4C 00 44 00 53 00   O.K.F.I.E.L.D.S.
001B0:  03 00                                             ..
```

If the account exists, the response contains vast quantities of useful
information about the user. In the MSDN API, *similar* data structures
correspond approximately to what is seen here: the closest that could
be found was **USER_INFO_21**. In addition, **subauth.h** contains a
structure named **USER_ALL_INFORMATION** that looks pretty good.
Basically, other than the excessively long Net monitor output shown
here, nothing is specifically documented:

```
****************************************************************************
Frame   Time      Src MAC Addr    Dst MAC Addr    Protocol   Description
592     289.974 EMERY            brookfields     R_LOGON    RPC Server response

  MSRPC: c/o RPC Response:     call 0x6  context 0x0  hint 0x198  cancels 0x0
  R_LOGON: RPC Server response logon:NetrLogonSamLogon(..)
        R_LOGON: PNETLOGON_AUTHENTICATOR ReturnAuthenticator {..}
            R_LOGON: NETLOGON_CREDENTIAL Credential {..}
                R_LOGON: CHAR data [..] = E1 3D 15 96 F9 F4 0E 7D
            R_LOGON: DWORD timestamp = 0 (0x0)
        R_LOGON: PNETLOGON_VALIDATION ValidationInformation {..}
            R_LOGON: Switch Value = 3 (0x3)
            R_LOGON: PNETLOGON_VALIDATION_SAM_INFO2 ValidationSam2 {..}
                R_LOGON: OLD_LARGE_INTEGER LogonTime {..}
                R_LOGON: OLD_LARGE_INTEGER LogoffTime {..}
                R_LOGON: OLD_LARGE_INTEGER KickOffTime {..}
                R_LOGON: OLD_LARGE_INTEGER PasswordLastSet {..}
```

```
              R_LOGON: OLD_LARGE_INTEGER PasswordCanChange {..}
              R_LOGON: OLD_LARGE_INTEGER PasswordMustChange {..}
              R_LOGON: UNICODE_STRING EffectiveName {..}
              R_LOGON: UNICODE_STRING FullName {..}
              R_LOGON: UNICODE_STRING LogonScript {..}
              R_LOGON: UNICODE_STRING ProfilePath {..}
              R_LOGON: UNICODE_STRING HomeDirectory {..}
              R_LOGON: UNICODE_STRING HomeDirectoryDrive {..}
              R_LOGON: USHORT LogonCount = 0 (0x0)
              R_LOGON: USHORT BadPasswordCount = 1 (0x1)
              R_LOGON: ULONG UserId = 1022 (0x3FE)
              R_LOGON: ULONG PrimaryGroupId = 513 (0x201)
              R_LOGON: ULONG GroupCount = 8 (0x8)
              R_LOGON: PGROUP_MEMBERSHIP GroupIds = 1473548 (0x167C0C)
              R_LOGON: ULONG UserFlags = 32 (0x20)
              R_LOGON: USER_SESSION_KEY UserSessionKey {..}
                  R_LOGON: CYPHER_BLOCK data [..]
                      R_LOGON: CYPHER_BLOCK data {..}
                      R_LOGON: CHAR data [..] = 00 00 00 00 00 00 00 00
                      R_LOGON: CYPHER_BLOCK data {..}
                          R_LOGON: CHAR data [..] = 00 00 00 00 00 00 00 00
              R_LOGON: UNICODE_STRING LogonServer {..}
              R_LOGON: UNICODE_STRING LogonDomainName {..}
              R_LOGON: PISID LogonDomainId = 1473612 (0x167C4C)
              R_LOGON: ULONG ExpansionRoom [..] = 00000000 00000000 00000000
➥00000000 00000000 00000000 00000000...
              R_LOGON: ULONG SidCount = 0 (0x0)
              R_LOGON: PNETLOGON_SID_AND_ATTRIBUTES ExtraSids = 0 (0x0)
              R_LOGON: USHORT * Buffer [..] = lkcl
              R_LOGON: PGROUP_MEMBERSHIP GroupIds [..]
              R_LOGON: USHORT * Buffer [..] = EMERY
              R_LOGON: USHORT * Buffer [..] = ROCKNROLL
              R_LOGON: PISID LogonDomainId {..}
                  R_LOGON: UCHAR Revision = 1 (0x1)
                  R_LOGON: UCHAR SubAuthorityCount = 4 (0x4)
                  R_LOGON: SID_IDENTIFIER_AUTHORITY IdentifierAuthority {..}
                      R_LOGON: UCHAR Value [..] = 00 00 00 00 00 05
                  R_LOGON: ULONG SubAuthority [..] = 00000015 2625004A 1345390C
➥05EE08E3
      R_LOGON: PBOOLEAN Authoritative = 1 (0x1)
      R_LOGON: Return Value = 0 (0x0)


00080:                         4C 53 16 00 E1 3D   ..........LS...=
00090:  15 96 F9 F4 0E 7D 00 00 00 00 03 00 00 00 40 7B   .....}........@{
000A0:  16 00 00 00 00 00 00 00 00 00 FF FF FF FF FF FF   ................
000B0:  FF 7F FF FF FF FF FF FF FF 7F 40 F9 AE 8A 49 25   ........@...I%
000C0:  BE 01 40 F9 AE 8A 49 25 BE 01 40 F9 AE 8A 09 47   ..@...I%..@....G
000D0:  BE 01 08 00 0A 00 64 7C 16 00 00 00 00 00 00 00   ......d¦........
000E0:  00 00 00 00 00 00 00 00 00 00 00 00 00 00 00 00   ................
000F0:  00 00 00 00 00 00 00 00 00 00 00 00 00 00 00 00   ................
00100:  00 00 00 00 01 00 FE 03 00 00 01 02 00 00 08 00   ................
00110:  00 00 0C 7C 16 00 20 00 00 00 00 00 00 00 00 00   ...¦.. .........
00120:  00 00 00 00 00 00 00 00 00 00 00 0A 00 0C 00 6E 7C   ..............n¦
00130:  16 00 12 00 14 00 7A 7C 16 00 4C 7C 16 00 00 00   ......z¦..L¦....
```

```
00140:   00 00 00 00 00 00 00 00 00 00 00 00 00 00 00 00    ...............
00150:   00 00 00 00 00 00 00 00 00 00 00 00 00 00 00 00    ...............
00160:   00 00 00 00 00 00 00 00 00 00 00 00 00 00 05 00    ...............
00170:   00 00 00 00 00 00 04 00 00 00 6C 00 6B 00 63 00    .........l.k.c.
00180:   6C 00 08 00 00 00 01 02 00 00 07 00 00 00 00 02    l..............
00190:   00 00 07 00 00 00 02 02 00 00 07 00 00 00 E9 03    ...............
001A0:   00 00 07 00 00 00 EB 03 00 00 07 00 00 00 EC 03    ...............
001B0:   00 00 07 00 00 00 ED 03 00 00 07 00 00 00 F6 03    ...............
001C0:   00 00 07 00 00 00 06 00 00 00 00 00 00 00 05 00    ...............
001D0:   00 00 45 00 4D 00 45 00 52 00 59 00 00 00 0A 00    ..E.M.E.R.Y.....
001E0:   00 00 00 00 00 00 09 00 00 00 52 00 4F 00 43 00    ..........R.O.C.
001F0:   4B 00 4E 00 52 00 4F 00 4C 00 4C 00 08 00 04 00    K.N.R.O.L.L.....
00200:   00 00 01 04 00 00 00 00 00 05 15 00 00 00 4A 00    ..............J.
00210:   25 26 0C 39 45 13 E3 08 EE 05 01 00 00 00 00 00    %&.9E..........
00220:   00 00                                              ..
```

If there is an error, the response contains a valid Credential Chain, but it returns a NULL pointer to the User Information plus a non-zero status code. In this example, the error message is **NT_STATUS_ PASSWORD_MUST_CHANGE**:

```
*************************************************************************
Frame   Time      Src MAC Addr    Dst MAC Addr    Protocol   Description
564     279.472 EMERY             brookfields     R_LOGON    RPC Server response

  MSRPC: c/o RPC Response:       call 0x5  context 0x0  hint 0x20  cancels 0x0
  R_LOGON: RPC Server response logon:NetrLogonSamLogon(..)
       R_LOGON: PNETLOGON_AUTHENTICATOR ReturnAuthenticator {..}
            R_LOGON: NETLOGON_CREDENTIAL Credential {..}
                 R_LOGON: CHAR data [..] = A3 7B E6 3C B9 60 A6 0E
            R_LOGON: DWORD timestamp = 0 (0x0)
       R_LOGON: PNETLOGON_VALIDATION ValidationInformation {..}
            R_LOGON: Switch Value = 3 (0x3)
       R_LOGON: PBOOLEAN Authoritative = 1 (0x1)
       R_LOGON: Return Value = 3221226020 (0xC0000224)

00080:                           4C 53 16 00 A3 7B    .. .......LS...{
00090:   E6 3C B9 60 A6 0E 00 00 00 00 03 00 00 00 00 00    .<.`............
000A0:   00 00 01 5D 88 8A 24 02 00 C0                      ...]..$...
```

An NT Workstation responds to the **NT_STATUS_PASSWORD_ MUST_CHANGE** error code by displaying a dialog box that warns you that your password will soon expire and asks if you wish to change it now. Any other error message will not allow the user to proceed: they will be returned to the Domain Login dialog box.

### Network Logon
The purpose of a Network Logon is for a Workstation that is a member of a Domain to verify an SMB Client, even though the Workstation does not own the Domain's SAM database. The

Workstation has to contact the Domain Controller to allow the SMB Client access to the Workstation's resources. This is also known as *Pass-Through Authentication.*

Microsoft has a different version of Pass-Through Authentication, which is fully documented in Microsoft's CIFS documentation (at ftp://ftp.microsoft.com/developr/drg/CIFS). The CIFS version is also problematic if a connection needs to be reestablished; in addition, it is less secure.

A Network Logon contains the following information:

- Domain Name
- Logon Identity (purpose unknown)
- User Name
- Workstation Name
- 8-byte NTLM Challenge
- 24-byte LM Response
- 24-byte NT Response

The 8-byte challenge was sent to the SMB Client by the Workstation that is a member of the Domain. The two 24-byte responses are returned to the Workstation from the SMB Client. The Workstation itself does not have a copy of the Domain SAM Database, so it uses the Pass-Through Logon. The Workstation must trust and respect the Domain Controller's response. A **NetrSamLogon** request follows:

```
***************************************************************************
Frame   Time    Src MAC Addr   Dst MAC Addr   Protocol   Description
51      15.761  FERENGI        REGENT         R_LOGON    RPC Client call

  MSRPC: c/o RPC Request:      call 0x18  opnum 0x2  context 0x0  hint 0x142
  R_LOGON: RPC Client call logon:NetrLogonSamLogon(..)
      R_LOGON: LOGONSRV_HANDLE LogonServer = \\REGENT
      R_LOGON: wchar_t ComputerName = STEELEYE
      R_LOGON: PNETLOGON_AUTHENTICATOR Authenticator {..}
          R_LOGON: NETLOGON_CREDENTIAL Credential {..}
              R_LOGON: CHAR data [..] = 0F 31 3B 4A DE F0 7C DB
          R_LOGON: DWORD timestamp = 922136537 (0x36F6AFD9)
      R_LOGON: PNETLOGON_AUTHENTICATOR ReturnAuthenticator {..}
          R_LOGON: NETLOGON_CREDENTIAL Credential {..}
              R_LOGON: CHAR data [..] = 00 00 00 00 00 00 00 00
          R_LOGON: DWORD timestamp = 922136537 (0x36F6AFD9)
      R_LOGON: NETLOGON_LOGON_INFO_CLASS LogonLevel = 2 (0x2)
      R_LOGON: PNETLOGON_LEVEL LogonInformation {..}
          R_LOGON: Switch Value = 2 (0x2)
          R_LOGON: PNETLOGON_NETWORK_INFO LogonNetwork {..}
              R_LOGON: NETLOGON_LOGON_IDENTITY_INFO Identity {..}
                  R_LOGON: UNICODE_STRING LogonDomainName {..}
```

```
                  R_LOGON: USHORT Length = 10 (0xA)
                  R_LOGON: USHORT MaximumLength = 10 (0xA)
                  R_LOGON: USHORT * Buffer = 4 (0x4)
             R_LOGON: ULONG ParameterControl = 0 (0x0)
             R_LOGON: OLD_LARGE_INTEGER LogonId {..}
                  R_LOGON: ULONG LowPart = 1600028946 (0x5F5E8112)
                  R_LOGON: LONG HighPart = 0 (0x0)
             R_LOGON: UNICODE_STRING UserName {..}
                  R_LOGON: USHORT Length = 8 (0x8)
                  R_LOGON: USHORT MaximumLength = 8 (0x8)
                  R_LOGON: USHORT * Buffer = 4 (0x4)
             R_LOGON: UNICODE_STRING Workstation {..}
                  R_LOGON: USHORT Length = 20 (0x14)
                  R_LOGON: USHORT MaximumLength = 20 (0x14)
                  R_LOGON: USHORT * Buffer = 4 (0x4)
         R_LOGON: LM_CHALLENGE LmChallenge {..}
             R_LOGON: CHAR data [..] = B4 39 CF 59 DF C0 67 3E
         R_LOGON: STRING NtChallengeResponse {..}
             R_LOGON: USHORT Length = 24 (0x18)
             R_LOGON: USHORT MaximumLength = 24 (0x18)
             R_LOGON: PCHAR Buffer = 1 (0x1)
         R_LOGON: STRING LmChallengeResponse {..}
             R_LOGON: USHORT Length = 24 (0x18)
             R_LOGON: USHORT MaximumLength = 24 (0x18)
             R_LOGON: PCHAR Buffer = 1 (0x1)
         R_LOGON: USHORT * Buffer [..] = 0054 0045 0053 0054 0031
         R_LOGON: USHORT * Buffer [..] = 0074 0065 0073 0074
         R_LOGON: USHORT * Buffer [..] = 005C 005C 0053 0054 0045 0045 004C
➥0045 0059 0045
         R_LOGON: PCHAR Buffer [..] = E1 6F 2E BC 07 7F
                          F5 2B DC 16 C8 69 05 91 17 4B 3D F9 45 67 70 FD DF 09
         R_LOGON: PCHAR Buffer [..] = 72 FB 58 C1 EB D3
                          EB 09 AB 6C 2E F9 51 D5 E4 56 12 C1 0F 59 6C 18 23 C5
     R_LOGON: NETLOGON_VALIDATION_INFO_CLASS ValidationLevel = 3 (0x3)


00080:            05 00 00 03 10 00 00 00 5A 01    PE\..........Z.
00090:  00 00 18 00 00 00 42 01 00 00 00 00 02 00 01 00    ......B.........
000A0:  00 00 09 00 00 00 00 00 00 00 09 00 00 00 5C 00    ..............\.
000B0:  5C 00 52 00 45 00 47 00 45 00 4E 00 54 00 00 00    \.R.E.G.E.N.T...
000C0:  00 00 01 00 00 00 09 00 00 00 00 00 00 00 09 00    ................
000D0:  00 00 53 00 54 00 45 00 45 00 4C 00 45 00 59 00    ..S.T.E.E.L.E.Y.
000E0:  45 00 00 00 00 00 01 00 00 00 0F 31 3B 4A DE F0    E..........1;J..
000F0:  7C DB D9 AF F6 36 01 00 00 00 00 00 00 00 00 00    |....6..........
00100:  00 00 D9 AF F6 36 02 00 02 00 01 00 00 00 0A 00    .....6..........
00110:  0A 00 04 00 00 00 00 00 00 00 12 81 5E 5F 00 00    ............^_..
00120:  00 00 08 00 08 00 04 00 00 00 14 00 14 00 04 00    ................
00130:  00 00 B4 39 CF 59 DF C0 67 3E 18 00 18 00 01 00    ...9.Y..g>......
00140:  00 00 18 00 18 00 01 00 00 00 05 00 00 00 00 00    ................
00150:  00 00 05 00 00 00 54 00 45 00 53 00 54 00 31 00    ......T.E.S.T.1.
00160:  00 00 04 00 00 00 00 00 00 00 04 00 00 00 74 00    ..............t.
00170:  65 00 73 00 74 00 0A 00 00 00 00 00 00 00 0A 00    e.s.t...........
00180:  00 00 5C 00 5C 00 53 00 54 00 45 00 45 00 4C 00    ..\.\.S.T.E.E.L.
00190:  45 00 59 00 45 00 18 00 00 00 00 00 00 00 18 00    E.Y.E...........
001A0:  00 00 E1 6F 2E BC 07 7F F5 2B DC 16 C8 69 05 91    ...o....+...i..
```

```
001B0:   17 4B 3D F9 45 67 70 FD DF 09 18 00 00 00 00 00    .K=.Egp.........
001C0:   00 00 18 00 00 00 72 FB 58 C1 EB D3 EB 09 AB 6C    ......r.X......l
001D0:   2E F9 51 D5 E4 56 12 C1 0F 59 6C 18 23 C5 03 00    ..Q..V...Yl.#...
```

If the account exists, the response contains pretty much the same
information as the Interactive Logon response. The basic User
Account details are the same. The password fields and other key fields
are slightly different. In particular, the User Session Key contains
**MD4(NT Password Hash)**, which is reversibly obfuscated with a
cypher key, where the cypher key is the Session Key calculated in the
setup of the NETLOGON Credential Chain.

Also, the **ExpansionRoom** field contains eight weird bytes. In NT
4.0 SP1 and below, incredibly, this was the first actual eight bytes of
the user's LM password hash. Now, whatever information is transmitted is reversibly encrypted with a cypher stream, using the same
Session Key previously mentioned. A **NetrSamLogon** response
follows:

```
**************************************************************************
Frame   Time    Src MAC Addr   Dst MAC Addr   Protocol   Description
52      15.766  REGENT         FERENGI        R_LOGON    RPC Server response

  MSRPC: c/o RPC Response:     call 0x18  context 0x0  hint 0x144  cancels 0x0
  R_LOGON: RPC Server response logon:NetrLogonSamLogon(..)
      R_LOGON: PNETLOGON_AUTHENTICATOR ReturnAuthenticator {..}
          R_LOGON: NETLOGON_CREDENTIAL Credential {..}
              R_LOGON: CHAR data [..] = 82 F3 81 50 54 4B 18 40
              R_LOGON: DWORD timestamp = 922136537 (0x36F6AFD9)
          R_LOGON: PNETLOGON_VALIDATION ValidationInformation {..}
              R_LOGON: Switch Value = 3 (0x3)
              R_LOGON: PNETLOGON_VALIDATION_SAM_INFO2 ValidationSam2 {..}
                  R_LOGON: OLD_LARGE_INTEGER LogonTime {..}
                  R_LOGON: OLD_LARGE_INTEGER LogoffTime {..}
                  R_LOGON: OLD_LARGE_INTEGER KickOffTime {..}
                  R_LOGON: OLD_LARGE_INTEGER PasswordLastSet {..}
                  R_LOGON: OLD_LARGE_INTEGER PasswordCanChange {..}
                  R_LOGON: OLD_LARGE_INTEGER PasswordMustChange {..}
                  R_LOGON: UNICODE_STRING EffectiveName {..}
                  R_LOGON: UNICODE_STRING FullName {..}
                  R_LOGON: UNICODE_STRING LogonScript {..}
                  R_LOGON: UNICODE_STRING ProfilePath {..}
                  R_LOGON: UNICODE_STRING HomeDirectory {..}
                  R_LOGON: UNICODE_STRING HomeDirectoryDrive {..}
                  R_LOGON: USHORT LogonCount = 25 (0x19)
                  R_LOGON: USHORT BadPasswordCount = 0 (0x0)
                  R_LOGON: ULONG UserId = 1002 (0x3EA)
                  R_LOGON: ULONG PrimaryGroupId = 513 (0x201)
                  R_LOGON: ULONG GroupCount = 1 (0x1)
                  R_LOGON: PGROUP_MEMBERSHIP GroupIds = 1476660 (0x168834)
                  R_LOGON: ULONG UserFlags = 288 (0x120)
                  R_LOGON: USER_SESSION_KEY UserSessionKey {..}
                      R_LOGON: CYPHER_BLOCK data [..]
```

```
                R_LOGON: CYPHER_BLOCK data {..}
                        R_LOGON: CHAR data [..] = 4D F7 55 1D 23 A0 D6 63
                R_LOGON: CYPHER_BLOCK data {..}
                        R_LOGON: CHAR data [..] = A0 08 85 B2 2D 1B B6 9C
        R_LOGON: UNICODE_STRING LogonServer {..}
        R_LOGON: UNICODE_STRING LogonDomainName {..}
        R_LOGON: PISID LogonDomainId = 1476668 (0x16883C)
        R_LOGON: ULONG ExpansionRoom [..] = 186A6D6C 7090DEC1...
        R_LOGON: ULONG SidCount = 0 (0x0)
        R_LOGON: PNETLOGON_SID_AND_ATTRIBUTES ExtraSids = 0 (0x0)
        R_LOGON: PGROUP_MEMBERSHIP GroupIds [..]
            R_LOGON: PGROUP_MEMBERSHIP GroupIds {..}
                R_LOGON: ULONG RelativeId = 513 (0x201)
                R_LOGON: ULONG Attributes = 7 (0x7)
        R_LOGON: USHORT * Buffer [..] = 0052 0045 0047 0045 004E 0054
        R_LOGON: USHORT * Buffer [..] = 0054 0045 0053 0054 0031
        R_LOGON: PISID LogonDomainId {..}
            R_LOGON: UCHAR Revision = 1 (0x1)
            R_LOGON: UCHAR SubAuthorityCount = 4 (0x4)
            R_LOGON: SID_IDENTIFIER_AUTHORITY IdentifierAuthority {..}
                R_LOGON: UCHAR Value [..] = 00 00 00 00 00 05
            R_LOGON: ULONG SubAuthority [..] = 00000015 23FD786B 71DB117C
➡069E3812
    R_LOGON: PBOOLEAN Authoritative = 1 (0x1)
    R_LOGON: Return Value = 0 (0x0)


00070:       05 00 02 03 10 00 00 00 5C 01 00 00 18 00    .Z........\.....
00080:    00 00 44 01 00 00 00 00 00 00 BC 8D 16 00 82 F3    ..D.............
00090:    81 50 54 4B 18 40 D9 AF F6 36 03 00 00 00 68 87    .PTK.@...6....h.
000A0:    16 00 B0 A7 A1 F7 8D 71 BE 01 FF FF FF FF FF FF    .......q........
000B0:    FF 7F FF FF FF FF FF FF FF 7F 00 B1 A8 29 C0 5A    ..........).Z
000C0:    BE 01 00 B1 A8 29 C0 5A BE 01 FF FF FF FF FF FF    .....).Z........
000D0:    FF 7F 00 00 00 00 00 00 00 00 00 00 00 00 00 00    ...............
000E0:    00 00 00 00 00 00 00 00 00 00 00 00 00 00 00 00    ...............
000F0:    00 00 00 00 00 00 00 00 00 00 00 00 00 00 00 00    ...............
00100:    00 00 19 00 00 00 EA 03 00 00 01 02 00 00 01 00    ...............
00110:    00 00 34 88 16 00 20 01 00 00 4D F7 55 1D 23 A0    ..4... ...M.U.#.
00120:    D6 63 A0 08 85 B2 2D 1B B6 9C 0C 00 0E 00 54 88    .c...-.......T.
00130:    16 00 0A 00 0C 00 62 88 16 00 3C 88 16 00 6C 6D    ......b...<...lm
00140:    6A 18 C1 DE 90 70 00 00 00 00 00 00 00 00 00 00    j....p..........
00150:    00 00 00 00 00 00 00 00 00 00 00 00 00 00 00 00    ...............
00160:    00 00 00 00 00 00 00 00 00 00 00 00 00 00 01 00    ...............
00170:    00 00 01 02 00 00 07 00 00 00 07 00 00 00 00 00    ...............
00180:    00 00 06 00 00 00 52 00 45 00 47 00 45 00 4E 00    ......R.E.G.E.N.
00190:    54 00 06 00 00 00 00 00 00 00 05 00 00 00 54 00    T.............T.
00 1A0:   45 00 53 00 54 00 31 00 45 00 04 00 00 00 01 04    E.S.T.1.E.......
001B0:    00 00 00 00 00 05 15 00 00 00 6B 78 FD 23 7C 11    ..........kx.#¦.
001C0:    DB 71 12 38 9E 06 01 11 DB 71 00 00 00 00          .q.8.....q....
```

## LanManager Login Functions

The LanManager API (transported by **SMBtrans2** calls over
**\PIPE\LANMAN**) provides totally different but equivalent

functionality. For example, **NetUserGetInfo** is used by Windows 95 Workstations to obtain the location of a user's profile. It is worthwhile emphasising that the concept of a "Domain Login" is completely alien to Windows 95: it does no such thing.

When a user manually types in a User name, Domain name, and password, the Windows 95 Workstation first attempts to locate a Domain Controller. If this succeeds, it will then follow up with an anonymous IPC$ connection and will issue a **NetUserGetInfo** call. The request contains the User name, and the response contains the user's profile: their full name, the logon path, and so on. The Logon Path contains the location of the user's profile. This is where the User name, Domain name, and password are used.

An authenticated **SMBsessionsetupX** is then sent, followed by **SMBtconX** to the share containing the profile, and then normal SMB file access is used to obtain the USER.DAT or USER.MAN profile. At *this* point, before the Server responds to the **SMBsessionsetupX**, it calls **LsaLogonUserEx** to verify the user. This call is what makes the user appear to "log on" to the Domain Controller.

The key distinction here is that Windows NT users logging in to a Domain Controller have to go through the complex verification process in order to "log on" to the Domain before the Workstation can even consider downloading the user's profile. With the undocumented modifications in NT 4.0 Service Pack 4 that encrypt the **NetrSamLogon** calls, there is no longer an easy, publicly known way for a malicious user to track NETLOGON traffic or disrupt it. If at some point in the future the new method becomes public knowledge, this may no longer be the case.

### 4.1.6: NetrSamLogoff

A user can be logged off a Domain by either closing the NETLOGON pipe or by sending a **NetrSamLogoff** call. Typically, a **NetrSamLogoff** will be explicitly sent when one user logs on immediately after another user has logged off. The Workstation may already have a NETLOGON resource open, and it will be reused.

A **NetrSamLogoff** request has exactly the same format as a **NetrSamLogon** request, including the User name, Domain name, password, and the Workstation that the user is logging in from. The obfuscated fields used to store encrypted 16-byte LM and NT password hashes are all set to zero, as shown here:

```
****************************************************************************
Frame   Time     Src MAC Addr   Dst MAC Addr   Protocol   Description
608     341.160  brookfields    EMERY          R_LOGON    RPC Client call
```

```
MSRPC: c/o RPC Request:      call 0x7  opnum 0x3  context 0x0  hint 0x10A
R_LOGON: RPC Client call logon:NetrLogonSamLogoff(..)
    R_LOGON: LOGONSRV_HANDLE LogonServer = \\EMERY
    R_LOGON: wchar_t ComputerName = BROOKFIELDS
    R_LOGON: PNETLOGON_AUTHENTICATOR Authenticator {..}
        R_LOGON: NETLOGON_CREDENTIAL Credential {..}
            R_LOGON: CHAR data [..] = CE F9 2B F7 D5 DC B0 21
        R_LOGON: DWORD timestamp = 913410079 (0x3671881F)
    R_LOGON: PNETLOGON_AUTHENTICATOR ReturnAuthenticator {..}
        R_LOGON: NETLOGON_CREDENTIAL Credential {..}
            R_LOGON: CHAR data [..] = D0 BA 1A 50 0B 00 0C 00
        R_LOGON: DWORD timestamp = 1408944 (0x157FB0)
    R_LOGON: NETLOGON_LOGON_INFO_CLASS LogonLevel = 1 (0x1)
    R_LOGON: PNETLOGON_LEVEL LogonInformation {..}
        R_LOGON: Switch Value = 1 (0x1)
        R_LOGON: PNETLOGON_INTERACTIVE_INFO LogonInteractive {..}
            R_LOGON: NETLOGON_LOGON_IDENTITY_INFO Identity {..}
                R_LOGON: UNICODE_STRING LogonDomainName {..}
                R_LOGON: ULONG ParameterControl = 0 (0x0)
                R_LOGON: OLD_LARGE_INTEGER LogonId {..}
                    R_LOGON: ULONG LowPart = 8415 (0x20DF)
                    R_LOGON: LONG HighPart = 0 (0x0)
                R_LOGON: UNICODE_STRING UserName {..}
                R_LOGON: UNICODE_STRING Workstation {..}
            R_LOGON: LM_OWF_PASSWORD LmOwfPassword {..}
            R_LOGON: NT_OWF_PASSWORD NtOwfPassword {..}
            R_LOGON: USHORT * Buffer [..] = ROCKNROLL
            R_LOGON: USHORT * Buffer [..] = lkcl
            R_LOGON: USHORT * Buffer [..] = BROOKFIELDS
```

```
000A0:                   60 D2 14 00 08 00 00 00 00 00   ......`.........
000B0:  00 00 08 00 00 00 5C 00 5C 00 45 00 4D 00 45 00   ......\.\.E.M.E.
000C0:  52 00 59 00 00 00 E4 B7 1A 50 0C 00 00 00 00 00   R.Y......P......
000D0:  00 00 0C 00 00 00 42 00 52 00 4F 00 4F 00 4B 00   ......B.R.O.O.K.
000E0:  46 00 49 00 45 00 4C 00 44 00 53 00 00 00 BC FC   F.I.E.L.D.S.....
000F0:  C9 00 CE F9 2B F7 D5 DC B0 21 1F 88 71 36 C8 FC   ....+....!..q6..
00100:  C9 00 D0 BA 1A 50 0B 00 0C 00 B0 7F 15 00 01 00   .....P..........
00110:  01 00 1C FD C9 00 12 00 14 00 A2 36 15 00 00 00   ...........6....
00120:  00 00 DF 20 00 00 00 00 00 00 08 00 0A 00 98 36   ... ...........6
00130:  15 00 16 00 18 00 E0 67 14 00 00 00 00 00 00 00   .......g........
00140:  00 00 00 00 00 00 00 00 00 00 00 00 00 00 00 00   ................
00150:  00 00 00 00 00 00 00 00 00 00 0A 00 00 00 00 00   ................
00160:  00 00 09 00 00 00 52 00 4F 00 43 00 4B 00 4E 00   ......R.O.C.K.N.
00170:  52 00 4F 00 4C 00 4C 00 00 00 05 00 00 00 00 00   R.O.L.L.........
00180:  00 00 04 00 00 00 6C 00 6B 00 63 00 6C 00 0C 00   ......l.k.c.l...
00190:  00 00 00 00 00 00 0B 00 00 00 42 00 52 00 4F 00   ..........B.R.O.
001A0:  4F 00 4B 00 46 00 49 00 45 00 4C 00 44 00 53 00   O.K.F.I.E.L.D.S.
```

A **NetrSamLogoff** response contains the usual Credential Challenge plus only a return status code. The only known error codes are those related to credential validation problems.

```
**********************************************************************
Frame   Time    Src MAC Addr   Dst MAC Addr   Protocol  Description

 MSRPC: c/o RPC Response:      call 0x7  context 0x0  hint 0x14  cancels 0x0
 R_LOGON: RPC Server response logon:NetrLogonSamLogoff(..)
     R_LOGON: PNETLOGON_AUTHENTICATOR ReturnAuthenticator {..}
        R_LOGON: NETLOGON_CREDENTIAL Credential {..}
            R_LOGON: CHAR data [..] = 07 50 4D AD D3 67 BD CD
        R_LOGON: DWORD timestamp = 1408944 (0x157FB0)
     R_LOGON: Return Value = 0 (0x0)

00080:                            4C 53 16 00 07 50   ..........LS...P
00090:  4D AD D3 67 BD CD B0 7F 15 00 00 00 00 00      M..g.........
```

## 4.2: NETLOGON Security Issues

There are a number of security flaws in the implementation of the
NETLOGON API:

- Use of anonymous IPC$ for communication.
- Well-known initial value for Trust Account Passwords.
- **NetrSamLogon** responds with verbose error codes.
- Interactive logins send the actual NT and LM hashes.
- Network logins send a User Session Key (equivalent to the NT
  hash for certain security-related operations).
- Network logins send the first eight bytes of the user's LM hash.
- The Credential Chain does not protect the payload.

Of these issues, only the last two have been addressed. Sending the
first eight bytes of a user's LM password hash was modified in NT
4.0 Service Pack 2, and the **NetrSamLogon** and **NetrSamLogoff** calls
are now encrypted in NT 4.0 Service Pack 4. These security flaws are
discussed in the sections that follow.

### 4.2.1: Anonymous IPC$ Risks

Anonymous IPC$ connections are a potential security risk. Other
DCE/RPC pipes, such as **\PIPE\srvsvc**, are used to obtain information
about the Server, such as **NetServerGetInfo**. **\PIPE\lsarpc** is used to
obtain the Security Identifier (SID) of the Primary Domain Controller,
which is done over an anonymous IPC$ connection.

It is suspected that part of the design of the NETLOGON calls was
made bearing in mind that an anonymous IPC$ connection would
already be established. Even if this were not the case, the likely reason
that anonymous IPC$ connections are used by the NETLOGON pipe

is because there is nothing to log in with until users are validated (a circular argument if ever there was one). The Credential Chain uses the Trust Account Password as well as the user's password so the user is known to be logging in from a Workstation that's known to be a member of the Domain.

So what is a potential solution to this? The simple solution is to make an authenticated **SMBsessionsetupX** using the user's details: User name, password, and Domain name. This will result in an internal call to the Local Security Authority on the Server. If that call is successful, the Client can issue an IPC$ **SMBtconX** on the authenticated SMB session.

Internally, the LSA will have noted that the user is logged in by allocating a *Local User ID*, which is associated with the SMB session. Then it makes the usual series of NETLOGON calls. When the **NetrSamLogon** call is made, *another* internal call to the LSA is made with the user's details. Yet another Local User ID is allocated, which is associated with both the NETLOGON session and the SMB session. No bonus points are allocated for this approach: it makes the Domain Controller take *two* user validation hits. In addition, a method will have to be added whereby the user's password can be changed at the next logon. If the password has expired, the **SMBsessionsetupX** will be refused and the NETLOGON session denied.

The other alternative is to use the Workstation Trust Account Password to authenticate the **SMBsessionsetupX** connection. However, this approach is already used for another purpose. Workstation Trust Account **SMBsessionsetupX** login requests are refused with a special error code: **NT_STATUS_NOLOGON_WORKSTATION_TRUST_ACCOUNT**. This error message indicates that the Trust Account already exists when the Workstation is added to the Domain. Furthermore, it verifies that the shared secret (the Trust Account password) is properly synchronised between the Workstation and the Domain Controller.

So, no ordinary logins are allowed. However, it is possible to request *Guest Access* in **SMBsessionsetupX** connections, and that avenue could potentially be used to solve the problem. In fact, this approach could be used to ensure that no anonymous IPC$ connections ever be used at any time in a Domain environment. Only when down-level machines (such as Windows 95 and below) are involved would anonymous IPC$ connections be required, and this could be enabled with a Registry setting.

Additionally, this approach would solve the problem of the user's password expiring and Account Lockout, because the Workstation Trust Account SMB session would be open. However, the User Login over the NETLOGON session could still be refused as required.

## 4.2.2: Well-Known Trust Account Passwords

A Workstation Trust Account Password's initial value is set to the Workstation name in lowercase. When an NT 3.5 or 4.0 Workstation is added to a Domain using the Network Control Panel dialog box, an Administrator User name and password is sometimes required. If the Workstation has been added and removed in the past and is now being returned to the Domain, the Workstation Trust Account Password will have already been changed by a **NetrServerPasswordSet** call, so the previous Trust Account Password may be out of sync. Or, the Administrator forgot to run SRVMGR.EXE and add the Workstation to the Domain.

In each case, whether you use the Network Control Panel dialog box or SRVMGR.EXE, the Workstation Trust Account password is set or reset to the same initial value. This means that if a malicious party sniffs the first login of a user and has the entire NETLOGON conversation, she can also calculate the same Session Key and potentially hijack or disrupt the NETLOGON session. In addition, if the malicious party captures all **NetrServerPasswordSet** calls right from the start, they can *continue* to decode all NETLOGON traffic from that Workstation.

This problem could be avoided if a random initial password is used, when the Administrator's User name and password were used in the Network Control Panel dialog to add the Workstation to the Domain. The malicious party would have to have the Administrator's password to decode NETLOGON traffic. But if they had the Administrator's password, they probably wouldn't bother with this relatively complex approach: it's game over anyway.

## 4.2.3: NetrSamLogon Error Codes

The following is a partial list of error codes that can be returned in **NetrSamLogon** responses:

- NT_STATUS_NO_SUCH_USER
- NT_STATUS_WRONG_PASSWORD
- NT_STATUS_LOGON_FAILURE
- NT_STATUS_ACCOUNT_RESTRICTION

- **NT_STATUS_INVALID_LOGON_HOURS**
- **NT_STATUS_INVALID_WORKSTATION**
- **NT_STATUS_PASSWORD_EXPIRED**
- **NT_STATUS_ACCOUNT_DISABLED**
- **NT_STATUS_PASSWORD_MUST_CHANGE**

This gives far too much information away to a potentially malicious party. Standard security procedure dictates that only *one* error code *ever* be returned. Here is a breakdown of what can be inferred from some of these NT error codes:

- **NT_STATUS_NO_SUCH_USER.** A Domain Controller is informing a malicious party that they need not bother with that User name: try another one.
- **NT_STATUS_WRONG_PASSWORD.** A Domain Controller is informing a malicious party that they have correctly guessed the User name and need only attempt to crack the password.
- **NT_STATUS_PASSWORD_MUST_CHANGE.** A Domain Controller is informing a malicious party that the User name and password are correct, but the password is of no use because it has expired. Maybe this User name and password can be tried somewhere else where it hasn't expired; maybe at some point in the future, the password will be valid again, depending on the Domain policy restrictions.
- **NT_STATUS_INVALID_WORKSTATION.** A Domain Controller is informing a malicious party that a user is restricted to logging in from a particular set of Workstations. A successful attempt to break into one of these Workstations would then allow the use of that account.

Any well-written and properly deployed Security Analysis tool should, therefore, make use of this information to alert Administrators of attacks in progress and of any potential security problems. Highlighting some of these problems with security tools simply makes users more aware of them. At the time of writing, there is no actual solution to stop Windows NT from returning such verbose information.

## 4.2.4: Interactive Logins Send NT and LM Passwords

The 8-byte Session Key, calculated from the Workstation Trust Account Password in the setup of the Credential Chain, is used to encrypt the actual cleartext-equivalent 16-byte NT and LM User password hashes in the interactive **NetrSamLogon** call. The initial value for the Trust Account Password is the Workstation name in lowercase. Therefore, the first time a user logs in to a Domain from a Workstation, the password is being sent obfuscated but ultimately in an easily decryptable manner. If a malicious party has undetected but constant access to NETLOGON traffic over a period of time, *all* logins from that Workstation can be decoded.

The solution for Microsoft to implement is simple: do not use the Interactive Login, use the Network Login instead. The difference is that the Workstation generates an 8-byte challenge internally and calculates the LM and NT 24-byte responses itself. The Server will calculate the two 24-byte responses from the 8-byte challenge and its LM and NT 16-byte cleartext-equivalent password hashes, and checks them against the responses calculated by the Workstation. This proves to the Server that the user knows the password, but the cleartext-equivalent passwords themselves are never sent over-the-wire.

An attacker *could* do the same thing in a brute-force attack, namely from enumerating a dictionary, generating 16-byte password hashes, and then comparing the 24-byte responses from the 8-byte challenge with the captured 24-byte responses. However, having the 16-byte password hashes in the first place, which could be generated from a complex, non-dictionary word, makes the attacker's job computationally less expensive.

## 4.2.5: Network Logins Send Half the LM Password

This issue has already been addressed in NT 4.0 Service Pack 2. However, it is not known whether the issue has been addressed in NT 3.51 with a hotfix or in the various ports of NT to Unix. The **NetrSamLogon** response contains an Expansion Room field. It was noted in the Interactive Login response that this is all zeros, but in the Network Login response, the first eight bytes were identical to the first eight bytes of the LM password hash.

The first eight bytes of the LM password hash are calculated by uppercasing the first seven characters of the user's cleartext password and using that as a DES key to encrypt an eight-byte well-known data block.

This is (or was) a significant security risk because the first eight bytes of the LM password hash are used to calculate the cypher stream in NTLM version 1 Secure Service Provider DCE/RPC sessions, described in Section 1.5.4.3. The implications of this are that any malicious party that observes a **NetrSamLogon** response from an NT 4.0 Server with Service Pack 1 and below will be able to decode encrypted DCE/RPC sessions.

The fix by Microsoft has been to replace these eight bytes in the Expansion Room field with a Session Key *based* on the LM password. No analysis of the replacement data is known of by the author at the time of writing.

## 4.2.6: Network Logins Send a User Session Key

The User Session Key (MD4 of the user's 16-byte NT hash) is used in certain critical places instead of the NTLM 8-byte challenge/24-byte response system. This makes it critical to protect. Fortunately, the User Session Key is reversibly encrypted in exactly the same way the 16-byte LM and NT hashes are sent, making this as secure (or as insecure) as the Interactive Logon.

Unfortunately, this does not protect against attacks when a Workstation Trust Account Password is known (for example, when a Workstation has just been added to a Domain). An 8-byte challenge plus the two 24-byte responses are sniffed from network traffic. A malicious party can establish a network logon session by pretending to be the Workstation for which the Trust Account password is known. The challenge and responses captured are sent to the Domain Controller, which then issues a valid response containing that user's Session Key.

Until Microsoft has produced a fix for this problem, the exact details of the attack analysis cannot be published: this would be highly irresponsible. Further information is likely to be found, should the problem be addressed, on the following Web sites:

- Microsoft at http://www.microsoft.com/
- Ntbugtraq at http://www.ntbugtraq.com/
- Internet Security Systems Inc. at http://www.iss.net/

## 4.2.7: Credential Chain

The Credential Chain that is attached to **NetrServerPasswordSet**, **NetrSamLogon,** and **NetrSamLogoff** is calculated independently of the contents of the packets in which it is placed. A malicious party that is either in control of a router through which the NETLOGON traffic is being sent or who can track NETLOGON traffic in real time and send, at a critical point, a fake response to a Workstation, can send false responses without the Workstation or the user being aware that anything might be wrong. For example, they could send a false **NetrSamLogon** response indicating that the logon has succeeded instead of failed. For example, they could modify the group to which the user belongs to grant Local Administrator rights.

A solution to this is to enable *SMB signing* between the Client and Server. Given that the DCE/RPC traffic uses SMB as its transport, this will stop a malicious party from sending any false packets or from tampering with packets. SMB signing is, however, computationally expensive.

Therefore, Microsoft added to NT 4.0 Service Pack 4 an extra negotiation bit (0x4000 0000) in the NETLOGON **NetrServerAuthenticate2** call. If this bit is set in both the request and the response by the Client and the Server, following the setup of the Credential Chain, a second NETLOGON pipe is opened.

While the first NETLOGON pipe is still open, encryption is negotiated over the second pipe. The **NetrSamLogon** and all other calls are sent over the second encrypted pipe.

It is worth mentioning that the new method works only between Service Pack 4 (and above) machines. Some sites cannot use Service Pack 4 because certain critical third-party services or device drivers do not work. Additionally, there is no way to disable the backward-compatible NETLOGON system (documented in this chapter) for better security through obscurity.

No further information is available as to the details or the security of this method, either in the form of documentation from Microsoft or in the form of published research by a third party—yet.

## 4.3: Summary

The NETLOGON system is a comprehensive system to provide secure, centralised Login Services. It provides a means to authenticate users and to obtain full account information. It uses (and only uses) LM and NT 16-byte password hashes as the ultimate basis for authenticating users.

Unfortunately, it looks like the NETLOGON system was initially designed without consultation from any security experts. As this is a critical component of Microsoft's Domain Protocol, Microsoft's Strategic Business Policy of ensuring that critical components are not revealed to competitors is actively enforced. This policy is constantly maintained by modifying the protocol whenever correct information on a critical component becomes publicly available.

Hopefully, Microsoft will properly consult with security experts before fixing any problems that are found by themselves or other sources. There can be, however, no substitute for full disclosure. Unfortunately, Microsoft cannot risk publishing such information because the company has been advised by lawyers that they risk being sued for compromising the security of their customers' sites. However, until Microsoft provides full disclosure, no independent experts (including experts independent of one another) can be consulted to verify whether the job has been done properly.

# 5

# \PIPE\srvsvc: NT Administrative Services

Windows NT's Server functionality, which includes SMB File Sharing, is provided by the **Server** service. The **\PIPE\srvsvc** pipe enables queries to be made to the **Server** service for Server information and remote management of the Server's resources, including available shares, files currently open, and session connections.

All these functions are correctly decoded by Microsoft Network Monitor. Netmon's parser was generated from Microsoft's Interface Definition Language (IDL) files. Sample traces, created mainly from routine use of Server Manager on a Windows NT client, are included in this chapter.

The direct use of some of the RPC functions in Windows client applications is discouraged in favour of the **WNet\*** Win32 interface in **lmserver.h, lmshare.h,** and related files, as two new APIs have been developed by Microsoft: **WNet\*** and **NP\***. The **WNet\*** API supports Client-side browsing by calling the **NP\*** API of browsing services that are installed on a Workstation. Two types of commonly available browsing services are "Client for NetWare Services" and "Client for Microsoft Networks." The new **WNet\*** API has been developed by Microsoft so that future browsing and file services can be added seamlessly and without Microsoft or third-party programs needing to be rewritten. However, to properly integrate with Windows NT Domains and support NT Administrative tools such as Server Manager, Servers will need to support a large number of the **\PIPE\srvsvc** RPC entrypoints. Even the "Client for Microsoft Networks" browser service, an implementation of the **NP\*** API, has to call some of these entrypoints. For these and other reasons, these RPC calls are described in the following sections.

# 5.1: srvsvc Calls

This section describes some of the \PIPE\srvsvc services in detail.
Samba properly supports only NetrServerGetInfo and
NetrRemoteTOD, as these are the only two essential routines for
Primary Domain Controller functionality, and **NetrShareEnum** and
**NetrShareGetInfo**. All the rest are management routines, accessible
from tools such as Server Manager for Domains. The full list of
functions in this chapter are listed here:

- NetrServerGetInfo
- NetrServerSetInfo
- NetrShareEnum
- NetrShareGetInfo
- NetrShareGetInfo
- NetrShareAdd
- NetrShareDel
- NetrSessionEnum
- NetrConnectionEnum
- NetrFileEnum
- NetrFileClose
- NetrRemoteTOD

This pipe can be accessed anonymously. Fortunately, some of the info
levels of these calls require higher privileges than anonymous access.
Some, such as NetrTransportEnum, do not.

## 5.1.1: NetrServerGetInfo

This function is used to obtain general Server information, from simple information, such as name and platform, to detailed configuration
and performance statistics. For instance, in the normal course of a
user logging into a Domain, the Workstation needs to check whether
the server it is accessing is in fact a Domain Controller. The MSDN
function prototype, which is automatically generated from its IDL
definition, is shown here:

```
NET_API_STATUS NET_API_FUNCTION
NetServerGetInfo (
    IN  LPTSTR  servername OPTIONAL,
    IN  DWORD   level,
    OUT LPBYTE  *bufptr
    );
```

There are a number of different information levels are available, depending on the type of information desired. The most common information level is 102, shown in the following traces and listed here:

```
typedef struct _SERVER_INFO_102 {
        DWORD           sv102_platform_id;
        LPTSTR          sv102_name;
        DWORD           sv102_version_major;
        DWORD           sv102_version_minor;
        DWORD           sv102_type;
        LPTSTR          sv102_comment;
        DWORD           sv102_users;
        LONG            sv102_disc;
        BOOL            sv102_hidden;
        DWORD           sv102_announce;
        DWORD           sv102_anndelta;
        DWORD           sv102_licenses;
        LPTSTR          sv102_userpath;
} SERVER_INFO_102, *PSERVER_INFO_102, *LPSERVER_INFO_102;
```

The other general information levels are 100 and 101, which include slightly less information. Server-specific performance and configuration information is provided by 4xx and 5xx, while individual properties can be queried via 1xxx. Note the large number of SERVER_INFO structures in **lmserver.h**. The higher information levels may indeed be used by NT performance tuning utilities but are unlikely to be useful for any other implementation.

An attempt to re-create an IDL definition for this function is shown here, which is very similar to the auto-generated MSDN function prototype, above. The [in] and [in out] parameters are sent over-the-wire in the request, and the [in out] and [out] parameters are sent back over-the-wire in the response.

```
typedef union _SERVER_INFO switch (DWORD dwLevel) ctr {
        case 100: SERVER_INFO_100 *sv100;
        case 101: SERVER_INFO_101 *sv101;
        case 102: SERVER_INFO_102 *sv102;
} SERVER_INFO;


STATUS NetrSrvGetInfo(          /* Function 0x15 */
                [in,unique] LPWSTR          pszServerName,
                     [in] DWORD             dwLevel,
                    [out] SERVER_INFO*      pServerInfo
                    );
```

The **NetServerGetInfo** request names the target server and specifies the desired information level:

```
**********************************************************************
Frame   Time    Src MAC Addr    Dst MAC Addr    Protocol  Description
1       0.000   CLIENT1         SERVER00        R_SRVSVC  RPC Client call
```

```
MSRPC: c/o RPC Request:        call 0x1  opnum 0x15  context 0x0  hint 0x2C
R_SRVSVC: RPC Client call srvsvc:NetrServerGetInfo(..)
    R_SRVSVC: SRVSVC_HANDLE ServerName = \\SERVER00
    R_SRVSVC: DWORD Level = 102 (0x66)


000A0:                      CC 82 31 00 0B 00 00 00 00 00   ........1.......
000B0:  00 00 0B 00 00 00 5C 00 5C 00 53 00 45 00 52 00   ......\.\.S.E.R.
000C0:  56 00 45 00 52 00 30 00 30 00 00 00 08 00 66 00   V.E.R.0.0...:..f.
000D0:  00 00                                             ..
```

The response is the desired SERVER_INFO structure and a status
code, as usual. Note that due to RPC marshalling the actual strings
appear after the structure, immediately preceded by size_is and
length_is attributes.

```
********************************************************************************
Frame   Time    Src MAC Addr   Dst MAC Addr   Protocol  Description
2       0.000   SERVER00       CLIENT1        R_SRVSVC  RPC Server response


MSRPC: c/o RPC Response:       call 0x1  context 0x0  hint 0xB4  cancels 0x0
R_SRVSVC: RPC Server response srvsvc:NetrServerGetInfo(..)
    R_SRVSVC: LPSERVER_INFO InfoStruct {..}
        R_SRVSVC: Switch Value = 102 (0x66)
        R_SRVSVC: LPSERVER_INFO_102 ServerInfo102 {..}
            R_SRVSVC: DWORD sv102_platform_id = 500 (0x1F4)
            R_SRVSVC: LPTSTR sv102_name = 1470348 (0x166F8C)
            R_SRVSVC: DWORD sv102_version_major = 4 (0x4)
            R_SRVSVC: DWORD sv102_version_minor = 0 (0x0)
            R_SRVSVC: DWORD sv102_type = 69635 (0x11003)
            R_SRVSVC: LPTSTR sv102_comment = 1470366 (0x166F9E)
            R_SRVSVC: DWORD sv102_users = 10 (0xA)
            R_SRVSVC: LONG sv102_disc = 15 (0xF)
            R_SRVSVC: DWORD sv102_hidden = 0 (0x0)
            R_SRVSVC: DWORD sv102_announce = 240 (0xF0)
            R_SRVSVC: DWORD sv102_anndelta = 3000 (0xBB8)
            R_SRVSVC: DWORD sv102_licenses = 0 (0x0)
            R_SRVSVC: LPTSTR sv102_userpath = 1470418 (0x166FD2)
            R_SRVSVC: LPTSTR sv102_name = SERVER00
            R_SRVSVC: LPTSTR sv102_comment = NCSA Student Resources PC
            R_SRVSVC: LPTSTR sv102_userpath = c:\
    R_SRVSVC: Return Value = 0 (0x0)


00080:                          66 00 00 00 58 6F          f...Xo
00090:  16 00 F4 01 00 00 8C 6F 16 00 04 00 00 00 00 00   .......o........
000A0:  00 00 03 10 01 00 9E 6F 16 00 0A 00 00 00 0F 00   .......o........
000B0:  00 00 00 00 00 00 F0 00 00 00 B8 0B 00 00 00 00   ................
000C0:  00 00 D2 6F 16 00 09 00 00 00 00 00 00 00 09 00   ...o............
000D0:  00 00 53 00 45 00 52 00 56 00 45 00 52 00 30 00   ..S.E.R.V.E.R.0.
```

```
000E0:   30 00 00 00 75 00 1A 00 00 00 00 00 00 00 1A 00    0...u..........
000F0:   00 00 4E 00 43 00 53 00 41 00 20 00 53 00 74 00    ..N.C.S.A. .S.t.
00100:   75 00 64 00 65 00 6E 00 74 00 20 00 52 00 65 00    u.d.e.n.t. .R.e.
00110:   73 00 6F 00 75 00 72 00 63 00 65 00 73 00 20 00    s.o.u.r.c.e.s. .
00120:   50 00 43 00 00 00 04 00 00 00 00 00 00 00 04 00    P.C............
00130:   00 00 63 00 3A 00 5C 00 00 00 00 00 00 00 00       ..c.:.\.......
```

## 5.1.2: NetrServerSetInfo

**NetrServerSetInfo** is used to set configurable server options such as the comment field. The MSDN function prototype is shown here:

```
NET_API_STATUS NET_API_FUNCTION
NetServerSetInfo (
    IN  LPTSTR  servername OPTIONAL,
    IN  DWORD   level,
    IN  LPBYTE  buf,
    OUT LPDWORD ParmError OPTIONAL
    );
```

Administrative privileges are required on the target Server. To avoid inadvertently changing elements to undesirable values, an application should always use **NetrServerGetInfo** to retrieve a SERVER_INFO structure at the desired level, to make the required modifications, and to call **NetrServerSetInfo** with the modified structure.

```
*******************************************************************************
Frame   Time    Src MAC Addr    Dst MAC Addr    Protocol  Description
1       0.000   CLIENT1         SERVER00        R_SRVSVC  RPC Client call


  MSRPC: c/o RPC Request:       call 0x1  opnum 0x16  context 0x0  hint 0xE0
  R_SRVSVC: RPC Client call srvsvc:NetrServerSetInfo(..)
      R_SRVSVC: SRVSVC_HANDLE ServerName = \\SERVER00
      R_SRVSVC: DWORD Level = 102 (0x66)
      R_SRVSVC: LPSERVER_INFO ServerInfo {..}
          R_SRVSVC: Switch Value = 102 (0x66)
          R_SRVSVC: LPSERVER_INFO_102 ServerInfo102 {..}
              R_SRVSVC: DWORD sv102_platform_id = 500 (0x1F4)
              R_SRVSVC: LPTSTR sv102_name = 3277964 (0x32048C)
              R_SRVSVC: DWORD sv102_version_major = 4 (0x4)
              R_SRVSVC: DWORD sv102_version_minor = 0 (0x0)
              R_SRVSVC: DWORD sv102_type = 69635 (0x11003)
              R_SRVSVC: LPTSTR sv102_comment = 3278880 (0x320820)
              R_SRVSVC: DWORD sv102_users = 10 (0xA)
              R_SRVSVC: LONG sv102_disc = 15 (0xF)
              R_SRVSVC: DWORD sv102_hidden = 0 (0x0)
              R_SRVSVC: DWORD sv102_announce = 240 (0xF0)
              R_SRVSVC: DWORD sv102_anndelta = 3000 (0xBB8)
              R_SRVSVC: DWORD sv102_licenses = 0 (0x0)
              R_SRVSVC: LPTSTR sv102_userpath = 1378652 (0x15095C)
              R_SRVSVC: LPTSTR sv102_name = \\SERVER00
              R_SRVSVC: LPTSTR sv102_comment = Windows NT Test Server
              R_SRVSVC: LPTSTR sv102_userpath = c:\
```

```
000A0:                   8C 04 32 00 0B 00 00 00 00 00        ..2.......
000B0:   00 00 0B 00 00 00 5C 00 5C 00 53 00 45 00 52 00    ......\.\.S.E.R.
000C0:   56 00 45 00 52 00 30 00 30 00 00 00 08 00 66 00    V.E.R.0.0.....f.
000D0:   00 00 66 00 00 00 E0 08 15 00 F4 01 00 00 8C 04    ..f.............
000E0:   32 00 04 00 00 00 00 00 00 00 03 10 01 00 20 08    2............. .
000F0:   32 00 0A 00 00 00 0F 00 00 00 00 00 00 00 F0 00    2...............
00100:   00 00 B8 0B 00 00 00 00 00 00 5C 09 15 00 0B 00    ..........\.....
00110:   00 00 00 00 00 00 0B 00 00 00 5C 00 5C 00 53 00    ..........\.\.S.
00120:   45 00 52 00 56 00 45 00 52 00 30 00 30 00 00 00    E.R.V.E.R.0.0...
00130:   5C 00 17 00 00 00 00 00 00 00 17 00 00 00 57 00    \.............W.
00140:   69 00 6E 00 64 00 6F 00 77 00 73 00 20 00 4E 00    i.n.d.o.w.s. .N.
00150:   54 00 20 00 54 00 65 00 73 00 74 00 20 00 53 00    T. .T.e.s.t. .S.
00160:   65 00 72 00 76 00 65 00 72 00 00 00 00 00 04 00    e.r.v.e.r.......
00170:   00 00 00 00 00 00 04 00 00 00 63 00 3A 00 5C 00    ..........c.:.\.
00180:   00 00 00 00 00 00                                  ......
```

The response contains a "ParmError" value, which specifies which parameter is invalid (or zero if the change succeeded) and the actual status code, indicating whether the change succeeded:

```
**************************************************************************
Frame   Time    Src MAC Addr   Dst MAC Addr   Protocol  Description
2       0.000   SERVER00       CLIENT1        R_SRVSVC  RPC Server response


  MSRPC: c/o RPC Response:    call 0x1  context 0x0  hint 0x8  cancels 0x0
  R_SRVSVC: RPC Server response srvsvc:NetrServerSetInfo(..)
     R_SRVSVC: Return Value = 0 (0x0)



00080:                            00 00 00 00 00 00        ......
00090:   00 00                                             ..
```

### 5.1.3: NetrShareEnum

**NetrShareEnum** is used to retrieve information about the shares offered by the Server, including "hidden" shares (those ending with $). An array of SHARE_INFO structures is returned. The MSDN function prototype is shown here:

```
NET_API_STATUS NET_API_FUNCTION
NetShareEnum (
    IN  LPTSTR        servername,
    IN  DWORD         level,
    OUT LPBYTE        *bufptr,
    IN  DWORD         prefmaxlen,
    OUT LPDWORD       entriesread,
    OUT LPDWORD       totalentries,
    IN OUT LPDWORD    resume_handle
    );
```

As with Server information, different information levels are available. The most commonly observed info level, level 2, is shown in the following traces and listed here from the MSDN:

```
typedef struct _SHARE_INFO_2 {
    LPTSTR  shi2_netname;
    DWORD   shi2_type;
    LPTSTR  shi2_remark;
    DWORD   shi2_permissions;
    DWORD   shi2_max_uses;
    DWORD   shi2_current_uses;
    LPTSTR  shi2_path;
    LPTSTR  shi2_passwd;
} SHARE_INFO_2, *PSHARE_INFO_2, *LPSHARE_INFO_2;
```

Levels 0 and 1 provide less information. In line with the normal convention levels, 5xx is Server-specific, while 1xxx retrieves particular attributes. See **lmshare.h** in the Win32 SDK for full details of all structures.

The query contains the target Server name and a container into which the entries are to be returned. PreferredMaximumLength is a hint to the volume of (unmarshalled) data desired—if that volume is exceeded STATUS_MORE_ENTRIES is returned.

```
******************************************************************************
Frame   Time    Src MAC Addr   Dst MAC Addr   Protocol   Description
1       0.000   CLIENT1        SERVER00       R_SRVSVC   RPC Client call


    MSRPC: c/o RPC Request:      call 0x1  opnum 0xF  context 0x0  hint 0x44
    R_SRVSVC: RPC Client call srvsvc:NetrShareEnum(..)
        R_SRVSVC: SRVSVC_HANDLE ServerName = \\SERVER00
        R_SRVSVC: LPSHARE_ENUM_STRUCT InfoStruct {..}
            R_SRVSVC: DWORD Level = 2 (0x2)
            R_SRVSVC: _SHARE_ENUM_UNION ShareInfo {..}
                R_SRVSVC: Switch Value = 2 (0x2)
                R_SRVSVC: SHARE_INFO_2_CONTAINER *Level2 {..}
                    R_SRVSVC: DWORD EntriesRead = 0 (0x0)
                    R_SRVSVC: LPSHARE_INFO_2 Buffer = 0 (0x0)
        R_SRVSVC: DWORD PreferredMaximumLength = 4294967295 (0xFFFFFFFF)


000A0:                   AC EB 12 00 0B 00 00 00 00 00    ..........
000B0:   00 00 0B 00 00 00 5C 00 5C 00 53 00 45 00 52 00    ......\.\.S.E.R.
000C0:   56 00 45 00 52 00 30 00 30 00 00 00 08 00 02 00    V.E.R.0.0.......
000D0:   00 00 02 00 00 00 A8 EA 12 00 00 00 00 00 00 00    ................
000E0:   00 00 FF FF FF FF 00 00 00 00                      ..........
```

Assuming the call is successful, the container is filled with an array of the requested structure. The strings are marshalled at the end in the usual manner. The total number of shares provided by the Server is also indicated (even if not all are present in this enumeration because of PreferredMaximumLength). The EntriesRead parameter indicates exactly how many shares were returned with this **NetrShareEnum** response.

```
****************************************************************************
Frame   Time    Src MAC Addr    Dst MAC Addr    Protocol  Description
2       0.000   SERVER00        CLIENT1         R_SRVSVC  RPC Server response


 MSRPC: c/o RPC Response:       call 0x1  context 0x0  hint 0x208  cancels 0x0
 R_SRVSVC: RPC Server response srvsvc:NetrShareEnum(..)
    R_SRVSVC: LPSHARE_ENUM_STRUCT InfoStruct {..}
        R_SRVSVC: DWORD Level = 2 (0x2)
        R_SRVSVC: _SHARE_ENUM_UNION ShareInfo {..}
            R_SRVSVC: Switch Value = 2 (0x2)
            R_SRVSVC: SHARE_INFO_2_CONTAINER *Level2 {..}
                R_SRVSVC: DWORD EntriesRead = 4 (0x4)
                R_SRVSVC: LPSHARE_INFO_2 Buffer = 1521976 (0x173938)
                R_SRVSVC: LPSHARE_INFO_2 Buffer [..]
                    R_SRVSVC: LPSHARE_INFO_2 Buffer {..}
                        R_SRVSVC: LPTSTR shi2_netname = 1530110 (0x1758FE)
                        R_SRVSVC: DWORD shi2_type = 2147483648 (0x80000000)
                        R_SRVSVC: LPTSTR shi2_remark = 1530124 (0x17590C)
                        R_SRVSVC: DWORD shi2_permissions = 0 (0x0)
                        R_SRVSVC: DWORD shi2_max_uses = 4294967295 (0xFFFFFFFF)
                        R_SRVSVC: DWORD shi2_current_uses = 0 (0x0)
                        R_SRVSVC: LPTSTR shi2_path = 1530150 (0x175926)
                        R_SRVSVC: LPTSTR shi2_passwd = 0 (0x0)
                    + R_SRVSVC: LPSHARE_INFO_2 Buffer {..}
                    + R_SRVSVC: LPSHARE_INFO_2 Buffer {..}
                      R_SRVSVC: LPSHARE_INFO_2 Buffer {..}
                        R_SRVSVC: LPTSTR shi2_netname = 1529972 (0x175874)
                        R_SRVSVC: DWORD shi2_type = 0 (0x0)
                        R_SRVSVC: LPTSTR shi2_remark = 1529982 (0x17587E)
                        R_SRVSVC: DWORD shi2_permissions = 0 (0x0)
                        R_SRVSVC: DWORD shi2_max_uses = 4294967295 (0xFFFFFFFF)
                        R_SRVSVC: DWORD shi2_current_uses = 0 (0x0)
                        R_SRVSVC: LPTSTR shi2_path = 1530018 (0x1758A2)
                        R_SRVSVC: LPTSTR shi2_passwd = 0 (0x0)
                    R_SRVSVC: LPSHARE_INFO_2 Buffer = ADMIN$
                    R_SRVSVC: LPTSTR shi2_remark = Remote Admin
                    R_SRVSVC: LPTSTR shi2_path = C:\WINNT
                    R_SRVSVC: LPSHARE_INFO_2 Buffer = IPC$
                    R_SRVSVC: LPTSTR shi2_remark = Remote IPC
                    R_SRVSVC: LPTSTR shi2_path =
                    R_SRVSVC: LPSHARE_INFO_2 Buffer = C$
                    R_SRVSVC: LPTSTR shi2_remark = Default share
                    R_SRVSVC: LPTSTR shi2_path = C:\
                    R_SRVSVC: LPSHARE_INFO_2 Buffer = TEMP
                    R_SRVSVC: LPTSTR shi2_remark = Temporary Storage
                    R_SRVSVC: LPTSTR shi2_path = C:\temp
        R_SRVSVC: LPDWORD TotalEntries = 4 (0x4)
        R_SRVSVC: Return Value = 0 (0x0)


 00080:                          02 00 00 00 02 00           ......
 00090:  00 00 34 29 17 00 04 00 00 00 38 39 17 00 04 00   ..4)......89....
```

```
000A0:  00 00 FE 58 17 00 00 00 00 80 0C 59 17 00 00 00    ...X.......Y....
000B0:  00 00 FF FF FF FF 00 00 00 00 26 59 17 00 00 00    ..........&Y....
000C0:  00 00 DC 58 17 00 03 00 00 80 E6 58 17 00 00 00    ...X.......X....
000D0:  00 00 FF FF FF FF 01 00 00 00 FC 58 17 00 00 00    ...........X....
000E0:  00 00 B2 58 17 00 00 00 00 80 B8 58 17 00 00 00    ...X.......X....
000F0:  00 00 FF FF FF FF 00 00 00 00 D4 58 17 00 00 00    ...........X....
00100:  00 00 74 58 17 00 00 00 00 00 7E 58 17 00 00 00    ..tX......~X....
00110:  00 00 FF FF FF FF 00 00 00 00 A2 58 17 00 00 00    ...........X....
00120:  00 00 07 00 00 00 00 00 00 00 07 00 00 00 41 00    ..............A.
00130:  44 00 4D 00 49 00 4E 00 24 00 00 00 00 00 0D 00    D.M.I.N.$.......
00140:  00 00 00 00 00 00 0D 00 00 00 52 00 65 00 6D 00    ..........R.e.m.
00150:  6F 00 74 00 65 00 20 00 41 00 64 00 6D 00 69 00    o.t.e. .A.d.m.i.
00160:  6E 00 00 00 00 00 09 00 00 00 00 00 00 00 09 00    n...............
00170:  00 00 43 00 3A 00 5C 00 57 00 49 00 4E 00 4E 00    ..C.:.\.W.I.N.N.
00180:  54 00 00 00 45 00 05 00 00 00 00 00 00 00 05 00    T...E...........
00190:  00 00 49 00 50 00 43 00 24 00 00 00 00 00 0B 00    ..I.P.C.$.......
001A0:  00 00 00 00 00 00 0B 00 00 00 52 00 65 00 6D 00    ..........R.e.m.
001B0:  6F 00 74 00 65 00 20 00 49 00 50 00 43 00 00 00    o.t.e. .I.P.C...
001C0:  45 00 01 00 00 00 00 00 00 00 01 00 00 00 00 00    E...............
001D0:  4C 00 03 00 00 00 00 00 00 00 03 00 00 00 43 00    L.............C.
001E0:  24 00 00 00 00 00 0E 00 00 00 00 00 00 00 0E 00    $...............
001F0:  00 00 44 00 65 00 66 00 61 00 75 00 6C 00 74 00    ..D.e.f.a.u.l.t.
00200:  20 00 73 00 68 00 61 00 72 00 65 00 00 00 04 00    .s.h.a.r.e.....
00210:  00 00 00 00 00 00 04 00 00 00 43 00 3A 00 5C 00    ..........C.:.\.
00220:  00 00 05 00 00 00 00 00 00 00 05 00 00 00 54 00    ..............T.
00230:  45 00 4D 00 50 00 00 00 00 00 12 00 00 00 00 00    E.M.P...........
00240:  00 00 12 00 00 00 54 00 65 00 6D 00 70 00 6F 00    ......T.e.m.p.o.
00250:  72 00 61 00 72 00 79 00 20 00 53 00 74 00 6F 00    r.a.r.y. .S.t.o.
00260:  72 00 61 00 67 00 65 00 00 00 08 00 00 00 00 00    r.a.g.e.........
00270:  00 00 08 00 00 00 43 00 3A 00 5C 00 74 00 65 00    ......C.:.\.t.e.
00280:  6D 00 70 00 00 00 00 00 04 00 00 00 00 00 00 00    m.p.............
00290:  00 00                                              ..
```

The resume handle, which in the example above is NULL, is used to resume the enumeration if the PreferredMaximumLength buffer size was too small to fit all the share information. A second and subsequent call to **NetrShareEnum** is made, passing the resume handle returned from the previous call to the next call, until such time as one of the calls returns a NULL resume handle. The resume handle should never be modified by the caller: doing so could result in an infinite loop of NetrShareEnum calls.

### Note

*There was a bug in the implementation of **NetrShareEnum** where the resume handle is not correctly implemented in Windows NT. This results in an infinite loop when using multiple **NetrShareEnum** calls to obtain large numbers of shares. **NetrShareEnumSticky** should be used instead.*

## 5.1.4: NetrShareEnumSticky

**NetrShareEnumSticky** is functionally the same as **NetrShareEnum**, except that hidden shares are not listed. There was also a bug in the MSDN **NetrShareEnum** API call whereby the enumeration failed to work for lists of shares that were too large for one **NetrShareEnum** call. Rather than return the next set of results, the **NetrShareEnum** call does not use the resume handle correctly, which results in an infinite loop of **NetrShareEnum** calls. The MSDN function prototype is shown here:

```
NET_API_STATUS NET_API_FUNCTION
NetShareEnumSticky (
    IN  LPTSTR      servername,
    IN  DWORD       level,
    OUT LPBYTE      *bufptr,
    IN  DWORD       prefmaxlen,
    OUT LPDWORD     entriesread,
    OUT LPDWORD     totalentries,
    IN OUT LPDWORD  resume_handle
    );
```

The **NetrShareEnumSticky** request, which uses exactly the same format as the **NetrShareEnum** request, is shown here:

```
***************************************************************************
Frame   Time    Src MAC Addr   Dst MAC Addr   Protocol   Description
1       0.000   CLIENT1        SERVER00       R_SRVSVC   RPC Client call


  MSRPC: c/o RPC Request:      call 0x1  opnum 0x24  context 0x0  hint 0x44
  R_SRVSVC: RPC Client call srvsvc:NetrShareEnumSticky(..)
      R_SRVSVC: SRVSVC_HANDLE ServerName = \\SERVER00
      R_SRVSVC: LPSHARE_ENUM_STRUCT InfoStruct {..}
          R_SRVSVC: DWORD Level = 2 (0x2)
          R_SRVSVC: _SHARE_ENUM_UNION ShareInfo {..}
              R_SRVSVC: Switch Value = 2 (0x2)
              R_SRVSVC: SHARE_INFO_2_CONTAINER *Level2 {..}
                  R_SRVSVC: DWORD EntriesRead = 0 (0x0)
                  R_SRVSVC: LPSHARE_INFO_2 Buffer = 0 (0x0)
      R_SRVSVC: DWORD PreferredMaximumLength = 4294967295 (0xFFFFFFFF)


000A0:                   DC DD 12 00 0B 00 00 00 00 00    ..........
000B0:  00 00 0B 00 00 00 5C 00 5C 00 53 00 45 00 52 00    ......\.\.S.E.R.
000C0:  56 00 45 00 52 00 30 00 30 00 00 00 08 00 02 00    V.E.R.0.0.......
000D0:  00 00 02 00 00 00 D8 DC 12 00 00 00 00 00 00 00    ................
000E0:  00 00 FF FF FF FF 00 00 00 00                      ..........
```

The response is in exactly the same format as the **NetrShareEnum** response, except of course that hidden shares are not returned:

```
*****************************************************************************
Frame   Time    Src MAC Addr   Dst MAC Addr   Protocol  Description
2       0.000   SERVER00       CLIENT1        R_SRVSVC  RPC Server response


   MSRPC: c/o RPC Response:     call 0x1  context 0x0  hint 0xA8  cancels 0x0
   R_SRVSVC: RPC Server response srvsvc:NetrShareEnumSticky(..)
       R_SRVSVC: LPSHARE_ENUM_STRUCT InfoStruct {..}
           R_SRVSVC: DWORD Level = 2 (0x2)
           R_SRVSVC: _SHARE_ENUM_UNION ShareInfo {..}
               R_SRVSVC: Switch Value = 2 (0x2)
               R_SRVSVC: SHARE_INFO_2_CONTAINER *Level2 {..}
                   R_SRVSVC: DWORD EntriesRead = 1 (0x1)
                   R_SRVSVC: LPSHARE_INFO_2 Buffer = 1521976 (0x173938)
                   R_SRVSVC: LPSHARE_INFO_2 Buffer [..]
                       R_SRVSVC: LPSHARE_INFO_2 Buffer {..}
                           R_SRVSVC: LPTSTR shi2_netname = 1530106 (0x1758FA)
                           R_SRVSVC: DWORD shi2_type = 0 (0x0)
                           R_SRVSVC: LPTSTR shi2_remark = 1530116 (0x175904)
                           R_SRVSVC: DWORD shi2_permissions = 0 (0x0)
                           R_SRVSVC: DWORD shi2_max_uses = 4294967295 (0xFFFFFFFF)
                           R_SRVSVC: DWORD shi2_current_uses = 0 (0x0)
                           R_SRVSVC: LPTSTR shi2_path = 1530152 (0x175928)
                           R_SRVSVC: LPTSTR shi2_passwd = 0 (0x0)
                       R_SRVSVC: LPSHARE_INFO_2 Buffer = TEMP
                       R_SRVSVC: LPTSTR shi2_remark = Temporary Storage
                       R_SRVSVC: LPTSTR shi2_path = C:\temp
           R_SRVSVC: LPDWORD TotalEntries = 1 (0x1)
       R_SRVSVC: Return Value = 0 (0x0)


00080:                               02 00 00 00 02 00         ......
00090:  00 00 34 29 17 00 01 00 00 00 38 39 17 00 01 00  ..4)......89....
000A0:  00 00 FA 58 17 00 00 00 00 00 04 59 17 00 00 00  ...X.......Y....
000B0:  00 00 FF FF FF FF 00 00 00 00 28 59 17 00 00 00  ..........(Y....
000C0:  00 00 05 00 00 00 00 00 00 00 05 00 00 00 54 00  ..............T.
000D0:  45 00 4D 00 50 00 00 00 00 00 12 00 00 00 00 00  E.M.P...........
000E0:  00 00 12 00 00 00 54 00 65 00 6D 00 70 00 6F 00  ......T.e.m.p.o.
000F0:  72 00 61 00 72 00 79 00 20 00 53 00 74 00 6F 00  r.a.r.y. .S.t.o.
00100:  72 00 61 00 67 00 65 00 00 00 08 00 00 00 00 00  r.a.g.e.........
00110:  00 00 08 00 00 00 43 00 3A 00 5C 00 74 00 65 00  ......C.:.\.t.e.
00120:  6D 00 70 00 00 00 01 00 00 00 00 00 00 00 00 00  m.p.............
00130:  00 00                                            ..
```

## 5.1.5: NetrShareGetInfo

This function is used to retrieve share information for a specific share.
See the "NetrShareEnum" section earlier in this chapter for a summary of the information levels available. Level 2 from the MSDN is shown here:

```
typedef struct _SHARE_INFO_2 {
    LPTSTR  shi2_netname;
```

```
    DWORD    shi2_type;
    LPTSTR   shi2_remark;
    DWORD    shi2_permissions;
    DWORD    shi2_max_uses;
    DWORD    shi2_current_uses;
    LPTSTR   shi2_path;
    LPTSTR   shi2_passwd;
} SHARE_INFO_2, *PSHARE_INFO_2, *LPSHARE_INFO_2;
```

Level 1501 is particularly important in Windows NT, as it is used to retrieve Security information (specifically, a **security descriptor**, which describes access rights) for the share object. The MSDN function prototype is shown here:

```
NET_API_STATUS NET_API_FUNCTION
NetShareGetInfo (
    IN  LPTSTR   servername,
    IN  LPTSTR   netname,
    IN  DWORD    level,
    OUT LPBYTE   *bufptr
    );
```

The query specifies the target Server and share name, and the desired information level.

```
************************************************************************
Frame   Time    Src MAC Addr   Dst MAC Addr   Protocol   Description
1       0.000   CLIENT1        SERVER00       R_SRVSVC   RPC Client call


    MSRPC: c/o RPC Request:      call 0x1  opnum 0x10  context 0x0  hint 0x44
    R_SRVSVC: RPC Client call srvsvc:NetrShareGetInfo(..)
        R_SRVSVC: SRVSVC_HANDLE ServerName = \\SERVER00
        R_SRVSVC: wchar_t NetName = TEMP
        R_SRVSVC: DWORD Level = 2 (0x2)


000A0:                    1C E3 12 00 0B 00 00 00 00 00          ..........
000B0:   00 00 0B 00 00 00 5C 00 5C 00 53 00 45 00 52 00   ......\.\.S.E.R.
000C0:   56 00 45 00 52 00 30 00 30 00 00 00 08 00 05 00   V.E.R.0.0.......
000D0:   00 00 00 00 00 00 05 00 00 00 54 00 45 00 4D 00   ..........T.E.M.
000E0:   50 00 00 00 FF FF 02 00 00 00                     P.........
```

Assuming the share exists, the response is a SHARE_INFO structure containing the requested data.

```
************************************************************************
Frame   Time    Src MAC Addr   Dst MAC Addr   Protocol   Description
2       0.000   SERVER00       CLIENT1        R_SRVSVC   RPC Server response


    MSRPC: c/o RPC Response:     call 0x1  context 0x0  hint 0x90  cancels 0x0
    R_SRVSVC: RPC Server response srvsvc:NetrShareGetInfo(..)
        R_SRVSVC: LPSHARE_INFO InfoStruct {..}
```

```
        R_SRVSVC: Switch Value = 2 (0x2)
        R_SRVSVC: LPSHARE_INFO_2 ShareInfo2 {..}
            R_SRVSVC: LPTSTR shi2_netname = 1530106 (0x1758FA)
            R_SRVSVC: DWORD shi2_type = 0 (0x0)
            R_SRVSVC: LPTSTR shi2_remark = 1530116 (0x175904)
            R_SRVSVC: DWORD shi2_permissions = 0 (0x0)
            R_SRVSVC: DWORD shi2_max_uses = 4294967295 (0xFFFFFFFF)
            R_SRVSVC: DWORD shi2_current_uses = 0 (0x0)
            R_SRVSVC: LPTSTR shi2_path = 1530152 (0x175928)
            R_SRVSVC: LPTSTR shi2_passwd = 0 (0x0)
            R_SRVSVC: LPTSTR shi2_netname = TEMP
            R_SRVSVC: LPTSTR shi2_remark = Temporary Storage
            R_SRVSVC: LPTSTR shi2_path = C:\temp
    R_SRVSVC: Return Value = 0 (0x0)
```

```
00080:                         02 00 00 00 38 39        ....89
00090:  17 00 FA 58 17 00 00 00 00 00 04 59 17 00 00 00  ...X.......Y....
000A0:  00 00 FF FF FF FF 00 00 00 00 28 59 17 00 00 00  ..........(Y....
000B0:  00 00 05 00 00 00 00 00 00 00 05 00 00 00 54 00  ..............T.
000C0:  45 00 4D 00 50 00 00 00 00 00 12 00 00 00 00 00  E.M.P...........
000D0:  00 00 12 00 00 00 54 00 65 00 6D 00 70 00 6F 00  ......T.e.m.p.o.
000E0:  72 00 61 00 72 00 79 00 20 00 53 00 74 00 6F 00  r.a.r.y. .S.t.o.
000F0:  72 00 61 00 67 00 65 00 00 00 08 00 00 00 00 00  r.a.g.e.........
00100:  00 00 08 00 00 00 43 00 3A 00 5C 00 74 00 65 00  ......C.:.\.t.e.
00110:  6D 00 70 00 00 00 00 00 00 00                    m.p.......
```

## 5.1.6: NetrShareSetInfo

The **NetrShareSetInfo** function is used to set share options such as
path and comment. It is complemented by the **NetrShareGetInfo** function. The user must either have sufficient privileges to manage shares
(usually the Power Users group is used for this purpose), or be the
owner of the share object. The MSDN function prototype is shown
here:

```
NET_API_STATUS NET_API_FUNCTION
NetShareSetInfo (
    IN  LPTSTR  servername,
    IN  LPTSTR  netname,
    IN  DWORD   level,
    IN  LPBYTE  buf,
    OUT LPDWORD parm_err
);
```

As always, an application should use **NetrShareGetInfo** to retrieve a
SHARE_INFO structure at the desired level, make the required modifications, and call **NetrShareSetInfo** with that structure.

```
***************************************************************************
Frame   Time    Src MAC Addr   Dst MAC Addr   Protocol   Description
1       0.000   CLIENT1        SERVER00       R_SRVSVC   RPC Client call
```

```
    MSRPC: c/o RPC Request:        call 0x1  opnum 0x11  context 0x0  hint 0xE4
    R_SRVSVC: RPC Client call srvsvc:NetrShareSetInfo(..)
        R_SRVSVC: SRVSVC_HANDLE ServerName = \\SERVER00
        R_SRVSVC: wchar_t NetName = TEMP
        R_SRVSVC: DWORD Level = 2 (0x2)
        R_SRVSVC: LPSHARE_INFO ShareInfo {..}
            R_SRVSVC: Switch Value = 2 (0x2)
            R_SRVSVC: LPSHARE_INFO_2 ShareInfo2 {..}
                R_SRVSVC: LPTSTR shi2_netname = 3280832 (0x320FC0)
                R_SRVSVC: DWORD shi2_type = 0 (0x0)
                R_SRVSVC: LPTSTR shi2_remark = 3280736 (0x320F60)
                R_SRVSVC: DWORD shi2_permissions = 0 (0x0)
                R_SRVSVC: DWORD shi2_max_uses = 4294967295 (0xFFFFFFFF)
                R_SRVSVC: DWORD shi2_current_uses = 0 (0x0)
                R_SRVSVC: LPTSTR shi2_path = 3280800 (0x320FA0)
                R_SRVSVC: LPTSTR shi2_passwd = 2005533904 (0x778A04D0)
                R_SRVSVC: LPTSTR shi2_netname = TEMP
                R_SRVSVC: LPTSTR shi2_remark = Temporary Storage
                R_SRVSVC: LPTSTR shi2_path = c:\temp
                R_SRVSVC: LPTSTR shi2_passwd =
```

```
000A0:                    94 E0 12 00 0B 00 00 00 00 00        ..........
000B0:   00 00 0B 00 00 00 5C 00 5C 00 53 00 45 00 52 00    ......\.\.S.E.R.
000C0:   56 00 45 00 52 00 30 00 30 00 00 00 08 00 05 00    V.E.R.0.0.......
000D0:   00 00 00 00 00 00 05 00 00 00 54 00 45 00 4D 00    ..........T.E.M.
000E0:   50 00 00 00 00 00 02 00 00 00 02 00 00 00 08 50    P..............P
000F0:   14 00 C0 0F 32 00 00 00 00 00 60 0F 32 00 00 00    ....2...`.2...
00100:   00 00 FF FF FF FF 00 00 00 00 A0 0F 32 00 D0 04    ............2...
00110:   8A 77 05 00 00 00 00 00 00 00 05 00 00 00 54 00    .w............T.
00120:   45 00 4D 00 50 00 00 00 0C 00 12 00 00 00 00 00    E.M.P...........
00130:   00 00 12 00 00 00 54 00 65 00 6D 00 70 00 6F 00    ......T.e.m.p.o.
00140:   72 00 61 00 72 00 79 00 20 00 53 00 74 00 6F 00    r.a.r.y. .S.t.o.
00150:   72 00 61 00 67 00 65 00 00 00 08 00 00 00 00 00    r.a.g.e.........
00160:   00 00 08 00 00 00 63 00 3A 00 5C 00 74 00 65 00    ......c.:.\.t.e.
00170:   6D 00 70 00 00 00 01 00 00 00 00 00 00 00 01 00    m.p.............
00180:   00 00 00 00 00 00 00 00 00 00                      ..........
```

The response contains a "ParmError" value, which specifies which
parameter is invalid (or zero if the change succeeded) and the actual
status code, indicating whether the change succeeded:

```
*****************************************************************************
Frame   Time    Src MAC Addr   Dst MAC Addr   Protocol   Description
2       0.000   SERVER00       CLIENT1        R_SRVSVC   RPC Server response
```

```
    MSRPC: c/o RPC Response:       call 0x1  context 0x0  hint 0x8  cancels 0x0
    R_SRVSVC: RPC Server response srvsvc:NetrShareSetInfo(..)
        R_SRVSVC: Return Value = 0 (0x0)
```

```
00080:                    00 00 00 00 00 00        ......
00090:   00 00                                      ..
```

## 5.1.7: NetrShareAdd

This function is used to create a new share on the target Server, based on a given SHARE_INFO structure. The MSDN function prototype is shown here:

```
NET_API_STATUS NET_API_FUNCTION
NetShareAdd (
    IN  LPTSTR  servername,
    IN  DWORD   level,
    IN  LPBYTE  buf,
    OUT LPDWORD parm_err
    );
```

All attributes are set to their default values. The user must of course have sufficient privileges to create shares.

```
*****************************************************************************
Frame   Time    Src MAC Addr   Dst MAC Addr   Protocol   Description
1       0.000   CLIENT1        SERVER00       R_SRVSVC   RPC Client call


  MSRPC: c/o RPC Request:        call 0x1  opnum 0xE  context 0x0  hint 0xCC
  R_SRVSVC: RPC Client call srvsvc:NetrShareAdd(..)
      R_SRVSVC: SRVSVC_HANDLE ServerName = \\SERVER00
      R_SRVSVC: DWORD Level = 2 (0x2)
      R_SRVSVC: LPSHARE_INFO InfoStruct {..}
          R_SRVSVC: Switch Value = 2 (0x2)
          R_SRVSVC: LPSHARE_INFO_2 ShareInfo2 {..}
              R_SRVSVC: LPTSTR shi2_netname = 3249584 (0x3195B0)
              R_SRVSVC: DWORD shi2_type = 0 (0x0)
              R_SRVSVC: LPTSTR shi2_remark = 3249488 (0x319550)
              R_SRVSVC: DWORD shi2_permissions = 0 (0x0)
              R_SRVSVC: DWORD shi2_max_uses = 4294967295 (0xFFFFFFFF)
              R_SRVSVC: DWORD shi2_current_uses = 0 (0x0)
              R_SRVSVC: LPTSTR shi2_path = 3249552 (0x319590)
              R_SRVSVC: LPTSTR shi2_passwd = 2005533904 (0x778A04D0)
              R_SRVSVC: LPTSTR shi2_netname = TEMP
              R_SRVSVC: LPTSTR shi2_remark = Temporary Storage
              R_SRVSVC: LPTSTR shi2_path = c:\temp
              R_SRVSVC: LPTSTR shi2_passwd =


000A0:                   74 E0 12 00 0B 00 00 00 00 00     t.........
000B0:  00 00 0B 00 00 00 5C 00 5C 00 53 00 45 00 52 00   ......\.\.S.E.R.
000C0:  56 00 45 00 52 00 30 00 30 00 00 00 08 00 02 00   V.E.R.0.0.......
000D0:  00 00 02 00 00 00 E0 A2 14 00 B0 95 31 00 00 00   ............1...
000E0:  00 00 50 95 31 00 00 00 00 00 FF FF FF FF 00 00   ..P.1...........
000F0:  00 00 90 95 31 00 D0 04 8A 77 05 00 00 00 00 00   ....1....w......
00100:  00 00 05 00 00 00 54 00 45 00 4D 00 50 00 00 00   ......T.E.M.P...
00110:  FF FF 12 00 00 00 00 00 00 00 12 00 00 00 54 00   ..............T.
00120:  65 00 6D 00 70 00 6F 00 72 00 61 00 72 00 79 00   e.m.p.o.r.a.r.y.
00130:  20 00 53 00 74 00 6F 00 72 00 61 00 67 00 65 00    .S.t.o.r.a.g.e.
00140:  00 00 08 00 00 00 00 00 00 00 08 00 00 00 63 00   ..............c.
00150:  3A 00 5C 00 74 00 65 00 6D 00 70 00 00 00 01 00   :.\.t.e.m.p.....
```

```
00160:  00 00 00 00 00 00 01 00 00 00 00 00 30 00 00 00    ............0...
00170:  00 00                                               ..
```

The response contains a NULL pointer and a status return code. The error codes 0x0, indicating success, or NT_STATUS_ACCESS_DENIED are expected:

```
*************************************************************************
Frame   Time    Src MAC Addr   Dst MAC Addr   Protocol  Description
2       0.000   SERVER00       CLIENT1        R_SRVSVC  RPC Server response


  MSRPC: c/o RPC Response:     call 0x1  context 0x0  hint 0x8  cancels 0x0
  R_SRVSVC: RPC Server response srvsvc:NetrShareAdd(..)
      R_SRVSVC: Return Value = 0 (0x0)



00080:                         00 00 00 00 00 00 00         ......
00090:  00 00                                               ..
```

## 5.1.8: NetrShareDel

This function removes the specified share from the target Server. The MSDN function prototype is shown here:

```
NET_API_STATUS NET_API_FUNCTION
NetShareDel    (
    IN  LPTSTR  servername,
    IN  LPTSTR  netname,
    IN  DWORD   reserved
    );
```

The delete, which contains the name of the share to be removed, takes effect immediately. The user must of course have sufficient privileges to delete shares.

```
*************************************************************************
Frame   Time    Src MAC Addr   Dst MAC Addr   Protocol  Description
1       0.000   CLIENT1        SERVER00       R_SRVSVC  RPC Client call


  MSRPC: c/o RPC Request:      call 0x1  opnum 0x12  context 0x0  hint 0x44
  R_SRVSVC: RPC Client call srvsvc:NetrShareDel(..)
      R_SRVSVC: SRVSVC_HANDLE ServerName = \\SERVER00
      R_SRVSVC: wchar_t NetName = TEMP
      R_SRVSVC: DWORD Reserved = 0 (0x0)



00080:                                              05 00    ..
00090:  00 03 10 00 00 00 5C 00 00 00 00 01 00 00 00 44 00   ......\.......D.
000A0:  00 00 00 00 12 00 1C E3 12 00 0B 00 00 00 00 00     ................
000B0:  00 00 0B 00 00 00 5C 00 5C 00 53 00 45 00 52 00     ......\.\.S.E.R.
000C0:  56 00 45 00 52 00 30 00 30 00 00 00 08 00 05 00     V.E.R.0.0.......
000D0:  00 00 00 00 00 00 05 00 00 00 54 00 45 00 4D 00     ..........T.E.M.
000E0:  50 00 00 00 FF FF 00 00 00 00                       P.........
```

The response contains a status return code. The error codes 0x0, indicating success, or NT_STATUS_ACCESS_DENIED, are expected:

```
***************************************************************************
Frame   Time    Src MAC Addr   Dst MAC Addr   Protocol  Description
2       0.000   SERVER00       CLIENT1        R_SRVSVC  RPC Server response


 MSRPC: c/o RPC Response:     call 0x1  context 0x0  hint 0x4  cancels 0x0
 R_SRVSVC: RPC Server response srvsvc:NetrShareDel(..)
     R_SRVSVC: Return Value = 0 (0x0)


00080:                        00 00 00 00                       ....
```

## 5.1.9: NetrSessionEnum

This function is used to enumerate the users which are currently connected to the Server and related information. In the SMB protocol one of the first requests sent by a client is the Session Setup request (SMB_COM_SESSION_SETUP_ANDX)—this creates a new **session** based on the specified User Credentials. The MSDN function prototype is shown here:

```
NET_API_STATUS NET_API_FUNCTION
NetSessionEnum (
    IN  LPTSTR      servername OPTIONAL,
    IN  LPTSTR      UncClientName OPTIONAL,
    IN  LPTSTR      username OPTIONAL,
    IN  DWORD       level,
    OUT LPBYTE      *bufptr,
    IN  DWORD       prefmaxlen,
    OUT LPDWORD     entriesread,
    OUT LPDWORD     totalentries,
    IN OUT LPDWORD  resume_handle OPTIONAL
    );
```

Session information comes in a number of information levels. The simplest, level 0, can be seen in the traces below—it simply enumerates connected clients. Other defined levels include 1, 2, 10, and 502, which give progressively more information about the session and also require progressively higher access rights to obtain. Level 2 is shown here, from the MSDN. See **lmshare.h** for a complete definition of all structures.

```
typedef struct _SESSION_INFO_2 {
    LPTSTR    sesi2_cname;             // client name (no backslashes)
    LPTSTR    sesi2_username;
    DWORD     sesi2_num_opens;
    DWORD     sesi2_time;
    DWORD     sesi2_idle_time;
```

```
    DWORD       sesi2_user_flags;
    LPTSTR      sesi2_cltype_name;
} SESSION_INFO_2, *PSESSION_INFO_2, *LPSESSION_INFO_2;
```

As with all the enumeration requests, the request consists of a container into which the entries should be returned, and a preferred maximum length. See the "**NetrShareEnum**" section earlier in this chapter for more information on how to use this.

```
**************************************************************************
Frame   Time    Src MAC Addr   Dst MAC Addr   Protocol  Description
1       0.000   CLIENT1        SERVER00       R_SRVSVC  RPC Client call


  MSRPC: c/o RPC Request:      call 0x1  opnum 0xC  context 0x0  hint 0x4C
  R_SRVSVC: RPC Client call srvsvc:NetrSessionEnum(..)
      R_SRVSVC: SRVSVC_HANDLE ServerName = \\SERVER00
      R_SRVSVC: PSESSION_ENUM_STRUCT InfoStruct {..}
        R_SRVSVC: DWORD Level = 0 (0x0)
        R_SRVSVC: _SESSION_ENUM_UNION SessionInfo {..}
          R_SRVSVC: Switch Value = 0 (0x0)
          R_SRVSVC: SESSION_INFO_0_CONTAINER *Level0 {..}
            R_SRVSVC: DWORD EntriesRead = 0 (0x0)
            R_SRVSVC: LPSESSION_INFO_0 Buffer = 0 (0x0)
      R_SRVSVC: DWORD PreferredMaximumLength = 4294967295 (0xFFFFFFFF)


000A0:                88 EE 12 00 0B 00 00 00 00 00     ·   ..........
000B0:  00 00 0B 00 00 00 5C 00 5C 00 53 00 45 00 52 00   ......\.\.S.E.R.
000C0:  56 00 45 00 52 00 30 00 30 00 00 00 08 00 00 00
V.E.R.0.0.......
000D0:  00 00 00 00 00 00 00 00 00 00 00 00 00 00 88 ED
................
000E0:  12 00 00 00 00 00 00 00 00 00 FF FF FF FF 00 00
................
000F0:  00 00                                                 ..
```

The container is filled, and the total number of sessions tracked by the Server is also returned.

```
**************************************************************************
Frame   Time    Src MAC Addr   Dst MAC Addr   Protocol  Description
2       0.000   SERVER00       CLIENT1        R_SRVSVC  RPC Server response


  MSRPC: c/o RPC Response:      call 0x1  context 0x0  hint 0x44  cancels 0x0
  R_SRVSVC: RPC Server response srvsvc:NetrSessionEnum(..)
      R_SRVSVC: PSESSION_ENUM_STRUCT InfoStruct {..}
        R_SRVSVC: DWORD Level = 0 (0x0)
        R_SRVSVC: _SESSION_ENUM_UNION SessionInfo {..}
          R_SRVSVC: Switch Value = 0 (0x0)
          R_SRVSVC: SESSION_INFO_0_CONTAINER *Level0 {..}
```

```
              R_SRVSVC: DWORD EntriesRead = 1 (0x1)
              R_SRVSVC: LPSESSION_INFO_0 Buffer = 1521976 (0x173938)
              R_SRVSVC: LPSESSION_INFO_0 Buffer [..]
                  R_SRVSVC: LPSESSION_INFO_0 Buffer {..}
                      R_SRVSVC: LPTSTR sesi0_cname = 1530152 (0x175928)
                  R_SRVSVC: LPSESSION_INFO_0 Buffer = CLIENT1
      R_SRVSVC: LPDWORD TotalEntries = 1 (0x1)
      R_SRVSVC: Return Value = 0 (0x0)
```

```
00080:                          00 00 00 00 00 00          ......
00090:  00 00 3C 29 17 00 01 00 00 00 38 39 17 00 01 00   ..<).......89....
000A0:  00 00 28 59 17 00 08 00 00 00 00 00 00 00 08 00   ..(Y............
000B0:  00 00 43 00 4C 00 49 00 45 00 4E 00 54 00 31 00   ..C.L.I.E.N.T.1.
000C0:  00 00 01 00 00 00 00 00 00 00 00 00 00 00         ..............
```

## 5.1.10: NetrSessionDel

**NetrSessionDel** forcibly disconnects a client. The MSDN function
prototype is shown here:

```
NET_API_STATUS NET_API_FUNCTION
NetSessionDel (
    IN  LPTSTR      servername OPTIONAL,
    IN  LPTSTR      UncClientName,
    IN  LPTSTR      username
    );
```

The calling user must have Administrative privileges. Data may be lost
if the Client was relying on the Server for storage, so this facility
should be used sparingly.

The request specifies the Client and the User name associated with
the session to be destroyed.

```
*************************************************************************
Frame  Time    Src MAC Addr   Dst MAC Addr   Protocol   Description
1      0.000   CLIENT1        SERVER00       R_SRVSVC   RPC Client call
```

```
  MSRPC: c/o RPC Request:      call 0x1  opnum 0xD  context 0x0  hint 0x6E
  R_SRVSVC: RPC Client call srvsvc:NetrSessionDel(..)
      R_SRVSVC: SRVSVC_HANDLE ServerName = \\SERVER00
      R_SRVSVC: wchar_t ClientName = \\CLIENT2
      R_SRVSVC: wchar_t UserName = matthewc
```

```
000A0:                    6C 04 32 00 0B 00 00 00 00 00   l.2.......
000B0:  00 00 0B 00 00 00 5C 00 5C 00 53 00 45 00 52 00   ......\.\.S.E.R.
000C0:  56 00 45 00 52 00 30 00 30 00 00 00 08 00 B0 1A   V.E.R.0.0.......
000D0:  32 00 0A 00 00 00 00 00 00 00 0A 00 00 00 5C 00   2.............\.
000E0:  5C 00 43 00 4C 00 49 00 45 00 4E 00 54 00 32 00   \.C.L.I.E.N.T.2.
000F0:  00 00 90 1B 32 00 09 00 00 00 00 00 00 00 09 00   ....2..........
00100:  00 00 6D 00 61 00 74 00 74 00 68 00 65 00 77 00   ..m.a.t.t.h.e.w.
00110:  63 00 00 00                                       c...
```

The response contains just a status code, indicating whether the deletion was successful or not.

```
***********************************************************************
Frame   Time    Src MAC Addr   Dst MAC Addr   Protocol  Description
2       0.000   SERVER00       CLIENT1        R_SRVSVC  RPC Server response


  MSRPC: c/o RPC Response:      call 0x1  context 0x0  hint 0x4  cancels 0x0
  R_SRVSVC: RPC Server response srvsvc:NetrSessionDel(..)
      R_SRVSVC: Return Value = 0 (0x0)


00080:                              00 00 00 00                     ....
```

## 5.1.11: NetrConnectionEnum

**NetrConnectionEnum** enumerates active share connections. The MSDN function prototype is shown here:

```
NET_API_STATUS NET_API_FUNCTION
NetConnectionEnum (
    IN  LPTSTR   servername OPTIONAL,
    IN  LPTSTR   qualifier,
    IN  DWORD    level,
    OUT LPBYTE   *bufptr,
    IN  DWORD    prefmaxlen,
    OUT LPDWORD  entriesread,
    OUT LPDWORD  totalentries,
    IN OUT LPDWORD resume_handle OPTIONAL
    );
```

A share connect, or *tree connect*, happens when an SMB client sends an **SMB_COM_TREE_CONNECT_ANDX** or **SMB_COM_TREE_CONNECT** request to access a specific share.

This RPC is of the same format as **NetrShareEnum** and **NetrSessionEnum**. A request is shown here:

```
***********************************************************************
Frame   Time    Src MAC Addr   Dst MAC Addr   Protocol  Description
1       0.000   CLIENT1        SERVER00       R_SRVSVC  RPC Client call


  MSRPC: c/o RPC Request:       call 0x1  opnum 0x8  context 0x0  hint 0x68
  R_SRVSVC: RPC Client call srvsvc:NetrConnectionEnum(..)
      R_SRVSVC: SRVSVC_HANDLE ServerName = \\SERVER00
      R_SRVSVC: wchar_t Qualifier = \\CLIENT1
      R_SRVSVC: LPCONNECT_ENUM_STRUCT InfoStruct {..}
          R_SRVSVC: DWORD Level = 1 (0x1)
          R_SRVSVC: _CONNECT_ENUM_UNION ConnectInfo {..}
              R_SRVSVC: Switch Value = 1 (0x1)
              R_SRVSVC: CONNECT_INFO_1_CONTAINER *Level1 {..}
```

```
            R_SRVSVC: DWORD EntriesRead = 0 (0x0)
            R_SRVSVC: LPCONNECTION_INFO_1 Buffer = 0 (0x0)
       R_SRVSVC: DWORD PreferredMaximumLength = 4294967295 (0xFFFFFFFF)


000A0:                    08 E9 12 00 0B 00 00 00 00 00     ..........
000B0:   00 00 0B 00 00 00 5C 00 5C 00 53 00 45 00 52 00   ......\.\.S.E.R.
000C0:   56 00 45 00 52 00 30 00 30 00 00 00 08 00 50 9C   V.E.R.0.0.....P.
000D0:   31 00 0A 00 00 00 00 00 00 00 0A 00 00 00 5C 00   1.............\.
000E0:   5C 00 43 00 4C 00 49 00 45 00 4E 00 54 00 31 00   \.C.L.I.E.N.T.1.
000F0:   00 00 01 00 00 00 01 00 00 00 00 00 E8 12 00 00   ................
00100:   00 00 00 00 00 00 FF FF FF FF 00 00 00 00          ..............
```

Connection information (CONNECTION_INFO) is available in levels
0 and 1. Level 0 includes only the connection ID (referred to as the
*Tree ID*, or TID, in the SMB protocol), while level 1 (shown here
from the MSDN) includes user and share information. For a complete
list of all CONNECTION_INFO structures, see **lmshare.h**).

```
typedef struct _CONNECTION_INFO_1 {
    DWORD    coni1_id;
    DWORD    coni1_type;
    DWORD    coni1_num_opens;
    DWORD    coni1_num_users;
    DWORD    coni1_time;
    LPTSTR   coni1_username;
    LPTSTR   coni1_netname;
} CONNECTION_INFO_1, *PCONNECTION_INFO_1, *LPCONNECTION_INFO_1;
```

An array of CONNECTION_INFO structures at the requested info
level is shown in the response, as follows.

```
*******************************************************************************
Frame   Time    Src MAC Addr   Dst MAC Addr   Protocol   Description
2       0.000   SERVER00       CLIENT1        R_SRVSVC   RPC Server response


MSRPC: c/o RPC Response:     call 0x1  context 0x0  hint 0x78  cancels 0x0
R_SRVSVC: RPC Server response srvsvc:NetrConnectionEnum(..)
     R_SRVSVC: LPCONNECT_ENUM_STRUCT InfoStruct {..}
        R_SRVSVC: DWORD Level = 1 (0x1)
        R_SRVSVC: _CONNECT_ENUM_UNION ConnectInfo {..}
           R_SRVSVC: Switch Value = 1 (0x1)
           R_SRVSVC: CONNECT_INFO_1_CONTAINER *Level1 {..}
              R_SRVSVC: DWORD EntriesRead = 1 (0x1)
              R_SRVSVC: LPCONNECTION_INFO_1 Buffer = 1521976 (0x173938)
              R_SRVSVC: LPCONNECTION_INFO_1 Buffer [..]
                 R_SRVSVC: LPCONNECTION_INFO_1 Buffer {..}
                    R_SRVSVC: DWORD coni1_id = 6 (0x6)
                    R_SRVSVC: DWORD coni1_type = 3 (0x3)
                    R_SRVSVC: DWORD coni1_num_opens = 1 (0x1)
                    R_SRVSVC: DWORD coni1_num_users = 1 (0x1)
                    R_SRVSVC: DWORD coni1_time = 183 (0xB7)
```

```
                            R_SRVSVC: LPTSTR coni1_username = 1530150 (0x175926)
                            R_SRVSVC: LPTSTR coni1_netname = 1530140 (0x17591C)
                        R_SRVSVC: LPTSTR coni1_username = matthewc
                        R_SRVSVC: LPTSTR coni1_netname = IPC$
        R_SRVSVC: LPDWORD TotalEntries = 1 (0x1)
        R_SRVSVC: Return Value = 0 (0x0)
```

```
00080:                              01 00 00 00 01 00          ......
00090:  00 00 58 29 17 00 01 00 00 00 38 39 17 00 01 00   ..X)......89....
000A0:  00 00 06 00 00 00 03 00 00 00 01 00 00 00 01 00   ................
000B0:  00 00 B7 00 00 00 26 59 17 00 1C 59 17 00 09 00   ......&Y...Y....
000C0:  00 00 00 00 00 00 09 00 00 00 6D 00 61 00 74 00   ..........m.a.t.
000D0:  74 00 68 00 65 00 77 00 63 00 00 00 00 00 05 00   t.h.e.w.c.......
000E0:  00 00 00 00 00 00 05 00 00 00 49 00 50 00 43 00   ..........I.P.C.
000F0:  24 00 00 00 32 00 01 00 00 00 00 00 00 00 00 00   $...2...........
00100:  00 00                                             ..
```

## 5.1.12: NetrFileEnum

NetrFileEnum enumerates the files that are currently open on behalf of Clients. Only information levels 2 and 3 are supported—level 2 includes only the file ID, whereas level 3 also includes user and path information (listed here from the MSDN). lmshare.h) contains the definitions for all these structures.

```
typedef struct _FILE_INFO_3 {
    DWORD     fi3_id;
    DWORD     fi3_permissions;
    DWORD     fi3_num_locks;
    LPTSTR    fi3_pathname;
    LPTSTR    fi3_username;
} FILE_INFO_3, *PFILE_INFO_3, *LPFILE_INFO_3;
```

Again NetrShareEnum should be consulted for a discussion of the format of this RPC, as it is very similar. The request contains the info level required.

```
*****************************************************************************
Frame   Time    Src MAC Addr   Dst MAC Addr   Protocol   Description
0       0.000   CLIENT1        SERVER00       R_SRVSVC   RPC Client call
```

```
MSRPC: c/o RPC Request:      call 0x1  opnum 0x9  context 0x0  hint 0x50
R_SRVSVC: RPC Client call srvsvc:NetrFileEnum(..)
    R_SRVSVC: SRVSVC_HANDLE ServerName = \\SERVER00
    R_SRVSVC: PFILE_ENUM_STRUCT InfoStruct {..}
      R_SRVSVC: DWORD Level = 3 (0x3)
      R_SRVSVC: _FILE_ENUM_UNION FileInfo {..}
        R_SRVSVC: Switch Value = 3 (0x3)
        R_SRVSVC: FILE_INFO_3_CONTAINER *Level3 {..}
            R_SRVSVC: DWORD EntriesRead = 0 (0x0)
            R_SRVSVC: LPFILE_INFO_3 Buffer = 0 (0x0)
```

```
       R_SRVSVC: DWORD PreferredMaximumLength = 4096 (0x1000)
       R_SRVSVC: LPDWORD ResumeHandle = 0 (0x0)


000A0:                     08 EE 12 00 0B 00 00 00 00 00     ..........
000B0:  00 00 0B 00 00 00 00 5C 00 5C 00 53 00 45 00 52 00
......\.\.S.E.R.
000C0:  56 00 45 00 52 00 30 00 30 00 00 00 08 00 00 00
V.E.R.0.0.......
000D0:  00 00 00 00 00 00 00 03 00 00 00
```

The response contains a list of files that are currently in use by remote
Clients. If info level 3 is requested, the user that has each file open is
also shown.

```
********************************************************************************
Frame   Time    Src MAC Addr    Dst MAC Addr   Protocol   Description
2       0.000   SERVER00        CLIENT1        R_SRVSVC   RPC Server response


  MSRPC: c/o RPC Response:     call 0x1  context 0x0  hint 0x84  cancels 0x0
  R_SRVSVC: RPC Server response srvsvc:NetrFileEnum(..)
      R_SRVSVC: PFILE_ENUM_STRUCT InfoStruct {..}
          R_SRVSVC: DWORD Level = 3 (0x3)
          R_SRVSVC: _FILE_ENUM_UNION FileInfo {..}
              R_SRVSVC: Switch Value = 3 (0x3)
              R_SRVSVC: FILE_INFO_3_CONTAINER *Level3 {..}
                  R_SRVSVC: DWORD EntriesRead = 1 (0x1)
                  R_SRVSVC: LPFILE_INFO_3 Buffer = 1521976 (0x173938)
                  R_SRVSVC: LPFILE_INFO_3 Buffer [..]
                      R_SRVSVC: LPFILE_INFO_3 Buffer {..}
                          R_SRVSVC: DWORD fi3_id = 4 (0x4)
                          R_SRVSVC: DWORD fi3_permissions = 35 (0x23)
                          R_SRVSVC: DWORD fi3_num_locks = 0 (0x0)
                          R_SRVSVC: LPTSTR fi3_pathname = 1526046 (0x17491E)
                          R_SRVSVC: LPTSTR fi3_username = 1526028 (0x17490C)
                      R_SRVSVC: LPTSTR fi3_pathname = \PIPE\srvsvc
                      R_SRVSVC: LPTSTR fi3_username = matthewc
          R_SRVSVC: LPDWORD TotalEntries = 1 (0x1)
          R_SRVSVC: LPDWORD ResumeHandle = 4 (0x4)
          R_SRVSVC: Return Value = 0 (0x0)


00080:                          03 00 00 00 03 00           ......
00090:  00 00 3C 29 17 00 01 00 00 00 38 39 17 00 01 00   ..<).......89....
000A0:  00 00 04 00 00 00 23 00 00 00 00 00 00 00 1E 49   ......#........I
000B0:  17 00 0C 49 17 00 0D 00 00 00 00 00 00 00 0D 00   ...I............
000C0:  00 00 5C 00 50 00 49 00 50 00 45 00 5C 00 73 00   ..\.P.I.P.E.\.s.
000D0:  72 00 76 00 73 00 76 00 63 00 00 00 4E 00 09 00   r.v.s.v.c...N...
000E0:  00 00 00 00 00 00 09 00 00 00 6D 00 61 00 74 00   ..........m.a.t.
000F0:  74 00 68 00 65 00 77 00 63 00 00 00 53 00 01 00   t.h.e.w.c...S...
00100:  00 00 4C 29 17 00 04 00 00 00 00 00 00 00         ..L).........
```

## 5.1.13: NetrFileClose

**NetrFileClose** is used to forcibly close a file that has been opened by a Client. Again this could result in data loss, so it should be used sparingly. The request contains the file id to be closed, which you must previously have obtained using **NetrFileEnum**.

```
*********************************************************************
Frame   Time    Src MAC Addr    Dst MAC Addr    Protocol  Description
1       0.000   CLIENT1         SERVER00        R_SRVSVC  RPC Client call


  MSRPC: c/o RPC Request:       call 0x1  opnum 0xB  context 0x0  hint 0x2C
 R_SRVSVC: RPC Client call srvsvc:NetrFileClose(..)
    R_SRVSVC: SRVSVC_HANDLE ServerName = \\SERVER00
    R_SRVSVC: DWORD FileId = 154 (0x9A)


000A0:                    60 1B 32 00 0B 00 00 00 00 00     `.2.......
000B0:  00 00 0B 00 00 00 5C 00 5C 00 53 00 45 00 52 00    ......\.\.S.E.R.
000C0:  56 00 45 00 52 00 30 00 30 00 00 00 08 00 9A 00    V.E.R.0.0.......
000D0:  00 00                                              ..
```

The response contains a status code, indicating whether the file close succeeded or not.

```
*********************************************************************
Frame   Time    Src MAC Addr    Dst MAC Addr    Protocol  Description
2       0.000   SERVER00        CLIENT1         R_SRVSVC  RPC Server response


  MSRPC: c/o RPC Response:      call 0x1  context 0x0  hint 0x4  cancels 0x0
 R_SRVSVC: RPC Server response srvsvc:NetrFileClose(..)
    R_SRVSVC: Return Value = 0 (0x0)


00080:                    00 00 00 00                       ....
```

## 5.1.14: NetrRemoteTOD

**NetrRemoteTOD** is used to obtain the time of day (TOD) or complete date information at the remote Server. The MSDN function prototype is shown here:

```
NET_API_STATUS NET_API_FUNCTION
NetRemoteTOD (
    IN LPCWSTR UncServerName,
    OUT LPBYTE *BufferPtr
    );
```

Only one info level is supported:

```
*********************************************************************
Frame   Time    Src MAC Addr    Dst MAC Addr    Protocol  Description
1       0.000   CLIENT1         SERVER00        R_SRVSVC  RPC Client call
```

```
MSRPC: c/o RPC Request:      call 0x1  opnum 0x1C  context 0x0  hint 0x26
R_SRVSVC: RPC Client call srvsvc:NetrRemoteTOD(..)
    R_SRVSVC: SRVSVC_HANDLE ServerName = \\SERVER00
```

```
000A0:                   D8 37 14 00 0B 00 00 00 00 00        .7.......
000B0:  00 00 0B 00 00 00 5C 00 5C 00 53 00 45 00 52 00    ......\.\.S.E.R.
000C0:  56 00 45 00 52 00 30 00 30 00 00 00                V.E.R.0.0...
```

The tod_elapsedt field represents the number of seconds elapsed since 00:00:00 on January 1, 1970, Coordinated Universal Time (UTC). The tod_timezone field specifies the time by which the local time zone differs from UTC, in minutes. The tod_weekday parameter is expressed as days since Sunday. The tod_interval represents the granularity of the remote clock tick, in ten-thousandths (0.0001) of seconds. All other fields should be self-explanatory.

```
*******************************************************************************
Frame  Time   Src MAC Addr   Dst MAC Addr   Protocol  Description
2      0.000  SERVER00       CLIENT1        R_SRVSVC  RPC Server response
```

```
MSRPC: c/o RPC Response:      call 0x1  context 0x0  hint 0x38  cancels 0x0
R_SRVSVC: RPC Server response srvsvc:NetrRemoteTOD(..)
    R_SRVSVC: LPTIME_OF_DAY_INFO BufferPtr {..}
        R_SRVSVC: DWORD tod_elapsedt = 928570886 (0x3758DE06)
        R_SRVSVC: DWORD tod_msecs = 346364686 (0x14A51B0E)
        R_SRVSVC: DWORD tod_hours = 8 (0x8)
        R_SRVSVC: DWORD tod_mins = 21 (0x15)
        R_SRVSVC: DWORD tod_secs = 26 (0x1A)
        R_SRVSVC: DWORD tod_hunds = 68 (0x44)
        R_SRVSVC: LONG tod_timezone = 4294966696 (0xFFFFFDA8)
        R_SRVSVC: DWORD tod_tinterval = 310 (0x136)
        R_SRVSVC: DWORD tod_day = 5 (0x5)
        R_SRVSVC: DWORD tod_month = 6 (0x6)
        R_SRVSVC: DWORD tod_year = 1999 (0x7CF)
        R_SRVSVC: DWORD tod_weekday = 6 (0x6)
    R_SRVSVC: Return Value = 0 (0x0)
```

```
00080:                      B0 9E 16 00 06 DE        ......
00090:  58 37 0E 1B A5 14 08 00 00 00 15 00 00 00 1A 00    X7..............
000A0:  00 00 44 00 00 00 A8 FD FF FF 36 01 00 00 05 00    ..D.......6.....
000B0:  00 00 06 00 00 00 CF 07 00 00 06 00 00 00 00 00    ................
000C0:  00 00                                              ..
```

# 5.2: Other \PIPE\srvsvc Functions

There are a number of other semi-documented **\PIPE\srvsvc** functions, including **NetrShareCheck, NetrSessionGetInfo, NetrFileGetInfo,**

**NetTransportEnum,** and **NetrRemoteComputerSupports,** which have not been seen "in the wild" and so are not described in detail here.

The **NetDfs*** API, also a part of **\PIPE\srvsvc** in Service Pack 3 and above, provides support for the remote management of a Distributed File System on a Server. This API is used by the DFSADMIN.EXE tool, available as part of DFS 4.1 from Microsoft's Web site.

## 5.3: Summary

For the committed **\PIPE\srvsvc** implementor, the form of most of these functions can be deduced from network traces and/or the MSDN prototypes, using this chapter as a guide. The MSDN prototypes, listed in **lmserver.h** and **lmshare.h,** were automatically generated from the original Interface Definition Language (IDL) files. Some functions in this API *have* been made obsolete, but for backward compatibility fortunately those functions are still published, albeit without any explanation, in Microsoft's MSDN.

A number of these functions provide too much information anonymously in some of their info levels. **NetTransportEnum** is a good example: this function provides the MAC addresses of network cards, which can be used to compromise a host on a local area network. **NetServerGetInfo** can be used to anonymously determine whether a host is a Primary Domain Controller or not, at which point it can be subjected to a more determined attack.

The style of each of the RPC pipes varies significantly, from which we can deduce that different teams at Microsoft were responsible for developing each RPC pipe. **\PIPE\srvsvc** is one of the better, self-consistent, useable APIs available, and it makes very efficient use of network bandwidth, due to well-designed IDL files.

# 6

## *\PIPE\winreg:*
## *NT Registry Services*

This chapter covers Windows NT's Remote Registry service. The
Windows NT Registry tools **REGEDIT.EXE** and **REGEDT32.EXE**
can be used to manipulate keys and values, including changing access
rights on keys.

The Windows NT Registry is used by programs and by the operating system to store configuration information. It was designed to
replace SYSTEM.INI, WIN.INI, and other such files. There has been
much confusion as to exactly where in the Registry it is acceptable for
programs to put configuration information. As a result, many programs have been installed with Administrator privileges on the multi-
user operating system Windows NT whilst the same programs install
"without problems" on the single-user system known as Windows 95.

The Registry functions are not decoded by Microsoft Network
Monitor (**NETMON.EXE**). However, the MSDN file **winreg.h** looks
as if it is directly generated from the Interface Definition Language
(IDL) files. This gives sufficient information to decode the data over-
the-wire and implement it as commands in Samba's rpcclient tool.
This was done as an academic exercise and also for the thrill of being
able to provide an Administrator with the capability to remotely shut
down a Windows NT system from a Unix command prompt.

The network traffic observed and the actual use of the MSDN
Registry API are sometimes odd and inefficient, which is related to
the original design of the IDL files for certain functions. Some of
these, therefore, *may* be good examples of how not to design remote
functions.

# 6.1: winreg pipe

This section describes almost all the remote Registry function calls. Specifically, the ASCII versions are not included, and **RegGetKeySecurity** is not included. As **Netmon** does not decode remote Registry, it has been necessary to use the debug output from rpcclient log files to illustrate each call.

The functions described in this chapter are listed here. The names are prefixed with *Reg*. These names follow the naming convention consistent with almost all other remote services.

- **RegOpenHKLM**
- **RegOpenHKU**
- **RegOpenKey**
- **RegClose**
- **RegFlushKey**
- **RegGetVersion**
- **RegQueryInfoKey**
- **RegEnumKey**
- **RegCreateKey**
- **RegDeleteKey**
- **RegDeleteValue**
- **RegCreateValue**
- **RegEnumValue**
- **RegGetKeySecurity**
- **RegSetKeySecurity**
- **RegShutdown**

Attentive MSDN users will have noticed that there is no function called **RegConnectRegistry** listed above. This is presumably because it is redirected to call either **RegOpenHKLM** or **RegOpenHKU**.

Typical access to a remote Registry starts with either **RegOpenHKLM** or **RegOpenHKU**, depending on whether **HIVE_KEY_LOCAL_MACHINE** (known as HKLM for short), or **HIVE_KEY_USERS** (known as HKU for short) is to be opened. **RegOpenHKLM** or **RegOpenHKU** could be followed by **RegOpenKey**, for example on **HKLM\System**, followed by **RegQueryInfoKey** to find out how many keys and values there are under **HKLM\System**. The amount of network traffic generated by running **REGEDIT.EXE** or **REGEDT32.EXE** can be considerably high. Some keys, such as **HKLM\System\CurrentControlSet\Control\ Services**, contain around 200 keys.

This service cannot be accessed anonymously by default. Additionally, certain actions, such as shutting down the Server, require Administrator-level privileges. Also, if a key is to be deleted, then the user must have the right to perform the delete action on that key. If delete rights have not been granted or if delete rights are not requested, then the delete fails.

Examining **winreg.h** shows that there are two versions of all functions. Both ASCII (eight bits per character) and UNICODE (sixteen bits per character) are supported. The functions that have been observed are from running **REGEDT32.EXE**, and these are UNICODE. The ASCII versions of these functions are identical except that where UNICODE strings are shown, ASCII is used instead. The MSRPC Operation Code is also different, representing the ASCII equivalent of the same function.

## 6.1.1: RegOpenHKLM

This is one of the first calls that must be made. **RegOpenHKLM** opens **HIVE_KEY_LOCAL_MACHINE**, known as HKLM for short. The MSDN API presumably calls this from **RegConnectRegistry**, shown here:

```
LONG
RegConnectRegistry(
    LPCWSTR lpMachineName,
    HKEY hKey,
    PHKEY phkResult
    );
```

The request contains information that is not obvious, so it is simply repeated verbatim here. The argument named here as level may actually be an access mask. According to **winnt.h**, the value 0x02000000 represents **MAXIMUM_ALLOWED** permissions.

```
000000 reg_io_q_open_hklm
    0000 ptr       : 00000001
    0004 unknown_0: 84e0
    0006 unknown_1: 0000
    0008 level     : 02000000
```

The response contains a Policy Handle that can be used in subsequent calls to represent HKLM:

```
000018 reg_io_r_open_hklm
    000018 smb_io_pol_hnd
        0018 data: 00 00 00 00 88 3c 7d 89 d5 49 d3 11 82 ba 00 10 4b 97 32 2e
    002c status: 00000000
```

The handle must be freed with a call to **RegClose,** after it is no longer needed. Failure to make this call may result in resource leaks on some Servers.

## 6.1.2: RegOpenHKU

This is one of the first calls that must be made. **RegOpenHKU** opens **HIVE_KEY_USERS,** known as HKU for short. The MSDN API presumably calls this from **RegConnectRegistry,** shown here:

```
LONG
RegConnectRegistry(
    LPCWSTR lpMachineName,
    HKEY hKey,
    PHKEY phkResult
    );
```

The request contains information that is not obvious, so it is simply repeated verbatim here. The argument named as level may actually be an access mask. According to **winnt.h,** the value 0x02000000 represents **MAXIMUM_ALLOWED** permissions.

```
000000 reg_io_q_open_hku
    0000 ptr      : 00000001
    0004 unknown_0: 84e0
    0006 unknown_1: 0000
    0008 level    : 02000000
```

The response contains a Policy Handle that can be used in subsequent calls to represent HKU:

```
000018 reg_io_r_open_hku
    000018 smb_io_pol_hnd
        0018 data: 00 00 00 00 c7 3c 7d 89 d5 49 d3 11 82 ba 00 10 4b 97 32 2e
    002c status: 00000000
```

The handle must be freed with a call to **RegClose,** after it is no longer needed. Failure to make this call may result in resource leaks on some Servers.

## 6.1.3: RegOpenKey .

**RegOpenKey** opens a Registry key. The MSDN function is **RegOpenKeyEx,** shown here:

```
LONG
RegOpenKeyEx(
    HKEY hKey,
    LPCWSTR lpSubKey,
    DWORD ulOptions,
    REGSAM samDesired,
    PHKEY phkResult
    );
```

This example is opening HKLM\System, as the first argument is
a Policy Handle returned from calling **RegOpenHKLM**, and the
second argument is the UNICODE string "system." The unknown_1
argument is actually an access mask. According to **winnt.h**, the value
0x02000000 represents **MAXIMUM_ALLOWED** permissions.

```
000000 reg_io_q_open_entry
    000000 smb_io_pol_hnd
        0000 data: 00 00 00 00 92 97 0a e6 99 4a d3 11 b0 cf 00 10 4b 97 33 32
    000014 smb_io_unihdr
        0014 uni_str_len: 000e
        0016 uni_max_len: 000e
        0018 buffer      : 00000001
    00001c smb_io_unistr2
        001c uni_max_len: 00000007
        0020 undoc       : 00000000
        0024 uni_str_len: 00000007
        0028 buffer      : s.y.s.t.e.m...
    0038 unknown_0: 00000000
    003c unknown_1: 02000000
```

The response contains a valid handle that can be used in subsequent
calls to represent the key opened (with the permissions requested) and
a status code. The status error code can indicate, for example, that the
user does not have sufficient privileges or that the key does not exist.

```
000018 reg_io_r_open_entry
    000018 smb_io_pol_hnd
        0018 data: 00 00 00 00 93 97 0a e6 99 4a d3 11 b0 cf 00 10 4b 97 33 32
    002c status: 00000000
```

In subsequent calls that use the handle returned, the permissions specified in the access mask parameter will be validated against the type of
operation being requested. For example, if write permission is not
requested in the **RegOpenKey** call and the handle returned from this
call to **RegOpenKey** is used in a subsequent call to **RegCreateKey**, the
**RegCreateKey** call will fail.

The handle must be freed with a call to **RegClose**, after it is no
longer needed. Failure to make this call may result in resource leaks
on some Servers.

## 6.1.4: RegClose

**RegClose** is used to free a handle. The MSDN function name is
**RegCloseKey**, shown here:

```
LONG
RegCloseKey (
    HKEY hKey
    );
```

The implementation of this function should inform the Server that any resources needed to service requests that used the handle are no longer needed.

```
000000 reg_io_q_close
    000000 smb_io_pol_hnd
        0000 data: 00 00 00 00 88 3c 7d 89 d5 49 d3 11 82 ba 00 10 4b 97 32 2e
```

The response usually contains an empty handle and a status code of 0x0, indicating that the handle and its associated resources were successfully freed. If the handle was invalid (for example, it has already been freed), then an appropriate non-zero status code is returned from this function.

```
000018 reg_io_r_close
    000018 smb_io_pol_hnd
        0018 data: 00 00 00 00 00 00 00 00 00 00 00 00 00 00 00 00 00 00 00 00
    002c status: 00000000
```

### 6.1.5: RegFlushKey

**RegFlushKey** ensures that modifications to a key are actually updated into the Registry. The MSDN function prototype is shown here:

```
LONG
RegFlushKey (
    HKEY hKey
    ;
```

This function takes a handle that must have been opened with **RegOpenKey, RegOpenHKLM,** or **RegOpenHKU.**

```
000000 reg_io_q_flush_key
    000000 smb_io_pol_hnd
        0000 data: 00 00 00 00 94 3c 7d 89 d5 49 d3 11 82 ba 00 10 4b 97 32 2e
```

A status code, indicating whether the call succeeded or failed, is returned:

```
000018 reg_io_r_flush_key
    0018 status: 00000000
```

### 6.1.6: RegGetVersion

**RegGetVersion** is called as part of an enumeration sequence. Its purpose is not exactly clear, and its function prototype is not listed in the MSDN. A construction of what its prototype is likely to be is shown here:

```
STATUS RegGetVersion(
    IN  HANDLE hKey,
    OUT DWORD dwVersion
);
```

Network traces show that **RegGetVersion** is called prior to each
**RegEnumValue** and **RegEnumKey** call in the enumeration sequence.
The handle parameter is the key that is being enumerated for its sub-
keys and values.

```
000000 reg_io_q_get_version
   000000 smb_io_pol_hnd
       0000 data: 00 00 00 00 88 3c 7d 89 d5 49 d3 11 82 ba 00 10 4b 97 32 2e
```

The response contains a version number 0x000000005 (and no other
value has ever been empirically observed in any network traffic when
using **REGEDT32.EXE**) and a status code.

```
000018 reg_io_r_get_version
   0018 unknown: 00000005
   001c status: 00000000
```

## 6.1.7: RegQueryInfoKey

**RegQueryInfoKey** obtains information about a key. Its MSDN function prototype is shown here. This prototype is automatically generated from its IDL definition.

```
LONG
RegQueryInfoKey(
    HKEY hKey,
    LPWSTR lpClass,
    LPDWORD lpcbClass,
    LPDWORD lpReserved,
    LPDWORD lpcSubKeys,
    LPDWORD lpcbMaxSubKeyLen,
    LPDWORD lpcbMaxClassLen,
    LPDWORD lpcValues,
    LPDWORD lpcbMaxValueNameLen,
    LPDWORD lpcbMaxValueLen,
    LPDWORD lpcbSecurityDescriptor,
    PFILETIME lpftLastWriteTime
    );
```

An attempt to re-create an IDL definition for this function is shown
here, which is very similar to the auto-generated MSDN function prototype, above. The [in] and [in out] parameters are sent over-the-wire
in the request, and the [in out] and [out] parameters are sent back
over-the-wire in the response.

```
STATUS RegQueryInfoKey( /* Function 0x10 */
                [in] HANDLE        hKey,
        [in,out,ref] UNICODE_STRING* lpClass,
               [out] DWORD*         lpcbSubKeys,
               [out] DWORD*         lpcbMaxSubKeyLen,
               [out] DWORD*         lpcbMaxClassLen,
               [out] DWORD*         lpcValues,
               [out] DWORD*         lpcbMaxValueNameLen,
```

```
                          [out] DWORD*          lpcbMaxValueLen,
                          [out] DWORD*          lpcbSecurityDescriptor,
                          [out] FILETIME*       lpftLastWriteTime
                          );
```

The first argument in the request is the handle of the key to be
queried, and the second argument, according to the MSDN, is a class
name string.

```
000000 reg_io_q_query_key
    000000 smb_io_pol_hnd
        0000 data: 00 00 00 00 93 97 0a e6 99 4a d3 11 b0 cf 00 10 4b 97 33 32
    000014 smb_io_unihdr
        0014 uni_str_len: 0000
        0016 uni_max_len: 0000
        0018 buffer     : 00000000
    00001c smb_io_unistr2 - NULL
```

The response contains the number of subkeys and number of values in
the key. The length of the longest key name and the longest value
name are also returned, to make enumeration easier. The response
also contains the class name string (which can be zero length), the last
time that the key was modified, and also the security descriptor buffer
size for this key. In this example, there are no values, only subkeys.

```
000018 reg_io_r_query_key
    000018 smb_io_unihdr
        0018 uni_str_len: 0002
        001a uni_max_len: 0000
        001c buffer      : 00000000
    000020 smb_io_unistr2 - NULL
    0020 num_subkeys    : 00000006
    0024 max_subkeylen  : 00000042
    0028 mak_subkeysize : 00000000
    002c num_values     : 00000000
    0030 max_valnamelen : 00000000
    0034 max_valbufsize : 00000000
    0038 sec_desc       : 00000140
    00003c smb_io_time mod_time
        003c low : 523ac880
        0040 high: 01bbb682
    0044 status: 00000000
```

This is where the design of the Registry API starts to get a bit odd.
Why is the class name string parameter being sent in both the request
and the response, when the only useful information that comes back is
in the response? Why are we interested in the length of the longest key
and value names, and why are we interested in the size of the security
descriptor buffer?

## 6.1.8: RegEnumKey

**RegEnumKey** is called repeatedly to enumerate subkeys in a key. The MSDN prototype is shown here:

```
LONG
RegEnumKeyEx(
    HKEY hKey,
    DWORD dwIndex,
    LPWSTR lpName,
    LPDWORD lpcbName,
    LPDWORD lpReserved,
    LPWSTR lpClass,
    LPDWORD lpcbClass,
    PFILETIME lpftLastWriteTime
    );
```

The request is shown here. The only significant parameters are the Policy Handle of the key to be enumerated and the index indicating which of the subkeys is to be returned in the response.

```
000000 reg_io_q_enum_key
    000000 smb_io_pol_hnd
        0000 data: 00 00 00 00 88 3c 7d 89 d5 49 d3 11 82 ba 00 10 4b 97 32 2e
    0014 key_index: 00000000
    0018 key_name_len: 0000
    001a unknown_1: 0414
    001c ptr1: 00000001
    0020 unknown_2: 0000020a
    0024 pad1: 00 00 00 00 00 00 00 00
    002c ptr2: 00000001
    0030 pad2: 00 00 00 00 00 00 00 00
    0038 ptr3: 00000001
    00003c smb_io_time
        003c low : ffffffff
        0040 high: 7fffffff
```

The response fills in the parameters, including those that were really not supposed to have been sent over in the request. These include the key name, class name (here shown as pad2 because that was not known at the time of writing this function in rpcclient!), and the subkey's last modified time.

```
000018 reg_io_r_enum_key
    0018 key_name_len: 0012
    001a unknown_1: 0414
    001c ptr1: 0014f600
    0020 unknown_2: 0000020a
    0024 unknown_3: 00000000
    000028 smb_io_unistr3 key_name
        0028 uni_str_len: 00000009
        002c unistr: H.A.R.D.W.A.R.E...
    0040 ptr2: 0014e988
    0044 pad2: 00 00 00 00 00 00 00 00
```

```
004c ptr3: 0014e994
000050 smb_io_time
    0050 low : b2b2b2b2
    0054 high: b2b2b2b2
0058 status: 00000000
```

Almost every parameter listed in the request also appears in the
response, and can contain complete garbage in the request (which is
replaced in the response). This is completely unnecessary, and a waste
of network bandwidth, particularly because this function can be called
very frequently. The key name and key class strings need not appear
in the request, and neither should the key last write time. Presumably
the IDL definition for **RegEnumKey** shows these parameters as **[in
out]** parameters when they should only be **[out]**.

## 6.1.9: RegCreateKey

**RegCreateKey** creates a subkey. The MSDN prototype is shown here:

```
LONG
RegCreateKeyEx(
    HKEY hKey,
    LPCWSTR lpSubKey,
    DWORD Reserved,
    LPWSTR lpClass,
    DWORD dwOptions,
    REGSAM samDesired,
    LPSECURITY_ATTRIBUTES lpSecurityAttributes,
    PHKEY phkResult,
    LPDWORD lpdwDisposition
    );
```

The request contains a handle to a key in which the subkey and all its
attributes are to be created, which includes the subkey name, class
name, and a security descriptor.

```
000000 reg_io_q_create_key
    000000 smb_io_pol_hnd
        0000 data: 00 00 00 00 c5 3c 7d 89 d5 49 d3 11 82 ba 00 10 4b 97 32 2e
    000014 smb_io_unihdr
        0014 uni_str_len: 000a
        0016 uni_max_len: 000a
        0018 buffer     : 00000001
    00001c smb_io_unistr2
        001c uni_max_len: 00000005
        0020 undoc      : 00000000
        0024 uni_str_len: 00000005
        0028 buffer     : t.e.s.t...
    000034 smb_io_unihdr
        0034 uni_str_len: 0002
        0036 uni_max_len: 0002
        0038 buffer     : 00000001
```

```
00003c smb_io_unistr2
    003c uni_max_len: 00000001
    0040 undoc        : 00000000
    0044 uni_str_len: 00000001
    0048 buffer       : ..
004c reserved: 00000000
000050 sec_io_access sam_access
    0050 mask: 00020019
0054 ptr1: 00000001
0058 sec_info: 0000000c
005c ptr2: 00000001
0068 ptr3: 00000001
00006c sec_io_desc_buf data
    0070 undoc   : 00000000
    000078 sec_io_desc sec
        0078 revision : 0001
        007a type     : 8000
        007c off_owner_sid: 00000000
        0080 off_grp_sid : 00000000
        0084 off_sacl    : 00000000
        0088 off_dacl    : 00000000
    006c max_len: 00000014
    0074 len    : 00000014
000060 smb_io_hdrbuf hdr_sec
    0060 buf_max_len: 00000014
    0064 buf_len    : 00000014
0090 unknown_2: 00000000
```

The response contains a handle to the subkey that was created, a Disposition parameter (shown here as unknown), and a status code.

```
000018 reg_io_r_create_key
    000018 smb_io_pol_hnd
        0018 data: 00 00 00 00 c6 3c 7d 89 d5 49 d3 11 82 ba 00 10 4b 97 32 2e
    002c unknown: 00000000
    0030 status: 00000000
```

There is a parameter listed in the request, referred to as **unknown_2**, after the security descriptor. This is likely to be the Disposition parameter, according to the MSDN prototype. Exactly what it is doing in the request data is not known by the author, particularly when the MSDN makes it clear that the Disposition is a pointer that only receives information.

The handle must be freed with a call to **RegClose**, after it is no longer needed. Failure to make this call may result in resource leaks on some Servers.

### 6.1.10: RegDeleteKey

**RegDeleteKey** removes a subkey from the Registry. The MSDN prototype is shown here:

```
LONG
RegDeleteKey(
    HKEY hKey,
    LPCWSTR lpSubKey
    );
```

The first parameter in the request is a handle representing the key from which the named subkey, the second parameter, is to be removed.

```
000000 reg_io_q_delete_key
    000000 smb_io_pol_hnd
        0000 data: 00 00 00 00 9c 3c 7d 89 d5 49 d3 11 82 ba 00 10 4b 97 32 2e
    000014 smb_io_unihdr
        0014 uni_str_len: 000a
        0016 uni_max_len: 000a
        0018 buffer     : 00000001
    00001c smb_io_unistr2
        001c uni_max_len: 00000005
        0020 undoc       : 00000000
        0024 uni_str_len: 00000005
        0028 buffer     : t.e.s.t...
```

The response contains the status code. In this example, the subkey contained further values and subkeys. Consequently, the subkey could not be deleted and an **NT_STATUS_ACCESS_VIOLATION** error code was returned. This call can be rejected because the user does not have sufficient access rights to remove subkeys from this key, or because the handle in the request was not opened with delete rights.

```
000018 reg_io_r_delete_key
    0018 status: 00000005
REG_DELETE_KEY: NT_STATUS_ACCESS_VIOLATION
```

### 6.1.11: RegDeleteValue

**RegDeleteValue** removes a value from the Registry. The MSDN prototype is shown here:

```
LONG
RegDeleteValue(
    HKEY hKey,
    LPCWSTR lpValueName
    );
```

The first parameter in the request is a handle representing the key from which the named value, the second parameter, is to be removed.

```
000000 reg_io_q_delete_val
    000000 smb_io_pol_hnd
```

```
     0000 data: 00 00 00 00 96 3c 7d 89 d5 49 d3 11 82 ba 00 10 4b 97 32 2e
000014 smb_io_unihdr
     0014 uni_str_len: 000c
     0016 uni_max_len: 000c
     0018 buffer     : 00000001
00001c smb_io_unistr2
     001c uni_max_len: 00000006
     0020 undoc      : 00000000
     0024 uni_str_len: 00000006
     0028 buffer     : d.w.o.r.d...
```

The response contains the status code. A status code of 0x0 was returned in this example, indicating that the value was successfully removed. This call can be rejected because the user does not have sufficient access rights to remove values from this key.

```
000018 reg_io_r_delete_val
     0018 status: 00000000
```

## 6.1.12: RegCreateValue

**RegCreateValue** adds a new value to a Registry subkey. The MSDN function prototype for **RegSetValueEx** is shown here:

```
LONG
RegSetValueEx(
    HKEY hKey,
    LPCWSTR lpValueName,
    DWORD Reserved,
    DWORD dwType,
    CONST BYTE* lpData,
    DWORD cbData
    );
```

The first parameter in the request is a handle representing the key to which the named value, the second parameter, is to be added. The third parameter tells us what kind of data the fourth parameter is. In this example, the fourth parameter is a UNICODE string, so parameter 3 is set to 0x1 (which is defined as REG_SZ in **winnt.h**).

```
000000 reg_io_q_create_val
     000000 smb_io_pol_hnd
         0000 data: 00 00 00 00 9a 3c 7d 89 d5 49 d3 11 82 ba 00 10 4b 97 32 2e
     000014 smb_io_unihdr hdr_name
         0014 uni_str_len: 000e
         0016 uni_max_len: 000e
         0018 buffer     : 00000001
     00001c smb_io_unistr2 uni_name
         001c uni_max_len: 00000007
         0020 undoc      : 00000000
         0024 uni_str_len: 00000007
         0028 buffer     : s.t.r.i.n.g...
     0038 type: 00000001
```

```
00003c smb_io_buffer3 buf_value
   003c uni_max_len: 0000000e
   0040 buffer    : s.t.r.i.n.g...
   004e buf_len   : 0000000e
```

The response contains the status code. A status code of 0x0 was returned in this example, indicating that the value was successfully created. This call can be rejected because the user does not have sufficient access rights to add values to this key.

```
000018 reg_io_r_create_val
   0018 status: 00000000
```

## 6.1.13: RegEnumValue

**RegEnumValue** is called repeatedly to enumerate values contained in a key. The MSDN function prototype is shown here:

```
LONG
RegEnumValue(
    HKEY hKey,
    DWORD dwIndex,
    LPWSTR lpValueName,
    LPDWORD lpcbValueName,
    LPDWORD lpReserved,
    LPDWORD lpType,
    LPBYTE lpData,
    LPDWORD lpcbData
    );
```

The first parameter in the request is a handle representing the key to be enumerated. The second parameter is the index of the value to be returned, starting out at zero in the first call and incrementing with subsequent calls until all values have been enumerated. The rest of the request is, putting it bluntly, a mess. Amongst other things, it contains a length-limited NULL UNICODE string representing the name of the value and the maximum length of the name. It also contains a pointer to the type of the value, which is uninitialised in the request.

```
000000 reg_io_q_enum_val
   000000 smb_io_pol_hnd
      0000 data: 00 00 00 00 92 3c 7d 89 d5 49 d3 11 82 ba 00 10 4b 97 32 2e
   0014 val_index: 00000000
   000018 smb_io_unihdr hdr_name
      0018 uni_str_len: 0000
      001a uni_max_len: 0024
      001c buffer     : 00000001
   000020 smb_io_unistr2 uni_name
      0020 uni_max_len: 00000012
      0024 undoc      : 00000000
      0028 uni_str_len: 00000000
      002c buffer     :
```

```
002c ptr_type: 00000001
0030 type: 00000000
0034 ptr_value: 00000001
000038 smb_io_buffer2 buf_value
     0038 buf_max_len: 000031f5
     003c undoc      : 00000000
     0040 buf_len    : 00000000
     0044 buffer     :
0044 ptr1: 00000001
0048 len_value1: 000031f5
004c ptr2: 00000001
0050 len_value2: 00000000
```

The response contains the name of the value being enumerated plus the value and its type. These are the parameters that were inappropriately uninitialised in the request.

```
000018 reg_io_r_enum_val
     000018 smb_io_unihdr hdr_name
          0018 uni_str_len: 000e
          001a uni_max_len: 0024
          001c buffer      : 00148fb0
     000020 smb_io_unistr2 uni_name
          0020 uni_max_len: 00000012
          0024 undoc       : 00000000
          0028 uni_str_len: 00000007
          002c buffer      : r.e.g._.s.z...
     003c ptr_type: 0014e988
     0040 type: 00000001
     0044 ptr_value: 0014f600
     000048 smb_io_buffer2 buf_value
          0048 buf_max_len: 00000018
          004c undoc       : 00000000
          0050 buf_len     : 00000018
          0054 buffer      : s.t.r.i.n.g. .d.a.t.a...
     006c ptr1: 0014e9a0
     0070 len_value1: 00000018
     0074 ptr2: 0014e9a8
     0078 len_value2: 00000018
     007c status: 00000000
```

The design of this function is terrible. The only parameters that really need to be sent in the request are the handle and the index. The purpose of the IDL **[in]** and **[out]** specifiers are to indicate which parameters are to be sent in the request and which are going to be modified and sent back in the response, or both sent in the request, modified, and returned in the response. **winreg** designers have failed to use these specifiers correctly, which results in uninitialised variables—such as the type parameter—being sent over-the-wire. Failure to use **[in]** and **[out]** specifiers correctly results in the IDL compiler not being able to fully optimise the marshalling/unmarshalling code that turns over-the-wire data into function parameters and vice-versa. Sending uninitialised variables over-the-wire is such a waste of network bandwidth that there should be a law against it.

There is also absolutely no need to impose a requirement to set the maximum length of the value's name in the **RegEnumValue** call, mandating that **RegQueryInfoKey** be called first to obtain the maximum string length of all value names in a key. The string should be returned in the request *regardless* of its length, and the caller should decide what to do with the string, if anything.

### 6.1.14: RegGetKeySecurity

**RegGetKeySecurity** is used to obtain the security descriptor associated with a Registry key. The security descriptor controls the access rights of users to perform certain operations, such as delete, enumerate, and modify. The MSDN prototype for **RegGetKeySecurity** is shown here:

```
LONG
RegGetKeySecurity (
    HKEY hKey,
    SECURITY_INFORMATION SecurityInformation,
    PSECURITY_DESCRIPTOR pSecurityDescriptor,
    LPDWORD lpcbSecurityDescriptor
    );
```

The first parameter in the request indicates what kind of security information should be returned in the security descriptor. For example, it can be used to ask who the owner of the object is (in this case, the object is a registry key). The second parameter indicates, in a badly designed manner, the maximum size of the buffer in which the security descriptor should be returned.

```
000000 reg_io_q_get_key_sec
    000000 smb_io_pol_hnd
        0000 data: 00 00 00 00 c1 3c 7d 89 d5 49 d3 11 82 ba 00 10 4b 97 32 2e
    0014 sec_info: 00000007
    0018 ptr     : 00000001
    000024 sec_io_desc_buf data
        0028 undoc  : 00000000
        0024 max_len: 00000000
        002c len    : 00000000
    00001c smb_io_hdrbuf hdr_sec
        001c buf_max_len: 00000000
        0020 buf_len    : 00000000
```

The response indicates that the maximum size of the buffer was too small, which resulted in a Win32 status code, defined in **winerror.h** as **ERROR_INSUFFICIENT_BUFFER**. The security descriptor buffer is

modified to contain the new recommended buffer size, but it still does
not contain the security descriptor (or even a part of it).

```
000000 reg_io_q_get_key_sec
    000000 smb_io_pol_hnd
        0000 data: 00 00 00 00 c1 3c 7d 89 d5 49 d3 11 82 ba 00 10 4b 97 32 2e
    0014 sec_info: 00000007
    0018 ptr     : 00000001
    000024 sec_io_desc_buf data
        0028 undoc  : 00000000
        0024 max_len: 00000140
        002c len    : 00000000
    00001c smb_io_hdrbuf hdr_sec
        001c buf_max_len: 00000140
        0020 buf_len    : 00000000
```

Following the failure of the first request, the second request contains
the modified security descriptor buffer with the newly recommended
buffer size.

```
000018 reg_io_r_get_key_sec
    0018 ptr     : 0014b330
    00001c smb_io_hdrbuf
        001c buf_max_len: 00000140
        0020 buf_len    : 00000000
    000024 sec_io_desc_buf
        0024 max_len: 00000140
        0028 undoc  : 00000000
        002c len    : 00000000
    0030 status: 0000007a
```

At last, a security descriptor is returned, shown here:

```
000018 reg_io_r_get_key_sec
    0018 ptr     : 00152928
    00001c smb_io_hdrbuf
        001c buf_max_len: 00000140
        0020 buf_len    : 00000140
    000024 sec_io_desc_buf
        0024 max_len: 00000140
        0028 undoc  : 00000000
        002c len    : 00000140
        000030 sec_io_desc sec
            0030 revision : 0001
            0032 type     : 8004
            0034 off_owner_sid: 00000114
            0038 off_grp_sid  : 00000124
            003c off_sacl     : 00000000
            0040 off_dacl     : 00000014
            000044 sec_io_acl dacl
                0044 revision: 0002
                0046 size     : 0100
                0048 num_aces : 00000003
                00004c sec_io_ace ace[00]:
```

```
            004c type : 00
            004d flags: 02
            004e size : 0014
            000050 sec_io_access info
                0050 mask: 00020019
            000054 smb_io_dom_sid sid
                0054 sid_rev_num: 01
                0055 num_auths  : 01
                0056 id_auth[0..5] : 00 00 00 00 00 01
                005c sub_auths : 00000000
        000060 sec_io_ace ace[01]:
            0060 type : 00
            0061 flags: 02
            0062 size : 0018
            000064 sec_io_access info
                0064 mask: 0003001f
            000068 smb_io_dom_sid sid
                0068 sid_rev_num: 01
                0069 num_auths  : 02
                006a id_auth[0..5] : 00 00 00 00 00 05
                0070 sub_auths : 00000020 00000220
        000078 sec_io_ace ace[02]:
            0078 type : 00
            0079 flags: 02
            007a size : 0014
            00007c sec_io_access info
                007c mask: 000f003f
            000080 smb_io_dom_sid sid
                0080 sid_rev_num: 01
                0081 num_auths  : 01
                0082 id_auth[0..5] : 00 00 00 00 00 05
                0088 sub_auths : 00000012
    000144 smb_io_dom_sid owner_sid
        0144 sid_rev_num: 01
        0145 num_auths  : 02
        0146 id_auth[0..5] : 00 00 00 00 00 05
        014c sub_auths : 00000020 00000220
    000154 smb_io_dom_sid grp_sid
        0154 sid_rev_num: 01
        0155 num_auths  : 05
        0156 id_auth[0..5] : 00 00 00 00 00 05
        015c sub_auths : 00000015 7ecf65a0 5f9b4b78 70877ce7 00000201
0170 status: 00000000
```

A detailed description of the contents of a security descriptor is beyond the scope of this book. There is an entire MSDN set of functions responsible for tearing apart and reconstructing security descriptors. However, to assist the reader, the output from Samba's rpcclient command **reggetsec** is shown here. This command was used to generate the same debug output shown above.

```
smb: \> reggetsec hklm\system
reggetsec hklm\system

        Security Descriptor          revision: 1          type:      8004
        ...................
        ACL     Num ACEs:            3            revision:          2
        ...
        ACE
                Permissions:        Read
                SID:      S-1-1-0
        ACE
                Permissions:        Query Set Create Enum Notify Delete ReadControl
                SID:      S-1-5-32-544
        ACE
                Permissions:        Full Control
                SID:      S-1-5-18

        Owner SID:              S-1-5-32-544
        Parent SID:            S-1-5-21-2127521184-1604012920-1887927527-513

smb: \> quit
quit
```

**winnt.h** shows that the Security ID (SID) **S-1-1-0** represents **Everyone,** so in this example, Read permission is granted to everyone on **HKLM\System.** In addition, a more complex set of permissions is granted to **S-1-5-32-544, Domain Administrator Group,** and full control is granted to **S-1-5-18,** which represents **Local System.** In other words, normal users can read this key, whilst Domain Administrators get to do things such as add, delete, and modify, and the Operating System can do anything it likes.

## 6.1.15: RegSetKeySecurity

This function changes the security settings (access rights) of a Registry key. At the time of writing of this chapter, this call is not fully understood; an NT status code 0x539 is returned by the prototype **regsetsec** command in Samba's rpcclient tool. Rather than potentially provide misleading information, this function is not documented here.

## 6.1.16: RegShutdown

**RegShutdown** is the best remote function in the entire MSRPC API set. It requires Administrator privileges to be run, and it can be used to shut down, and optionally restart, a remote Windows NT host. The MSDN function prototype, named **InitiateSystemShutdown,** is listed here:

```
BOOL
InitiateSystemShutdownW(
    LPWSTR lpMachineName,
    LPWSTR lpMessage,
```

```
DWORD dwTimeout,
BOOL bForceAppsClosed,
BOOL bRebootAfterShutdown
);
```

The request contains a message reported in an onscreen pop-up, in case someone is using the host interactively at the time. The timeout parameter, in seconds, is the time left for the interactive user to perform a mad scramble to find a way to stop the countdown. The two Boolean parameters here are actually individual 8-bit values that have been combined by mistake into the field shown here as flags. In other words, flags must be set to 0x0100 in order for a reboot to take place, 0x0001 for all applications to be forcibly closed, and 0x0101 for both actions to take place.

```
000000 reg_io_q_shutdown
    0000 ptr_0: 00000001
    0004 ptr_1: 00000001
    0008 ptr_2: 00000001
    00000c smb_io_unihdr hdr_msg
        000c uni_str_len: 0002
        000e uni_max_len: 0002
        0010 buffer     : 00000001
    000014 smb_io_unistr2 uni_msg
        0014 uni_max_len: 00000001
        0018 undoc      : 00000000
        001c uni_str_len: 00000001
        0020 buffer     : ..
    0024 timeout: 00000014
    0028 flags  : 0000
```

The response contains a status code indicating whether the shutdown was initiated or not. This function schedules a shutdown; it does not wait for the shutdown to actually take place before replying, because by that time the remote host will not be capable of replying!

```
000018 reg_io_r_shutdown
    0018 status: 00000000
```

## 6.2: Summary

The Windows Registry API does exactly what it is designed to do: it provides remote management of a Windows Registry, which includes the creation, removal, and enumeration of keys and values. It's just not very efficient over-the-wire in certain areas, which tells us that the designers of this API had a poor understanding of how MSRPC works, and they should have been instructed to examine network traces of programs that access a registry remotely, prior to finalising the API.

# 7

## \PIPE\svcctl: NT Service Control Services

This pipe provides remote management of Windows NT Services. This includes adding, changing default startup mode, starting, stopping, and removing services. On Windows NT, services are managed locally from the Services Network Control Panel and remotely from Server Manager for Domains by selecting Computer | Services from the menu.

A small subset of these functions, as an academic exercise, has been implemented in Samba's rpcclient tool. Enough calls were implemented sufficiently to enumerate all services on a remote Windows NT host. The eventual intent was to provide a means by which, through Samba, Unix services such as FTP'd and HTTP'd could be started and stopped using Samba's rpcclient tool or Windows NT's Server Manager for Domains.

Microsoft Network Monitor (Netmon) does not decode any of these functions. However, all are listed as part of the MSDN API, in **winsvc.h**. Therefore it is a relatively simple task to match the network traffic to actual function arguments. The only difficult function was **SvcEnumServicesStatus**, for reasons described in detail later on. The difficulties were related to the enumeration method chosen by the team that implemented this service. This function is therefore not fully understood, and under certain circumstances, Samba's rpcclient tool has been known to fail to obtain a list of services from a Windows NT Server, when that list is known to be large.

## 7.1: svcctl pipe

This section describes some individual services function calls in detail. As Netmon does not decode this service, Samba debug output is used in this chapter to illustrate each call. Due to the nature of some of these calls (they contain relative offsets), the data is not processed sequentially. However, each and every byte of the data stream *is* covered in the debug output, just not in order. Also, due to the amount of data that can be transferred with some of these calls, the debug output has had regular, repetitive sections removed to improve readability.

The functions described in this chapter are included in the following list. The names are prefixed here with **Svc**, but in a break from the practice of the majority of the Windows NT MSRPC services, this is not the case in the MSDN API naming convention.

- SvcOpenSCMananger
- SvcEnumServicesStatus
- SvcOpenService
- SvcQueryServiceConfig
- SvcClose

Typically, calling **SvcOpenSCManager** produces a complete list of services. This returns a handle, which is used as one of the arguments to **SvcEnumServicesStatus**. This will return a buffer with an array of services currently installed on the server. Then, to list more information on each service, **SvcOpenService** is called, and returns a handle that is used to call **SvcQueryServiceConfig**. **SvcClose** must be called with each handle opened with **SvcOpenService**. Finally, calling **SvcClose** with the handle from **SvcOpenSCManager** frees up any resources that the Server needed to use since the **SvcOpenSCManager** call.

This service cannot be accessed anonymously by default. Additionally, certain actions, such as stopping a service, require Administrator-level privileges. Enumerating services appears to require user rights (including, but not limited to, Administrator rights).

Examining **winsvc.h** shows that there are two versions of all functions, for example, **OpenSCManagerA** and **OpenSCManagerW**. Both ASCII (eight bits per character) and UNICODE (sixteen bits per character) are supported. The functions described in this chapter are from running the Services Network Control Panel, and these are all UNICODE. The ASCII versions of these functions will be an identical format over-the-wire to their UNICODE counterparts, except that ASCII strings are used instead of UNICODE, and the MSRPC Operation Code will be different, representing the ASCII equivalent of the same function.

## 7.1.1: SvcOpenSCManager

**SvcOpenSCManager** is the first call that must be made. It is known in the MSDN as **OpenSCManager**, which is shown here:

```
SC_HANDLE
OpenSCManager(
    LPCWSTR lpMachineName,
    LPCWSTR lpDatabaseName,
    DWORD   dwDesiredAccess
    );
```

The level of access privileges required must be specified as one of the arguments. In this example, **winsvc.h** and **winnt.h** show that the rights requested are SC_MANAGER_ENUMERATE_SERVICE and GENERIC_READ.

```
SVC Open SC_MAN
000000 svc_io_q_open_sc_man
    0000 ptr_srv_name: 00000001
    000004 smb_io_unistr2
        0004 uni_max_len: 0000000b
        0008 undoc      : 00000000
        000c uni_str_len: 0000000b
        0010 buffer     : \.\.S.T.E.E.L.E.Y.E...
    0028 ptr_db_name: 00000000
    00002c smb_io_unistr2 - NULL
    002c des_access: 80000004
```

The response contains a handle, with which the access requested is associated. If the user does not have the rights to request this level of privilege, or even have the rights to call **SvcOpenSCManager** at all, then a status code NT_STATUS_ACCESS_DENIED is returned.

```
000018 svc_io_r_open_sc_man
    000018 smb_io_pol_hnd
        0018 data: 00 00 00 00 b1 a1 3c 2d 9c 43 d3 11 82 b9 00 10 4b 97 32 2e
    002c status     : 00000000
```

In all subsequent calls that use the handle returned, the associated access rights in the request will be verified against the type of call being made and the privileges of the user making the call. The handle must be freed with a call to **SvcClose**, after it is no longer needed. Failure to do this may result in resource leaks on some Servers.

## 7.1.2: SvcEnumServicesStatus

**SvcEnumServicesStatus** enumerates a list of services on a remote machine, known in the MSDN as **EnumServicesStatus()**, which is shown here:

```
BOOL
EnumServicesStatus(
```

```
SC_HANDLE                hSCManager,
DWORD                    dwServiceType,
DWORD                    dwServiceState,
LPENUM_SERVICE_STATUSW   lpServices,
DWORD                    cbBufSize,
LPDWORD                  pcbBytesNeeded,
LPDWORD                  lpServicesReturned,
LPDWORD                  lpResumeHandle
);
```

The mechanism by which this is done, or even by which this function call is used, is very unclear, as will be explained in this section. The function call contains, amongst other parameters, a handle (from a **SvcOpenSCManager** call), a maximum buffer size, and an enumeration handle. The maximum buffer size is set to an arbitrarily large number, for example, 2048 bytes.

```
smb_io_enum_hnd
000000 svc_io_q_enum_svcs_status
    000000 smb_io_pol_hnd
        0000 data: 00 00 00 00 b1 a1 3c 2d 9c 43 d3 11 82 b9 00 10 4b 97 32 2e
    0014 service_type : 00000030
    0018 service_state: 00000003
    001c buf_size     : 00000800
    000020 smb_io_enum_hnd resume_hnd
        0020 ptr_hnd: 00000000
```

The response contains a list of services, an array of MSDN **ENUM_SERVICE_STATUS** structures, shown here:

```
typedef struct _ENUM_SERVICE_STATUS {
    LPWSTR         lpServiceName;
    LPWSTR         lpDisplayName;
    SERVICE_STATUS ServiceStatus;
} ENUM_SERVICE_STATUS, *LPENUM_SERVICE_STATUS;

typedef struct _SERVICE_STATUS {
    DWORD   dwServiceType;
    DWORD   dwCurrentState;
    DWORD   dwControlsAccepted;
    DWORD   dwWin32ExitCode;
    DWORD   dwServiceSpecificExitCode;
    DWORD   dwCheckPoint;
    DWORD   dwWaitHint;
} SERVICE_STATUS, *LPSERVICE_STATUS;
```

There is a status code (0x0) indicating that this call contains all, or the last part, of the list of services. The resume handle is NULL. Samba's debug log output appears to be out of sequence here because in fact it *is* actually processed out of sequence. The data itself arrives over-the-wire in sequence. The buf_size argument indicates the number of bytes in the data stream that contain the list of services, so Samba's

marshalling code jumps over that section temporarily. The number of
services in the buffer must be read first, even though it is later in the
data stream than the buffer itself. After this buffer size is known, the
correct number of services in the buffer can be processed.

```
000018 svc_io_r_enum_svcs_status
    0018 buf_size: 00000fa4
    0fc0 more_buf_size: 00000000
    0fc4 num_svcs: 00000026
    000fc8 smb_io_enum_hnd resume_hnd
        0fc8 ptr_hnd: 00000000
    0fcc dos_status: 00000000
    001c srvc_offset: 00000f94
    0020 disp_offset: 00000f84
    000024 svc_io_svc_status status
        0024 svc_type: 00000020
        0028 current_state: 00000004
        002c controls_accepted: 00000001
        0030 win32_exit_code: 00000000
        0034 svc_specific_exit_code: 00000000
        0038 check_point: 00000000
        003c wait_hint: 00000000
    000fb0 smb_io_unistr srvc[00] A.l.e.r.t.e.r.
    000fa0 smb_io_unistr disp[00] A.l.e.r.t.e.r.
    0040 srvc_offset: 00000f74
    0044 disp_offset: 00000f52
    000048 svc_io_svc_status status
        0048 svc_type: 00000020
        004c current_state: 00000004
        0050 controls_accepted: 00000005
        0054 win32_exit_code: 00000000
        0058 svc_specific_exit_code: 00000000
        005c check_point: 00000000
        0060 wait_hint: 00000000
    000f90 smb_io_unistr srvc[01] B.r.o.w.s.e.r.
    000f6e smb_io_unistr disp[01] C.o.m.p.u.t.e.r. B.r.o.w.s.e.r.
    0064 srvc_offset: 00000f42
    0068 disp_offset: 00000f22
    ...
    ...
    ...
    0550 srvc_offset: 0000059e
    0554 disp_offset: 00000562
    000558 svc_io_svc_status status
        0558 svc_type: 00000010
        055c current_state: 00000004
        0560 controls_accepted: 00000007
        0564 win32_exit_code: 00000000
        0568 svc_specific_exit_code: 00000000
        056c check_point: 00000000
        0570 wait_hint: 00000000
    0005ba smb_io_unistr srvc[37] W.i.n.s.
    00057e smb_io_unistr disp[37] W.i.n.d.o.w.s. .I.n.t.e.r.n.e.
                                  t. .N.a.m.e. .S.e.r.v.i.c.e.
```

Shown below is a response indicating that the buffer size specified is too small. It is a Win32 error code, ERROR_MORE_DATA. The buffer (which is not included in this debug output) is still contained in the response, and is sent with as many entries as will fit in the buffer. The resume handle is still NULL.

```
000018 svc_io_r_enum_svcs_status
  0018 buf_size: 00000800
  081c more_buf_size: 000007a4
  0820 num_svcs: 00000013
  000824 smb_io_enum_hnd resume_hnd
      0824 ptr_hnd: 00000000
  0828 dos_status: 000000ea
  ...
  ...
  ...
```

The workings of this enumeration function have no logical explanation. The use of relative offsets rather than the network data pointers makes it difficult to parse. The failure of the server-side implementation of this function on Windows NT to use the resume handle makes it necessary to repeatedly call this function, ignoring the partial list of results returned by the server so far. As there appears to be no logical connection between the arbitrary initial size of the buffer and the arbitrary suggested size returned by the server, this can only be done by increasing the buffer size by an arbitrary amount in each request until such time as it is large enough to contain a list of all services in a response. As the buffer is filled each time with an incomplete list of services and the ERROR_MORE_DATA status code returned, and the buffer used in the response is in fact as large as is requested, this is a serious waste of bandwidth. And why is this function using Win32 error codes rather than NT status codes?

### 7.1.3: SvcOpenService

**SvcOpenService** is used to open a service. It is known as **OpenService** in the MSDN, which is shown here:

```
SC_HANDLE
OpenService(
    SC_HANDLE    hSCManager,
    LPCWSTR      lpServiceName,
    DWORD        dwDesiredAccess
    );
```

Access rights, indicating or limiting the types of operations that are intended to be made on the service, are also included. In this example,

**winsvc.h** and **winnt.h** show us that the rights requested are SERVICE_
QUERY_CONFIG and GENERIC_READ because this specific query
was in fact followed up with a call to **SvcQueryServiceConfig**.

```
000000 svc_io_q_open_service
   000000 smb_io_pol_hnd
      0000 data: 00 00 00 00 b2 a1 3c 2d 9c 43 d3 11 82 b9 00 10 4b 97 32 2e
   000014 smb_io_unistr2
      0014 uni_max_len: 00000008
      0018 undoc      : 00000000
      001c uni_str_len: 00000008
      0020 buffer     : A.l.e.r.t.e.r...
   0030 des_access: 80000001
```

The response contains a handle, with which the access rights requested
are associated. If the user does not have the rights to request this level
of privilege, or even have the rights to call **SvcOpenService** at all, then
a status code NT_STATUS_ACCESS_DENIED is returned.

```
000018 svc_io_r_open_service
   000018 smb_io_pol_hnd
      0018 data: 00 00 00 00 b3 a1 3c 2d 9c 43 d3 11 82 b9 00 10 4b 97 32 2e
   002c status     : 00000000
```

In all subsequent calls that use the handle returned, the associated
access rights in the request will be verified against the type of call
being made and the privileges of the user making the call.

The handle must be freed with a call to **SvcClose**, after it is no
longer needed. Failure to do this may result in resource leaks on some
servers.

## 7.1.4: SvcQueryServiceConfig

**SvcQueryServiceConfig** is used to obtain detailed information about a
service. It is known in the MSDN as **QueryServiceConfig**, which is
shown here. This function prototype is automatically generated from
its IDL definition.

```
QueryServiceConfig(
   SC_HANDLE                hService,
   LPQUERY_SERVICE_CONFIGW  lpServiceConfig,
   DWORD                    cbBufSize,
   LPDWORD                  pcbBytesNeeded
   );
```

An attempt to re-create an IDL definition for this function is shown
here, which is very similar to the auto-generated MSDN function prototype, in the above example. The [in] and [in out] parameters are sent
over-the-wire in the request, and the [in out] and [out] parameters are
sent back over-the-wire in the response.

```
typedef byte HANDLE[20];

STATUS QueryServiceConfigW(      /* Function 0x11 */
                 [in] HANDLE                hSCManager,
                 [out] QUERY_SERVICE_CONFIGW* lpServiceConfig,
                 [in] DWORD                 cbBufSize,
                 [out] DWORD*               pcbBytesNeeded
                      );
```

The handle passed here as the only argument must be from a
**SvcOpenService** call where the access rights requested must include bit
**SERVICE_QUERY_CONFIG** set. The expected size of the buffer is
also passed as an argument, shown here as buf_size, which in this
example is set to 2048 bytes.

```
SVC Query Service Config
000000 svc_io_q_query_svc_config
    000000 smb_io_pol_hnd
        0000 data: 00 00 00 00 b3 a1 3c 2d 9c 43 d3 11 82 b9 00 10 4b 97 32 2e
    0014 buf_size: 00000800
```

The response contains detailed information about the status of the service, which is listed in **winsvc.h** as the **QUERY_SERVICE_CONFIG**
structure, shown here:

```
typedef struct _QUERY_SERVICE_CONFIG {
    DWORD    dwServiceType;
    DWORD    dwStartType;
    DWORD    dwErrorControl;
    LPWSTR   lpBinaryPathName;
    LPWSTR   lpLoadOrderGroup;
    DWORD    dwTagId;
    LPWSTR   lpDependencies;
    LPWSTR   lpServiceStartName;
    LPWSTR   lpDisplayName;
} QUERY_SERVICE_CONFIG, *LPQUERY_SERVICE_CONFIG;
```

The parameter buf_size is reset to the size of the
**QUERY_SERVICE_CONFIG** structure. A DOS status code is
returned.

```
000018 svc_io_r_query_svc_config
    000018 svc_io_query_svc_cfg cfg
        0018 service_type          : 00000020
        001c start_type            : 00000002
        0020 error_control         : 00000001
        0024 ptr_bin_path_name     : 00187ba4
        0028 ptr_load_order_grp    : 00187ba2
        002c tag_id                : 00000000
        0030 ptr_dependencies      : 00187b7c
        0034 ptr_service_start_name: 00187b64
        0038 ptr_display_name      : 00187b54
        00003c smb_io_unistr2 uni_bin_path_name
            003c uni_max_len: 00000022
            0040 undoc      : 00000000
```

```
       0044 uni_str_len: 00000022

       0048 buffer      : C.:.\.W.I.N.N.T.S.R.V.\.S.y.s.t.e.m.3.2.\.
                          s.e.r.v.i.c.e.s...e.x.e...
   00008c smb_io_unistr2 uni_load_order_grp
       008c uni_max_len: 00000001
       0090 undoc       : 00000000
       0094 uni_str_len: 00000001
       0098 buffer      : ..
   00009c smb_io_unistr2 uni_dependencies
       009c uni_max_len: 00000013
       00a0 undoc       : 00000000
       00a4 uni_str_len: 00000013
       00a8 buffer      : L.a.n.m.a.n.W.o.r.k.s.t.a.t.i.o.n./...
   0000d0 smb_io_unistr2 uni_service_start_name
       00d0 uni_max_len: 0000000c
       00d4 undoc       : 00000000
       00d8 uni_str_len: 0000000c
       00dc buffer      : L.o.c.a.l.S.y.s.t.e.m...
   0000f4 smb_io_unistr2 uni_display_name
       00f4 uni_max_len: 00000008
       00f8 undoc       : 00000000
       00fc uni_str_len: 00000008
       0100 buffer      : A.l.e.r.t.e.r...
 0110 buf_size: 000000c8
 0114 status  : 00000000
```

Presumably, as in the rest of these badly designed functions, if the buffer size is too small, a DOS error code (not an NT status code) **ERROR_MORE_DATA** is returned; part of the structure is sent (wasting network bandwidth), and the application must make this call a second time with the newly discovered buffer size (wasting further network bandwidth).

## 7.1.5: SvcClose

**SvcClose** is used to free a handle. It is known in the MSDN as **CloseServiceHandle**, which is shown here:

```
BOOL
CloseServiceHandle(
    SC_HANDLE   hSCObject
    );
```

Its implementation should inform the server that any resources needed to service requests that used that handle can now also be freed.

```
000000 svc_io_q_close
    000000 smb_io_pol_hnd
       0000 data: 00 00 00 00 b1 a1 3c 2d 9c 43 d3 11 82 b9 00 10 4b 97 32 2e
```

The response usually contains an empty handle and a status code of 0x0, indicating that the handle and its associated resources have been

successfully freed. If the handle was already freed, then the Win32
error code (not an NT status code) ERROR_INVALID_HANDLE is
returned.

```
000018 svc_io_r_close
    000018 smb_io_pol_hnd
       0018 data: 00 00 00 00 00 00 00 00 00 00 00 00 00 00 00 00 00 00 00 00
    002c status: 00000000
```

## 7.2: Summary

Services Control is a well-implemented service, the workings of which
can be fully deduced using the MSDN and this chapter as a guide. The
exception is **SvcEnumServicesStatus**, which is a classic example of how
not to implement an enumeration call.

Services Control is a thorough, rich API that provides the capability
to control services, including running them as a specific user (that is,
as if the user actually logged in and started the service). This level of
control gives us a glimpse of the comprehensive and powerful nature
of the Windows NT operating system and the potential for abuse that
this provides.

# 8

# \PIPE\samr: NT SAM Database Management Services

This pipe provides functions that manage a Server or Workstation's SAM (Security Accounts Manager) Database. It is undocumented, and some of the reasons for this are good ones. The documented API in the MSDN is the set of functions such as **NetQueryDisplayInfo,** **NetQueryUserGroups,** and so forth. Where appropriate, the MSDN function that generates one or more DCE/RPC calls will be mentioned in this chapter because its parameters often have some relevance. The use of the documented MSDN API enables developers to write Account Management programs that can be used regardless of the underlying Accounts database. It also guarantees that the level of support required for Windows NT Users and their profiles is provided by an Accounts database implementer.

The programs "User Manager for Domains" and "Server Manager for Domains" were observed in operation over a network and the resultant traffic decoded over a period of six months. The task is still unfinished, but has yielded sufficient information to provide, amongst other things, NT Domain Group Management from a Unix command-line tool in the Samba suite, rpcclient. The debug output from this tool and from running a Samba server, smbd, is shown in this chapter because Microsoft's NetMonitor tool unfortunately does not provide any information on the **samr pipe.**

## 8.1: Warning: You Are on Your Own

Firstly, the **samr pipe** is an internal, undocumented API. This gives Microsoft the flexibility of changing or replacing it at will whilst supporting a fully documented higher-level API that is unlikely to change. With the introduction of LDAP to Windows NT 5.0, Microsoft is replacing the SAM Database, but still maintaining backward compatibility with NT 3.51 and 4.0 Domains.

Secondly, as this API is completely undocumented, particularly in NetMonitor, there is absolutely no way of guaranteeing that the interpretation of the DCE/RPC packets described in this chapter is correct. Also, some of the packets are sent over an encrypted pipe. As has been mentioned before and is worthwhile emphasising, the NT Domains for Unix project has been a network reverse engineering project; there are going to be gaps in the deduction process that simply cannot be filled. Moreover, it doesn't matter. The deduction process works whether there are or are not differences between the operation of different programs or the operation of the same program in different ways. If no changes in a completely undocumented DCE/RPC packet are ever observed for all instances of that packet on a Windows NT network, then who cares? Only the purists, and for them there is always the option of a Microsoft Source Code License.

In short, although it has been demonstrated using Samba and the rpcclient utility that the functions described here do the job, anyone wishing to actually rely on this and use the information so gained, *be warned*.

## 8.2: samr pipe

The following list of function names was obtained from a QuickView on a Checked Build version of **SAMSRV.DLL**:

- SamrAddMemberToAlias
- SamrAddMemberToGroup
- SamrAddMultipleMembersToAlias
- SamrChangePasswordUser
- SamrCloseHandle
- SamrConnect
- SamrCreateAliasInDomain
- SamrCreateGroupInDomain
- SamrCreateUserInDomain

- SamrDeleteAlias
- SamrDeleteGroup
- SamrDeleteUser
- SamrEnumerateAliasesInDomain
- SamrEnumerateDomainsInSamServer
- SamrEnumerateGroupsInDomain
- SamrEnumerateUsersInDomain
- SamrGetUserDomainPasswordInformation
- SamrLookupDomainInSamServer
- SamrLookupIdsInDomain
- SamrLookupNamesInDomain
- SamrOpenAlias
- SamrOpenDomain
- SamrOpenGroup
- SamrOpenUser
- SamrQueryDisplayInformation
- SamrQueryInformationAlias
- SamrQueryInformationDomain
- SamrQueryInformationUser
- SamrQuerySecurityObject
- SamrRemoveMemberFromAlias
- SamrRemoveMemberFromForiegnDomain
- SamrRemoveMemberFromGroup
- SamrRemoveMultipleMembersFromAlias
- SamrSetInformationAlias
- SamrSetInformationDomain
- SamrSetInformationGroup
- SamrSetInformationUser
- SamrSetMemberAttributesOfGroup
- SamrSetSecurityObject
- SamrShutdownSamServer
- SamrTestPrivateFunctionsDomain
- SamrTestPrivateFunctionsUser

This list is extremely useful in deducing what the DCE/RPC Operations do, by a process of elimination. It also helps by providing a naming convention—one less item to have to worry about. It is suspected, however, that other functions are available via the **samr pipe** that are not actually exported from **SAMSRV.DLL**.

The functions included in the list can be used to add, modify, and remove Users, Groups, and Aliases. The design of this API allows for the manipulation of any SAM Database, as named by its Security Identifier (SID). A Windows NT Workstation or stand-alone Server has a local SAM Database for which it is responsible, whilst an NT Domain Controller is only responsible for the primary Domain SAM. In both cases, there is also a second hidden Domain, the well-known Domain BUILTIN (SID S-1-5-32, see winnt.h), which contains well-known aliases such as "Administrators" and "Power Users." The main function of the BUILTIN Domain is to provide a well-known set of SIDs for user roles, so that permissions can be preserved to some extent when a server changes Domains.

It is worth mentioning that the SAM API refers to Groups and Aliases, whilst all the MSDN documentation refers to Global Groups and Local Groups respectively. This chapter predominantly uses the SAM API terminology. The distinction between Groups and Aliases *is* important. From the perspective of a User, Users can be added to both Groups and Aliases (but only Groups and Aliases of the user's Domain). From the perspective of Groups, Groups can have *only* users in their Domain added to them. From the perspective of an Alias, Aliases can have *anything* added to them from *any* SAM database, including Workstation SAM Databases.

Examination of the MSDN documentation shows the following groups of functions:

- User Functions
  - NetUserAdd
  - NetUserChangePassword
  - NetUserDel
  - NetUserEnum
  - NetUserGetGroups
  - NetUserGetInfo
  - NetUserGetLocalGroups
  - NetUserSetGroups
  - NetUserSetInfo

- Local Group Functions
  - NetLocalGroupAdd
  - NetLocalGroupAddMembers
  - NetLocalGroupDel
  - NetLocalGroupDelMember
  - NetLocalGroupDelMembers
  - NetLocalGroupEnum
  - NetLocalGroupGetInfo
  - NetLocalGroupGetMembers
  - NetLocalGroupSetInfo
  - NetLocalGroupSetMembers
- Domain Group Functions
  - NetGroupAdd
  - NetGroupAddUser
  - NetGroupDel
  - NetGroupDelUser
  - NetGroupEnum
  - NetGroupGetInfo
  - NetGroupGetUsers
  - NetGroupSetInfo
  - NetGroupSetUsers
- Miscellaneous Functions
  - NetQueryDisplayInfo
  - NetUserChangePassword

The lists of functions here are independent of the underlying implementation. One of the purposes of this chapter is to help tie these documented MSDN calls with the undocumented over-the-wire SAM Database calls. Sometimes an MSDN function results in multiple DCE/RPC calls. For example, a **NetLocalGroupGetMembers** call returns a list of names, but the **SamrEnumDomainAliases** function returns a list of Relative Identifiers (RIDs), so a follow-up call to **SamrLookupRids** is required in order to deliver the goods.

## 8.3: Domain Access Functions

This set of functions describes how to connect to a SAM server and to a Domain, and how this is done from both the Windows 95 and Windows NT versions of User Manager for Domains (**USRMGR.EXE**), and Server Manager for Domains (**SRVMGR.EXE**). This set of functions also includes enumeration and resolution functions that are carried out at the Domain level. These include:

- **SamrLookupRids** and **SamrLookupNames**, to resolve Relative Identifiers (RIDs) in a Domain to names, and vice-versa.

- **SamrEnumDomainUsers**, **SamrEnumDomainGroups**, and **SamrEnumDomainAliases**, which enumerate Users, Groups, and Aliases in a Domain. **SamrEnumDomainGroups** can be used only on a Domain Controller, not a Workstation.

- **SamrQueryDisplayInfo**, which provides a quick way of obtaining a list of Account information. The information is typically displayed onscreen.

### 8.3.1: SamrConnect

The **SamrConnect** request is the first call that must be made on the **samr pipe**. The name of the calling Workstation and an unknown parameter are passed as arguments.

Due to an error in the Microsoft interface definition for this function, only a single UNICODE character of the Workstation name is passed over-the-wire (and because the Workstation name is in the UNC form **\\SERVER** this is always \ = 0x005c). If you look carefully at the hex dump you can see another word following this, but that is simply padding. No value other than 0x20 has been observed for the second, unknown parameter.

```
000000 samr_io_q_connect
   0000 ptr_srv_name: 00000001
   0004 srv_name:     005c
   0024 unknown_0   : 00000020

[020]    01 00 00 00 5c 00 01  00 20 00 00 00          ........ .....
```

The **SamrConnect** response contains a Policy Handle and a status code.

```
000018 samr_io_r_connect
   000018 smb_io_pol_hnd connect_pol
      0018 data: 00 00 00 00 01 00 00 00 00 00 00 00 31 70 8a 36 5b 1c 00 00
   002c status: 00000000
```

```
[010]                          00 00 00 00 01 00 00   ........ ........
[020] 00 00 00 00 00 31 70 8A  36 5B 1C 00 00 00 00 00   .....1p. 6[......
[030] 00                                              .
```

The Policy Handle, if successfully obtained, must be freed up by
**SamrCloseHandle** after it is no longer needed.

There is no documented MSDN equivalent to this call; however, all
MSDN calls that are made from a Windows 95 box result initially in
**SamrConnect** being called, and will be followed up with a call to
**SamrCloseHandle** after the MSDN call is complete.

Part of the process behind the MSDN functions is to detect whether
the remote target is LanManager-compatible or Windows NT-
LanManager-compatible. Even if the detection is successful, occasionally a LanManager-style call will be made by the Client. (Over SMB
**IPC$** an **SMBtrans2** call is made on **\PIPE\LANMAN**.) If this occurs
it is up to the recipient of this call to send an error message that indicates that the buffer for the results is too small, and the Windows NT
Client will follow up with a DCE/RPC equivalent to the same call. For
example, in the LanManager call **RNetGroupGetUsers**, the error code
that the server returns is 0x08AC (please don't ask what this means).
This results in the Client following up with a
**SamrQueryGroupMembers** call over the **samr pipe** using DCE/RPC.

### 8.3.2: SamrConnect2

This is exactly the same as the **SamrConnect** call described previously
except the faulty interface definition has been fixed, resulting in the
correct Server name being sent over-the-wire. Windows NT Clients use
this version in preference to the first one.

As before, the request contains the Server name and an unknown
parameter that seems to be always 0x20:

```
000000 samr_io_q_connect2
   0000 ptr_srv_name: 00000001
   000004 smb_io_unistr2
      0004 uni_max_len: 00000009
      0008 undoc      : 00000000
      000c uni_str_len: 00000009
      0010 buffer     : \.\.K.N.I.G.H.T...
   0024 unknown_0    : 00000020
```

```
[020]    01 00 00 00 09 00 00  00 00 00 00 00 09 00 00   ........ ........
[030] 00 5C 00 5C 00 4B 00 4E  00 49 00 47 00 48 00 54  .\.\.K.N .I.G.H.T
[040] 00 00 00 00 00 20 00 00  00                       ..... .. .
```

The response contains the Policy Handle and status code.

```
000018 samr_io_r_connect2
   000018 smb_io_pol_hnd connect_pol
```

```
          0018 data: 00 00 00 00 01 00 00 00 00 00 00 00 31 70 8a 36 5b 1c 00 00
       002c status: 00000000
```

```
[010]                              00 00 00 00 01 00 00   ........ ........
[020] 00 00 00 00 00 31 70 8A  36 5B 1C 00 00 00 00 00   .....1p. 6[......
[030] 00                                                  .
```

### 8.3.3: SamrCloseHandle

After any Policy Handles allocated by any SAM Database calls are no longer needed they must be freed with a call to **SamrCloseHandle**. The request contains the Policy Handle.

```
000000 samr_io_q_close_hnd
    000000 smb_io_pol_hnd pol
        0000 data: 00 00 00 00 04 00 00 00 00 00 00 00 31 70 8a 36 5b 1c 00 00
```

```
[020]    00 00 00 00 04 00 00  00 00 00 00 00 31 70 8A   ........ .....1p.
[030] 36 5B 1C 00 00                                     6[...
```

The **SamrCloseHandle** response contains a blank Policy Handle and a status code. Only a Policy Handle that has been allocated by a SAM Database call and has not already been closed can be closed; an error code should be returned otherwise.

```
000018 samr_io_r_close_hnd
    000018 smb_io_pol_hnd pol
        0018 data: 00 00 00 00 00 00 00 00 00 00 00 00 00 00 00 00 00 00 00 00
       002c status: 00000000
```

```
[010]                              00 00 00 00 00 00 00   ........ ........
[020] 00 00 00 00 00 00 00 00  00 00 00 00 00 00 00 00   ........ ........
[030] 00                                                  .
```

There is no documented MSDN equivalent to this call; however, it is frequently used in combination with other SAM database calls as a direct result of the use of MSDN calls.

### 8.3.4: SamrOpenDomain

Following a **SamrConnect** call, a **SamrOpenDomain** call must be made with a SID. The SID can be the well-known SID **S-1-5-32** if the BUILTIN Domain is to be queried, or it can be the SID of the SAM database for which the server is responsible. In the case of a Workstation this will be the local SAM Database, and in the case of a Domain Controller it will be the Domain SAM Database. The SID of the SAM database for which a host is responsible can be obtained with **LsaQueryInfoPolicy**, part of the Local Security Authority (LSA) API.

The **SamrOpenDomain** request contains the Policy Handle returned by the **SamrConnect** or **SamrConnect2** call, and a Domain SID.

```
000000 samr_io_q_open_domain
    000000 smb_io_pol_hnd connect_pol
        0000 data: 00 00 00 00 01 00 00 00 00 00 00 00 31 70 8a 36 5b 1c 00 00
    0014 flags: 00000304
    000018 smb_io_dom_sid2 sid
        0018 num_auths: 00000004
        00001c smb_io_dom_sid sid
            001c sid_rev_num: 01
            001d num_auths  : 04
            001e id_auths    : 00 00 00 00 00 05
            0024 sub_auths : 00000015 466e2442 08de9320 b8c519a4

[020]    00 00 00 00 01 00 00  00 00 00 00 00 31 70 8A   ........ .....1p.
[030] 36 5B 1C 00 00 04 03 00  00 04 00 00 00 01 04 00   6[...... ........
[040] 00 00 00 00 05 15 00 00  00 42 24 6E 46 20 93 DE   ........ .B$nF ..
[050] 08 A4 19 C5 B8                                     .....
```

The **SamrOpenDomain** response contains a Policy Handle and a status code.

```
000018 samr_io_r_open_domain
    000018 smb_io_pol_hnd domain_pol
        0018 data: 00 00 00 00 02 00 00 00 00 00 00 00 01 79 8a 36 c1 1c 00 00
    002c status: 00000000

[010]                          00 00 00 00 02 00 00   ........ ........
[020] 00 00 00 00 00 01 79 8A  36 C1 1C 00 00 00 00 00   ......y. 6.......
[030] 00                                                 .
```

The Policy Handle, if successfully obtained, must be freed by **SamrCloseHandle** after it is no longer needed.

There is no documented MSDN equivalent to this call; however, it is frequently used in combination with other SAM database calls as a direct result of the use of MSDN calls.

## 8.3.5: SamrQueryInformationDomain

**SamrQueryInformationDomain** is used to obtain information about a SAM Database. Only one info level has been observed to date, and that level tells us how many Users, Groups, and Aliases are in the Domain. Additionally, there is a number that increments each time the SAM Database is modified.

The request contains the Policy Handle representing the Domain, and the info level required.

```
000000 samr_io_q_query_dom_info
    000000 smb_io_pol_hnd domain_pol
        0000 data: 00 00 00 00 c7 35 58 ec 90 5d d3 11 9e cd 83 c5 61 b1 64 14
    0014 switch_value: 0002

[020] 00 00 00 00 C7 35 58 EC  90 5D D3 11 9E CD 83 C5   .....5X. .].....
[030] 61 B1 64 14 02 00 00 00                            a.d.....
```

The response contains a Domain information structure at the level requested. The purpose of most of the items in this info level cannot be determined easily. The server name and Domain name are obvious. The number of Users, Groups, and Aliases in the Domain required several modifications to the database to determine their purpose, and the sequence number incremented each time the database was modified.

```
000018 samr_io_r_query_dom_info
    0018 ptr_0        : 0014d3e0
    001c switch_value: 0002
    000020 sam_io_unk_info2 unk_inf2
        0020 unknown_0: 00000000
        0024 unknown_1: 80000000
        0028 unknown_2: 00000000
        002c ptr_0: 0014dad8
        000030 smb_io_unihdr hdr_domain
            0030 uni_str_len: 000c
            0032 uni_max_len: 000e
            0034 buffer      : 0014f830
        000038 smb_io_unihdr hdr_server
            0038 uni_str_len: 0000
            003a uni_max_len: 0000
            003c buffer      : 0014d850
        0040 seq_num : 0000000a
        0044 unknown_3 : 00000000
        0048 unknown_4 : 00000001
        004c unknown_5 : 00000003
        0050 unknown_6 : 00000001
        0054 num_domain_usrs : 00000003
        0058 num_domain_grps: 00000001
        005c num_local_grps: 00000001
        0060 padding: 00 00 00 00 00 00 00 00 00 00 00 00
        00006c smb_io_unistr2 uni_domain
            006c uni_max_len: 00000007
            0070 undoc       : 00000000
            0074 uni_str_len: 00000006
            0078 buffer      : K.N.I.G.H.T.
        000084 smb_io_unistr2 uni_server
            0084 uni_max_len: 00000000
            0088 undoc       : 00000000
            008c uni_str_len: 00000000
            0090 buffer      :
    0090 status      : 00000000


    [010]                        E0 D3 14 00 02 00 58 EC      . ......X.
    [020] 00 00 00 00 00 00 00 80  00 00 00 00 D8 DA 14 00   ........ ........
    [030] 0C 00 0E 00 30 F8 14 00  00 00 00 00 50 D8 14 00   ....0... ....P...
    [040] 0A 00 00 00 00 00 00 00  01 00 00 00 03 00 00 00   ........ ........
    [050] 01 00 00 00 03 00 00 00  01 00 00 00 01 00 00 00   ........ ........
    [060] 00 00 00 00 00 00 00 00  00 00 00 00 07 00 00 00   ........ ........
    [070] 00 00 00 00 06 00 00 00  4B 00 4E 00 49 00 47 00   ........ K.N.I.G.
    [080] 48 00 54 00 00 00 00 00  00 00 00 00 00 00 00 00   H.T..... ........
    [090] 00 00 00 00                                        ....
```

## 8.3.6: SamrLookupRids

**SamrLookupRids** resolves User, Group, and Alias names in a Domain, from Relative Identifiers (RIDs). The function prototype, if it was known, could look something like this:

```
NTSTATUS SamrLookupRids(
        IN  PHANDLE pSamHnd,
        IN  DWORD   numRids,
        IN  DWORD   flags,
        IN  PVOID   pRids,
        OUT DWORD   *pnumNames,
        OUT PUNISTR pNames,
        OUT DWORD   *pnumTypes,
        OUT DWORD   *pTypes);
```

The **SamrLookupRids** request includes a Domain Policy Handle plus a list of RIDs. In this way, full SIDs such as **S-1-5-32-0x220** can be resolved by opening a Domain Handle of **S-1-5-32** with a **SamrOpenDomain** call, followed by a **SamrLookupRids** call with a RID of 0x220. A definition for **S-1-5-32** and **S-1-5-32-0x220** can be found in **winnt.h**. There appears to be a flags field, the use or purpose of which is unknown, so Samba's rpcclient tool uses the value observed in Network traffic: 0x3e8. In the following example, a resolution of the Domain RID of 0x57e is being requested.

```
000000 samr_io_q_lookup_rids
    000000 smb_io_pol_hnd pol
        0000 data: 00 00 00 00 02 00 00 00 00 00 00 00 31 70 8a 36 5b 1c 00 00
        0014 num_rids1: 00000001
        0018 flags    : 000003e8
        001c ptr      : 00000000
        0020 num_rids2: 00000001
        0024 rid[00]  : 0000057e

[020]    00 00 00 00 02 00 00  00 00 00 00 00 31 70 8A  ........ .....1p.
[030] 36 5B 1C 00 00 01 00 00  00 E8 03 00 00 00 00 00  6[...... ........
[040] 00 01 00 00 00 7E 05 00  00                       .....~.. .
```

The **SamrLookupRids** response lists an array of names followed by an array of types. The type field appears to match up with the Windows NT enumeration **SID_NAME_USE**. It tells us the type of each individual name, which will have been resolved from a RID:

- **0x1** User name
- **0x2** Domain Group name
- **0x3** Domain name
- **0x4** Alias (Local Group) name
- **0x5** Well-known Group name

- **0x6** Deleted name
- **0x7** Invalid name
- **0x8** Unknown name

If a RID is unknown in a Domain, then the pointer to the name will be NULL, the type field for that entry will be marked as Unknown (0x8), and the return status is set to the informational warning, 0x107. If all RIDs are unknown then the return status is set to the error code 0xC0000073 (**NT_STATUS_NONE_MAPPED**). In the example shown here, the RID in the preceding request resolves to an Alias (0x4) called "NTlocalgroup":

```
000018 samr_io_r_lookup_rids
    0018 num_names1: 00000001
    001c ptr_names : 00000001
    0020 num_names2: 00000001
    000024 smb_io_unihdr
        0024 uni_str_len: 0018
        0026 uni_max_len: 0018
        0028 buffer     : 00000001
    00002c smb_io_unistr2
        002c uni_max_len: 0000000c
        0030 undoc      : 00000000
        0034 uni_str_len: 0000000c
        0038 buffer     : N.T.l.o.c.a.l.g.r.o.u.p.
    0050 num_types1: 00000001
    0054 ptr_types : 00000001
    0058 num_types2: 00000001
    005c type[00]  : 00000004
    0060 status: 00000000


[010]                          01 00 00 00 01 00 00  .L...... ........
[020] 00 01 00 00 00 18 00 18  00 01 00 00 00 0C 00 00  ........ ........
[030] 00 00 00 00 00 0C 00 00  00 4E 00 54 00 6C 00 6F  ........ .N.T.l.o
[040] 00 63 00 61 00 6C 00 67  00 72 00 6F 00 75 00 70  .c.a.l.g .r.o.u.p
[050] 00 01 00 00 00 01 00 00  00 01 00 00 00 04 00 00  ........ ........
[060] 00 00 00 00 00                                    .....
```

**USRMGR.EXE** uses this function to resolve the names of RIDs listed in a Domain Group; a Domain Policy Handle will already be open on the Domain SID and in addition, a Domain Group on a Domain Controller cannot contain anything other than RIDs for users relative to its own Domain.

In contrast, Aliases (more commonly referred to as Local Groups) contain a list of full SIDs describing their members: the Domain SID component concatenated with the RID component representing the member. To resolve the list of SIDs into names when viewing the members of a Local Group, **USRMGR.EXE** uses an **LsaLookupSids** call—not a **SamrLookupRids** call. For SIDs that *are* in the Server's Domain, exactly the same information will be given but just via a different code path. Unlike **SamrLookupRids**, the **LsaLookupSids** call is designed to handle multiple Domain SIDs—Trusted Domains as well as its own SAM Database—by making a follow-up call to **LsaLookupSids** to the Trusted Domain. The **SamrLookupRids** call is an exclusive interface to a particular SAM Database only.

The **SamrLookupRids** function does not have an equivalent MSDN call, but it pops up frequently. For example, the MSDN **NetUserGetGroups** call requires a list of Domain Group names, and so is constructed from two calls: **SamrQueryUserGroups** and **SamrLookupRids**. **SamrQueryUserGroups** returns only RIDs, so the entire list of RIDs returned is passed on to a **SamrLookupRids** call. Only then can the implementation of the **NetUserGetGroups** function return a list of Group Names.

### 8.3.7: SamrLookupNames

**SamrLookupNames** resolves User, Group, and Alias names in a Domain to Relative Identifiers (RIDs). The function prototype, if it was known, could look something like this:

```
STATUS SamrLookupNamesInDomain(
                    IN HANDLE          hDomain,
                    IN DWORD           dwNames,
                    IN DWORD           dwFlags,
                    IN DWORD           dwReserved,
                    IN UNICODE_STRING  pNames[*],
                    OUT DWORD*         dwRids,
                    OUT DWORD*         pRids[*],
                    OUT DWORD*         dwTypes,
                    OUT SID_ENUM*      pTypes
                        );
```

An attempt to re-create an Interface Definition Language (IDL) definition for this function is shown next. It is very similar to the preceding auto-generated MSDN function prototype. The **[in]** and **[in out]** parameters are sent over-the-wire in the request, and the **[in out]** and **[out]** parameters are sent over-the-wire in the response.

```
STATUS SamrLookupNamesInDomain( /* Function 0x11 */
                        [in] HANDLE          hDomain,
                        [in] DWORD           dwNames,
                        [in] DWORD           dwFlags,
                        [in] DWORD           dwReserved,
         [in,ref,size_is(dwNames)] UNICODE_STRING* pNames,
                        [out] DWORD*         dwRids,
```

```
       [out,size_is(,*dwRids)]  DWORD**           pRids,
                       [out]  DWORD*            dwTypes,
      [out,size_is(,*dwTypes)]  SID_NAME_USE**   pTypes
                            );
```

The **SamrLookupNames** request includes a Domain Policy Handle
plus a list of names to be resolved to RIDs (and their type) in that
Domain. There appears to be a flags field, the use or purpose of which
is unknown, so Samba's rpcclient tool uses the value observed in
Network traffic: 0x3e8. In this example, a resolution of two Domain
names **Guests** and **test** is being requested.

```
000000 samr_io_q_lookup_names
   000000 smb_io_pol_hnd pol
      0000 data: 00 00 00 00 16 98 25 50 63 5d d3 11 9e cc d7 20 92 94 16 14
   0014 num_names1: 00000002
   0018 flags     : 000003e8
   001c ptr       : 00000000
   0020 num_names2: 00000002
   000024 smb_io_unihdr
      0024 uni_str_len: 000c
      0026 uni_max_len: 000c
      0028 buffer     : 00000001
   00002c smb_io_unihdr
      002c uni_str_len: 0008
      002e uni_max_len: 0008
      0030 buffer     : 00000001
   000034 smb_io_unistr2
      0034 uni_max_len: 00000006
      0038 undoc      : 00000000
      003c uni_str_len: 00000006
      0040 buffer     : G.u.e.s.t.s.
   00004c smb_io_unistr2
      004c uni_max_len: 00000004
      0050 undoc      : 00000000
      0054 uni_str_len: 00000004
      0058 buffer     : t.e.s.t.


[020] 00 00 00 00 16 98 25 50   63 5D D3 11 9E CC D7 20   ......%P c].....
[030] 92 94 16 14 02 00 00 00   E8 03 00 00 00 00 00 00   ........ ........
[040] 02 00 00 00 0C 00 0C 00   01 00 00 00 08 00 08 00   ........ ........
[050] 01 00 00 00 06 00 00 00   00 00 00 00 06 00 00 00   ........ ........
[060] 47 00 75 00 65 00 73 00   74 00 73 00 04 00 00 00   G.u.e.s. t.s.....
[070] 00 00 00 00 04 00 00 00   74 00 65 00 73 00 74 00   ........ t.e.s.t.
```

The **SamrLookupNames** response lists an array of RIDs followed by
an array of types. The type field appears to match up with the
Windows NT enumeration SID_NAME_USE. It tells us the type of
each individual RID, which will have been resolved from a name:

- **0x1** User name
- **0x2** Domain Group name

- **0x3** Domain name

- **0x4** Alias (Local Group) name

- **0x5** Well-known Group name

- **0x6** Deleted name

- **0x7** Invalid name

- **0x8** Unknown name

If any name is unknown in a Domain, then the RID is set to 0, the type field for that entry will be marked as Unknown (0x8), and the return status is set to the informational warning, 0x107. If all names are unknown then the return status is set to the error code 0xC0000073 (**NT_STATUS_NONE_MAPPED**). In the following example, the response tells us that the name **Guests** is unknown in the Domain and the name **test** is a user with RID 1001.

```
[010]                         02 00 00 00 50 85 14 00         ....P...
[020] 02 00 00 00 00 00 00 00  E9 03 00 00 02 00 00 00  ........ ........
[030] 40 86 14 00 02 00 00 00  08 00 00 00 01 00 00 00  @....... ........
[040] 07 01 00 00                                          ....

000018 samr_io_r_lookup_names
    0018 num_rids1: 00000002
    001c ptr_rids : 00148550
    0020 num_rids2: 00000002
    0024 rid[00]  : 00000000
    0028 rid[01]  : 000003e9
    002c num_types1: 00000002
    0030 ptr_types : 00148640
    0034 num_types2: 00000002
    0038 type[00]  : 00000008
    003c type[01]  : 00000001
    0040 status: 00000107
```

This function does not have an equivalent in the MSDN.

## 8.3.8: SamrQueryDisplayInfo

**SamrQueryDisplayInfo** is one of the first calls made by **USRMGR.EXE** and **SRVMGR.EXE**. It can return a list of Users, a list of Servers, or a list of Groups. It can be called by the Windows NT implementation of the MSDN API **NetQueryDisplayInformation**, shown here.

```
NET_API_STATUS NetQueryDisplayInformation(
                    IN  LPWSTR ServerName,
                    IN  DWORD Level,
                    IN  DWORD Index,
                    IN  DWORD EntriesRequested,
```

```
            IN  DWORD PreferredMaximumLength,
            OUT LPDWORD ReturnedEntryCount,
            OUT PVOID *SortedBuffer
                );
```

**NetQueryDisplayInformation** returns an array of structures, one of which is the **NET_DISPLAY_USER** structure when info level 1 is requested. As the following examples are with info level 1, this structure is shown here:

```
typedef struct _NET_DISPLAY_USER {
    LPWSTR    usri1_name;
    LPWSTR    usri1_comment;
    DWORD     usri1_flags;
    LPWSTR    usri1_full_name;
    DWORD     usri1_user_id;
    DWORD     usri1_next_index;
} NET_DISPLAY_USER, *PNET_DISPLAY_USER;
```

The request contains an info level, starting index, maximum number of structures to be returned, plus a maximum amount of space that also limits the number of structures to be returned.

```
make_samr_q_query_dispinfo
000000 samr_io_q_query_dispinfo
   000000 smb_io_pol_hnd domain_pol
      0000 data: 00 00 00 00 37 36 58 ec 90 5d d3 11 9e cd 83 c5 61 b1 64 14
   0014 switch_level: 0001
   0018 start_idx   : 00000000
   001c max_entries : ffffffff
   0020 max_size    : 0000ffff

[020] 00 00 00 00 37 36 58  EC 90 5D D3 11 9E CD 83 C5   ....76X. .]......
[030] 61 B1 64 14 01 00 00  00 00 00 00 00 FF FF FF FF   a.d..... ........
[040] FF FF 00 00                                        ....
```

The response contains an array of structures requested, starting at the index number requested. In the following example, Users were requested. The SAM for which this Workstation is responsible has only three Users, and even so the amount of data returned is quite large, so it has been truncated.

```
000018 samr_io_r_query_dispinfo
   0018 total_size  : 00000174
   001c data_size   : 00000174
   0020 switch_level: 0001
   0024 num_entries : 00000003
   0028 ptr_entries : 00156d30
   002c num_entries2: 00000003
   000030 sam_io_sam_dispinfo_1 users
      000030 sam_io_sam_entry1
         0030 user_idx : 00000001
         0034 rid_user : 000001f4
```

```
        0038 acb_info : 0210
        003a pad      : 0000
        00003c smb_io_unihdr unihdr
        000044 smb_io_unihdr unihdr
        00004c smb_io_unihdr unihdr
    000054 sam_io_sam_entry1
        0054 user_idx : 00000002
        0058 rid_user : 000001f5
        005c acb_info : 0211
        005e pad      : 0000
        000060 smb_io_unihdr unihdr
        000068 smb_io_unihdr unihdr
        000070 smb_io_unihdr unihdr
    000078 sam_io_sam_entry1
        0078 user_idx : 00000003
        007c rid_user : 000003e9
        0080 acb_info : 0015
        0082 pad      : 0000
        000084 smb_io_unihdr unihdr
        00008c smb_io_unihdr unihdr
        000094 smb_io_unihdr unihdr
    00009c sam_io_sam_str1
        00009c smb_io_unistr2 unistr2
            009c uni_max_len: 0000000d
            00a0 undoc      : 00000000
            00a4 uni_str_len: 0000000d
            00a8 buffer     : Administrator
        0000c2 smb_io_unistr2 unistr2
            00c4 uni_max_len: 00000036
            00c8 undoc      : 00000000
            00cc uni_str_len: 00000036
            00d0 buffer     : Built-in account for administering the ...
        00013c smb_io_unistr2 - NULL unistr2
    00013c sam_io_sam_str1
        00013c smb_io_unistr2 unistr2
            013c uni_max_len: 00000005
            0140 undoc      : 00000000
            0144 uni_str_len: 00000005
            0148 buffer     : Guest
        000152 smb_io_unistr2 unistr2
            0154 uni_max_len: 00000038
            0158 undoc      : 00000000
            015c uni_str_len: 00000038
            0160 buffer     : Built-in account for guest access to the ...
        0001d0 smb_io_unistr2 - NULL unistr2
    0001d0 sam_io_sam_str1
        0001d0 smb_io_unistr2 unistr2
            01d0 uni_max_len: 00000004
            01d4 undoc      : 00000000
            01d8 uni_str_len: 00000004
            01dc buffer     : test
        0001e4 smb_io_unistr2 - NULL unistr2
        0001e4 smb_io_unistr2 - NULL unistr2
01e4 status: 00000000
```

This is another example of how to perform enumeration with multiple calls. **SamrQueryDisplayInfo** allocates a unique index with each structure returned. The caller indicates where to start in the list and the maximum number of structures to return. This is in contrast to some of the other enumeration systems implemented in the Windows NT APIs, where an opaque handle is returned from one call, which must be passed on to the next call.

### 8.3.9: SamrEnumDomainUsers

The **SamrEnumDomainUsers** call obtains a list of users in a Domain. Its closest MSDN equivalent is **NetUserEnum,** shown here:

```
STATUS NetUserEnum(
            IN    LPWSTR servername,
            IN    DWORD level,
            IN    DWORD filter,
            OUT   LPBYTE *bufptr,
            OUT   DWORD prefmaxlen,
            OUT   LPDWORD entriesread,
            OUT   LPDWORD totalentries,
            OUT   LPDWORD resume_handle
            );
```

The Domain Policy Handle is clearly seen; however, the best guess as to what the other request parameters are is listed here. These are most likely to be 16-bit and so must be padded to 4-byte boundaries, although the first parameter after the Domain Policy Handle may be a 32-bit Enumeration Handle. The possible purpose of the **acb_mask** parameter is to exclude certain Users, for example by setting the ACB_DISABLED bit (0x1), which presumably will exclude all disabled User Accounts. The purpose of some of these parameters is not known for certain. However, regardless of the actual purpose of these parameters, typical values are shown here:

```
000000 samr_io_q_enum_dom_users
    000000 smb_io_pol_hnd pol
        0000 data: 00 00 00 00 02 00 00 00 00 00 00 00 31 70 8a 36 5b 1c 00 00
    0014 req_num_entries: 0000
    0016 unknown_0     : 0000
    0018 acb_mask      : 0000
    001a unknown_1     : 0000
    001c max_size      : 0000ffff

[000] 5C 50 49 50 45 5C 00 00  00 05 00 00 03 10 00 00   \PIPE\.. ........
[010] 00 38 00 00 00 0A 00 00  00 20 00 00 00 00 00 0D   .8...... . ......
[020] 00 00 00 00 00 02 00 00  00 00 00 00 00 31 70 8A   ........ .....1p.
[030] 36 5B 1C 00 00 00 00 00  00 00 00 00 00 FF FF 00   6[...... ........
[040] 00                                                 .
```

The **SamrEnumDomainUsers** response contains a list of RIDs plus User names. Because the response is quite long, the *smb_io_unihdr* and *smb_io_unistr2* references have been pared down; normally a Samba debug log shows the length and size of the UNICODE strings as well. Unlike the **SamrQueryDisplayInfo** call, the list contains just the User names plus the RIDs associated with each User: the **SamrQueryDisplayInfo** call also includes the comment field for each Account.

```
000018 samr_io_r_enum_dom_users
    0018 unknown_0   : 00000000
    001c ptr_entries1: 00000001
    0020 num_entries2: 00000005
    0024 ptr_entries2: 00000001
    0028 num_entries3: 00000005
    00002c sam_io_sam_entry
        002c rid: 000003e8
        000030 smb_io_unihdr unihdr
    000038 sam_io_sam_entry
        0038 rid: 00001388
        00003c smb_io_unihdr unihdr
    000044 sam_io_sam_entry
        0044 rid: 0000138c
        000048 smb_io_unihdr unihdr
    000050 sam_io_sam_entry
        0050 rid: 000403dc
        000054 smb_io_unihdr unihdr
    00005c sam_io_sam_entry
        005c rid: 000403d8
        000060 smb_io_unihdr unihdr
    000068 smb_io_unistr2
        0074 buffer      : r.o.o.t.
    00007c smb_io_unistr2
        0088 buffer      : l.k.c.l.
    000090 smb_io_unistr2
        009c buffer      : t.e.s.t.
    0000a4 smb_io_unistr2
        00b0 buffer      : 6.5.5.3.3.
    0000ba smb_io_unistr2
        00c8 buffer      : 6.5.5.3.2.
    00d4 num_entries4: 00000005
    00d8 status: 00000000


[010]                       00 00 00 00 01 00 00   ........ ........
[020] 00 05 00 00 00 01 00 00  00 05 00 00 00 E8 03 00   ........ ........
[030] 00 08 00 08 00 01 00 00  00 88 13 00 00 08 00 08   ........ ........
[040] 00 01 00 00 00 8C 13 00  00 08 00 08 00 01 00 00   ........ ........
[050] 00 DC 03 04 00 0A 00 0A  00 01 00 00 00 D8 03 04   ........ ........
[060] 00 0A 00 0A 00 01 00 00  00 04 00 00 00 00 00 00   ........ ........
[070] 00 04 00 00 00 72 00 6F  00 6F 00 74 00 04 00 00   .....r.o .o.t....
[080] 00 00 00 00 00 04 00 00  00 6C 00 6B 00 63 00 6C   ........ .l.k.c.l
[090] 00 04 00 00 00 00 00 00  00 04 00 00 00 74 00 65   ........ .....t.e
```

```
[0A0] 00 73 00 74 00 05 00 00   00 00 00 00 00 05 00 00   .s.t....  ........
[0B0] 00 36 00 35 00 35 00 33   00 33 00 00 00 05 00 00   .6.5.5.3 .3......
[0C0] 00 00 00 00 00 05 00 00   00 36 00 35 00 35 00 33   ........ .6.5.5.3
[0D0] 00 32 00 00 00 05 00 00   00 00 00 00 00 00         .2......  .....
```

The likely members for the structure that contains User Information, from which the DCE/RPC parsing code is generated, are shown here:

```
typedef struct
{
        DWORD           UserRid;
        PUNICODE_STRING pUserName;

} SAM_DOM_USER, *PSAM_DOM_USER;
```

The function prototype is likely to be as follows:

```
NTSTATUS SamrEnumDomUsers(
    IN  PHANDLE       pDomainHnd,
        PENUMHND      pEnumerationHandle,
    IN  WORD          acb_mask,
    IN  WORD          max_size,
    OUT DWORD         *pNumUsers,
    OUT PSAM_DOM_USER pUserInfo);
```

After a little bit more thought, it is considered likely that the first four bytes after the Domain Policy Handle in the request and the first four bytes in the response *could* be an Enumeration Handle. This would make this a typical-style Enumeration function, similar to **NetrFileEnum** and other **srvsvc pipe** functions. This *could* lend weight to the conclusion that the **max_size** parameter has been correctly identified.

Typical Enumeration functions work in this manner: you start with a NULL Enumeration Handle (32 bits, all zero) on the first call. On return from the call, the pointers to the number of structures and the array of structures will have been set. If there are additional structures to return, the Enumeration Handle is set to an appropriate value that must be treated as opaque by the caller of the function. The caller can check whether the Enumeration Handle is zero or non-zero. If nonzero, the Enumeration function must be called again, this time with the opaque Enumeration Handle.

Sometimes there is also a parameter that specifies the total number of structures that will be enumerated across the multiple calls to the Enumeration function. The **SamrEnumDomainUsers** function does not appear to have this parameter. Sometimes the Enumeration structure members have an index associated with each member. It has been observed that this is not the case here.

There is another style of Enumeration function, one that involves returning pointers to a buffer and the size of the buffer. This style of function returns a non-zero status code to indicate that the buffer size requested is too small, and is typically used for medium to small numbers of entries (around 200 bytes to 4096 bytes). The **SamrEnumDomainUsers** function can potentially return several thousand Users, potentially returning megabytes of data across multiple calls to **SamrEnumDomainUsers**. It would therefore be unwise for the Microsoft SAM Database API developers to have used that Enumeration style here, so we can conclude that it is almost definitely not being used.

The closest equivalent MSDN call to **SamrEnumDomainUsers** is the **NetUserEnum** call. **NetUserEnum** is likely to be implemented as a **SamrOpenDomain**, followed by a **SamrEnumDomainUsers**, followed by a **SamrCloseHandle** with the Domain Policy Handle.

## 8.3.10: SamrEnumDomainGroups

The **SamrEnumDomainGroups** call obtains a list of Domain Groups in a Domain. Its closest MSDN equivalent is **NetGroupEnum**, shown here:

```
STATUS NetGroupEnum(
            IN      LPWSTR servername,
            IN      DWORD level,
            OUT     LPBYTE *bufptr,
            IN      DWORD prefmaxlen,
            OUT     LPDWORD entriesread,
            OUT     LPDWORD totalentries,
            IN OUT LPDWORD resume_handle
              );
```

**SamrEnumDomainGroups** supports a number of information levels. Samba supports only one of these in order to satisfy the demands of **USRMGR.EXE**—level 3. **SamrEnumDomainGroups** is structured so that it can be called many times, as a prodigious number of Domain Groups may exist.

The **SamrEnumDomainGroups** request, unlike the User and Alias Enumeration functions, contains an information level. Like these two other calls, it contains a Domain Policy Handle. The rest of the request is unknown. Shown here are typical values and possible descriptions:

```
000000 samr_io_q_enum_dom_groups
    000000 smb_io_pol_hnd pol
        0000 data: 00 00 00 00 02 00 00 00 00 00 00 00 fc 93 92 36 f5 06 00 00
    0014 switch_level: 0003
    0016 unknown_0   : 0000
    0018 start_idx   : 00000000
    001c unknown_1   : 000007d0
    0020 max_size    : 0000ffff
```

```
[020]    00 00 00 00 02 00 00   00 00 00 00 00 FC 93 92    ........ ........
[030]    36 F5 06 00 00 03 00 00   00 00 00 00 00 D0 07 00    6....... ........
[040]    00 FF FF 00 00                                       .....
```

The **SamrEnumDomainGroups** response contains an array of Domain Group member structures at the informational level requested. The only level observed has been 0x3. There are two members (**unknown_0** and **unknown_1**) whose purpose is completely mystical—never mind; you can't have everything. Typical values are shown. A level 0x3 request will result in the Domain Group's Relative Identifier (RID), SE_GROUP attributes, Name, and description being returned for each and every Domain Group in the requested Domain.

```
000018 samr_io_r_enum_dom_groups
    0018 unknown_0     : 00000492
    001c unknown_1     : 0000049a
    0020 switch_level  : 00000003
    0024 num_entries   : 00000004
    0028 ptr_entries   : 00000001
    002c num_entries2  : 00000004
    000030 sam_io_sam_entry3
        0030 grp_idx: 00000001
        0034 rid_grp: 000403e1
        0038 attr   : 00000007
        00003c smb_io_unihdr unihdr
        000044 smb_io_unihdr unihdr
    00004c sam_io_sam_entry3
        004c grp_idx: 00000002
        0050 rid_grp: 00000200
        0054 attr   : 00000007
        000058 smb_io_unihdr unihdr
        000060 smb_io_unihdr unihdr
    000068 sam_io_sam_entry3
        0068 grp_idx: 00000003
        006c rid_grp: 00000201
        0070 attr   : 00000007
        000074 smb_io_unihdr unihdr
        00007c smb_io_unihdr unihdr
    000084 sam_io_sam_entry3
        0084 grp_idx: 00000004
        0088 rid_grp: 00000202
        008c attr   : 00000007
        000090 smb_io_unihdr unihdr
        000098 smb_io_unihdr unihdr
    0000a0 sam_io_sam_str3
        0000a0 smb_io_unistr2 unistr2
            00ac buffer      : n.o.g.r.o.u.p.
        0000ba smb_io_unistr2 - NULL unistr2
    0000ba sam_io_sam_str3
        0000bc smb_io_unistr2 unistr2
            00c8 buffer      : D.o.m.a.i.n. .A.d.m.i.n.s.
        0000e2 smb_io_unistr2 - NULL unistr2
    0000e2 sam_io_sam_str3
```

```
      0000e4 smb_io_unistr2 unistr2
          00f0 buffer      : D.o.m.a.i.n. .U.s.e.r.s.
      000108 smb_io_unistr2 - NULL unistr2
    000108 sam_io_sam_str3
      000108 smb_io_unistr2 unistr2
          0114 buffer      : D.o.m.a.i.n. .G.u.e.s.t.s.
      00012e smb_io_unistr2 - NULL unistr2
    012e status: 00000000
```

```
[010]                         92 04 00 00 9A 04 00   ........ ........
[020]  00 03 00 00 00 04 00 00  00 01 00 00 00 04 00 00   ........ ........
[030]  00 01 00 00 00 E1 03 04  00 07 00 00 00 0E 00 0E   ........ ........
[040]  00 01 00 00 00 00 00 00  00 00 00 00 00 02 00 00   ........ ........
[050]  00 00 02 00 00 07 00 00  00 1A 00 1A 00 01 00 00   ........ ........
[060]  00 00 00 00 00 00 00 00  00 03 00 00 00 01 02 00   ........ ........
[070]  00 07 00 00 00 18 00 18  00 01 00 00 00 00 00 00   ........ ........
[080]  00 00 00 00 00 04 00 00  00 02 02 00 00 07 00 00   ........ ........
[090]  00 1A 00 1A 00 01 00 00  00 00 00 00 00 00 00 00   ........ ........
[0A0]  00 07 00 00 00 00 00 00  00 07 00 00 00 6E 00 6F   ........ .....n.o
[0B0]  00 67 00 72 00 6F 00 75  00 70 00 00 00 0D 00 00   .g.r.o.u .p......
[0C0]  00 00 00 00 00 0D 00 00  00 44 00 6F 00 6D 00 61   ........ .D.o.m.a
[0D0]  00 69 00 6E 00 20 00 41  00 64 00 6D 00 69 00 6E   .i.n. .A .d.m.i.n
[0E0]  00 73 00 00 00 0C 00 00  00 00 00 00 00 0C 00 00   .s...... ........
[0F0]  00 44 00 6F 00 6D 00 61  00 69 00 6E 00 20 00 55   .D.o.m.a .i.n. .U
[100]  00 73 00 65 00 72 00 73  00 0D 00 00 00 00 00 00   .s.e.r.s ........
[110]  00 0D 00 00 00 44 00 6F  00 6D 00 61 00 69 00 6E   .....D.o .m.a.i.n
[120]  00 20 00 47 00 75 00 65  00 73 00 74 00 73 00 00   . .G.u.e .s.t.s..
[130]  00 00 00                                           ...
```

The DCE/RPC format for the level 0x3 Domain Group member structure in this function is not known. From the observed network traffic, the format *could* look like this:

```
typedef struct
{
        DWORD group_index;
        DWORD group_rid;
        DWORD group_attributes;
        PUNICODE_STRING group_name;
        PUNICODE_STRING group_description;

} SAM_DOM_GROUP, *PSAM_DOM_GROUP;
```

The function prototype is likely to be as follows:

```
NTSTATUS SamrEnumDomGroups(
        IN   PHANDLE        pDomainHnd,
        IN   WORD           switch_level,
        IN   DWORD          start_idx,
        IN   DWORD          unknown,
        IN   WORD           max_size,
        OUT  DWORD          unknown_0,
        OUT  DWORD          unknown_1,
        OUT  DWORD          *pNumGroups,
        OUT  PSAM_DOM_GROUP pGroupInfo);
```

How do we guess that there is a **start_idx** parameter to this function, and how should it be used? Just like a lot of other Enumeration functions, a Domain Group Enumeration request contains four bytes (which in the first call are all set to zero) just after the **switch_value** parameter. Just like other Enumeration member structures, each Domain Group member structure contains an index. It is suspected that should there be more members outstanding that a status code *could* be returned, **STATUS_BUFFER_OVERFLOW**, and another **SamrEnumDomainGroups** call made with the **start_idx** parameter set to the same value as the last Domain Group member structure's index parameter. This is one approach that has been observed by other Enumeration functions.

However, unlike a lot of other Enumeration functions (for example the **NetrFileEnum** call in the **srvsvc pipe**), there is no parameter indicating the total number of Domain Group member structures in the Domain. **SamrEnumDomainGroups** *could* be similar to the **SvcEnumServicesStatus** call in the **svcctl pipe**. This is also unlikely because those types of Enumeration functions specify a maximum buffer size, indicate the total number of structures being returned, and also return a **STATUS_BUFFER_OVERFLOW** status code if the suggested maximum buffer size was too small.

There are many different Enumeration styles to choose from, which leads us to speculate that several different development teams made their mark—without any communication between them to provide some semblance of consistency to the DCE/RPC function suites. Not that it particularly matters, but it *is* a bit painful to observe how many possible ways Enumeration can be done.

The best guess, therefore, is that this is one of those "dummy" Enumeration functions that one of the Microsoft development teams has only partially implemented, namely: you are only ever expected to make one call to it. It's all very horrible, basically, and it potentially puts a maximum limit on the number of Domain Groups that can be dealt with. In fact, there *is* a hard limit on the number of groups in a Windows NT Domain. This limitation puts a cloud of uncertainty over how to deal with several hundred (or it could be several thousand) Domain Groups.

The closest MSDN equivalent to **SamrEnumDomainGroups** is the **NetGroupEnum** call. This is likely to be implemented as a call to **SamrOpenDomain**, followed by **SamrEnumDomainGroups**, followed by **SamrCloseHandle** with the Domain Policy Handle.

## 8.3.11: SamrEnumDomainAliases

The **SamrEnumDomainAliases** call obtains a list of Aliases in a Domain. Its closest MSDN equivalent is **NetLocalGroupEnum**, shown here:

```
STATUS NetLocalGroupEnum(
                IN      LPWSTR servername,
                IN      DWORD level,
                OUT     LPBYTE *bufptr,
                IN      DWORD prefmaxlen,
                OUT     LPDWORD entriesread,
                OUT     LPDWORD totalentries,
                IN OUT LPDWORD resumehandle
                    );
```

**SamrEnumDomainAliases** is pretty similar to the **SamrEnumDomainUsers** call. The **SamrEnumDomainAliases** request includes a Domain Policy Handle plus a couple of other parameters. The first seems to indicate where the Enumeration should begin, whereas the second hints at the maximum size of data that will be returned.

```
000000 samr_io_q_enum_dom_aliases
    000000 smb_io_pol_hnd pol
        0000 data: 00 00 00 00 15 00 00 00 00 00 00 00 3a 70 8a 36 5b 1c 00 00
    0014 unknown_0: 00000000
    0018 max_size : 0000ffff

[020]    00 00 00 00 15 00 00  00 00 00 00 00 3A 70 8A  ........ .....:p.
[030]  36 5B 1C 00 00 00 00 00  00 FF FF 00 00           6[...... .....
```

The **SamrEnumDomainAliases** response, like the **SamrEnumDomainUsers** response, contains a list of RIDs plus Alias names. The response shown here is in full (unlike the preceding **SamrEnumDomainUsers** response, which is pared down).

```
000018 samr_io_r_enum_dom_aliases
    0018 num_entries: 00000001
    001c ptr_entries: 00000001
    0020 num_entries2: 00000001
    0024 ptr_entries2: 00000001
    0028 num_entries3: 00000001
    00002c sam_io_sam_entry
        002c rid: 0000057e
        000030 smb_io_unihdr unihdr
            0030 uni_str_len: 0018
            0032 uni_max_len: 0018
            0034 buffer     : 00000001
    000038 smb_io_unistr2
        0038 uni_max_len: 0000000c
        003c undoc      : 00000000
        0040 uni_str_len: 0000000c
```

```
        0044 buffer      : N.T.l.o.c.a.l.g.r.o.u.p.
    005c num_entries4: 00000001
    0060 status: 00000000

[010]                                  01 00 00 00 01 00 00   .L...... ........
[020] 00 01 00 00 00 01 00 00  00 01 00 00 00 7E 05 00   ........ .....~..
[030] 00 18 00 18 00 01 00 00  00 0C 00 00 00 00 00 00   ........ ........
[040] 00 0C 00 00 00 4E 00 54  00 6C 00 6F 00 63 00 61   .....N.T .l.o.c.a
[050] 00 6C 00 67 00 72 00 6F  00 75 00 70 00 01 00 00   .l.g.r.o .u.p....
[060] 00 00 00 00 00 00                                  .....
```

When this call is made with a Domain Policy Handle associated with the well-known Domain SID **S-1-5-32**, it will return all (and will only return all) the well-known Aliases such as "Administrators," "Power Users," and so forth. For a Domain Policy Handle associated with the Server's Domain SID, it will return all the Aliases in the Domain, and it will *not* return the previously mentioned well-known Alias names because these are not *in* the SAM database associated with the Server's Domain SID; they are in the BUILTIN SAM database associated with the SID **S-1-5-32**. A declaration for the well-known Aliases and their associated RIDs can be found in **winnt.h**.

The likely members for the structure that contains Alias information, from which the DCE/RPC parsing code is generated, are shown here:

```
typedef struct
{
        DWORD           AliasRid;
        PUNICODE_STRING pAliasName;

} SAM_DOM_ALIAS, *PSAM_DOM_ALIAS;
```

The function prototype is likely to be as follows:

```
NTSTATUS SamrEnumDomAliases(
        IN  PHANDLE         pDomainHnd,
        IN  DWORD           unknown_0,
        IN  WORD            max_size,
        OUT DWORD           *pNumAliases,
        OUT PSAM_DOM_ALIAS pAliasInfo);
```

The closest MSDN equivalent to **SamrEnumDomainAliases** is the **NetLocalGroupEnum** call. This is likely to be implemented as a call to **SamrOpenDomain**, followed by **SamrEnumDomainAliases**, followed by **SamrCloseHandle** with the Domain Policy Handle.

## 8.4: Domain Group Functions
This group of functions deals specifically with Domain Groups, including how to create, delete, and modify them, and how to find out

what their members are. This group of functions works only on a
Domain Controller. None of them will work on a Workstation,
as a Workstation's Local SAM Database cannot hold any Domain
Groups.

## 8.4.1: SamrOpenGroup

**SamrOpenGroup** associates a Policy Handle with a Relative Identifier
(RID) in a domain. The function prototype for **SamrOpenGroup** probably looks like this:

```
NTSTATUS SamrOpenGroup(
       IN  PHANDLE  pDomainHnd,
       IN  SEC_INFO access_rights,
       IN  DWORD    GroupRid,
       OUT PHANDLE  pGroupHnd);
```

The request contains the Policy Handle representing the Domain, what
is believed to be a requested access mask, and the RID of the Domain
Group:

```
000000 samr_io_q_open_group
   000000 smb_io_pol_hnd domain_pol
      0000 data: 00 00 00 00 0f 00 00 00 00 00 00 00 37 70 8a 36 5b 1c 00 00
   0014 unknown  : 00000010
   0018 rid_group: 000403e1

[020]     00 00 00 00 0F 00 00  00 00 00 00 00 37 70 8A  ........ .....7p.
[030] 36 5B 1C 00 00 10 00 00  00 E1 03 04 00          6[...... .....
```

The **SamrOpenGroup** response contains a Policy Handle that has been
associated with the Domain Group and a status code. If the RID does
not exist in the Domain, the status code will be 0xC000 0066
(**NT_STATUS_NO_SUCH_GROUP**) and a Policy Handle will not be
returned.

```
000018 samr_io_r_open_group
   000018 smb_io_pol_hnd pol
      0018 data: 00 00 00 00 10 00 00 00 00 00 00 00 37 70 8a 36 5b 1c 00 00
   002c status: 00000000

[010]                          00 00 00 00 10 00 00  ........ ........
[020] 00 00 00 00 00 37 70 8A  36 5B 1C 00 00 00 00 00  .....7p. 6[......
[030] 00                                                .
```

The requested access mask will limit the kinds of operations that can
be carried out using the Domain Policy Handle returned by the
**SamrOpenGroup** call. In the instances where 0x00010 has been used
for this parameter (which represents Notify rights if the interpretation
of this parameter is correct), then **SamrQueryGroupInfo** and
**SamrQueryGroupMembers** are called. In the instances where 0x0001f

has been used (which represents Notify, Enumerate, Create, Set, and Query rights), then **SamrDeleteGroupMember**, **SamrDeleteGroup**, and **SamrAddGroupMember** are called.

Asking to open a Domain Group in the well-known Domain **S-1-5-32** will always fail. This is not for any specific reason—it is just because SAM Databases do not *have* any Domain Groups in the well-known Domain, only Aliases.

The Policy Handle returned by this call must be closed with a **SamrCloseHandle** call. Failure to do this may cause a Server to run out of resources. Using the Policy Handle after it has been closed will result in **NT_STATUS_INVALID_HANDLE** error messages being returned.

### 8.4.2: SamrQueryInformationGroup

**SamrQueryInformationGroup** corresponds to the MSDN function **NetGroupGetInfo**, which is used to obtain information about a Domain Group.

```
STATUS NetGroupGetInfo(
            IN  LPWSTR servername,
            IN  LPWSTR groupname,
            IN  DWORD level,
            OUT LPBYTE *bufptr
                );
```

As with all objects in the SAM, there are a number of information levels at which Domain Groups can be queried. The documented levels are 0, 1, 2, 1002, and 1005 (see **lmaccess.h**); these are all subsets of the **GROUP_INFO_2** structure:

```
typedef struct _GROUP_INFO_2 {
    LPWSTR    grpi2_name;
    LPWSTR    grpi2_comment;
    DWORD     grpi2_group_id;
    DWORD     grpi2_attributes;
}GROUP_INFO_2, *PGROUP_INFO_2;
```

However, the **SamrSetInformationGroup** call shown in the next section is at an information level of 4 (comment only), so there are clearly other undocumented information levels.

The **SamrQueryInformationGroup** request contains a handle to the group that is to be queried, and a 16-bit value indicating the required information level. The group handle must have been opened with sufficient rights to permit query.

```
000000 samr_io_q_query_groupinfo
    000000 smb_io_pol_hnd pol
        0000 data: 00 00 00 00 01 3b 28 cb 4c 5f d3 11 93 80 e7 74 bc bd 31 44
```

```
     0014 switch_level: 0001

[020]    00 00 00 00 01 3B 28  CB 4C 5F D3 11 93 80 E7  ......;( .L_.....
[030] 74 BC BD 31 44 01 00                             t..1D..
```

The response contains the requested **GROUP_INFO** structure, marshalled in the usual manner, and a status code.

```
000018 samr_io_r_query_groupinfo
   0018 ptr: 001791f8
   00001c samr_group_info_ctr ctr
      001c switch_value1: 0001
      001e switch_value2: cb28
      000020 samr_io_group_info1 group_info1
         000020 smb_io_unihdr hdr_acct_name
            0020 uni_str_len: 001a
            0022 uni_max_len: 001a
            0024 buffer     : 00178e90
         0028 unknown_1: 00000003
         002c unknown_2: 00000002
         000030 smb_io_unihdr hdr_acct_desc
            0030 uni_str_len: 003a
            0032 uni_max_len: 003a
            0034 buffer     : 0016e8f8
         000038 smb_io_unistr2 uni_acct_name
            0038 uni_max_len: 0000000d
            003c undoc      : 00000000
            0040 uni_str_len: 0000000d
            0044 buffer     : Trusted Users
         000060 smb_io_unistr2 uni_acct_desc
            0060 uni_max_len: 0000001d
            0064 undoc      : 00000000
            0068 uni_str_len: 0000001d
            006c buffer     : Users with special privileges
   00a8 status: 00000000

[010]                         F8 91 17 00 01 00 28  ........ .......(
[020] CB 1A 00 1A 00 90 8E 17  00 03 00 00 00 02 00 00  ........ ........
[030] 00 3A 00 3A 00 F8 E8 16  00 0D 00 00 00 00 00 00  .:.:.... ........
[040] 00 0D 00 00 00 54 00 72  00 75 00 73 00 74 00 65  .....T.r .u.s.t.e
[050] 00 64 00 20 00 55 00 73  00 65 00 72 00 73 00 70  .d. .U.s .e.r.s.p
[060] 00 1D 00 00 00 00 00 00  00 1D 00 00 00 55 00 73  ........ .....U.s
[070] 00 65 00 72 00 73 00 20  00 77 00 69 00 74 00 68  .e.r.s.  .w.i.t.h
[080] 00 20 00 73 00 70 00 65  00 63 00 69 00 61 00 6C  . .s.p.e .c.i.a.l
[090] 00 20 00 70 00 72 00 69  00 76 00 69 00 6C 00 65  . .p.r.i .v.i.l.e
[0A0] 00 67 00 65 00 73 00 00  00 00 00 00 00           .g.e.s.. .....
```

Note that the **GROUP_INFO** structure is referenced by a pointer; if
the call fails then the pointer is NULL and the status code follows
immediately after it.

### 8.4.3: SamrSetInformationGroup

**SamrSetInformationGroup** is exactly analogous to
**SamrQueryInformationGroup** described in the preceding section,
except that the **GROUP_INFO** structure is passed into the function
for the purpose of changing the SAM group information. Naturally,
the caller must have sufficient access rights to do this.

**SamrSetInformationGroup** corresponds to the MSDN function
**NetGroupSetInfo**, shown as follows:

```
STATUS NetGroupSetInfo(
            IN  LPWSTR servername,
            IN  LPWSTR groupname,
            IN  DWORD level,
            IN  LPBYTE buf,
            OUT LPDWORD parm_err
                );
```

The request contains a handle to the group to be changed, an arbitrary information level, and a **GROUP_INFO** structure at that information level containing the changes. To avoid inadvertent changes, the
original structure should always be retrieved with a
**SamrQueryInformationGroup** at the same information level, and the
necessary changes should be made to that structure.

```
000000 samr_io_q_set_groupinfo
    000000 smb_io_pol_hnd pol
        0000 data: 00 00 00 00 51 3a 28 cb 4c 5f d3 11 93 80 e7 74 bc bd 31 44
    000014 samr_group_info_ctr ctr
        0014 switch_value1: 0004
        0016 switch_value2: 0004
        000018 samr_io_group_info4 group_info4
            000018 smb_io_unihdr hdr_acct_desc
                0018 uni_str_len: 003a
                001a uni_max_len: 003a
                001c buffer     : 00000001
            000020 smb_io_unistr2 uni_acct_desc
                0020 uni_max_len: 0000001d
                0024 undoc      : 00000000
                0028 uni_str_len: 0000001d
                002c buffer     : Users with special privileges

[020]    00 00 00 00 51 3A 28  CB 4C 5F D3 11 93 80 E7   .....Q:( .L_.....
[030] 74 BC BD 31 44 04 00 04  00 3A 00 3A 00 01 00 00   t..1D... .:.:....
[040] 00 1D 00 00 00 00 00 00  00 1D 00 00 00 55 00 73   ........ .....U.s
[050] 00 65 00 72 00 73 00 20  00 77 00 69 00 74 00 68   .e.r.s.  .w.i.t.h
[060] 00 20 00 73 00 70 00 65  00 63 00 69 00 61 00 6C   . .s.p.e .c.i.a.l
[070] 00 20 00 70 00 72 00 69  00 76 00 69 00 6C 00 65   . .p.r.i .v.i.l.e
[080] 00 67 00 65 00 73 00 00  00                        .g.e.s.. .
```

The response contains the status code for the operation:

```
000018 samr_io_r_set_groupinfo
    0018 status: 00000000

[010]                           00 00 00 00          ........ .....
```

Note that the preceding traces show a **SamrSetGroupInformation** call at an information level of 4, which is undocumented. This particular level had to be implemented in Samba, however, because it is used by Windows NT to set the group comment when a new group is created.

## 8.4.4: SamrAddMemberToGroup

**SamrAddMemberToGroup** is used, as the name suggests, to add a User to a Domain group. It corresponds to the MSDN function **NetGroupAddUser**:

```
STATUS NetGroupAddUser(
                IN  LPWSTR servername,
                IN  LPWSTR GroupName,
                IN  LPWSTR username
                );
```

The request contains a group handle and the relative identifier (RID) of the User to be added to the Group, as well as an unknown quantity thought to represent a set of User attributes. The exact meaning of this is unknown, but it has always been observed to have the value 5.

```
000000 samr_io_q_add_groupmem
    000000 smb_io_pol_hnd pol
        0000 data: 00 00 00 00 55 3a 28 cb 4c 5f d3 11 93 80 e7 74 bc bd 31 44
    0014 rid   : 000006b6
    0018 unknown: 00000005

[020]   00 00 00 00 55 3A 28  CB 4C 5F D3 11 93 80 E7   .....U:( .L_.....
[030] 74 BC BD 31 44 B6 06 00  00 05 00 00 00           t..1D... .....
```

The response is a status code indicating whether the User has successfully been added to the Group.

```
000018 samr_io_r_add_groupmem
    0018 status: 00000000

[010]                           00 00 00 00          ........ .....
```

As is often the case for SAM functions, the RPC version takes a group handle and user RID, while the MSDN interface takes a Group name and a User name. The RPC version hides the implementation details from the programmer and provides extra portability between revisions of the security subsystem, at the expense of extra overhead for multiple calls.

### 8.4.5: SamrCreateGroupInDomain

**SamrCreateGroupInDomain** provides a means to add new Groups to the Security Access Manager database. It is normally accessed via the MSDN function **NetGroupAdd**:

```
STATUS NetGroupAdd(
          IN  LPWSTR servername,
          IN  DWORD level,
          OUT LPBYTE buf,
          OUT LPDWORD parm_err
          );
```

Unlike most Windows NT Add Object functions, which take in a structure at some information level and create the new object using that as a template, **SamrCreateGroupInDomain** takes only a Domain handle and Group name. Any other attributes to be set, including the comment, must be filled in with an explicit **SamrSetGroupInformation** call.

```
000000 samr_io_q_create_dom_group
    000000 smb_io_pol_hnd pol
        0000 data: 00 00 00 00 50 3a 28 cb 4c 5f d3 11 93 80 e7 74 bc bd 31 44
    000014 smb_io_unihdr hdr_acct_name
        0014 uni_str_len: 001a
        0016 uni_max_len: 001a
        0018 buffer     : 00000001
    00001c smb_io_unistr2 uni_acct_name
        001c uni_max_len: 0000000d
        0020 undoc      : 00000000
        0024 uni_str_len: 0000000d
        0028 buffer     : T.r.u.s.t.e.d. .U.s.e.r.s.
    0044 unknown_1: 0002
    0046 unknown_2: 0001

[020]    00 00 00 00 50 3A 28  CB 4C 5F D3 11 93 80 E7   .....P:( .L......
[030] 74 BC BD 31 44 1A 00 1A  00 01 00 00 00 0D 00 00   t..1D... ........
[040] 00 00 00 00 00 0D 00 00  00 54 00 72 00 75 00 73   ........ .T.r.u.s
[050] 00 74 00 65 00 64 00 20  00 55 00 73 00 65 00 72   .t.e.d.  .U.s.e.r
[060] 00 73 00 00 00 02 00 01  00                        .s...... .
```

The parameters marked by rpcclient as "unknown" seem to represent an access mask for the returned handle. In this case it is 0x00010002. The 2 allows "set value" (necessary for issuing the **SamrSetGroupInformation** call that normally follows the create), while the 1 allows "delete" (in case that fails).

The response contains a handle for the new Group (which is implicitly opened by the create), the newly assigned RID, and a status code.

```
000018 samr_io_r_create_dom_group
    000018 smb_io_pol_hnd pol
        0018 data: 00 00 00 00 51 3a 28 cb 4c 5f d3 11 93 80 e7 74 bc bd 31 44
    002c rid    : 00000754
```

```
     0030 status: 00000000

[010]                          00 00 00 00 51 3A 28   ........ .....Q:(
[020] CB 4C 5F D3 11 93 80 E7  74 BC BD 31 44 54 07 00   .L_..... t..1DT..
[030] 00 00 00 00 00                                .....
```

## 8.4.6: SamrDeleteGroup

**SamrDeleteGroup** is used to delete Groups. Somewhat counter-intuitively, the group to be deleted must be open; if successful this function destroys the open handle and replaces it with all zeros.

The corresponding MSDN function is called **NetGroupDel**, which hides these technicalities by simply accepting a Group name:

```
STATUS NetGroupDel(
            IN  LPWSTR servername,
            IN  LPWSTR groupname
              );
```

The **SamrDeleteGroup** request contains the handle of the Group to be deleted. This handle must have been opened with Delete rights.

```
000000 samr_io_q_delete_dom_group
    000000 smb_io_pol_hnd group_pol
        0000 data: 00 00 00 00 2b 3b 28 cb 4c 5f d3 11 93 80 e7 74 bc bd 31 44

[020]    00 00 00 00 2B 3B 28  CB 4C 5F D3 11 93 80 E7   .....+;( .L_.....
[030] 74 BC BD 31 44                             t..1D
```

The response contains the new value for the handle (technically speaking, the handle is an **[in out]** parameter to this function), which is all zeros—if the function is successful—and a status code as usual.

```
000018 samr_io_r_delete_dom_group
    000018 smb_io_pol_hnd pol
        0018 data: 00 00 00 00 00 00 00 00 00 00 00 00 00 00 00 00 00 00 00 00
    002c status: 00000000

[010]                          00 00 00 00 00 00 00   ........ ........
[020] 00 00 00 00 00 00 00 00  00 00 00 00 00 00 00 00   ........ ........
[030] 00
```

## 8.4.7: SamrRemoveMemberFromGroup

**SamrRemoveMemberFromGroup** is used to delete a single member from a Domain group. It corresponds to the MSDN function **NetGroupDelUser**. **SamrRemoveMemberFromGroup** is, not surprisingly, the opposite of **SamrAddMemberToGroup**.

```
STATUS NetGroupDelUser(
            IN  LPWSTR servername,
            IN  LPWSTR GroupName,
            IN  LPWSTR Username
              );
```

The request contains a handle to the group of which the User is currently a member, and the user's RID:

```
000000 samr_io_q_del_groupmem
   000000 smb_io_pol_hnd pol
      0000 data: 00 00 00 00 18 3b 28 cb 4c 5f d3 11 93 80 e7 74 bc bd 31 44
   0014 rid   : 000006b6

[020]    00 00 00 00 18 3B 28 CB 4C 5F D3 11 93 80 E7    ......;( .L_.....
[030] 74 BC BD 31 44 B6 06 00  00                        t..1D... .
```

The response contains a status code indicating whether the User was successfully removed from the Group:

```
000018 samr_io_r_del_groupmem
   0018 status: 00000000

[010]                           00 00 00 00              ........ .....
```

The most common failure conditions are **STATUS_NO_SUCH_USER**, if the RID is invalid, or **STATUS_MEMBER_NOT_IN_GROUP**.

## 8.4.8: SamrQueryGroupMembers

**SamrQueryGroupMembers** is used to enumerate the users in a given Group. It is not a "true" Enumeration function, however; there is no facility for limiting the output from a single call and resuming from that point. This presumably places an upper limit to the number of users that can be placed into a single Group, although at only 8 bytes per user this is probably similar to the hard limit imposed by the SAM database format.

**SamrQueryGroupMembers** is analogous to the MSDN function **NetGroupGetUsers**, although the MSDN function is more flexible in that it does provide for a maximum buffer size and resume handle. Presumably other database providers, such as NetWare NDS, are able to harness that functionality despite the limitation of **SamrQueryGroupMembers**.

```
STATUS NetGroupGetUsers(
            IN     LPWSTR servername,
            IN     LPWSTR groupname,
            IN     DWORD level,
            OUT    LPBYTE *bufptr,
            IN     DWORD prefmaxlen,
            OUT    LPDWORD entriesread,
            OUT    LPDWORD totalentries,
            IN OUT LPDWORD resumeHandle
                   );
```

The RPC request, surprisingly, contains only a group handle. As noted previously, there is no way of limiting the number of entries returned.

```
000000 samr_io_q_query_groupmem
    000000 smb_io_pol_hnd group_pol
        0000 data: 00 00 00 00 03 00 00 00 00 00 00 00 6e 09 ca 37 24 02 00 00

[020]             03 00 00  00 00 00 00 00 6E 09 CA 37      .... ....n..7
[030] 24 02 00 00                              $...
```

The response contains the total number of users in the group and two arrays, one containing each user's RID and the other containing the corresponding attributes.

```
000018 samr_io_r_query_groupmem
    0018 ptr: 00000001
    001c num_entries : 00000003
    0020 ptr_rids : 00000001
    0024 ptr_attrs: 00000001
    0028 num_rids: 00000003
    002c : 000003e8
    0030 : 000003ec
    0034 : 000003f0
    0038 num_attrs: 00000003
    003c : 00000007
    0040 : 00000007
    0044 : 00000007
    0048 status: 00000000

[010]                   00  01 00 00 00 03 00 00 00      ........
[020] 01 00 00 00 01 00 00 00  03 00 00 00 E8 03 00 00      ........ ........
[030] EC 03 00 00 F0 03 00 00  03 00 00 00 07 00 00 00      ........ ........
[040] 07 00 00 00 07 00 00 00  00 00 00 00                  ........ ....
```

# 8.5: Domain Alias Functions

This group of functions deals specifically with Aliases (also known as Local Groups): how to create, delete, and modify them, and how to find out what their members are. This group of functions works on both a Workstation as a Domain member and a Workstation that is not a member of a Domain because these have a Local SAM Database. Of course, they also work on a Domain Controller's SAM Database.

## 8.5.1: SamrOpenAlias

This function associates a Policy Handle with a Relative Identifier (RID) in a Domain. The function prototype for **SamrOpenAlias** probably looks like this:

```
NTSTATUS SamrOpenAlias(
        IN  PHANDLE  pDomainHnd,
        IN  SEC_INFO access_rights,
```

```
      IN  DWORD     AliasRid,
      OUT PHANDLE   pAliasHnd);
```

The request contains the Policy Handle representing the Domain, an unknown 32-bit parameter (probably the requested access rights), and the RID of the Domain Alias:

```
000000 samr_io_q_open_alias
   000000 smb_io_pol_hnd dom_pol
      0000 data: 00 00 00 00 15 00 00 00 00 00 00 00 3a 70 8a 36 5b 1c 00 00
   0014 unknown_0: 000f001f
   0018 rid_alias: 0000057e

[020]    00 00 00 00 15 00 00  00 00 00 00 00 3A 70 8A   ........ .....:p.
[030] 36 5B 1C 00 00 1F 00 0F  00 7E 05 00 00            6[...... .~...
```

The **SamrOpenAlias** response contains a Policy Handle that has been associated with the Domain Alias and a status code. If the RID does not exist in the Domain, the status code will be 0xC000 0181 (**NT_STATUS_NO_SUCH_ALIAS**) and a Policy Handle will not be returned.

```
000018 samr_io_r_open_alias
   000018 smb_io_pol_hnd pol
      0018 data: 00 00 00 00 16 00 00 00 00 00 00 00 3a 70 8a 36 5b 1c 00 00
   002c status: 00000000

[010]                          00 00 00 00 16 00 00     ........ ........
[020] 00 00 00 00 00 3A 70 8A  36 5B 1C 00 00 00 00 00   .....:p. 6[......
[030] 00                                                 .
```

The value for the unknown parameter in the request, 0xf001f, looks vaguely familiar. Examination of the Windows NT Security Information bits that are found in Access Control Entries leads us to speculate that this parameter may dictate the Access Rights being requested. This in turn will limit the kinds of operations that can be carried out using the Alias Policy Handle returned by the **SamrOpenAlias** call. If the **SamrOpenAlias** call is made requesting Full Control within a Security Context that does not have those rights (for example, an "Account Operator") then presumably a status code of 0xC000 0021 (**NT_STATUS_ACCESS_DENIED**) will be returned. If the **SamrOpenAlias** call is made (and granted) requesting Read Only rights, and a **SamrDeleteAlias** call is subsequently made with this Alias Policy Handle, the Delete should *not* be carried out. The only value observed to date represents Read, Write, Delete, Notify, Enumerate, Create, Set, and Query.

The Domain associated with the Domain Policy Handle in the request can be either be the SAM Database SID for which the Server is responsible or the well-known Domain SID **S-1-5-32**. For the well-known Domain SID, only the well-known Aliases such as Administrators, Power Users, Account Operators, and so forth can be opened. A declaration for the well-known Aliases and their RIDs can be found in **winnt.h**. For the SAM Database SID, any Aliases that have been added to the Domain can be opened. It *is* important to use the correct Domain Policy Handle because each Domain contains totally separate Users, Aliases, and Groups.

The Policy Handle returned by this call must be closed with a **SamrCloseHandle** call after it has been dealt with. Failure to do this may cause a Server to run out of resources. The use of the Policy Handle after it has been closed will result in NT_STATUS_INVALID_HANDLE error messages being returned.

## 8.5.2: SamrQueryInformationAlias

**SamrQueryInformationAlias** has not been observed in network traffic to date, and so is not documented here. Without example network traffic, it is difficult to ascertain the exact parameters of a function, although it is likely that the **SamrQueryInformationAlias** function will be very similar to **SamrSetInformationAlias**. The MSDN equivalent of **SamrQueryInformationAlias** is **NetLocalGroupGetInfo**, shown here:

```
STATUS NetLocalGroupGetInfo(
            IN  LPWSTR servername,
            IN  LPWSTR LocalGroupName,
            IN  DWORD level,
            OUT LPBYTE *bufptr
                );
```

## 8.5.3: SamrSetInformationAlias

**SamrSetInformationAlias** is used to modify attributes of an Alias (also known as a Local Group). Its MSDN equivalent, **NetLocalGroupSetInfo**, is shown here:

```
STATUS NetLocalGroupSetInfo(
            IN  LPWSTR servername,
            IN  LPWSTR LocalGroupName,
            IN  DWORD level,
            IN  LPBYTE buf,
            OUT LPDWORD parm_err
                );
```

**SamrSetInformationAlias** can be used to rename an Alias or to set its description. When a new Alias is added to a Domain with **SamrCreateAliasInDomain**, USRMGR.EXE follows up with a call to **SamrSetInformationAlias** to set the description of the Alias.

The request contains a Policy Handle, then an info level, followed by a structure. In this example, the info level is 3. The structure, presumably named **ALIAS_INFO_3**, contains the description of the Alias.

```
000000 samr_io_q_set_aliasinfo
   000000 smb_io_pol_hnd alias_pol
      0000 data: 00 00 00 00 24 97 25 50 63 5d d3 11 9e cc d7 20 92 94 16 14
   000014 samr_alias_info_ctr ctr
      0014 switch_value1: 0003
      0016 switch_value2: 0003
      000018 samr_io_alias_info3 alias_info3
         000018 smb_io_unihdr hdr_acct_desc
            0018 uni_str_len: 0000
            001a uni_max_len: 0000
            001c buffer     : 00000000
         000020 smb_io_unistr2 - NULL uni_acct_desc

[020] 00 00 00 00 24 97 25 50  63 5D D3 11 9E CC D7 20   ....$.%P c].....
[030] 92 94 16 14 03 00 03 00  00 00 00 00 00 00 00 00   ........ ........
```

The response is a status code acknowledging that the Alias was modified. Presumably if the call was made with a Policy Handle that does not have suitable access rights associated with it, an error status code **NT_STATUS_ACCESS_DENIED** is returned instead.

```
000018 samr_io_r_set_aliasinfo
   0018 status: 00000000

[010]                     00 00 00 00                    ....
```

### 8.5.4: SamrCreateAliasInDomain

**SamrCreateAliasInDomain** is used to add an Alias to a Domain. Its MSDN equivalent is **NetLocalGroupAdd**, shown here:

```
STATUS NetLocalGroupAdd(
            IN  LPWSTR servername,
            IN  DWORD level,
            IN  LPBYTE buf,
            OUT LPDWORD parm_err
               );
```

The request contains a Policy Handle associated with the domain to which the Alias is to be added, the name of the Alias, and a couple of unknown parameters that look vaguely familiar and could potentially be an access mask.

```
000000 samr_io_q_create_dom_alias
   000000 smb_io_pol_hnd dom_pol
      0000 data: 00 00 00 00 23 97 25 50 63 5d d3 11 9e cc d7 20 92 94 16 14
   000014 smb_io_unihdr hdr_acct_desc
      0014 uni_str_len: 000c
      0016 uni_max_len: 000c
```

```
    0018 buffer    : 00000001
00001c smb_io_unistr2 uni_acct_desc
    001c uni_max_len: 00000006
    0020 undoc     : 00000000
    0024 uni_str_len: 00000006
    0028 buffer    : a.l.i.a.s.1.
0034 unknown_1: 001f
0036 unknown_2: 000f
```

```
[020]     00 00 00 00 23 97 25  50 63 5D D3 11 9E CC D7   .....#.% Pc].....
[030] 20 92 94 16 14 0C 00 0C  00 01 00 00 00 06 00 00   ....... ........
[040] 00 00 00 00 00 06 00 00  00 61 00 6C 00 69 00 61   ........ .a.l.i.a
[050] 00 73 00 31 00 1F 00 0F  00                        .s.1.... .
```

The response contains a handle representing the Alias that has just been created, the RID of the new Alias in the Domain in which it was added, and a status code of 0x0. The Policy Handle is empty and a RID of 0x0 is returned if the status code is non-zero.

```
000018 samr_io_r_create_dom_alias
    000018 smb_io_pol_hnd alias_pol
        0018 data: 00 00 00 00 24 97 25 50 63 5d d3 11 9e cc d7 20 92 94 16 14
    002c rid: 000003e8
    0030 status: 00000000
```

```
[010]                         00 00 00 00 24 97 25   ........ .....$.%
[020] 50 63 5D D3 11 9E CC D7  20 92 94 16 14 E8 03 00   Pc]..... .......
[030] 00 00 00 00 00                                     .....
```

For the Alias to be created, the Domain Policy Handle in the request must have been opened with an appropriate access mask by a User with sufficient privileges. Otherwise, an NT_STATUS_ACCESS_DENIED error will be returned on the SamrCreateAliasInDomain call.

## 8.5.5: SamrQueryAliasMembers

SamrQueryAliasMembers lists all the members of an Alias. Its nearest MSDN equivalent is NetLocalGroupGetMembers, shown here:

```
STATUS NetLocalGroupGetMembers(
                IN    LPWSTR servername,
                IN    LPWSTR localgroupname,
                IN    DWORD level,
                OUT   LPBYTE *bufptr,
                IN    DWORD prefmaxlen,
                OUT   LPDWORD entriesread,
                OUT   LPDWORD totalentries,
                IN OUT LPDWORD resumehandle
                    );
```

The request contains a Policy Handle representing the Alias.

```
000000 samr_io_q_query_aliasmem
    000000 smb_io_pol_hnd alias_pol
        0000 data: 00 00 00 00 16 00 00 00 00 00 00 00 3a 70 8a 36 5b 1c 00 00

[020]    00 00 00 00 16 00 00  00 00 00 00 00 3A 70 8A    ........ .....:p.
[030] 36 5B 1C 00 00                                    6[...
```

The response contains an array of pointers to Security Identifiers
(SIDs) plus a status code. Each SID represents a member in the Alias.

```
000018 samr_io_r_query_aliasmem
    0018 num_sids : 00000002
    001c ptr: 00000001
    0020 num_sids1: 00000002
    0024 ptr_sid[00]: 00000001
    0028 ptr_sid[01]: 00000001
    00002c smb_io_dom_sid2
        002c num_auths: 00000005
        000030 smb_io_dom_sid sid
            0030 sid_rev_num: 01
            0031 num_auths  : 05
            0032 id_auths: 00 00 00 00 00 05
            0038 sub_auths : 00000015 466e2442 08de9320 b8c519a4 00001388
    00004c smb_io_dom_sid2
        004c num_auths: 00000005
        000050 smb_io_dom_sid sid
            0050 sid_rev_num: 01
            0051 num_auths  : 05
            0032 id_auths: 00 00 00 00 00 05
            0058 sub_auths : 00000015 466e2442 08de9320 b8c519a4 000003e8
    006c status: 00000000

[010]                    00 00  00 02 00 00 00 01 00 00   .X...... ........
[020] 00 02 00 00 00 01 00 00  00 01 00 00 00 05 00 00   ........ ........
[030] 00 01 05 00 00 00 00 00  05 15 00 00 00 42 24 6E   ........ .....B$n
[040] 46 20 93 DE 08 A4 19 C5  B8 88 13 00 00 05 00 00   F ...... ........
[050] 00 01 05 00 00 00 00 00  05 15 00 00 00 42 24 6E   ........ .....B$n
[060] 46 20 93 DE 08 A4 19 C5  B8 E8 03 00 00 00 00 00   F ...... ........
[070] 00                                                 .
```

## 8.5.6: SamrAddMemberToAlias

**SamrAddMemberToAlias** is used to add a member to an Alias. Its
MSDN equivalent is **NetLocalGroupAddMembers,** shown here:

```
STATUS NetLocalGroupAddMembers(
            IN  LPWSTR servername,
            IN  LPWSTR LocalGroupName,
            IN  DWORD level,
            IN  LPBYTE buf,
            OUT DWORD membercount
                );
```

A significant difference between these two functions is that
**SamrAddMemberToAlias** adds only one member at a time, whilst
the MSDN function replaces all existing members with new ones.

Alias members are specified by their full Security Identifier (SID).
This is in contrast to Group members, which are specified only by
Relative Identifier (RID). This appears to be an awkward mechanism,
particularly in that Users can only be joined to Aliases or Groups, but
it is in fact extremely powerful. Bear in mind that Aliases can also be
Group members. Therefore, it is possible to add a SID to an Alias,
then add that Alias to a Group, then make Users members of that
Group.

The request contains a Policy Handle representing the Alias to
which the member is to be added, plus the full SID of the member
to be added to the Alias.

```
make_samr_q_add_aliasmem
000000 samr_io_q_add_aliasmem
   000000 smb_io_pol_hnd alias_pol
      0000 data: 00 00 00 00 42 97 25 50 63 5d d3 11 9e cc d7 20 92 94 16 14
   000014 smb_io_dom_sid2 sid
      0014 num_auths: 00000005
      000018 smb_io_dom_sid sid
         0018 sid_rev_num: 01
         0019 num_auths  : 05
         001a id_auth[0..5] : 00 00 00 00 00 05
         0020 sub_auths : 00000015 31f31e7c 6984478a 724049dc 000001f4

[020] 00 00 00 00 42 97 25 50  63 5D D3 11 9E CC D7 20   ....B.%P c].....
[030] 92 94 16 14 05 00 00 00  01 05 00 00 00 00 00 05   ........ ........
[040] 15 00 00 00 7C 1E F3 31  8A 47 84 69 DC 49 40 72   ....¦..1 .G.i.I@r
[050] F4 01 00 00                                        ....
```

The response is a status code acknowledging that the member was
added to the Alias. Presumably, if the call was made with a Policy
Handle that does not have suitable access rights associated with it,
then an error status code **NT_STATUS_ACCESS_DENIED** is returned
instead.

```
000018 samr_io_r_add_aliasmem
   0018 status: 00000000
[010]                          00 00 00 00             ....
```

The SID is *not* validated at the time that it is added. Contrary to
appearances, when **USRMGR.EXE** is being used to add members to
Aliases, it is not the responsibility of **SamrAddMemberToAlias** to ver-
ify that the SID is anything other than complete garbage. Only when a
User action is performed will the SID members be checked against a
Security Descriptor. The member SID has relevance only if it appears

in an Access Control Entry in the Security Descriptor; otherwise, it is ignored.

### 8.5.7: SamrDeleteAlias

**SamrDeleteAlias** removes an Alias from a Domain. There must be no members in the Domain for this to succeed. **NetLocalGroupDel** is the nearest MSDN equivalent to this function, shown here:

```
STATUS NetLocalGroupDel(
            IN  LPWSTR servername,
            IN  LPWSTR LocalGroupName
               );
```

The request contains the handle of the Alias to be deleted. The handle must have been opened with the appropriate access rights (presumably delete must be included in there somewhere) by a user with sufficient privileges to request those access rights.

```
make_samr_q_delete_dom_alias

000000 samr_io_q_delete_dom_alias
   000000 smb_io_pol_hnd alias_pol
        0000 data: 00 00 00 00 56 3b 28 cb 4c 5f d3 11 93 80 e7 74 bc bd 31 44

[020]    00 00 00 00 56 3B 28  CB 4C 5F D3 11 93 80 E7    .....V;( .L_.....
[030] 74 BC BD 31 44                                      t..1D
```

The response contains an empty Policy Handle and a status code of 0x0 if the delete succeeds.

```
000018 samr_io_r_delete_dom_alias
   000018 smb_io_pol_hnd pol
        0018 data: 00 00 00 00 00 00 00 00 00 00 00 00 00 00 00 00 00 00 00 00
   002c status: 00000000

[010]                         00 00 00 00 00 00 00        ........ ........
[020] 00 00 00 00 00 00 00 00  00 00 00 00 00 00 00 00    ........ ........
[030] 00                                                  .
```

### 8.5.8: SamrRemoveMemberFromAlias

**SamrRemoveMemberFromAlias** removes a single member from an Alias. The nearest MSDN equivalent is **NetLocalGroupDeleteMembers,** shown here. The difference between these functions is that **SamrRemoveMemberFromAlias** removes only one member at a time, whilst **NetLocalGroupDeleteMembers** removes multiple members.

```
STATUS NetLocalGroupDelMembers(
            IN  LPWSTR servername,
            IN  LPWSTR LocalGroupName,
            IN  DWORD level,
```

```
             IN  LPBYTE buf,
             OUT DWORD membercount
                        );
```

The request contains a Policy Handle associated with the Alias from which the member is to be deleted, and the Security Identifier (SID) of the member to be deleted. The Policy Handle must have been opened with an access mask that includes delete rights, and it must have been opened by a User with sufficient privileges to request those rights.

```
000000 samr_io_q_del_aliasmem
   000000 smb_io_pol_hnd alias_pol
      0000 data: 00 00 00 00 14 98 25 50 63 5d d3 11 9e cc d7 20 92 94 16 14
   000014 smb_io_dom_sid2 sid
      0014 num_auths: 00000005
      000018 smb_io_dom_sid sid
         0018 sid_rev_num: 01
         0019 num_auths  : 05
         001a id_auth[0] : 00
         001b id_auth[1] : 00
         001c id_auth[2] : 00
         001d id_auth[3] : 00
         001e id_auth[4] : 00
         001f id_auth[5] : 05
         0020 sub_auths : 00000015 31f31e7c 6984478a 724049dc 000003e9

[020] 00 00 00 00 14 98 25 50  63 5D D3 11 9E CC D7 20   ......%P c].....
[030] 92 94 16 14 05 00 00 00  01 05 00 00 00 00 00 05   ........ ........
[040] 15 00 00 00 7C 1E F3 31  8A 47 84 69 DC 49 40 72   ....¦..1 .G.i.I@r
[050] E9 03 00 00                                         ....
```

The response contains an acknowledgment status code. If the User does not have the right to delete members, or if the SID is not a member of the Alias, then a non-zero status error code is returned.

```
000018 samr_io_r_del_aliasmem
   0018 status: 00000000

[010]                    00 00 00 00                        ....
```

# 8.6: Domain User Functions

This group of functions deals specifically with Users: how to create them, how to find out what Groups a User is in, how to change a User password. This group of functions works on both a Workstation as a Domain member and a Workstation that is not a member of a Domain, as these have a Local SAM Database. Of course, they also work on a Domain Controller's SAM Database.

## 8.6.1: SamrOpenUser

The function prototype for **SamrOpenUser** probably looks like this:

```
NTSTATUS SamrOpenUser(
        IN  PHANDLE  pDomainHnd,
        IN  SEC_INFO unknown_0,
        IN  DWORD    UserRid,
        OUT PHANDLE  pUserHnd);
```

### SamrOpenUser request:

```
000000 samr_io_q_open_user
    000000 smb_io_pol_hnd domain_pol
        0000 data: 00 00 00 00 02 00 00 00 00 00 00 00 31 70 8a 36 5b 1c 00 00
        0014 unknown_0: 0002011b
        0018 user_rid : 000003e8

[020]    00 00 00 00 02 00 00  00 00 00 00 00 31 70 8A  ........ .....1p.
[030] 36 5B 1C 00 00 1B 01 02  00 E8 03 00 00              6[...... .....
```

### SamrOpenUser response:

```
000018 samr_io_r_open_user
    000018 smb_io_pol_hnd user_pol
        0018 data: 00 00 00 00 04 00 00 00 00 00 00 00 31 70 8a 36 5b 1c 00 00
        002c status: 00000000

[010]                          00 00 00 00 04 00 00  ........ ........
[020] 00 00 00 00 00 31 70 8A  36 5B 1C 00 00 00 00 00  .....1p. 6[......
[030] 00                                              .
```

## 8.6.2: SamrCreateUserInDomain

**SamrCreateUserInDomain** adds a User to a Domain. The closest MSDN equivalent is **NetUserAdd**, shown here.

```
STATUS NetUserAdd(
                IN   LPWSTR servername,
                IN   DWORD level,
                OUT  LPBYTE buf,
                OUT  LPDWORD parm_err
                );
```

The request contains a Policy Handle of the Domain to which the User should be added, plus the name of the User and the type of account (Account Control Block). The Domain Policy Handle must have been opened with the appropriate access rights by a User with the privileges to request those rights. The following example adds an ordinary User account (**ACB_NORMAL**) named **test** to the Domain.

```
samr_make_samr_q_create_user
000000 samr_io_q_create_user
    000000 smb_io_pol_hnd domain_pol
```

```
        0000 data: 00 00 00 00 55 97 25 50 63 5d d3 11 9e cc d7 20 92 94 16 14
    000014 smb_io_unihdr unihdr
        0014 uni_str_len: 0008
        0016 uni_max_len: 0008
        0018 buffer     : 00000001
    00001c smb_io_unistr2 unistr2
        001c uni_max_len: 00000004
        0020 undoc      : 00000000
        0024 uni_str_len: 00000004
        0028 buffer     : t.e.s.t.
    0030 acb_info: 0010
    0034 unknown_1: e005000b

[020] 00 00 00 00 55 97 25 50  63 5D D3 11 9E CC D7 20   ....U.%P c].....
[030] 92 94 16 14 08 00 08 00  01 00 00 00 04 00 00 00   ........ ........
[040] 00 00 00 00 04 00 00 00  74 00 65 00 73 00 74 00   ........ t.e.s.t.
[050] 10 00 00 00 0B 00 05 E0                            .......
```

The response contains a Policy Handle representing the newly created User, the Relative Identifier (RID) of that User, a status code, and some unidentifiable information. A status error code will be returned if there is a problem, for example if the User name already exists.

```
000018 samr_io_r_create_user
    000018 smb_io_pol_hnd user_pol
        0018 data: 00 00 00 00 56 97 25 50 63 5d d3 11 9e cc d7 20 92 94 16 14
    002c unknown_0: 0007035f
    0030 user_rid : 000003e9
    0034 status: 00000000

[010]                          00 00 00 00 56 97 25 50       ....V.%P
[020] 63 5D D3 11 9E CC D7 20  92 94 16 14 5F 03 07 00   c]..... ...._...
[030] E9 03 00 00 00 00 00 00                            ........
```

The use of **NetUserAdd** probably results in calls to **SamrConnect,** **SamrOpenDomain, SamrCreateUser, SamrSetUserInfo,** and then three calls to **SamrCloseHandle** on to close the User, Domain, and connection Policy Handles.

## 8.6.3: SamrQueryUserInfo

**SamrQueryUserInfo** obtains information about a User in a Domain. Its nearest MSDN equivalent is **NetUserGetInfo,** and it's a long way away.

```
STATUS NetUserGetInfo(
                IN    LPWSTR servername,
                IN    LPWSTR username,
                IN    DWORD level,
                OUT   LPBYTE *bufptr
                   );
```

The **NetUserGetInfo** MSDN function can be used to return tens of different info levels. The largest documented such info level is the **USER_INFO_3** structure, shown here. It does not match up with anything like the info levels supported by **SamrQueryUserInfo,** but is about the closest available.

```
typedef struct _USER_INFO_3 {
    LPWSTR    usri3_name;
    LPWSTR    usri3_password;
    DWORD     usri3_password_age;
    DWORD     usri3_priv;
    LPWSTR    usri3_home_dir;
    LPWSTR    usri3_comment;
    DWORD     usri3_flags;
    LPWSTR    usri3_script_path;
    DWORD     usri3_auth_flags;
    LPWSTR    usri3_full_name;
    LPWSTR    usri3_usr_comment;
    LPWSTR    usri3_parms;
    LPWSTR    usri3_workstations;
    DWORD     usri3_last_logon;
    DWORD     usri3_last_logoff;
    DWORD     usri3_acct_expires;
    DWORD     usri3_max_storage;
    DWORD     usri3_units_per_week;
    PBYTE     usri3_logon_hours;
    DWORD     usri3_bad_pw_count;
    DWORD     usri3_num_logons;
    LPWSTR    usri3_logon_server;
    DWORD     usri3_country_code;
    DWORD     usri3_code_page;
    DWORD     usri3_user_id;
    DWORD     usri3_primary_group_id;
    LPWSTR    usri3_profile;
    LPWSTR    usri3_home_dir_drive;
    DWORD     usri3_password_expired;
}USER_INFO_3, *PUSER_INFO_3, *LPUSER_INFO_3;
```

The request contains a Policy Handle representing the User for which details are being requested, and an info level.

```
000000 samr_io_q_query_userinfo
    000000 smb_io_pol_hnd pol
        0000 data: 00 00 00 00 04 00 00 00 00 00 00 00 31 70 8a 36 5b 1c 00 00
    0014 switch_value: 0015

[020]    00 00 00 00 04 00 00   00 00 00 00 00 31 70 8A   ........ .....1p.
[030] 36 5B 1C 00 00 15 00 00   00                        6[...... .
```

The response shown here was chosen because it is used by **USR-MGR.EXE** when a User profile is selected. The information in it is

also fairly close to the **USER_INFO_3** structure. The interpretation of
some of the following data has been removed to improve readability.

```
000018 samr_io_r_query_userinfo
    0018 ptr          : 00000001
    001c switch_value: 0015
    000020 lsa_io_user_info
        000020 smb_io_time logon_time
        000028 smb_io_time logoff_time
        000030 smb_io_time kickoff_time
        000038 smb_io_time pass_last_set_time
        000040 smb_io_time pass_can_change_time
        000048 smb_io_time pass_must_change_time
        000050 smb_io_unihdr hdr_user_name
        000058 smb_io_unihdr hdr_full_name
        000060 smb_io_unihdr hdr_home_dir
        000068 smb_io_unihdr hdr_dir_drive
        000070 smb_io_unihdr hdr_logon_script
        000078 smb_io_unihdr hdr_profile_path
        000080 smb_io_unihdr hdr_acct_desc
        000088 smb_io_unihdr hdr_workstations
        000090 smb_io_unihdr hdr_unknown_str
        000098 smb_io_unihdr hdr_munged_dial
        00a0 lm_pwd        : 00 00 00 00 00 00 00 00 00 00 00 00 00 00 00 00
        00b0 nt_pwd        : 00 00 00 00 00 00 00 00 00 00 00 00 00 00 00 00
        00c0 user_rid      : 000003e8
        00c4 group_rid     : 000003e9
        00c8 acb_info      : 0010
        00cc unknown_3     : 00ffffff
        00d0 logon_divs    : 00a8
        00d4 ptr_logon_hrs : 00000001
        00d8 unknown_5     : 00020000
        00dc padding1      : 00 00 00 00 00 00 00 00
        0000e4 smb_io_unistr2 uni_user_name
            00f0 buffer      : r.o.o.t.
        0000f8 smb_io_unistr2 uni_full_name
            0104 buffer      :
        000104 smb_io_unistr2 uni_home_dir
            0110 buffer      : \.\.k.n.i.g.h.t.\.r.o.o.t.
        00012a smb_io_unistr2 uni_dir_drive
            0138 buffer      :
        000138 smb_io_unistr2 uni_logon_script
            0144 buffer      :
        000144 smb_io_unistr2 uni_profile_path
            0150 buffer      : \.\.k.n.i.g.h.t.\.r.o.o.t.\.p.r.o.f.i.l.e.
        00017a smb_io_unistr2 uni_acct_desc
            0188 buffer      :
        000188 smb_io_unistr2 uni_workstations
            0194 buffer      :
        000194 smb_io_unistr2 uni_unknown_str
            01a0 buffer      :
        0001a0 smb_io_unistr2 uni_munged_dial
            01ac buffer      :
```

```
          01ac unknown_6      : 000004ec
          01b0 padding4       : 00000000
          0001b4 sam_io_logon_hrs logon_hrs
              01b4 len  : 00000015
              01b8 hours: ffffffffffffffffffffffffffffffffffffffffff
      01d0 status: 00000000


[010]                          01 00 00 00 15 00 00   ........ ........
[020] 00 80 E9 A5 D4 DE B1 9D  01 80 E9 A5 D4 DE B1 9D   ........ ........
[030] 01 80 E9 A5 D4 DE B1 9D  01 80 E9 A5 D4 DE B1 9D   ........ ........
[040] 01 80 E9 A5 D4 DE B1 9D  01 80 E9 A5 D4 DE B1 9D   ........ ........
[050] 01 08 00 08 00 01 00 00  00 00 00 00 00 01 00 00   ........ ........
[060] 00 1A 00 1A 00 01 00 00  00 00 00 00 00 01 00 00   ........ ........
[070] 00 00 00 00 00 01 00 00  00 2A 00 2A 00 01 00 00   ........ .*.*....
[080] 00 00 00 00 00 01 00 00  00 00 00 00 00 01 00 00   ........ ........
[090] 00 00 00 00 00 01 00 00  00 00 00 00 00 01 00 00   ........ ........
[0A0] 00 00 00 00 00 00 00 00  00 00 00 00 00 00 00 00   ........ ........
[0B0] 00 00 00 00 00 00 00 00  00 00 00 00 00 00 00 00   ........ ........
[0C0] 00 E8 03 00 00 E9 03 00  00 10 00 00 00 FF FF FF   ........ ........
[0D0] 00 A8 00 00 00 01 00 00  00 00 00 02 00 00 00 00   ........ ........
[0E0] 00 00 00 00 00 04 00 00  00 00 00 00 00 04 00 00   ........ ........
[0F0] 00 72 00 6F 00 6F 00 74  00 00 00 00 00 00 00 00   .r.o.o.t ........
[100] 00 00 00 00 00 0D 00 00  00 00 00 00 00 0D 00 00   ........ ........
[110] 00 5C 00 5C 00 6B 00 6E  00 69 00 67 00 68 00 74   .\.\.k.n .i.g.h.t
[120] 00 5C 00 72 00 6F 00 6F  00 74 00 00 00 00 00 00   .\.r.o.o .t......
[130] 00 00 00 00 00 00 00 00  00 00 00 00 00 00 00 00   ........ ........
[140] 00 00 00 00 00 15 00 00  00 00 00 00 00 15 00 00   ........ ........
[150] 00 5C 00 5C 00 6B 00 6E  00 69 00 67 00 68 00 74   .\.\.k.n .i.g.h.t
[160] 00 5C 00 72 00 6F 00 6F  00 74 00 5C 00 70 00 72   .\.r.o.o .t.\.p.r
[170] 00 6F 00 66 00 69 00 6C  00 65 00 00 00 00 00 00   .o.f.i.l .e......
[180] 00 00 00 00 00 00 00 00  00 00 00 00 00 00 00 00   ........ ........
[190] 00 00 00 00 00 00 00 00  00 00 00 00 00 00 00 00   ........ ........
[1A0] 00 00 00 00 00 00 00 00  00 00 00 00 00 EC 04 00   ........ ........
[1B0] 00 00 00 00 00 15 00 00  00 FF FF FF FF FF FF FF   ........ ........
[1C0] FF FF FF FF FF FF FF FF  FF FF FF FF FF FF 00 00   ........ ........
[1D0] 00 00 00 00 00                                     .....
```

## 8.6.4: SamrQueryUserGroups

**SamrQueryUserGroups** obtains a list of Domain Groups to which a user belongs. Its closest MSDN equivalent is **NetUserGetGroups**, shown here.

```
STATUS NetUserGetGroups(
          IN    LPWSTR servername,
          IN    LPWSTR username,
          IN    DWORD level,
          OUT   LPBYTE *bufptr,
          IN    DWORD prefmaxlen,
          OUT   LPDWORD entriesread,
          OUT   LPDWORD totalentries
              );
```

One of the info levels supported by **NetUserGetGroups** is GROUP_USERS_INFO_1, shown here. This info level matches up with the information returned by **SamrQueryUserGroups**.

```
typedef struct _GROUP_USERS_INFO_1 {
    LPWSTR  grui1_name;
    DWORD   grui1_attributes;
} GROUP_USERS_INFO_1, *PGROUP_USERS_INFO_1, *LPGROUP_USERS_INFO_1;
```

The request contains a Policy Handle representing the User for which a list of Domain Groups is being requested.

```
000000 samr_io_q_query_usergroups
    000000 smb_io_pol_hnd pol
        0000 data: 00 00 00 00 6f 3b 28 cb 4c 5f d3 11 93 80 e7 74 bc bd 31 44

[020]    00 00 00 00 6F 3B 28  CB 4C 5F D3 11 93 80 E7   .....o;( .L_.....
[030] 74 BC BD 31 44                                    t..1D
```

The response contains an array of **GROUP_USERS_INFO_1** structures, each of which contains the Relative Identifier (RID) of a Group to which the User belongs.

```
000018 samr_io_r_query_usergroups
    0018 ptr_0       : 00154cb8
    001c num_entries : 00000002
    0020 ptr_1       : 0019afb8
    0024 num_entries2: 00000002
    000028 smb_io_gid
        0028 g_rid: 00000201
        002c attr : 00000007
    000030 smb_io_gid
        0030 g_rid: 0000066b
        0034 attr : 00000007
    0038 status: 00000000

[010]                         B8 4C 15 00 02 00 00   .$...... ..L.....
[020] 00 B8 AF 19 00 02 00 00  00 01 02 00 00 07 00 00   ........ ........
[030] 00 6B 06 00 00 07 00 00  00 00 00 00 00 00        .k...... .....
```

## 8.6.5: SamrQueryUserAliases

**SamrQueryUserAliases** obtains a list of Domain Aliases that a User is in. Its closest MSDN equivalent is **NetUserGetLocalGroups**, shown here.

```
STATUS NetUserGetLocalGroups(
                IN  LPWSTR servername,
                IN  LPWSTR username,
                IN  DWORD level,
                IN  DWORD flags,
                OUT LPBYTE *bufptr,
                IN  DWORD prefmaxlen,
```

```
        OUT LPDWORD entriesread,
        OUT LPDWORD totalentries
              );
```

The info level supported by **NetUserGetLocalGroups** is **LOCAL-GROUP_USERS_INFO_0**, shown here. This info level does not match up with the information returned by **SamrQueryUserAliases**, which returns Relative Identifiers (RIDs). A follow-up call to **SamrLookupRids** is therefore required to turn names into RIDs.

```
typedef struct _LOCALGROUP_USERS_INFO_0 {
    LPWSTR  lgrui0_name;
} LOCALGROUP_USERS_INFO_0, *PLOCALGROUP_USERS_INFO_0,
  *LPLOCALGROUP_USERS_INFO_0;
```

The request contains a Policy Handle representing the User for which a list of Domain Aliases is being requested.

```
000000 samr_io_q_query_useraliases
    000000 smb_io_pol_hnd pol
        0000 data: 00 00 00 00 02 00 00 00 00 00 00 00 31 70 8a 36 5b 1c 00 00
    0014 num_sids1: 00000001
    0018 ptr      : 00000001
    001c num_sids2: 00000001
    0020 ptr[00]: 00000001
    000024 smb_io_dom_sid2 sid[00]
        0024 num_auths: 00000005
        000028 smb_io_dom_sid sid
            0028 sid_rev_num: 01
            0029 num_auths  : 05
            002a id_auths   : 00 00 00 00 00 05
            0030 sub_auths : 00000015 466e2442 08de9320 b8c519a4 000003e8

[020]    00 00 00 00 02 00 00  00 00 00 00 00 31 70 8A  ........ ......1p.
[030] 36 5B 1C 00 00 01 00 00  00 01 00 00 00 01 00 00  6[...... ........
[040] 00 01 00 00 00 05 00 00  00 01 05 00 00 00 00 00  ........ ........
[050] 05 15 00 00 00 42 24 6E ˉ46 20 93 DE 08 A4 19 C5  .....B$n F ......
[060] B8 E8 03 00 00                                    .....
```

The response contains an array of Local Group RIDs, including each to which the User belongs.

```
000018 samr_io_r_query_useraliases
    0018 num_entries: 00000001
    001c ptr        : 00000001
    0020 num_entries2: 00000001
    0024 rid[00]: 0000057e
    0028 status: 00000000

[010]                          00 01 00 00 00 01 00 00  ........ ........
[020] 00 01 00 00 00 7E 05 00  00 00 00 00 00          .....~.. .....
```

### 8.6.6: SamrGetDomainPasswordInformation

**SamrGetDomainPasswordInformation** is associated with changing User passwords. It is likely to be a request for information regarding the format of passwords in the SAM Database.

The request contains a pointer to a UNICODE string with the name of the Workstation from which the call is being made:

```
make_samr_q_unknown_38
000000 samr_io_q_unknown_38
    0000 ptr: 00000001
    000004 smb_io_unihdr
        0004 uni_str_len: 0010
        0006 uni_max_len: 0010
        0008 buffer      : 00000001
    00000c smb_io_unistr2
        000c uni_max_len: 00000008
        0010 undoc        : 00000000
        0014 uni_str_len: 00000008
        0018 buffer      : \.\.K.N.I.G.H.T.

[000] 01 00 00 00 10 00 10 00   01 00 00 00 08 00 00 00   ........ ........
[010] 00 00 00 00 08 00 00 00   5C 00 5C 00 4B 00 4E 00   ........ \.\.K.N.
[020] 49 00 47 00 48 00 54 00                             I.G.H.T.
```

The response contains three unknown parameters and a status code. The three unknown parameters are considered to be 16 bits because the intermediate bytes in between them in the data stream change at random.

```
000018 samr_io_r_unknown_38
    0018 unk_0 : 0000
    001c unk_1 : 0000
    0020 unk_2 : 0000
    0024 status: 00000000

[000] 00 00 00 00 00 00 00 00   00 00 00 00 00 00 00 00   ........ ........
```

The purpose of this function is unknown. Its necessity is unknown. It's just that it is always immediately followed up with a **SamrChangePasswordUser** call. Both these calls are *often* made over an encrypted connection. The reason that they are sometimes *not* made over an encrypted connection is that the setup of the encrypted session can often fail.

### 8.6.7: SamrChangePasswordUser

**SamrChangePasswordUser** is used to change a User password. It is preceded by a call to **SamrGetDomainPasswordInformation**, which can only be presumed to affect the usage of **SamrChangePasswordUser**

in some way. However, no usage other than that shown here has yet
been observed.

The request contains the name of the Server on which the User
account is held, the User name, two encrypted password blocks, and
two password verifiers. The encrypted password blocks are each 516
bytes in length and so the request shown here has been shortened to
improve readability.

```
000000 samr_io_q_chgpasswd_user
    0000 ptr_0: 00000001
    000004 smb_io_unihdr
        0004 uni_str_len: 0010
        0006 uni_max_len: 0010
        0008 buffer     : 00000001
    00000c smb_io_unistr2
        000c uni_max_len: 00000008
        0010 undoc       : 00000000
        0014 uni_str_len: 00000008
        0018 buffer     : \.\.K.N.I.G.H.T.
    000028 smb_io_unihdr
        0028 uni_str_len: 0008
        002a uni_max_len: 0008
        002c buffer     : 00000001
    000030 smb_io_unistr2
        0030 uni_max_len: 00000004
        0034 undoc       : 00000000
        0038 uni_str_len: 00000004
        003c buffer     : r.o.o.t.
    000044 samr_io_enc_passwd nt_newpass
        0044 ptr: 00000001
        0048 pwd: df 44 e2 a4 eb c2 9d 69 ...
    00024c samr_io_enc_hash nt_oldhash
        024c ptr : 00000001
        0250 hash: 58 6f e7 0c a7 aa 1b 2a 92 0f 27 16 92 44 76 46
    0260 unknown: 00000001
    000264 samr_io_enc_passwd lm_newpass
        0264 ptr: 00000001
        0268 pwd: 26 86 0d 15 5f 44 58 3a ...
    00046c samr_io_enc_hash lm_oldhash
        046c ptr : 00000001
        0470 hash: b8 ca c2 a5 ee 65 36 f2 07 b5 2e ce d8 6a 80 fb


[000] 01 00 00 00 10 00 10 00  01 00 00 00 08 00 00 00   ........ ........
[010] 00 00 00 00 08 00 00 00  5C 00 5C 00 4B 00 4E 00   ........ \.\.K.N.
[020] 49 00 47 00 48 00 54 00  08 00 08 00 01 00 00 00   I.G.H.T. ........
[030] 04 00 00 00 00 00 00 00  04 00 00 00 72 00 6F 00   ........ ....r.o.
[040] 6F 00 74 00 01 00 00 00  DF 44 E2 A4 EB C2 9D 69   o.t..... .D.....i
...
...
[240]                          ... 01 00 00 00              ....
[250] 58 6F E7 0C A7 AA 1B 2A  92 0F 27 16 92 44 76 46   Xo.....* ..'..DvF
[260] 01 00 00 00 01 00 00 00  26 86 0D 15 5F 44 58 3A   ........ &..._DX:
```

```
...
...
[460]                                    ... 01 00 00 00              ....
[470] B8 CA C2 A5 EE 65 36 F2  07 B5 2E CE D8 6A 80 FB  .....e6. .....j..
```

The response contains a status code indicating whether the password change succeeded or not.

```
000018 samr_io_r_chgpasswd_user
   0018 status: 00000000
[000] 00 00 00 00                                     ....
```

# 8.7: samr Security Issues

There are a few security flaws in the **samr pipe** implementation, all associated with anonymous **IPC$** access:

- Polling for valid RIDs in a SAM database
- Resolution of Relative Identifiers (RIDs) to names and vice-versa
- Enumeration of all entries in the SAM database

Only the last of these issues has been addressed: the **SamrQueryDisplayInfo** call that provides a method to enumerate all entries in the SAM database. Apparently, Windows NT 5.0 in backward-compatibility mode should address the rest of these problems.

## 8.7.1: Polling for Valid RIDs

It is possible to deduce that a RID is valid by making individual **SamrOpenUser** calls with every single potential RID in a Domain (starting at 0x3fe and potentially going up to 0xffffffff). It is possible to obtain the user's profile and get full information about the User by following this up with a **SamrQueryUserInformation** call. This is quite a slow process, and it could be stopped by disallowing anonymous **IPC$** access.

## 8.7.2: RID-to-Name Conversion

An array of RIDs can be specified in a **SamrLookupRids** call. All that needs to be done is to enumerate through all RIDs, or specifically the well-known RIDs (for example the Administrator's RID), and the Server will respond with the User names or Group names, if the RID is valid in the Domain. After a RID is known to be valid then a **SamrQueryUserInfo**, **SamrQueryGroupInfo**, or **SamrQueryAliasInfo** call can be made. The use of **SamrLookupRids** calls is much faster than using **SamrOpenUser** calls, and it could be stopped by disallowing anonymous **IPC$** access.

### 8.7.3: Enumeration of SAM Database

With the **SamrQueryDisplayInfo** call a complete list of User names and their RIDs can be obtained. This issue has been resolved by Microsoft: it has been described as the "Red Button bug." Their solution was to require a DWORD Registry Value "RestrictAnonymous" with a value of 0x1 to be placed in HKLM\System\CurrentControlSet\Control\Lsa. It is slightly bizarre: this restriction does not nearly go far enough, what with all other methods available to obtain SAM database information (including **LsaLookupSids** and so forth).

### Solution

The solution to these security problems is very simple: Deny all anonymous **IPC$** access from the **samr pipe**. If you run **USRMGR.EXE** you may be forgiven for thinking that the SAM Database is secure just because **USRMGR.EXE** cannot give you any useful information except when it is run by an Administrator, as a member of the Account Operators Local Group or as a member of the Domain Admins Domain Group. The restriction is *mostly* due to validation checks on your access rights carried out by **USRMGR.EXE** itself. All that malicious users need to do is either use standard MSDN API calls such as **NetQueryDisplayInfo** or to write their own DCE/RPC calls, and they can obtain information about a Domain.

Windows NT 5.0 apparently will be introducing a new level to RestrictAnonymous, with a value of 0x2 for this Registry Value. Apparently it will restrict the **lsarpc pipe** as well as the **samr pipe**, hopefully to the extent that is required. If this affects the operation of any programs (whether part of Microsoft's Administrative suite or a third party) then those programs are going to have to be updated. This is a small price to pay for proper security because those programs should never have been capable of obtaining the information that they could, without the proper access rights.

## 8.8: Summary

The **samr pipe** provides an impressive, well-designed mechanism by which User accounts can be remotely managed. It is the author's opinion that this API could be submitted as an Internet Draft RFC. The only criticisms are with the security implications of Windows NT's implementation of this API, not with the design of the API itself. Fortunately, Microsoft is aware of the issues concerned and is addressing them, most notably by deprecating this API with the introduction of NT 5.0 Domains.

# 9

# \PIPE\EVENTLOG: NT Event Log Service

This chapter covers Windows NT's remote Event Log service. The Windows NT event log tool **EVENTVWR.EXE** can be used to view system, security, and application events, and to clear event logs. The Event Log is used by the Windows NT operating system and some applications to log informational warnings, debug information, and critical errors.

The **EVENTLOG** functions are not decoded by Microsoft Network Monitor (**NETMON.EXE**). However, the MSDN file **winnt.h** contains function prototypes for all of them. It is therefore a relatively simple task to match MSDN functions to network data obtained from running **EVENTVWR.EXE**, which is done in this chapter for a small subset of the **EVENTLOG API**.

Samba's rpcclient tool provides an implementation of an event log viewer command, sufficient to read and display events. This was done as an academic exercise, which happens to benefit Unix-oriented Windows NT Administrators. Future versions of Samba's rpcclient tool may include commands to clear an event log, set the maximum log size, and so forth. In addition, Samba's own log files could potentially be presented as a Windows NT Event Log, such that **EVENTVWR.EXE** and rpcclient could be used to manage Samba log files.

## 9.1: EVENTLOG Calls

This section describes some of the **\PIPE\EVENTLOG** functions in detail. As Microsoft Network Monitor does not decode this service, Samba debug output is used in this chapter to illustrate each call. The MSDN function prototypes are shown in each section as well to make it easier for the reader to see how the network traffic matches with the function.

The functions described in this chapter are listed here.

- OpenEventLog
- GetNumberOfEventLogRecords
- ReadEventLog
- CloseEventLog

Typically, to view a list of events, **OpenEventLog** must be called with the name of the log to be viewed. This is followed by a call to **GetNumberOfEventLogRecords** to find out how many events there are, and then repeated calls to ReadEventLog. Finally, **CloseEventLog** is called with the Policy Handle returned from the **OpenEventLog** call, freeing up any resources that the Server needed to use.

This pipe cannot be accessed as an anonymous user. Additionally, certain actions, such as clearing an event log, require Administrator-level privileges. Viewing the contents of an event log appears to only require guest user rights or above.

## 9.1.1: OpenEventLog

**OpenEventLog** is the first function call that must be made. The MSDN function prototype is shown here:

```
HANDLE
OpenEventLog (
    LPCWSTR lpUNCServerName,
    LPCWSTR lpSourceName
    );
```

The request contains the name of the event log to be opened, plus a few other parameters, one of which is an unknown string. In the following example, the event log being opened is the system log.

```
000000 eventlog_io_q_open
    0000 ptr0: 00000001
    0004 unk0: 005c
    0006 unk1: 0001
    000008 smb_io_unihdr hdr_source
        0008 uni_str_len: 000c
        000a uni_max_len: 000c
        000c buffer     : 00000001
    000010 smb_io_unistr2 uni_source
        0010 uni_max_len: 00000006
        0014 undoc      : 00000000
        0018 uni_str_len: 00000006
        001c buffer     : s.y.s.t.e.m.
```

```
000028 smb_io_unihdr hdr_unk
     0028 uni_str_len: 0000
     002a uni_max_len: 0000
     002c buffer     : 00000000
000030 smb_io_unistr2 - NULL uni_unk
0030 unk6: 00000001
0034 unk7: 00000001
```

The response contains a handle to the event log requested. A status code is also returned, indicating whether the request succeeded or whether the user had the rights to open the event log requested, as indicated by returning an NT status code of **NT_STATUS_PRIVI-LEGE_NOT_HELD**.

```
000018 eventlog_io_r_open
   000018 smb_io_pol_hnd
       0018 data: 00 00 00 00 15 88 4c c5 9b 51 d3 11 b0 d1 00 00 00 00 00 00
   002c status: 00000000
```

The handle must be freed with a call to **CloseEventLog** after it is no longer needed. Failure to do this may result in resource leaks on some servers.

The data over-the-wire for this function does not match up well with the MSDN prototype: there are a couple of unidentified and unidentifiable parameters. It would therefore appear that the Event Log MSDN API has been massaged in some way.

## 9.1.2: GetNumberOfEventLogRecords

**GetNumberOfEventLogRecords** finds out how many records are in an event log. The MSDN function prototype is shown here:

```
BOOL
GetNumberOfEventLogRecords (
    HANDLE hEventLog,
    PDWORD NumberOfRecords
    );
```

An attempt to re-create an Interface Definition Language (IDL) definition for this function is shown here, which is very similar to the auto-generated MSDN function prototype, above. The **[in]** and **[in out]** parameters are sent over-the-wire in the request, and the **[in out]** and **[out]** parameters are sent over-the-wire in the response.

```
NTSTATUS GetNumberOfEventLogRecords(
            [in] HANDLE pHandle,
            [out] PDWORD pNumberOfRecords
              );
```

The request contains all **[in]** and **[in out]** parameters, in this case the handle representing the event log, which was obtained from an

**OpenEventLog** call:

```
000000 eventlog_io_q_numofeventlogrec
    000000 smb_io_pol_hnd
        0000 data: 00 00 00 00 15 88 4c c5 9b 51 d3 11 b0 d1 00 00 00 00 00 00
```

The response contains all **[in out]** and **[out]** parameters, in this case the number of records in the log and a status code indicating whether the request succeeded or not:

```
000018 eventlog_io_r_numofeventlogrec
    0018 number: 00000612
    001c status: 00000000
```

## 9.1.3: ReadEventLog

**ReadEventLog** obtains individual entries in the event log. The MSDN function prototype is shown here:

```
BOOL
ReadEventLog (
        HANDLE      hEventLog,
        DWORD       dwReadFlags,
        DWORD       dwRecordOffset,
        LPVOID      lpBuffer,
        DWORD       nNumberOfBytesToRead,
        DWORD       *pnBytesRead,
        DWORD       *pnMinNumberOfBytesNeeded
        );
```

The request contains a handle to the event log to be read; a flags field, which is used to indicate the order in which the records are to be scanned; an index of the record required; and a maximum buffer size for the record to be returned in:

```
000000 eventlog_io_q_readeventlog
    000000 smb_io_pol_hnd
        0000 data: 00 00 00 00 15 88 4c c5 9b 51 d3 11 b0 d1 00 00 00 00 00 00
    0014 flags: 00000009
    0018 offset: 00000000
    001c number_of_bytes: 00000000
```

This response contains the size of the buffer, as we sent the previous request with a buffer size of zero. The error message returned is a Windows NT status code **NT_STATUS_BUFFER_TOO_SMALL**:

```
000018 eventlog_io_r_readeventlog
    0018 number_of_bytes: 00000000
    001c sent_size: 00000000
    0020 real_size: 00000088
    0024 status: c0000023
```

The request is then sent a second time, this time with the advised size
of the buffer from the previous call:

```
000000 eventlog_io_q_readeventlog
    000000 smb_io_pol_hnd
        0000 data: 00 00 00 00 15 88 4c c5 9b 51 d3 11 b0 d1 00 00 00 00 00 00
    0014 flags: 00000009
    0018 offset: 00000000
    001c number_of_bytes: 00000088
```

The **EVENTLOGRECORD** structure contained this time in the
response is shown here:

```
typedef struct _EVENTLOGRECORD {
    DWORD   Length;         // Length of full record
    DWORD   Reserved;       // Used by the service
    DWORD   RecordNumber;   // Absolute record number
    DWORD   TimeGenerated;  // Seconds since 1-1-1970
    DWORD   TimeWritten;    // Seconds since 1-1-1970
    DWORD   EventID;
    WORD    EventType;
    WORD    NumStrings;
    WORD    EventCategory;
    WORD    ReservedFlags;  // For use with paired events (auditing)
    DWORD   ClosingRecordNumber; // For use with paired events (auditing)
    DWORD   StringOffset;   // Offset from beginning of record
    DWORD   UserSidLength;
    DWORD   UserSidOffset;
    DWORD   DataLength;
    DWORD   DataOffset;     // Offset from beginning of record
    //
    // Then follow:
    //
    // WCHAR SourceName[]
    // WCHAR Computername[]
    // SID   UserSid
    // WCHAR Strings[]
    // BYTE  Data[]
    // CHAR  Pad[]
    // DWORD Length;
    //
} EVENTLOGRECORD, *PEVENTLOGRECORD;
```

The response also contains the size of the buffer in various places,
which is an artifact of the IDL definition for this function. The status
code of 0x0 indicates that the buffer size was sufficient:

```
000018 eventlog_io_r_readeventlog
    0018 number_of_bytes: 00000088
    00001c eventlog_io_eventlog
        001c size: 00000088
        0020 reserved: 654c664c
        0024 recordnumber: 00000612
        0028 creationtime: 37b4471d
```

```
002c writetime: 37b4471d
0030 eventnumber: 40001f4f
0034 eventtype: 0004
0036 num_of_strings: 0001
0038 category: 0000
003a reserved_flag: 0000
003c closingrecord: 00000000
0040 stringoffset: 00000056
0044 sid_length: 00000000
0048 sid_offset: 00000056
004c data_length: 00000000
0050 data_offset: 00000080
000054 smb_io_unistr B.R.O.W.S.E.R.
000064 smb_io_unistr R.E.G.E. N.T.
000072 smb_io_unistr \.D.e.v.i.c.e.\.N.e.t.B.T._.E.1.9.0.x.1.
009c size2: 00000000
00a0 sent_size: 00000088
00a4 real_size: 00000088
00a8 status: 00000000
```

This function call can be repeated several thousand times to read all events. This mechanism is far less efficient than it could be. The designers of this function chose to implement a mechanism that effectively doubles the round-trip time over a network required to read a complete event log. Proper IDL design might possibly have avoided this redundant network traffic.

### 9.1.4: CloseEventLog

CloseEventLog is used to free a handle. The MSDN function proto-type is shown here:

```
BOOL
CloseEventLog (
    HANDLE hEventLog
    );
```

The request contains the handle to be freed:

```
000000 eventlog_io_q_close
000000 smb_io_pol_hnd
  0000 data: 00 00 00 00 0f 88 4c c5 9b 51 d3 11 b0 d1 00 00 00 00 00 00
```

The response usually contains an empty handle and a status code of 0x0, indicating that the handle and its associated resources have been successfully freed. If the handle was already freed then the Win32 error code (not an NT status code) **ERROR_INVALID_HANDLE** is returned.

```
000018 eventlog_io_r_close
000018 smb_io_pol_hnd
  0018 data: 00 00 00 00 00 00 00 00 00 00 00 00 00 00 00 00 00 00 00 00
002c status: 00000000
```

## 9.2: Summary

The Event Log API presents a structured mechanism for application writers to report errors. Additionally, programmers can take advantage of the structured format to write programs that generate reports from these event logs. The Event Log API is therefore very useful and practical. Using this chapter as a guide, the form of most of the \PIPE\EVENTLOG functions can be deduced from network traces and/or the MSDN prototypes. More third-party developers now have a means to take advantage of this API, both server-side and client-side.

# Samba
# Source Code

This Appendix contains a copy of the GNU Public License (GPL) and some Samba Source Code that is released under that license. Please read the license carefully before proceeding. If you do not agree to or do not understand the terms of the GPL then please do not read or use any of the Source Code in this chapter.

If you are working for a commercial organisation, it is recommended that you consult your legal department with respect to the GPL, as they are likely to advise that you should tear out these pages and burn them. Or words to that effect.

Samba Source Code is available from http://samba.org/, ftp://samba.org/ and mirror sites across the world, such as ftp://sunsite.unc.edu/ and ftp://sunsite.doc.ic.ac.uk/. You can also obtain Samba Source using Concurrent Version System (cvs), by following the instructions at http://samba.org/cvs.html.

## A.1: GNU Public License

This section contains a printed copy of the GNU Public License. It should also be contained in the Samba Source archives.

```
                GNU GENERAL PUBLIC LICENSE
                 Version 2, June 1991

Copyright (C) 1989, 1991 Free Software Foundation, Inc.
            675 Mass Ave, Cambridge, MA 02139, USA
Everyone is permitted to copy and distribute verbatim copies
of this license document, but changing it is not allowed.


                     Preamble

  The licenses for most software are designed to take away your
freedom to share and change it.  By contrast, the GNU General Public
```

License is intended to guarantee your freedom to share and change free
Software—to make sure the software is free for all its users. This
General Public License applies to most of the Free Software
Foundation's software and to any other program whose authors commit to
using it. (Some other Free Software Foundation software is covered by
the GNU Library General Public License instead.) You can apply it to
your programs, too.

When we speak of free software, we are referring to freedom, not
price. Our General Public Licenses are designed to make sure that you
have the freedom to distribute copies of free software (and charge for
this service if you wish), that you receive source code or can get it
if you want it, that you can change the software or use pieces of it
in new free programs; and that you know you can do these things.

To protect your rights, we need to make restrictions that forbid
anyone to deny you these rights or to ask you to surrender the rights.
These restrictions translate to certain responsibilities for you if you
distribute copies of the software, or if you modify it.

For example, if you distribute copies of such a program, whether
gratis or for a fee, you must give the recipients all the rights that
you have. You must make sure that they, too, receive or can get the
source code. And you must show them these terms so they know their
rights.

We protect your rights with two steps: (1) copyright the software, and
(2) offer you this license which gives you legal permission to copy,
distribute and/or modify the software.

Also, for each author's protection and ours, we want to make certain
that everyone understands that there is no warranty for this free
software. If the software is modified by someone else and passed on, we
want its recipients to know that what they have is not the original, so
that any problems introduced by others will not reflect on the original
authors' reputations.

Finally, any free program is threatened constantly by software
patents. We wish to avoid the danger that redistributors of a free
program will individually obtain patent licenses, in effect making the
program proprietary. To prevent this, we have made it clear that any
patent must be licensed for everyone's free use or not licensed at all.

The precise terms and conditions for copying, distribution and
modification follow.

—
GNU GENERAL PUBLIC LICENSE
TERMS AND CONDITIONS FOR COPYING, DISTRIBUTION AND MODIFICATION

0. This License applies to any program or other work which contains
a notice placed by the copyright holder saying it may be distributed
under the terms of this General Public License. The "Program", below,
refers to any such program or work, and a "work based on the Program"

means either the Program or any derivative work under copyright law:
that is to say, a work containing the Program or a portion of it,
either verbatim or with modifications and/or translated into another
language. (Hereinafter, translation is included without limitation in
the term "modification".)  Each licensee is addressed as "you".

Activities other than copying, distribution and modification are not
covered by this License; they are outside its scope.  The act of
running the Program is not restricted, and the output from the Program
is covered only if its contents constitute a work based on the
Program (independent of having been made by running the Program).
Whether that is true depends on what the Program does.

1. You may copy and distribute verbatim copies of the Program's
source code as you receive it, in any medium, provided that you
conspicuously and appropriately publish on each copy an appropriate
copyright notice and disclaimer of warranty; keep intact all the
notices that refer to this License and to the absence of any warranty;
and give any other recipients of the Program a copy of this License
along with the Program.

You may charge a fee for the physical act of transferring a copy, and
you may at your option offer warranty protection in exchange for a fee.

2. You may modify your copy or copies of the Program or any portion
of it, thus forming a work based on the Program, and copy and
distribute such modifications or work under the terms of Section 1
above, provided that you also meet all of these conditions:

a) You must cause the modified files to carry prominent notices
stating that you changed the files and the date of any change.

b) You must cause any work that you distribute or publish, that in
whole or in part contains or is derived from the Program or any
part thereof, to be licensed as a whole at no charge to all third
parties under the terms of this License.

c) If the modified program normally reads commands interactively
when run, you must cause it, when started running for such
interactive use in the most ordinary way, to print or display an
announcement including an appropriate copyright notice and a
notice that there is no warranty (or else, saying that you provide
a warranty) and that users may redistribute the program under
these conditions, and telling the user how to view a copy of this
License.  (Exception: if the Program itself is interactive but
does not normally print such an announcement, your work based on
the Program is not required to print an announcement.)

These requirements apply to the modified work as a whole.  If
identifiable sections of that work are not derived from the Program,
and can be reasonably considered independent and separate works in
themselves, then this License, and its terms, do not apply to those
sections when you distribute them as separate works.  But when you

distribute the same sections as part of a whole which is a work based
on the Program, the distribution of the whole must be on the terms of
this License, whose permissions for other licensees extend to the
entire whole, and thus to each and every part regardless of who wrote it.

Thus, it is not the intent of this section to claim rights or contest
your rights to work written entirely by you; rather, the intent is to
exercise the right to control the distribution of derivative or
collective works based on the Program.

In addition, mere aggregation of another work not based on the Program
with the Program (or with a work based on the Program) on a volume of
a storage or distribution medium does not bring the other work under
the scope of this License.

   3. You may copy and distribute the Program (or a work based on it,
under Section 2) in object code or executable form under the terms of
Sections 1 and 2 above provided that you also do one of the following:

   a) Accompany it with the complete corresponding machine-readable
   source code, which must be distributed under the terms of Sections
   1 and 2 above on a medium customarily used for software interchange; or,

   b) Accompany it with a written offer, valid for at least three
   years, to give any third party, for a charge no more than your
   cost of physically performing source distribution, a complete
   machine-readable copy of the corresponding source code, to be
   distributed under the terms of Sections 1 and 2 above on a medium
   customarily used for software interchange; or,

   c) Accompany it with the information you received as to the offer
   to distribute corresponding source code. (This alternative is
   allowed only for noncommercial distribution and only if you
   received the program in object code or executable form with such
   an offer, in accord with Subsection b above.)

The source code for a work means the preferred form of the work for
making modifications to it. For an executable work, complete source
code means all the source code for all modules it contains, plus any
associated interface definition files, plus the scripts used to
control compilation and installation of the executable. However, as a
special exception, the source code distributed need not include
anything that is normally distributed (in either source or binary
form) with the major components (compiler, kernel, and so on) of the
operating system on which the executable runs, unless that component
itself accompanies the executable.

If distribution of executable or object code is made by offering
access to copy from a designated place, then offering equivalent
access to copy the source code from the same place counts as
distribution of the source code, even though third parties are not
compelled to copy the source along with the object code.

–

4. You may not copy, modify, sublicense, or distribute the Program except as expressly provided under this License. Any attempt otherwise to copy, modify, sublicense or distribute the Program is void, and will automatically terminate your rights under this License. However, parties who have received copies, or rights, from you under this License will not have their licenses terminated so long as such parties remain in full compliance.

5. You are not required to accept this License, since you have not signed it. However, nothing else grants you permission to modify or distribute the Program or its derivative works. These actions are prohibited by law if you do not accept this License. Therefore, by modifying or distributing the Program (or any work based on the Program), you indicate your acceptance of this License to do so, and all its terms and conditions for copying, distributing or modifying the Program or works based on it.

6. Each time you redistribute the Program (or any work based on the Program), the recipient automatically receives a license from the original licensor to copy, distribute or modify the Program subject to these terms and conditions. You may not impose any further restrictions on the recipients' exercise of the rights granted herein. You are not responsible for enforcing compliance by third parties to this License.

7. If, as a consequence of a court judgment or allegation of patent infringement or for any other reason (not limited to patent issues), conditions are imposed on you (whether by court order, agreement or otherwise) that contradict the conditions of this License, they do not excuse you from the conditions of this License. If you cannot distribute so as to satisfy simultaneously your obligations under this License and any other pertinent obligations, then as a consequence you may not distribute the Program at all. For example, if a patent license would not permit royalty-free redistribution of the Program by all those who receive copies directly or indirectly through you, then the only way you could satisfy both it and this License would be to refrain entirely from distribution of the Program.

If any portion of this section is held invalid or unenforceable under any particular circumstance, the balance of the section is intended to apply and the section as a whole is intended to apply in other circumstances.

It is not the purpose of this section to induce you to infringe any patents or other property right claims or to contest validity of any such claims; this section has the sole purpose of protecting the integrity of the free software distribution system, which is implemented by public license practices. Many people have made generous contributions to the wide range of software distributed through that system in reliance on consistent application of that system; it is up to the author/donor to decide if he or she is willing to distribute software through any other system and a licensee cannot impose that choice.

This section is intended to make thoroughly clear what is believed to be a consequence of the rest of this License.

8. If the distribution and/or use of the Program is restricted in certain countries either by patents or by copyrighted interfaces, the original copyright holder who places the Program under this License may add an explicit geographical distribution limitation excluding those countries, so that distribution is permitted only in or among countries not thus excluded. In such case, this License incorporates the limitation as if written in the body of this License.

9. The Free Software Foundation may publish revised and/or new versions of the General Public License from time to time. Such new versions will be similar in spirit to the present version, but may differ in detail to address new problems or concerns.

Each version is given a distinguishing version number. If the Program specifies a version number of this License which applies to it and "any later version", you have the option of following the terms and conditions either of that version or of any later version published by the Free Software Foundation. If the Program does not specify a version number of this License, you may choose any version ever published by the Free Software Foundation.

10. If you wish to incorporate parts of the Program into other free programs whose distribution conditions are different, write to the author to ask for permission. For software which is copyrighted by the Free Software Foundation, write to the Free Software Foundation; we sometimes make exceptions for this. Our decision will be guided by the two goals of preserving the free status of all derivatives of our free software and of promoting the sharing and reuse of software generally.

NO WARRANTY

11. BECAUSE THE PROGRAM IS LICENSED FREE OF CHARGE, THERE IS NO WARRANTY FOR THE PROGRAM, TO THE EXTENT PERMITTED BY APPLICABLE LAW. EXCEPT WHEN OTHERWISE STATED IN WRITING THE COPYRIGHT HOLDERS AND/OR OTHER PARTIES PROVIDE THE PROGRAM "AS IS" WITHOUT WARRANTY OF ANY KIND, EITHER EXPRESSED OR IMPLIED, INCLUDING, BUT NOT LIMITED TO, THE IMPLIED WARRANTIES OF MERCHANTABILITY AND FITNESS FOR A PARTICULAR PURPOSE. THE ENTIRE RISK AS TO THE QUALITY AND PERFORMANCE OF THE PROGRAM IS WITH YOU. SHOULD THE PROGRAM PROVE DEFECTIVE, YOU ASSUME THE COST OF ALL NECESSARY SERVICING, REPAIR OR CORRECTION.

12. IN NO EVENT UNLESS REQUIRED BY APPLICABLE LAW OR AGREED TO IN WRITING WILL ANY COPYRIGHT HOLDER, OR ANY OTHER PARTY WHO MAY MODIFY AND/OR REDISTRIBUTE THE PROGRAM AS PERMITTED ABOVE, BE LIABLE TO YOU FOR DAMAGES, INCLUDING ANY GENERAL, SPECIAL, INCIDENTAL OR CONSEQUENTIAL DAMAGES ARISING OUT OF THE USE OR INABILITY TO USE THE PROGRAM (INCLUDING BUT NOT LIMITED TO LOSS OF DATA OR DATA BEING RENDERED INACCURATE OR LOSSES SUSTAINED BY YOU OR THIRD PARTIES OR A FAILURE OF THE PROGRAM TO OPERATE WITH ANY OTHER PROGRAMS), EVEN IF SUCH HOLDER OR OTHER PARTY HAS BEEN ADVISED OF THE POSSIBILITY OF SUCH DAMAGES.

END OF TERMS AND CONDITIONS

—

Appendix: How to Apply These Terms to Your New Programs

If you develop a new program, and you want it to be of the greatest
possible use to the public, the best way to achieve this is to make it
free software which everyone can redistribute and change under these terms.

To do so, attach the following notices to the program.  It is safest
to attach them to the start of each source file to most effectively
convey the exclusion of warranty; and each file should have at least
the "copyright" line and a pointer to where the full notice is found.

    <one line to give the program's name and a brief idea of what it does.>
    Copyright (C) 19yy  <name of author>

    This program is free software; you can redistribute it and/or modify
    it under the terms of the GNU General Public License as published by
    the Free Software Foundation; either version 2 of the License, or
    (at your option) any later version.

    This program is distributed in the hope that it will be useful,
    but WITHOUT ANY WARRANTY; without even the implied warranty of
    MERCHANTABILITY or FITNESS FOR A PARTICULAR PURPOSE.  See the
    GNU General Public License for more details.

    You should have received a copy of the GNU General Public License
    along with this program; if not, write to the Free Software
    Foundation, Inc., 675 Mass Ave, Cambridge, MA 02139, USA.

Also add information on how to contact you by electronic and paper mail.

If the program is interactive, make it output a short notice like this
when it starts in an interactive mode:

    Gnomovision version 69, Copyright (C) 19yy name of author
    Gnomovision comes with ABSOLUTELY NO WARRANTY; for details type `show w'.
    This is free software, and you are welcome to redistribute it
    under certain conditions; type `show c' for details.

The hypothetical commands `show w' and `show c' should show the appropriate
parts of the General Public License.  Of course, the commands you use may
be called something other than `show w' and `show c'; they could even be
mouse-clicks or menu items—whatever suits your program.

You should also get your employer (if you work as a programmer) or your
school, if any, to sign a "copyright disclaimer" for the program, if
necessary.  Here is a sample; alter the names:

    Yoyodyne, Inc., hereby disclaims all copyright interest in the program
    `Gnomovision' (which makes passes at compilers) written by James Hacker.

```
<signature of Ty Coon>, 1 April 1989
Ty Coon, President of Vice
```

This General Public License does not permit incorporating your program into
proprietary programs.  If your program is a subroutine library, you may
consider it more useful to permit linking proprietary applications with the
library.  If this is what you want to do, use the GNU Library General

## A.2: source/credentials.c

This file is used by Samba (as both Client and Server) to calculate a
Credential chain, which is attached to **NETLOGON pipe** calls. A verbose description of the Credential chain can be found in the section on
**NETLOGON** Credential Chain. A detailed description can be found
in Appendix B, Section B.3.3.

```
/*
   Unix SMB/Netbios implementation.
   Version 1.9.
   code to manipulate domain credentials
   Copyright (C) Andrew Tridgell 1997-1998

   This program is free software; you can redistribute it and/or modify
   it under the terms of the GNU General Public License as published by
   the Free Software Foundation; either version 2 of the License, or
   (at your option) any later version.

   This program is distributed in the hope that it will be useful,
   but WITHOUT ANY WARRANTY; without even the implied warranty of
   MERCHANTABILITY or FITNESS FOR A PARTICULAR PURPOSE.  See the
   GNU General Public License for more details.

   You should have received a copy of the GNU General Public License
   along with this program; if not, write to the Free Software
   Foundation, Inc., 675 Mass Ave, Cambridge, MA 02139, USA.
*/

#include "includes.h"

extern int DEBUGLEVEL;


/***************************************************************************
represent a credential as a string
***************************************************************************/
char *credstr(uchar *cred)
{
        static fstring buf;
        slprintf(buf, sizeof(buf) - 1, "%02X%02X%02X%02X%02X%02X%02X%02X",
                     cred[0], cred[1], cred[2], cred[3],
                   cred[4], cred[5], cred[6], cred[7]);
        return buf;
}
```

```c
static void cred_hash1(unsigned char *out,unsigned char *in,unsigned char *key)
{
        unsigned char buf[8];

        smbhash(buf, in, key, 1);
        smbhash(out, buf, key+9, 1);
}

static void cred_hash2(unsigned char *out,unsigned char *in,unsigned char *key)
{
        unsigned char buf[8];
        static unsigned char key2[8];

        smbhash(buf, in, key, 1);
        key2[0] = key[7];
        smbhash(out, buf, key2, 1);
}

/***************************************************************************
  setup the session key.
Input: 8 byte challenge block
       8 byte server challenge block
      16 byte md4 encrypted password
Output:
      8 byte session key
 ***************************************************************************/
void cred_session_key(DOM_CHAL *clnt_chal, DOM_CHAL *srv_chal, char *pass,
                   uchar session_key[8])
{
        uint32 sum[2];
        unsigned char sum2[8];

        sum[0] = IVAL(clnt_chal->data, 0) + IVAL(srv_chal->data, 0);
        sum[1] = IVAL(clnt_chal->data, 4) + IVAL(srv_chal->data, 4);

        SIVAL(sum2,0,sum[0]);
        SIVAL(sum2,4,sum[1]);

        cred_hash1(session_key, sum2,(unsigned char *)pass);

        /* debug output */
        DEBUG(4,("cred_session_key\n"));

        DEBUG(5,("        clnt_chal: %s\n", credstr(clnt_chal->data)));
        DEBUG(5,("        srv_chal : %s\n", credstr(srv_chal->data)));
        DEBUG(5,("        clnt+srv : %s\n", credstr(sum2)));
        DEBUG(5,("        sess_key : %s\n", credstr(session_key)));
}


/***************************************************************************
```

```
create a credential

Input:
      8 byte sesssion key
      8 byte stored credential
      4 byte timestamp

Output:
      8 byte credential
*****************************************************************************/
void cred_create(uchar session_key[8], DOM_CHAL *stor_cred, UTIME timestamp,
                 DOM_CHAL *cred)
{
      DOM_CHAL time_cred;

      SIVAL(time_cred.data, 0, IVAL(stor_cred->data, 0) + timestamp.time);
      SIVAL(time_cred.data, 4, IVAL(stor_cred->data, 4));

      cred_hash2(cred->data, time_cred.data, session_key);

      /* debug output*/
      DEBUG(4,("cred_create\n"));

      DEBUG(5,("        sess_key : %s\n", credstr(session_key)));
      DEBUG(5,("        stor_cred: %s\n", credstr(stor_cred->data)));
      DEBUG(5,("        timestamp: %x\n"  , timestamp.time));
      DEBUG(5,("        timecred : %s\n", credstr(time_cred.data)));
      DEBUG(5,("        calc_cred: %s\n", credstr(cred->data)));
}


/*****************************************************************************
  check a supplied credential

Input:
      8 byte received credential
      8 byte sesssion key
      8 byte stored credential
      4 byte timestamp

Output:
      returns 1 if computed credential matches received credential
      returns 0 otherwise
*****************************************************************************/
int cred_assert(DOM_CHAL *cred, uchar session_key[8], DOM_CHAL *stored_cred,
                UTIME timestamp)
{
      DOM_CHAL cred2;

      cred_create(session_key, stored_cred, timestamp, &cred2);

      /* debug output*/
      DEBUG(4,("cred_assert\n"));
```

```
        DEBUG(5,("           challenge : %s\n", credstr(cred->data)));
        DEBUG(5,("           calculated: %s\n", credstr(cred2.data)));

        if (memcmp(cred->data, cred2.data, 8) == 0)
        {
                DEBUG(5, ("credentials check ok\n"));
                return True;
        }
        else
        {
                DEBUG(5, ("credentials check wrong\n"));
                return False;
        }
}


/****************************************************************************
  checks credentials; generates next step in the credential chain
 ****************************************************************************/
BOOL clnt_deal_with_creds(uchar sess_key[8],
                          DOM_CRED *sto_clnt_cred, DOM_CRED *rcv_srv_cred)
{
        UTIME new_clnt_time;
        uint32 new_cred;

        DEBUG(5,("clnt_deal_with_creds: %d\n", __LINE__));

        /* increment client time by one second */
        new_clnt_time.time = sto_clnt_cred->timestamp.time + 1;

        /* check that the received server credentials are valid */
        if (!cred_assert(&(rcv_srv_cred->challenge), sess_key,
                         &(sto_clnt_cred->challenge), new_clnt_time))
        {
                return False;
        }

        /* 1st 4 bytes of the new seed is old client 4 bytes + clnt time + 1 */
        new_cred = IVAL(sto_clnt_cred->challenge.data, 0);
        new_cred += new_clnt_time.time;

        /* store new seed in client credentials */
        SIVAL(sto_clnt_cred->challenge.data, 0, new_cred);

        DEBUG(5,("           new clnt cred: %s\n",
                credstr(sto_clnt_cred->challenge.data)));

        return True;
}
```

```
/******************************************************************************
   checks credentials; generates next step in the credential chain
 ******************************************************************************/
BOOL srv_deal_with_creds(uchar sess_key[8],
                         DOM_CRED *sto_clnt_cred,
                         DOM_CRED *rcv_clnt_cred, DOM_CRED *rtn_srv_cred)
{
        UTIME new_clnt_time;
        uint32 new_cred;

        DEBUG(5,("deal_with_creds: %d\n", __LINE__));

        /* check that the received client credentials are valid */
        if (!cred_assert(&(rcv_clnt_cred->challenge), sess_key,
                   &(sto_clnt_cred->challenge), rcv_clnt_cred->timestamp))
        {
                return False;
        }

        /* increment client time by one second */
        new_clnt_time.time = rcv_clnt_cred->timestamp.time + 1;

        /* 1st 4 bytes of the new seed is old client 4 bytes + clnt time + 1 */
        new_cred = IVAL(sto_clnt_cred->challenge.data, 0);
        new_cred += new_clnt_time.time;

        DEBUG(5,("deal_with_creds: new_cred[0]=%x\n", new_cred));

        /* doesn't matter that server time is 0 */
        rtn_srv_cred->timestamp.time = 0;

        DEBUG(5,("deal_with_creds: new_clnt_time=%x\n", new_clnt_time.time));

        /* create return credentials for inclusion in the reply */
        cred_create(sess_key, &(sto_clnt_cred->challenge), new_clnt_time,
                   &(rtn_srv_cred->challenge));

        DEBUG(5,("deal_with_creds: clnt_cred=%s\n",
                   credstr(sto_clnt_cred->challenge.data)));

        /* store new seed in client credentials */
        SIVAL(sto_clnt_cred->challenge.data, 0, new_cred);

        return True;
}
```

# A.3: include/rpc_atsvc.h

This file contains definitions used in Samba for DCE/RPC operation codes on \PIPE\atsvc.

```
/*
   Unix SMB/Netbios implementation.
```

```
Version 1.9.
Copyright (C) Matthew Chapman 1999
Copyright (C) Luke Kenneth Casson Leighton 1996-1999
Copyright (C) Andrew Tridgell 1992-1999

This program is free software; you can redistribute it and/or modify
it under the terms of the GNU General Public License as published by
the Free Software Foundation; either version 2 of the License, or
(at your option) any later version.

This program is distributed in the hope that it will be useful,
but WITHOUT ANY WARRANTY; without even the implied warranty of
MERCHANTABILITY or FITNESS FOR A PARTICULAR PURPOSE.  See the
GNU General Public License for more details.

You should have received a copy of the GNU General Public License
along with this program; if not, write to the Free Software
Foundation, Inc., 675 Mass Ave, Cambridge, MA 02139, USA.
*/

#ifndef _RPC_ATSVC_H
#define _RPC_ATSVC_H

#define AT_ADD_JOB      0x00
#define AT_DEL_JOB      0x01
#define AT_ENUM_JOBS    0x02
#define AT_QUERY_JOB    0x03

#endif /* _RPC_ATSVC_H */
```

# A.4: include/rpc_eventlog.h

This file contains definitions used in Samba for DCE/RPC operation codes on **\PIPE\eventlog**.

```
/*
   Unix SMB/Netbios implementation.
   Version 1.9.
   Interface header: Scheduler service
   Copyright (C) Luke Kenneth Casson Leighton 1996-1999
   Copyright (C) Andrew Tridgell               1992-1999
   Copyright (C) Jean-Francois Micouleau       1998-1999

   This program is free software; you can redistribute it and/or modify
   it under the terms of the GNU General Public License as published by
   the Free Software Foundation; either version 2 of the License, or
   (at your option) any later version.

   This program is distributed in the hope that it will be useful,
   but WITHOUT ANY WARRANTY; without even the implied warranty of
   MERCHANTABILITY or FITNESS FOR A PARTICULAR PURPOSE.  See the
   GNU General Public License for more details.
```

```
    You should have received a copy of the GNU General Public License
    along with this program; if not, write to the Free Software
    Foundation, Inc., 675 Mass Ave, Cambridge, MA 02139, USA.
*/


#ifndef _RPC_EVENTLOG_H
#define _RPC_EVENTLOG_H

#define EVENTLOG_OPEN 0x07
#define EVENTLOG_CLOSE 0x02
#define EVENTLOG_NUMOFEVENTLOGRECORDS 0x04
#define EVENTLOG_READEVENTLOG          0x0a

#endif /* _RPC_EVENTLOG_H */
```

## A.5: include/rpc_lsa.h

This file contains definitions used in Samba for DCE/RPC operation codes on \PIPE\lsarpc.

```
/*
    Unix SMB/Netbios implementation.
    Version 1.9.
    Copyright (C) Andrew Tridgell 1992-1997
    Copyright (C) Luke Kenneth Casson Leighton 1996-1997
    Copyright (C) Paul Ashton 1997

    This program is free software; you can redistribute it and/or modify
    it under the terms of the GNU General Public License as published by
    the Free Software Foundation; either version 2 of the License, or
    (at your option) any later version.

    This program is distributed in the hope that it will be useful,
    but WITHOUT ANY WARRANTY; without even the implied warranty of
    MERCHANTABILITY or FITNESS FOR A PARTICULAR PURPOSE.  See the
    GNU General Public License for more details.

    You should have received a copy of the GNU General Public License
    along with this program; if not, write to the Free Software
    Foundation, Inc., 675 Mass Ave, Cambridge, MA 02139, USA.
*/

#ifndef _RPC_LSA_H /* _RPC_LSA_H */
#define _RPC_LSA_H

enum SID_NAME_USE
{
        SID_NAME_USER    = 1, /* user */
        SID_NAME_DOM_GRP = 2, /* domain group */
        SID_NAME_DOMAIN  = 3, /* domain: don't know what this is */
        SID_NAME_ALIAS   = 4, /* local group */
        SID_NAME_WKN_GRP = 5, /* well-known group */
        SID_NAME_DELETED = 6, /* deleted account: needed for c2 rating */
```

```
            SID_NAME_INVALID = 7, /* invalid account */
            SID_NAME_UNKNOWN = 8  /* oops. */
};

/* ntlsa pipe */
#define LSA_CLOSE              0x00
#define LSA_QUERYINFOPOLICY    0x07
#define LSA_ENUMTRUSTDOM       0x0d
#define LSA_LOOKUPNAMES        0x0e
#define LSA_LOOKUPSIDS         0x0f
#define LSA_OPENPOLICY         0x06
#define LSA_OPENPOLICY2        0x2c
#define LSA_OPENSECRET         0x1c
#define LSA_QUERYSECRET        0x1e

#endif /* _RPC_LSA_H */
```

# A.6: include/rpc_netlogon.h

This file contains definitions used in Samba for DCE/RPC operation codes on **\PIPE\NETLOGON**.

```
/*
   Unix SMB/Netbios implementation.
   Version 1.9.
   Copyright (C) Andrew Tridgell 1992-1997
   Copyright (C) Luke Kenneth Casson Leighton 1996-1997
   Copyright (C) Paul Ashton 1997

   This program is free software; you can redistribute it and/or modify
   it under the terms of the GNU General Public License as published by
   the Free Software Foundation; either version 2 of the License, or
   (at your option) any later version.

   This program is distributed in the hope that it will be useful,
   but WITHOUT ANY WARRANTY; without even the implied warranty of
   MERCHANTABILITY or FITNESS FOR A PARTICULAR PURPOSE.  See the
   GNU General Public License for more details.

   You should have received a copy of the GNU General Public License
   along with this program; if not, write to the Free Software
   Foundation, Inc., 675 Mass Ave, Cambridge, MA 02139, USA.
*/

#ifndef _RPC_NETLOGON_H /* _RPC_NETLOGON_H */
#define _RPC_NETLOGON_H

/* NETLOGON pipe */
#define NET_REQCHAL           0x04
#define NET_SRVPWSET          0x06
#define NET_SAMLOGON          0x02
#define NET_SAMLOGOFF         0x03
#define NET_AUTH2             0x0f
```

```
#define NET_LOGON_CTRL2        0x0e
#define NET_TRUST_DOM_LIST     0x13

#define NET_SAM_SYNC           0x10
#define NET_SAM_DELTAS         0x07

#endif /* _RPC_NETLOGON_H */
```

## A.7: include/rpc_reg.h

This file contains definitions used in Samba for DCE/RPC operation codes on **\PIPE\winreg**.

```
/*
   Unix SMB/Netbios implementation.
   Version 1.9.
   Copyright (C) Andrew Tridgell 1992-1997
   Copyright (C) Luke Kenneth Casson Leighton 1996-1997
   Copyright (C) Paul Ashton 1997

   This program is free software; you can redistribute it and/or modify
   it under the terms of the GNU General Public License as published by
   the Free Software Foundation; either version 2 of the License, or
   (at your option) any later version.

   This program is distributed in the hope that it will be useful,
   but WITHOUT ANY WARRANTY; without even the implied warranty of
   MERCHANTABILITY or FITNESS FOR A PARTICULAR PURPOSE.  See the
   GNU General Public License for more details.

   You should have received a copy of the GNU General Public License
   along with this program; if not, write to the Free Software
   Foundation, Inc., 675 Mass Ave, Cambridge, MA 02139, USA.
*/

#ifndef _RPC_REG_H /* _RPC_REG_H */
#define _RPC_REG_H

/* winreg pipe defines */
#define REG_OPEN_HKLM       0x02
#define REG_OPEN_HKU        0x04
#define REG_FLUSH_KEY       0x0B
#define REG_UNK_1A          0x1a
#define REG_QUERY_KEY       0x10
#define REG_ENUM_KEY        0x09
#define REG_CREATE_KEY      0x06
#define REG_DELETE_KEY      0x07
#define REG_DELETE_VALUE    0x08
#define REG_CREATE_VALUE    0x16
#define REG_GET_KEY_SEC     0x0c
#define REG_SET_KEY_SEC     0x15
#define REG_ENUM_VALUE      0x0a
#define REG_OPEN_ENTRY      0x0f
```

```
#define REG_INFO           0x11
#define REG_CLOSE          0x05
#define REG_SHUTDOWN       0x18

#endif /* _RPC_REG_H */
```

# A.8: include/rpc_samr.h

This file contains definitions used in Samba for DCE/RPC operation
codes on **\PIPE\samr**.

```
/*
   Unix SMB/Netbios implementation.
   Version 1.9.
   Copyright (C) Andrew Tridgell 1992-1998
   Copyright (C) Luke Kenneth Casson Leighton 1996-1998
   Copyright (C) Paul Ashton 1997-1998

   This program is free software; you can redistribute it and/or modify
   it under the terms of the GNU General Public License as published by
   the Free Software Foundation; either version 2 of the License, or
   (at your option) any later version.

   This program is distributed in the hope that it will be useful,
   but WITHOUT ANY WARRANTY; without even the implied warranty of
   MERCHANTABILITY or FITNESS FOR A PARTICULAR PURPOSE.  See the
   GNU General Public License for more details.

   You should have received a copy of the GNU General Public License
   along with this program; if not, write to the Free Software
   Foundation, Inc., 675 Mass Ave, Cambridge, MA 02139, USA.
*/

#ifndef _RPC_SAMR_H /* _RPC_SAMR_H */
#define _RPC_SAMR_H

/********************************************************************
 the following information comes from a QuickView on samsrv.dll,
 and gives an idea of exactly what is needed:

x SamrAddMemberToAlias
x SamrAddMemberToGroup
SamrAddMultipleMembersToAlias
x SamrChangePasswordUser
x SamrCloseHandle
x SamrConnect
x SamrCreateAliasInDomain
x SamrCreateGroupInDomain
x SamrCreateUserInDomain
? SamrDeleteAlias
SamrDeleteGroup
SamrDeleteUser
x SamrEnumerateAliasesInDomain
```

```
      SamrEnumerateDomainsInSamServer
    x SamrEnumerateGroupsInDomain
    x SamrEnumerateUsersInDomain
      SamrGetUserDomainPasswordInformation
      SamrLookupDomainInSamServer
    ? SamrLookupIdsInDomain
    x SamrLookupNamesInDomain
    x SamrOpenAlias
    x SamrOpenDomain
    x SamrOpenGroup
    x SamrOpenUser
    x SamrQueryDisplayInformation
    x SamrQueryInformationAlias
      SamrQueryInformationDomain
    ? SamrQueryInformationUser
      SamrQuerySecurityObject
      SamrRemoveMemberFromAlias
      SamrRemoveMemberFromForiegnDomain
      SamrRemoveMemberFromGroup
      SamrRemoveMultipleMembersFromAlias
    x SamrSetInformationAlias
      SamrSetInformationDomain
    x SamrSetInformationGroup
    x SamrSetInformationUser
      SamrSetMemberAttributesOfGroup
      SamrSetSecurityObject
      SamrShutdownSamServer
      SamrTestPrivateFunctionsDomain
      SamrTestPrivateFunctionsUser


    ********************************************************************/


    #define SAMR_CONNECT_ANON       0x00
    #define SAMR_CLOSE_HND          0x01

    #define SAMR_QUERY_SEC_OBJECT   0x03
    #define SAMR_LOOKUP_DOMAIN      0x05
    #define SAMR_OPEN_DOMAIN        0x07

    #define SAMR_QUERY_DOMAIN_INFO 0x08

    #define SAMR_CREATE_DOM_GROUP   0x0a
    #define SAMR_ENUM_DOM_GROUPS    0x0b
    #define SAMR_ENUM_DOM_USERS     0x0d
    #define SAMR_CREATE_DOM_ALIAS   0x0e
    #define SAMR_ENUM_DOM_ALIASES   0x0f
    #define SAMR_QUERY_USERALIASES 0x10

    #define SAMR_LOOKUP_NAMES       0x11
    #define SAMR_LOOKUP_RIDS        0x12

    #define SAMR_OPEN_GROUP         0x13
    #define SAMR_QUERY_GROUPINFO    0x14
```

```
#define SAMR_SET_GROUPINFO      0x15
#define SAMR_ADD_GROUPMEM       0x16
#define SAMR_DELETE_DOM_GROUP   0x17
#define SAMR_DEL_GROUPMEM       0x18
#define SAMR_QUERY_GROUPMEM     0x19

#define SAMR_OPEN_ALIAS         0x1b
#define SAMR_QUERY_ALIASINFO    0x1c
#define SAMR_SET_ALIASINFO      0x1d
#define SAMR_DELETE_DOM_ALIAS   0x1e
#define SAMR_ADD_ALIASMEM       0x1f
#define SAMR_DEL_ALIASMEM       0x20
#define SAMR_QUERY_ALIASMEM     0x21

#define SAMR_OPEN_USER          0x22
#define SAMR_CREATE_USER        0x32
#define SAMR_SET_USERINFO       0x3A

#define SAMR_QUERY_USERINFO     0x24
#define SAMR_QUERY_USERGROUPS   0x27
#define SAMR_QUERY_DISPINFO     0x28

#define SAMR_GET_USRDOM_PWINFO 0x2c
#define SAMR_QUERY_DISPINFO3    0x30 /* Alias for SAMR_QUERY_DISPINFO
                                            with info level 3 */
#define SAMR_QUERY_DISPINFO4    0x33 /* Alias for SAMR_QUERY_DISPINFO
                                            with info level 4 */
#define SAMR_ADDMULTI_ALIASMEM 0x34

#define SAMR_CHGPASSWD_USER     0x37
#define SAMR_GET_DOM_PWINFO     0x38

#define SAMR_CONNECT            0x39

#endif /* _RPC_SAMR_H */
```

# A.9: include/rpc_spoolss.h

This file contains definitions used in Samba for DCE/RPC operation codes on \PIPE\spoolss.

```
/*
   Unix SMB/Netbios implementation.
   Version 1.9.
   SMB parameters and setup
   Copyright (C) Andrew Tridgell 1992-1998
   Copyright (C) Luke Kenneth Casson Leighton 1996-1998
   Copyright (C) Jean Francois Micouleau 1998-1999

   This program is free software; you can redistribute it and/or modify
   it under the terms of the GNU General Public License as published by
   the Free Software Foundation; either version 2 of the License, or
   (at your option) any later version.
```

```
        This program is distributed in the hope that it will be useful,
        but WITHOUT ANY WARRANTY, without even the implied warranty of
        MERCHANTABILITY or FITNESS FOR A PARTICULAR PURPOSE.  See the
        GNU General Public License for more details.

        You should have received a copy of the GNU General Public License
        along with this program; if not, write to the Free Software
        Foundation, Inc., 675 Mass Ave, Cambridge, MA 02139, USA.
*/

#ifndef _RPC_SPOOLSS_H /* _RPC_SPOOLSS_H */
#define _RPC_SPOOLSS_H


/* spoolss pipe: this are the calls which are not implemented ...
#define SPOOLSS_OPENPRINTER                             0x01
#define SPOOLSS_DELETEPRINTER                                      0x06
#define SPOOLSS_GETPRINTERDRIVER                        0x0b
#define SPOOLSS_DELETEPRINTERDRIVER                     0x0d
#define SPOOLSS_ADDPRINTPROCESSOR                       0x0e
#define SPOOLSS_GETPRINTPROCESSORDIRECTORY              0x10
#define SPOOLSS_ABORTPRINTER                            0x15
#define SPOOLSS_READPRINTER                             0x16
#define SPOOLSS_WAITFORPRINTERCHANGE                    0x1c
#define SPOOLSS_DELETEFORM                              0x1f
#define SPOOLSS_GETFORM                                            0x20
#define SPOOLSS_ADDPORT                                            0x25
#define SPOOLSS_CONFIGUREPORT                                      0x26
#define SPOOLSS_DELETEPORT                              0x27
#define SPOOLSS_CREATEPRINTERIC                                    0x28
#define SPOOLSS_PLAYGDISCRIPTONPRINTERIC                0x29
#define SPOOLSS_DELETEPRINTERIC                                    0x2a
#define SPOOLSS_ADDPRINTERCONNECTION                    0x2b
#define SPOOLSS_DELETEPRINTERCONNECTION                            0x2c
#define SPOOLSS_PRINTERMESSAGEBOX                       0x2d
#define SPOOLSS_ADDMONITOR                              0x2e
#define SPOOLSS_DELETEMONITOR                                      0x2f
#define SPOOLSS_DELETEPRINTPROCESSOR                    0x30
#define SPOOLSS_ADDPRINTPROVIDOR                        0x31
#define SPOOLSS_DELETEPRINTPROVIDOR                     0x32
#define SPOOLSS_RESETPRINTER                            0x34
#define SPOOLSS_FINDFIRSTPRINTERCHANGENOTIFICATION      0x36
#define SPOOLSS_FINDNEXTPRINTERCHANGENOTIFICATION       0x37
#define SPOOLSS_ROUTERFINDFIRSTPRINTERNOTIFICATIONOLD   0x39
#define SPOOLSS_REPLYOPENPRINTER                        0x3a
#define SPOOLSS_ROUTERREPLYPRINTER                      0x3b
#define SPOOLSS_REPLYCLOSEPRINTER                       0x3c
#define SPOOLSS_ADDPORTEX                               0x3d
#define SPOOLSS_REMOTEFINDFIRSTPRINTERCHANGENOTIFICATION0x3e
#define SPOOLSS_SPOOLERINIT                             0x3f
#define SPOOLSS_RESETPRINTEREX                                     0x40
#define SPOOLSS_ROUTERREFRESHPRINTERCHANGENOTIFICATION  0x42
```

```
*/

/* those are implemented */

#define SPOOLSS_ENUMPRINTERS                        0x00
#define SPOOLSS_SETJOB                                      0x02
#define SPOOLSS_GETJOB                                      0x03
#define SPOOLSS_ENUMJOBS                            0x04
#define SPOOLSS_ADDPRINTER                          0x05
#define SPOOLSS_SETPRINTER                          0x07
#define SPOOLSS_GETPRINTER                          0x08
#define SPOOLSS_ADDPRINTERDRIVER                    0x09
#define SPOOLSS_ENUMPRINTERDRIVERS                  0x0a
#define SPOOLSS_GETPRINTERDRIVERDIRECTORY           0x0c
#define SPOOLSS_ENUMPRINTPROCESSORS                 0x0f
#define SPOOLSS_STARTDOCPRINTER                             0x11
#define SPOOLSS_STARTPAGEPRINTER                    0x12
#define SPOOLSS_WRITEPRINTER                        0x13
#define SPOOLSS_ENDPAGEPRINTER                              0x14
#define SPOOLSS_ENDDOCPRINTER                               0x17
#define SPOOLSS_ADDJOB                                      0x18
#define SPOOLSS_SCHEDULEJOB                         0x19
#define SPOOLSS_GETPRINTERDATA                              0x1a
#define SPOOLSS_SETPRINTERDATA                              0x1b
#define SPOOLSS_CLOSEPRINTER                        0x1d
#define SPOOLSS_ADDFORM                                     0x1e
#define SPOOLSS_SETFORM                                     0x21
#define SPOOLSS_ENUMFORMS                           0x22
#define SPOOLSS_ENUMPORTS                           0x23
#define SPOOLSS_ENUMMONITORS                        0x24
#define SPOOLSS_ENUMPRINTPROCESSORDATATYPES         0x33
#define SPOOLSS_GETPRINTERDRIVER2                   0x35
/* find close printer notification */
#define SPOOLSS_FCPN                                        0x38
/* remote find first printer change notifyEx */
#define SPOOLSS_RFFPCNEX                            0x41
/* remote find next printer change notifyEx */
#define SPOOLSS_RFNPCNEX                            0x43
#define SPOOLSS_OPENPRINTEREX                               0x45
#define SPOOLSS_ADDPRINTEREX                        0x46
#define SPOOLSS_ENUMPRINTERDATA                             0x48

#endif /* _RPC_SPOOLSS_H */
```

# A.10: include/rpc_srvsvc.h

This file contains definitions used in Samba for DCE/RPC operation codes on **\PIPE\svcctl**.

```
/*
  Unix SMB/Netbios implementation.
  Version 1.9.
  Copyright (C) Andrew Tridgell 1992-1997
```

```
#ifndef _RPC_SRVSVC_H /* _RPC_SRVSVC_H */
#define _RPC_SRVSVC_H

/* srvsvc pipe */
#define SRV_NETCONNENUM        0x08
#define SRV_NETFILEENUM        0x09
#define SRV_NETSESSENUM        0x0c
#define SRV_NETSHAREENUM       0x0f
#define SRV_NET_SRV_GET_INFO 0x15
#define SRV_NET_SRV_SET_INFO 0x16
#define   SRV_NET_REMOTE_TOD    0x1c

#endif /* _RPC_SRVSVC_H */
```

# A.11: include/rpc_svcctl.h

This file contains definitions used in Samba for DCE/RPC operation codes on \PIPE\svcctl.

```
    You should have received a copy of the GNU General Public License
    along with this program; if not, write to the Free Software
    Foundation, Inc., 675 Mass Ave, Cambridge, MA 02139, USA.
*/


#ifndef _RPC_SVCCTL_H /* _RPC_SVCCTL_H */
#define _RPC_SVCCTL_H


/* svcctl pipe */
#define SVC_OPEN_SC_MAN       0x0f
#define SVC_ENUM_SVCS_STATUS 0x0e
#define SVC_QUERY_SVC_CONFIG 0x11
#define SVC_QUERY_DISP_NAME  0x14
#define SVC_OPEN_SERVICE     0x10
#define SVC_START_SERVICE    0x13
#define SVC_CLOSE            0x00

#endif /* _RPC_SVCCTL_H */
```

# A.12: include/rpc_wkssvc.h

This file contains definitions used in Samba for DCE/RPC operation codes on **\PIPE\wkssvc**.

```
/*
    Unix SMB/Netbios implementation.
    Version 1.9.
    Copyright (C) Andrew Tridgell 1992-1997
    Copyright (C) Luke Kenneth Casson Leighton 1996-1997
    Copyright (C) Paul Ashton 1997


    This program is free software; you can redistribute it and/or modify
    it under the terms of the GNU General Public License as published by
    the Free Software Foundation; either version 2 of the License, or
    (at your option) any later version.

    This program is distributed in the hope that it will be useful,
    but WITHOUT ANY WARRANTY; without even the implied warranty of
    MERCHANTABILITY or FITNESS FOR A PARTICULAR PURPOSE.  See the
    GNU General Public License for more details.

    You should have received a copy of the GNU General Public License
    along with this program; if not, write to the Free Software
    Foundation, Inc., 675 Mass Ave, Cambridge, MA 02139, USA.
*/

#ifndef _RPC_WKS_H /* _RPC_WKS_H */
#define _RPC_WKS_H

/* wkssvc pipe */
#define WKS_QUERY_INFO    ·0x00

#endif /* _RPC_WKS_H */
```

# B

# *Windows NT Password and Authentication Methods*

This appendix contains information on Windows NT password changing and authentication methods. If no detailed information is available, then that fact is also mentioned here because knowledge of the existence of a mechanism is better than nothing.

## B.1: Definitions

- **Add(A1,A2)** Intel byte-ordered addition of corresponding 4 byte words in arrays A1 and A2.
- **E(K,D)** DES ECB encryption of 8-byte data D using 7-byte key K.
- **D(K,D)** DES ECB decryption of 8-byte data D using 7-byte key K.
- **LM#()** LM (LAN Manager) 16-byte cleartext-equivalent password hash.
- **NT#()** NT 16-byte cleartext-equivalent password hash.
- **RC4(K,Lk,D,Ld)** RC4 encryption of data D of length Ld with key K of length Lk.
- **v[m..n(,l)]** subset of v from bytes m to n, optionally padded with byte 0x00 to length l.
- **v[m..n(,l,0xNN)]** subset of v from bytes m to n, optionally padded with byte 0xNN to length l.
- **MD4(D)** MD4 message digest of data D [RFC 1320].
- **MD5(D)** MD5 message digest of data D [RFC 1321].
- **Unicode(s)** Unicode string s.
- **UC(s)** ASCII string, all lowercase letters replaced with uppercase letters. Numeric and symbol characters unaffected.

- **{ NN NN NN .. }** Data bytes (sequential, hexadecimal).
- **CRC32(D)** 32-bit Cyclic Redundancy Check of data D.
- **cat(A,B)** Concatenate data A with data B.
- **MOD(I,M)** Modulo M of integer I (I Modulus M).
- **HMAC(K, D)** HMAC MD5 of data D using key K. See RFC 2104.
- **OWF** One-Way Function.

# B.2: Authentication Tokens

## B.2.1: LM 16-Byte Cleartext-Equivalent Password Hashes

LM hashes are generated as follows:

- UP = UC(s[0..13])
- KGS = 8-byte string with ASCII characters "KGS!@#$%"
- LM#[0.. 7] = E(UP[ 0.. 6], KGS)
- LM#[8..15] = E(UP[ 7..13], KGS)

A good description of LM hashes and their weaknesses has been written by Open Solution Providers (`http://www.osp.nl/infobase/ntpass.html`).

## B.2.2: NT 16-Byte Cleartext-Equivalent Password Hashes

NT hashes are generated as follows:

- Up = Unicode(password)
- NT# = MD4(Up)

## B.2.3: User Session Key

In a number of places, a User Session Key is used rather than an NT or LM password hash to encrypt or decrypt sensitive information. The 16-byte User Session Key is as important to protect as the 16-byte password hashes themselves, and should never be revealed over-the-wire. It is calculated as follows:

- NT# = NT Password Hash (see B.2.2)
- NTskey = MD4(NT#)

The User Session Key is known to be transmitted in the "Network" version of a **NETLOGON NetrSamLogon** response, and is known to be used in at least **LsaQuerySecretInfo** (see B.6.1) and **SamrSetInformationUser** (see

B.5.4) to obfuscate important data. It is also used as part of the Authentication Verification process in [MS-CHAP-v2].

It has been reported, but not yet independently confirmed, that the use of NTLMv2 results in a different User Session Key being negotiated for use on a per-session basis. More information on the NTLMv2 User Session Key will be available when more information is also available on the use of NTLMv2 in NTLMSSP (see B.4.2).

# B.3: User Authentication

## B.3.1: SMB NTLM Challenge/Response System

An NTLM 24-byte LM and NT response is generated from an 8-byte, one-time server-generated challenge and either the LM or the NT password hash. It is used to determine to a high degree of probability whether a Client knows a password, without actually transmitting the password itself over a network.

- CS-8 = 8-byte server-generated random challenge
- Resp[ 0..23] = 24-byte LM or NT response
- PW# = either LM# (see 12.2.1) or NT# (see B.2.2)
- PW21 = PW#[0..15(,21)]
- Resp[ 0.. 7] = E(PW21[ 0.. 6], CS-8)
- Resp[ 8..15] = E(PW21[ 7..13], CS-8)
- Resp[16..23] = E(PW21[14..21], CS-8)
- LMR-24 = Resp[0..23] from LM#
- NTR-24 = Resp[0..23] from NT#

## B.3.2: SMB NTLM Version 2 Challenge/Response

This algorithm has been added to Windows NT 4.0 Service Pack 4 and above. It is enabled by setting the LmCompatibilityLevel registry key to 0x5 on servers, and to 0x3 on workstations. This change (enabled after the obligatory reboot) will have the effect of disabling communication with non-NTLMv2 SMB servers. To maintain backward compatibility with non-NTLMv2 SMB servers, set LmCompatibilityLevel registry key to 0x4 on servers and to 0x2 on workstations.

An example NTLMv2 server's **SMBnegprot** response is shown here. The Server Challenge is shown at bytes 0x7F to 0x86.

```
SMB: R negotiate, Dialect # = 7
    SMB: SMB Status = Error Success
    SMB: Command = C negotiate
        SMB: Capabilities = 17405 (0x43FD)
        SMB: Encryption key length = 8 (0x8)
        SMB: Domain name = ROCKNROLL
```

```
00030:                               53 4D 42 72 00    !B.......a.SMBr.
00040:  00 00 00 98 03 00 00 00 00 00 00 00 00 00 00 00    ................
00050:  00 00 00 00 FE CA 00 00 00 00 11 07 00 03 32 00    ..............2.
00060:  01 00 04 11 00 00 00 00 00 01 00 00 00 00 00 FD 43    ...............C
00070:  00 00 10 DC 51 C0 C3 92 BE 01 F0 00 08 1C 00 52    ....Q..........R
00080:  AA C8 E8 2C 06 7F A1 52 00 4F 00 43 00 4B 00 4E    ...,.R.O.C.K.N
00090:  00 52 00 4F 00 4C 00 4C 00 00 00    .R.O.L.L...
```

An example NTLMv2 client's **SMBsessonsetupX** response is shown here. The client's LMv3 response is shown at bytes 0x77 to 0x8e, where the LMv3 challenge is at 0x87 to 0x8e (LMv3_CLI_CHAL) and bytes 0x77 to 0x86 are calculated below (LMv3_RESP). The client's NTv3 response is shown at bytes 0x8f to 0xd9, whereas the NTv2 challenge is at 0x9f to 0xd9 (NTv2_CLI_CHAL), and bytes 0x8f to 0x9e are calculated below (NTv3_RESP).

```
SMB: C session setup & X, Username = administrator
    SMB: SMB Status = Error Success
    SMB: Command = C session setup & X
        SMB: Password length = 24 (0x18)
        SMB: Unicode Password length = 74 (0x4A)
        SMB: Capabilities = 212 (0xD4)
        SMB: Account name = administrator
        SMB: Domain name = rocknroll
        SMB: Native OS = Windows NT 1381
        SMB: Native Lanman = Windows NT 4.0
```

```
00030:                               53 4D 42 73 00    !........>.SMBs.
00040:  00 00 00 18 03 80 00 00 00 A0 35 60 6E 03 21 85    ..........5`n.!.
00050:  00 00 00 00 FE CA 00 00 00 00 0D 75 00 12 01 04    ...........u....
00060:  11 32 00 00 00 00 00 00 00 18 00 4A 00 00 00 00    .2.........J....
00070:  00 D4 00 00 00 D5 00 38 6B AE 8A CC 93 36 FA 8F    .......8k....6..
00080:  A5 16 CA F6 03 77 B0 05 83 32 EC FA E4 F3 6D 1A    .....w...2....m.
00090:  AD 55 22 61 87 C5 4F 9D D2 7A A1 5C CC 21 43 01    .U"a..O..z.\.!C.
000A0:  01 00 00 00 00 00 00 00 F0 20 D0 B6 C2 92 BE 01 05    ......... ......
000B0:  83 32 EC FA E4 F3 6D 6F 00 6E 00 02 00 12 00 52    .2....mo.n.....R
000C0:  00 4F 00 43 00 4B 00 4E 00 52 00 4F 00 4C 00 4C    .O.C.K.N.R.O.L.L
000D0:  00 00 00 00 00 65 00 00 00 4E 61 00 64 00 6D 00    .....e...Na.d.m.
000E0:  69 00 6E 00 69 00 73 00 74 00 72 00 61 00 74 00    i.n.i.s.t.r.a.t.
000F0:  6F 00 72 00 00 00 72 00 6F 00 63 00 6B 00 6E 00    o.r...r.o.c.k.n.
00100:  72 00 6F 00 6C 00 6C 00 00 00 57 00 69 00 6E 00    r.o.l.l...W.i.n.
00110:  64 00 6F 00 77 00 73 00 20 00 4E 00 54 00 20 00    d.o.w.s. .N.T. .
00120:  31 00 33 00 38 00 31 00 00 00 00 00 57 00 69 00    1.3.8.1.....W.i.
00130:  6E 00 64 00 6F 00 77 00 73 00 20 00 4E 00 54 00    n.d.o.w.s. .N.T.
00140:  20 00 34 00 2E 00 30 00 00 00 00 00 00 00     .4..0.......
```

### B.3.2.1: Definitions

- **HMACT64** Same as HMAC_MD5 in RFC 2104, except key is truncated instead of MD5 hashed above length 64 bytes.
- **UserName** User name.
- **DomainName** User's Domain. If the user is logged in to a Workstation, then this will be the Workstation name. If the user is logged in to a Domain, then this will be the name of the Domain to which the user is logged in.

### B.3.2.2: NTv2 and LMv3 Challenge/Response

To generate an NTv2 or LMv3 Challenge:

- NTTime() = 8-byte current time (100ms since 01/Jan/1600)
- Cc = 8-byte random challenge
- Udom = Unicode(DomainName)
- NTv2_CLI_CHAL = (1, 1, TIME(), Cc, Udom)
- LMv2_CLI_CHAL = Cc

Example:

```
NTv2_CLI_CHAL:
[000] 01 01 00 00 00 00 00 00  F0 20 D0 B6 C2 92 BE 01   ........ . ......
[010] 05 83 32 EC FA E4 F3 6D  6F 00 6E 00 02 00 12 00   ..2....m o.n.....
[020] 52 00 4F 00 43 00 4B 00  4E 00 52 00 4F 00 4C 00   R.O.C.K. N.R.O.L.
[030] 4C 00 00 00 00 00 65 00  00 00                     L.....e. ..

LMv3_CLI_CHAL:
[000] 05 83 32 EC FA E4 F3 6D                            ..2....m
```

To generate an NTLMv2 OWF:

- NT# = NT Password Hash (see B.2.2)
- UUuser = Unicode(UC(UserName));
- Udom = Unicode(DomainName));
- Kr = HMACT64(NT#, UUuser, Udom))

Example:

```
UUuser:
[000] 41 00 44 00 4D 00 49 00  4E 00 49 00 53 00 54 00   A.D.M.I. N.I.S.T.
[010] 52 00 41 00 54 00 4F 00  52 00                     R.A.T.O. R.

Udom:
[000] 72 00 6F 00 63 00 6B 00  6E 00 72 00 6F 00 6C 00   r.o.c.k. n.r.o.l.
[010] 6C 00                                              l.
```

```
NT#:
[000] 0C B6 94 88 05 F7 97 BF  2A 82 80 79 73 B8 95 37  ........ *..ys..7

Kr:
[000] 40 E1 B3 24 07 04 C3 64  15 49 BA DC C3 25 F3 CE  @..$...d .I...%..
```

To generate an NTv2 or LMv3 Response:

- Cs = 8-byte random challenge.
- NTv2_Resp = HMACT64(Kr, (Cs, NTv2_CLI_CHAL))
- LMv2_Resp = HMACT64(Kr, (Cs, LMv2_CLI_CHAL))

Example:

```
SRV_CHAL:
[000] 52 AA C8 E8 2C 06 7F A1                           R...,...

NTv2_RESP:
[000] 1A AD 55 22 61 87 C5 4F  9D D2 7A A1 5C CC 21 43  ..U"a..O ..z.\.!C

LMv2_RESP:
[000] 38 6B AE 8A CC 93 36 FA  8F A5 16 CA F6 03 77 B0  8k....6. ......w.
```

### B.3.2.3: Notes

- The HMAC_MD5 algorithm used here truncates its key at 64 bytes. RFC 2104 will substitute key = MD5(Key) if the key is greater than 64 bytes. It just so happens that none of the keys in this example are longer than 64 bytes; they are only 16 bytes.
- All strings observed are Unicode. The User name is *likely* to be Unicode regardless of whether Unicode is negotiated at the SMB level (Server's **SMBnegprot** response). The Domain name is *suspected* to be the data that comes off the wire in the Client's **SMBsessonsetupX** request.
- The NULL character (actually, a NULL Unicode character) is *NOT* included in the HMAC_MD5 data.
- DomainName is the name of the Domain under which the user is logged in. This *can* be the Local Workstation. The user's Domain is sent as part of the **SMBsessonsetupX** request, and this string should be used unmodified (unlike the User name, which is uppercased).

## B.3.3: MSRPC NETLOGON Pipe Credential Chain

This section describes the DCE/RPC NETLOGON pipe "Interactive" and "Netlogon" Credential chain system. It uses Trust Account Passwords (Workstation or Inter-Domain) to protect users' passwords. Unfortunately, at the present time, these passwords are initialised to well-known values.

This section is relevant only to Windows NT 4.0 Service Pack 3 and below. When Windows NT 4.0 Service Pack 4 is applied to *all* Workstations and *all* Domain Controllers, a different NETLOGON system is negotiated and used, known as the NETLOGON Secure Channel (see B.3.4).

### B.3.3.1: Definitions

- **PW** MD4(wks_trust_password) == MD4(lsadump $wks_trust.acc) == pwdump(wks_trust$) == MD4(Unicode(workstation name, in lowercase)), initially.
- **Cred(K,D)** $E(K[7..7,7],E(K[0..6],D))$. Computes a Credential.
- **Time()** 4-byte current time.
- **Cc** 8-byte Client challenge.
- **Cs** 8-byte Server challenges.
- **Rc** 8-byte Client Credential.
- **Rs** 8-byte Server Credential.
- **C->S Net\*** Client sends data to Server using function named Net\*.
- **S->C Net\*** Server sends data to Client in modified parameters of function named Net\*.
- **C:** Client.
- **S:** Server.

### B.3.3.2: Protocol

- C: generates Cc
- S: generates Cs
- C->S NetrRequestChallenge: Cc
- S->C NetrRequestChallenge: Cs
- C & S: session key $Ks = E(PW[9..15],E(PW[0..6],Add(Cc,Cs)))$

- C: Rc = Cred(Ks,Cc)
- C->S NetrAuthenticate2: Rc
- S: Rs = Cred(Ks,Cs), assert(Rc == Cred(Ks,Cc))
- S->C NetrAuthenticate2: Rs
- C: assert(Rs == Cred(Ks,Cs))

On joining the Domain, the Client will optionally attempt to change its password to a random value. The Domain Controller may refuse to update the password, depending on Registry settings. This will also occur weekly afterwards.

- C: Tc = Time(), Rc' = Cred(Ks,Rc+Tc)
- C->S NetServerPasswordSet: Rc',Tc, rc4(Ks[0..7,16], LM#)
- C: Rc = Cred(Ks,Rc+Tc+1)
- S: assert(Rc' == Cred(Ks,Rc+Tc)), Ts = Time()
- S: Rs' = Cred(Ks,Rs+Tc+1)
- S->C NetServerPasswordSet: Rs',Ts
- C: assert(Rs' == Cred(Ks,Rs+Tc+1))
- S: Rs = Rs'

**Interactive NetrSamLogon**
User U with password P wishes to log in to the Domain (incidental data such as Workstation and Domain omitted).

- C: Tc = Time(), Rc' = Cred(Ks,Rc+Tc)
- C->S NetrSamLogon: Rc',Tc,U, rc4(Ks[0..7,16],16,NT#,16), rc4(Ks[0..7,16],16,LM#,16)
- S: assert(Rc' == Cred(Ks,Rc+Tc)) assert(passwords match in SAM)
- S: Ts = Time()
- S->C NetrSamLogon: Cred(Ks,Cred(Ks,Rc+Tc+1)), userinfo(logon script,UID,SIDs,etc.)
- C: assert(Rs == Cred(Ks,Cred(Rc+Tc+1))
- C: Rc = Cred(Ks,Rc+Tc+1)

**Network NetrSamLogon**

User U with password P wishes to access a Workstation in a Domain (incidental data such as Workstation and Domain omitted). The intermediate Workstation contacts Domain Controller.

- C: Tc = Time(), Rc' = Cred(Ks,Rc+Tc)
- C->S NetrSamLogon: Rc',Tc,U, (CS-8, LMR-24, NTR-24)
- S: assert(Rc' == Cred(Ks,Rc+Tc)) assert(passwords match in SAM)
- S: Ts = Time()
- S->C NetrSamLogon: Cred(Ks,Cred(Ks,Rc+Tc+1)), userinfo(logon script,UID,SIDs,etc.)
- C: assert(Rs == Cred(Ks,Cred(Rc+Tc+1))
- C: Rc = Cred(Ks,Rc+Tc+1)

### B.3.3.3: Credits and References

The original article is Paul Ashton's "NT Domain Member to Domain Controller Authentication Protocol." It can be found in *The NTBugtraq Archives* as Article 40, August 1997.

The Credential Chain was worked out by Paul Ashton and Luke Leighton.

# B.3.4: MSRPC NETLOGON "Secure Channel"

The **NETLOGON** "Secure Channel" has been added to NT 4.0 Service Pack 4 and above. The intent is to provide a more secure means to protect **\PIPE\NETLOGON**. An attacker can potentially modify the data stream, without knowing the Trust Account Password, when the **NETLOGON** "Secure Channel" is not negotiated.

An attacker's task as a "man in the middle" is made more difficult with the **NETLOGON** "Secure Channel." The Trust Account Password must be known in order to decrypt and observe the login taking place, and the attacker must then potentially modify and re-encrypt the NETLOGON channel.

### 12.3.4.1: Definitions

- **PW** MD4(wks_trust_password) == MD4(lsadump $wks_trust.acc) == pwdump(wks_trust$) == MD4(Unicode(workstation name, in lowercase)), initially.

- **Cred(K,D)** E(K[7..7,7],E(K[0..6],D)). Computes a Credential.
- **Time()** 4-byte current time.
- **Cc** 8-byte Client challenge.
- **Cs** 8-byte Server challenges.
- **Rc** 8-byte Client Credential.
- **Rs** 8-byte Server Credential.
- **C->S Net*** Client sends data to Server using function named Net*.
- **S->C Net*** Server sends data to Client in modified parameters of function named Net*.

### B.3.4.2: Protocol

- C: generates Cc
- S: generates Cs
- C->S NetrRequestChallenge: Cc
- S->C NetrRequestChallenge: Cs
- C & S: session key Ks = E(PW[9..15],E(PW[0..6],Add(Cc,Cs)))
- C: Rc = Cred(Ks,Cc)
- C->S NetrAuthenticate2: Rc
- S: Rs = Cred(Ks,Cs), assert(Rc == Cred(Ks,Cc))
- S->C NetrAuthenticate2: Rs
- C: assert(Rs == Cred(Ks,Cs))

At this point, if bit 31 of the **NetrAuthenticate2** negotiation flags is set, then a *second* MSRPC connection is opened whilst the first is also left open. The second MSRPC connection negotiates the encrypted **NETLOGON** secure channel system, and all subsequent MSRPC traffic on that connection is signed and sealed. The session key (Ks) from the first **NETLOGON** connection is used as the basis of the sign and seal encryption on the second channel.

### Definitions

- **HMACT64** Same as HMAC_MD5 in RFC 2104, except key is truncated instead of MD5 hashed above length 64 bytes.
- **DReq** Data stream of individual Request to be signed.
- **DResp** Data stream of individual Response to be signed.
- **Data** DReq or DResp.

- **SNS-8** (Secure NETLOGON Signature) { 77 00 7a 00 ff ff 00 00 }
- **00-4** { 00 00 00 00 }
- **e(N)** Encrypted form of N.
- **Si-8** 8-byte signature.
- **Sq-8** 8-byte sequence signature.
- **Verf** 24-byte Authentication Verifier.

### B.3.4.3: Calculation of Sequence Key
There is a key to encrypt/decrypt the 8-byte sequence number, calculated as follows:

- SqK = 16-byte key to encrypt Sq-8
- SqK = HMACT64(HMACT64(session key Ks, 00-4), e(Si-8))

### B.3.4.4: Calculation of Data Stream and Signature Key
There is a key to encrypt/decrypt both the variable length data stream and the 8-byte signature, calculated as follows:

- Nc-8 = 8-byte random nonce.
- F0-16 = { F0 F0 F0 F0 F0 F0 F0 F0 F0 F0 F0 F0 F0 F0 F0 F0 }
- KsF = Ks XOR F0-16 (that is, each byte of Ks XORed with 0xF0)
- DSK = HMACT64(HMACT64(KsF, 00-4), Sq-8)

### B.3.4.5: Authentication Verifier
When traffic is being signed, an Authentication Verifier is attached. It is calculated as follows:

- Si-16 = HMACT64(Ks, MD5( cat(00-4, SNS-8, Nc-8, Data) ) )
- Si-8[0..7] = Si-16[0..7]
- Verf = cat( SNS-8, e(Sq-8), e(Si-8), Nc-8 )

### B.3.4.6: Signed and Sealed Traffic
RC4 is used to encrypt the 8-byte signature, the 8-byte sequence number, and the data stream itself, with the keys calculated above, as follows:

- e(Si-8) = RC4(DSK, 16, Si-8, 8)
- e(Data) = RC4(DSK, 16, Data, Len(Data))
- e(Sq-8) = RC4(SqK, 16, Sq-8, 8)

### B.3.4.7: Credits

- Paul Leach (paulle@microsoft.com) for pointing out the KB article on how to mandate **NETLOGON** sign/seal.

# B.4: NTLM Secure Service Provider

## B.4.1: NTLMSSP Version 1

NTLM Secure Service Provider (NTLMSSP) can be used to sign and seal many types of traffic. It is best known for its use in encrypting the following traffic:

- DCE/RPC. Microsoft Exchange Server Administrative programs use NTLMSSP-encrypted DCE/RPC.
- MSRPC. Windows NT Password changes use NTLMSSP-encrypted MSRPC over connections to \PIPE\samr.
- HTTP.

An RC4 key is used to encrypt the data stream and an authentication verifier. The RC4 state is initialised from this key at the start and is not re-initialised.

### B.4.1.1: Calculation of NTLMSSP-v1 RC4 Key

The NTLMSSP-v1 key is generated from information gathered from the standard NTLM Challenge/Response system (see B.3.1). A variation of this scheme is then used once again to generate an RC4 key. This key is then used to sign and seal traffic.

- CS-8 = 8-byte server-generated random challenge
- LMR-24 - LM 24-byte response (see 12.3.1)
- LMBD-21 = LM#[0..15(,21-0xBD)]
- LMR-8 = LMR-24[0..7]
- LMV-24[ 0.. 7] = E(LMBD-21[ 0.. 6], LMR-8)
- LMV-24[ 8..15] = E(LMBD-21[ 7..13], LMR-8)
- LMV-24[16..23] = E(LMBD-21[14..21], LMR-8)

- 40-bit case:
  - SSPkey[0..4] = LMV-24[0..4]
  - SSPkey[5..7] = { E5 38 B0 }
  - SSPklen = 8
- 128-bit case:
  - SSPkey[0..15] = LMV-24[0..15]
  - SSPklen = 16

### B.4.1.2: Authentication Verifier
When traffic is being signed, an Authentication Verifier is attached. It is calculated as follows:

- DReq = Data stream of individual Request to be signed
- DResp = Data stream of individual Response to be signed
- AV[0..3] = { 00 00 00 00 }
- AV[4..7] = CRC32(Data Stream - DReq or DResp)
- AV[8..11] = { 00 00 00 00 }
- EncAV[0..3] = { 01 00 00 00 }
- EncAV[4..15] = RC4(SSPkey, SSPklen, AV, 12)

The CRC32 Algorithm used is available from *Dr. Dobb's Journal* (www.ddj.com/ftp/1992/1992.05/crcman.zip).

### B.4.1.3: Signed and Sealed Traffic
RC4 is used to obfuscate the first request data stream and the first request verifier, followed by the first response data stream and the first response verifier, followed by the second request data stream, and so forth. DReq and DReq are defined above in section B.4.1.2:

- EReq = cat(RC4(SSPkey, SSPklen, DReq, Len(DReq)), EncAV(DReq))
- ERes = cat(RC4(SSPkey, SSPklen, DRes, Len(DRes)), EncAV(DRes))

## B.4.2: MSRPC NTLMSSP Version 2
Undocumented. Same data format observed in SMB NTLMv2 challenge/response. Added to Windows NT 4.0 Service Pack 4 and above.

### B.4.3: MSRPC NTLMSSP Session Key Negotiation

Undocumented, both in NTLM version 1 and 2.

### B.4.4: NTLMSSP over HTTP

This mechanism, and details on the mechanism, is known to exist.

## B.5: Changing User Authentication Tokens

### B.5.1: Windows 95 SMB Password Change

Password changes are encrypted over **SMBtrans2** using the following method:

- OLM# = Old (previous) User's LM#
- PW = User's new Password
- PWbuf[0..511] = Initialised to Pseudo-Random data
- PWbuf[512..515] = Len(PW)
- PWbuf[511-Len(PW)..511] = PW
- EncPWbuf[0..515] = RC4(OLM#, 16, PWbuf, 516)

Password changes are verified over **SMBtrans2** using the following method:

- OLM# = Old (previous) User's LM#
- LM# = User's new LM#
- EncPWver[0.. 7] = E(OLM#[0.. 6], LM#[ 0.. 7])
- EncPWver[8..15] = E(OLM#[7..13], LM#[ 8..15])

This method is similar to those used to change Windows NT passwords (see 12.5.2) and to set user passwords with **SamrSetInformationUser** (see B.5.4).

### B.5.2: Windows NT MSRPC samr Password Change

Passwords are encrypted twice when changed over MSRPC **\PIPE\samr**. The two blocks contain exactly the same user's new password. The Windows NT Password Change function **SamrChangePasswordUser** contains two sets of encrypted password blocks and two verifiers. The first block uses the old NT Password Hash to encrypt the user's new password, as follows:

- ONT# = Old (previous) user's NT#
- PW = user's new password

- UPW = Unicode(PW)
- PWbuf[0..511] = Initialised to Pseudo-Random data
- PWbuf[512..515] = Len(PW)
- PWbuf[511-Len(PW)..511] = UPW
- EncPWbuf[0..515] = RC4(ONT#, 16, PWbuf, 516)

The new password in the first block is verified as follows:

- ONT# = Old (previous) user's NT#
- NT# = user's new NT#
- EncPWver[0.. 7] = E(ONT#[0.. 6], NT#[ 0.. 7])
- EncPWver[8..15] = E(ONT#[7..13], NT#[ 8..15])

This password change block and its verifier is identical to the [MS-CHAP-v2] Password Change (see 12.5.3). There is, however, a second block in the **SamrChangePasswordUser** function. The second block uses the old LM Password Hash to encrypt the user's new password, as follows:

- OLM# = Old (previous) user's LM#
- PW = user's new password
- UPW = Unicode(PW)
- PWbuf[0..511] = Initialised to Pseudo-Random data
- PWbuf[512..515] = Len(PW)
- PWbuf[511-Len(PW)..511] = UPW
- EncPWbuf[0..515] = RC4(OLM#, 16, PWbuf, 516)

The new password in the second block is verified as follows:

- ONT# = Old (previous) user's NT#
- LM# = user's new LM#
- EncPWver[0.. 7] = E(ONT#[0.. 6], LM#[ 0.. 7])
- EncPWver[8..15] = E(ONT#[7..13], LM#[ 8..15])

This method for changing passwords is similar to the methods used to change Windows 95 passwords (see B.5.2) and to set User passwords with **SamrSetInformationUser** (see B.5.4).

### B.5.3: MS-CHAP-v2 (PPP) Password Change

The IETF Draft RFC, draft-ietf-pppext-mschap-v2-03.txt, is a "work in progress" document and should only be and is only quoted here as such. It contains a section entitled "Change-Password Packet."

The method uses the old NT Password Hash to encrypt the user's new UNICODE password and uses the new NT Password Hash to encrypt the old NT Password Hash. This password change method is identical to the first block (not the second, which uses the old LM Password Hash) of the **SamrChangePasswordUser** Password change method (see 12.5.2).

Credits and Author
Thanks to the author, Glen Zorn, (gwz@acm.org), for permission to refer to sections of draft-ietf-pppext-mschap-v2-03.txt.

### B.5.4: MSRPC SamrSetInformationUser

#### B.5.4.1: Description
The following method is used to encrypt passwords as they are added to User accounts:

- SessK = MD4(Administrator's NT#)
- PW = User's new Password
- UPW = Unicode(PW)
- PWbuf[0..511] = Initialised to Pseudo-Random data
- PWbuf[512..515] = Len(PW)
- PWbuf[511-Len(UPW)..511] = UPW
- EncPWbuf[0..515] = RC4(SessK, 16, PWbuf, 516)

This method for changing passwords is similar to the methods used to change Windows 95 passwords (see B.5.2) and to change Windows NT passwords (see B.5.4).

#### B.5.4.2: Credits

- Paul Ashton (xml@mailandnews.com) for the original work on decoding **NETLOGON** (see B.3.3) and for helping extend the attack analysis.
- Luke Leighton (lkcl@iss.net) for decoding (guess-work!) **SamrSetInformationUser**, and further work on **NETLOGON** and the attack analysis.

- David LeBlanc (dleblanc@mindspring.com) for suggestions on security recommendations.

- Jeremy Allison (jra@samba.org) for helping extend the attack analysis.

- Mike Slifcak (mslifcak@iss.net) for review comments.

- Andre Frech (afrech@iss.net) for review comments.

## B.5.5: MSRPC SAM Database Replication: PDC/BDC Interaction

Primary Domain Controllers (PDCs) can share their Security Accounts Manager (SAM) database with Backup Domain Controllers (BDCs). Users can then log in to a Domain using any PDC or its BDCs. The login load is automatically distributed amongst the PDC and its BDCs. The load distribution can be influenced by careful design of a network's layout.

The SAM database must be replicated from the PDC to its BDCs. This replication is initiated by the BDC, as the BDC knows when it last (or if it ever) asked for an update. All details of all SAM database entries (users, which includes Workstation, Server, and Inter-Domain Trust Accounts; Domain Groups and their members; Local Groups and their members) can be requested.

In Service Pack 3 and below, the majority of this information is sent in-the-clear. The only encrypted component is the User password field, which contains the 16-byte cleartext equivalent LanManager hash (LM#) and NT hash (NT#). This obfuscated component is 68 bytes in length. The rest of the PDC-to-BDC replication is not described in detail here because it can be easily understood by examining a network trace, whereas the obfuscated component, containing the passwords, cannot.

In Service Pack 4 and above, the **NETLOGON** "Secure Channel" can be used. It must be installed on the PDC, and it must also be installed on each BDC for each individual PDC/BDC replication to negotiate the **NETLOGON** "Secure Channel." Under these circumstances, the entire SAM replication/synchronisation data is encrypted using the Server Trust Account Password as the basis for the sign and seal keys.

The process of adding a BDC to a Domain can be done in two ways. The first method is to install Windows NT Server as a BDC. If you have it connected to the network and the BDC network drivers successfully install, then a dialog box requests the Administrator's User name and password. This is the same as if you were adding a Workstation to a Domain from the Network Control Panel, and in fact exactly the same thing occurs: A **SAMRSETINFORMATIONUSER** call is made that adds a Server Trust Account Password using the Server's name in UNICODE lowercase. After this has been done, the BDC setup continues by opening a connection to **\PIPE\NETLOGON**, setting up a credential chain using the Server Trust Account Password, and then issuing **NetrSamSync** and **NetrSamDeltas** calls.

The second method is to skip this dialog box, reboot, connect the BDC to the network (install necessary network drivers and so forth) using Server Manager for Domains, and add a Server to the Domain with the BDC's name. In this case, a **SamrSetInformationUser** call sets up the Server Trust Account Password in the same way as described above. After the BDC comes online, it will sync with the PDC to obtain a copy of the SAM database over the **\PIPE\NETLOGON**, also in the same way as described above.

The following sections describe how the 68-byte password block is decrypted and the associated problems, and how to minimise the risks associated with these problems.

### B.5.5.1: SAM Replication Password Key
The key to encrypt/decrypt the 68-byte password block is the 16-byte Session Key (Ks) from the **NETLOGON** credential chain, which is actually 8 bytes padded to 16 bytes with zeros. This key is used as an RC4 key to all blocks, independent of each other. In other words, the RC4 XOR cypher stream is reset for each and every password block, and the same key is used to obfuscate each and every password block.

### B.5.5.2: SAM Password Hash Keys
After the 68-byte password block has been decrypted, it becomes clear exactly where the LM# and NT# are stored. These are *also* encrypted, and the encryption mechanism is identical to that used to store the LM# and the NT# in the Windows NT Registry. This mechanism, which is used in the PWDUMP utility written by Jeremy Allison (jra@samba.org) and which has an equivalent program in the Windows NT Server ResKit, is described in the following section.

### Definitions
- **User** A normal user, or a Trust Account, which includes Workstation (for Workstation logins), Server (that is, Backup Domain Controllers), and Inter-Domain.

- **RID** User's Relative ID (RID) in the SAM Database.
- **Key** Encryption key for password hashes.
- **nt#** Encrypted version of NT# in the 68-byte password block.
- **lm#** Encrypted version of LM# in the 68-byte password block.

### Protocol

- Key[0..4 ] = RID[0..3]
- Key[5..7 ] = RID[0..2]
- nt#[0..7 ] = E(Key, NT#[0..7 ])
- nt#[8..15] = E(Key, NT#[8..15])
- lm#[0..7 ] = E(Key, LM#[0..7 ])
- lm#[8..15] = E(Key, LM#[8..15])

### B.5.5.3: Credits

- MSRPC calls successfully decoded by Matthew Chapman (matty@samba.org), except the 68-byte Password field.
- 68-byte Password field successfully decoded by Luke Kenneth Casson Leighton (lkcl@samba.org).
- Password field decode implementation written by Matthew Chapman (matty@samba.org) and Luke Kenneth Casson Leighton (lkcl@samba.org), from which the specification in this document was written.
- Review comments from Kelley Blount (kblount@iss.net).

# B.6: Miscellaneous

## B.6.1: MSRPC LsarQuerySecretInfo

This DCE/RPC function call returns private information. The information is encrypted using MD4(NT#), known as the "User Session Key," which is also used in **SamrSetInformationUser** to encrypt the user's password (see B.5.4).

The User Session Key, a 16-byte quantity, is used round-robin to select 7-byte DES keys. Take the User Session Key and repeat it continuously. Take the first 7 bytes as the first DES key, then the second 7 bytes, and so on. If a key ever crosses a boundary between two repetitions of the User Session Key, then it is skipped. The "skipping" first occurs on the third 7 bytes, which "starts" at the 14th byte of the User Session Key and "ends" at the 5th byte.

Initialisation and Definitions are as follows:

- $N = 0$
- $M = 0$
- NTskey = User Session Key
- EncData = Encrypted Data

The following is repeated until the data is decrypted:

- $N = N + 7$
- $M = M + 7$
- If $(N + 7 > 16)$ Then $N = MOD((N + 7), 16)$
- Data[M..M+7] = D(NTskey[N..N+6], EncData[M..M+7]

**B.6.1.1: Credits**
Thanks to Matthew Chapman (matty@samba.org) for decoding (guess work!) **LsaRetrievePrivateData.**

## B.6.2: SMB Signing
Microsoft's CIFS Documentation (ftp://www.microsoft.com/developr/drg/CIFS) contains a document that specifies how SMB signing works. The relevant document by Paul Leach (paulle@microsoft.com) is a preliminary draft. As such, the author requests that it not be cited. It is the only known source of information on SMB signing.

# B.7: Credits

- Andre Frech (afrech@iss.net) for review comments.
- Mike Warfield (mhw@iss.net) for review comments.

# B.8: More Information

- Open Solution Providers (http://www/osp.nl/infobase/ntpass.html)
- L0pht Industries (http://www.l0pht.com)
- CIFS Documentation (ftp://www.microsoft.com/developr/drg/CIFS)
- CRC32—Dr Dobb's. (http://www.ddj.com/ftp/1992/1992.05/crcman.zip)
- MS-PPTP Analysis (http://www.counterpane.com/pptp-paper.html)
- NT Password Security (http://www.osp.nl/infobase/ntpass.html)
- MS-CHAP-v2—IETF Draft RFC (ftp://search.ietf.org/internet-drafts/draft-ietf-pppext-mschap-v2-03.txt)

# *Index*

# B

# C

## G-H

## I-J

## K-L

# M-N

## O-P

# Q-R

# Books for Technology Professionals

MACMILLAN
TECHNICAL
PUBLISHING
U·S·A

## Windows NT

### Windows NT Automated Deployment and Customization
by Richard Puckett
1st Edition
$32.00
ISBN: 1-57870-045-0

Time-saving advice that helps you install, update, and configure software on each of your clients, without having to visit each client. Control all clients remotely for tasks such as security and legal software use. Includes reference material on native NT tools, registry edits, and third-party tools.

### Windows NT Shell Scripting
by Tim Hill
1st Edition
$32.00
ISBN: 1-57870-047-7

A complete reference for Windows NT scripting, this book guides you through a high-level introduction to the shell language itself and the shell commands that are useful for controlling or managing different components of a network.

### Windows NT and UNIX Integration
by Gene Henriksen
1st Edition
$32.00
ISBN: 1-57870-048-5

This book provides you with an all-in-one guide to integrating NT and UNIX in the same network, beginning with the fundamentals of both NT and UNIX, and following with discussions of file sharing, proven solutions to the problems related to printing in an integrated environment, and more.

### Windows NT Device Driver Deployment
by Peter Viscarola and W. Anthony Mason
1st Edition
$50.00
ISBN: 1-57870-058-2

This title begins with an introduction to the general Windows NT operating system concepts relevant to drivers, then progresses to more detailed information about the operating system, such as interrupt management, synchronization issues, the I/O Subsystem, standard kernel mode drivers, and more.

### Windows NT Heterogeneous Networking
by Steven Thomas
1st Edition
$40.00
ISBN: 1-57870-064-7

A complete reference for internetworking all major systems with Windows NT, both at the OS and protocol levels, you'll find information on how to successfully develop an enterprise model as well as coverage of how to optimize hardware, domain controllers, and enterprise service traffic.

### Windows NT Thin Client Solutions

by Todd Mathers and
Shawn Genoway
1st Edition
$35.00
ISBN: 1-57870-065-5

Explore the cost-saving features of
Windows-Based Terminal Server—
which allows applications to be run on
a server—as well as the software based
upon Citrix's core ICA (Independent
Computing Architecture) protocol that
provides enterprise capability.

### Windows NT Win32 Perl Programming: The Standard Extensions

by Dave Roth
1st Edition
$40.00
ISBN: 1-57870-067-1

See numerous proven examples and
practical uses of Perl in solving everyday
Win32 problems. This is the only book
available with comprehensive coverage of
Win32 extensions, where most of the Perl
functionality resides in Windows settings.

### Windows NT Domain Architecture

by Gregg Branham
1st Edition
$38.00
ISBN: 1-57870-112-0

As Windows NT continues
to be deployed more and more in the
enterprise, the domain architecture for
the network becomes more critical as
the complexity increases. This book
contains the in-depth expertise that is
necessary to truly plan a complex
enterprise domain.

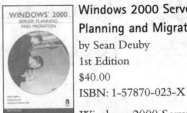

### Windows 2000 Server: Planning and Migration

by Sean Deuby
1st Edition
$40.00
ISBN: 1-57870-023-X

Windows 2000 Server:
Planning and Migration can quickly save
the NT professional thousands of dollars
and hundreds of hours. This title includes
authoritative information on key features
of Windows 2000 and offers recommendations on how to best position your NT
network for Windows 2000.

### Windows 2000 Quality of Service

by David Iseminger
1st Edition
$45.00
ISBN: 1-57870-115-5

As the traffic on networks
continues to increase, the strain on
network infrastructure and available
resources has also grown. Windows 2000
Quality of Service teaches network
engineers and administrators how to
define traffic control patterns and utilize
bandwidth and their networks.

### Windows NT Applications: Measuring and Optimizing Performance

by Paul Hinsberg
1st Edition
$45.00
ISBN: 1-57870-176-7

This book offers developers crucial
insight into the underlying structure of
Windows NT, as well as the methodology
and tools for measuring and ultimately
optimizing code performance.

## Windows 2000 and Mainframe Integration

by William Zack
1st Edition
$40.00
ISBN: 1-57870-200-3

*Windows 2000 and Mainframe Integration* provides mainframe computing professionals with the practical know-how to build and integrate Windows 2000 technologies into their current environment.

## Windows Script Host

by Tim Hill
1st Edition
$35.00
ISBN: 1-57870-139-2

*Windows Script Host* is one of the first books published about this powerful tool. The text focuses on system scripting and the VBScript language, using objects, server scriptlets, and ready-to-use script solutions.

# Programming

## Handbook of Programming Languages, Volume I

Edited by Peter Salus
1st Edition
$49.99
ISBN: 1-57870-008-6

This is the most comprehensive source on the principal object-oriented languages. It covers languages from Smalltalk to Java, with explanations of the languages' histories, descriptions of their syntax and semantics, how-to information and tips, and pointers to potential traps.

## Handbook of Programming Languages, Volume II

Edited by Peter Salus
1st Edition
$49.99
ISBN: 1-57870-009-4

The four most important imperative languages are covered in this title: Fortran, C, Turbo Pascal, and Icon. Evaluate them to find the best imperative language for your purpose at hand, and learn how these languages are related to each other historically and syntactically.

## Handbook of Programming Languages, Volume III

Edited by Peter Salus
1st Edition
$49.99
ISBN: 1-57870-010-8

Beginning with Jon Bentley's discussion of little languages, this book continues to discuss languages "specialized to a particular problem domain"—such as Perl, sed, awk, SQL, Tcl/Tk, Python, and more.

## Handbook of Programming Languages, Volume IV

Edited by Peter Salus
1st Edition
$49.99
ISBN: 1-57870-011-6

This book begins with the functional programming group, descended from John McCarthy's LISP of the late 1960s, and moves on to discuss its offspring: Emacs Lisp, Scheme, Guile, and CLOS.

## Smart Card Developers Kit

by Scott Guthery and
Tim Jurgensen

1st Edition
$79.99
ISBN: 1-57870-027-2

This is all the practical information a computing professional needs to write programs that use and run on smart cards. Smart card communications and commands, SDKs, terminal-side and card-side APIs, security, financial applications, and e-commerce are all covered in this title.

## Autoconf, Automake, and Libtool

by Ben Elliston, et al.
1st Edition
$34.99, Spring 2000
ISBN: 1-57870-190-2

This book is the first of its kind, authored by Open Source community luminaries and current maintainers of the tools, teaching developers how to boost their productivity and the portability of their applications using GNU autoconf, GNU automake, and GNU libtool.

## Delphi COM Programming

by Eric Harmon
1st Edition
$45.00, Winter 2000
ISBN: 1-57870-221-6

*Delphi COM Programming* is for all Delphi 4 and 5 programmers. After providing readers with an understanding of the COM framework, it offers a practical exploration of COM to enable Delphi developers to program component-based applications. Typical real-world scenarios, such as Windows Shell programming, automating Microsoft Agent, and creating and using ActiveX controls, are explored. Discussions of each topic are illustrated with detailed examples.

## glibc: A Comprehensive Reference to GNU/Linux libC

by Jeff Garzik
1st Edition
$40.00, Winter 2000
ISBN: 1-57870-202-X

*glibc: A Comprehensive Reference to GNU/Linux libC* comprises over 1,800 functions. A complete reference work—encompassing a single-volume version that gives quick coverage to each function. It includes an easily searched index to provide added value. The book content consists of an index of functions by category (networking, threading, string, etc), and then an alphabetical function listing.

# Networking

## LDAP: Programming Directory Enabled Applications

by Tim Howes and Mark Smith
$44.99
ISBN: 1-57870-000-0

This overview of the LDAP standard discusses its creation and history with the Internet Engineering Task Force, as well as the original RFC standard. LDAP also covers compliance trends, implementation, data packet handling in C++, client/server responsibilities and more.

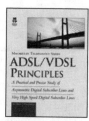

## ASDL/VSDL Principles

by Dennis Rushmayer
1st Edition
$44.99
ISBN: 1-57870-015-9

*ASDL/VSDL Principles* provides the communications and networking engineer with the practical explanations, technical detail, and in-depth insight needed to fully implement ASDL and VSDL. Coverage includes the fundamentals of the transmission theory and crosstalk in the outside plant, including the details of modeling and simulating the expected performance of ADSL and VDSL under different operating conditions.

## DSL: Specialization Techniques and Standards

by Walter Chen
1st Edition
$54.99
ISBN: 1-57870-017-5

DSL is ideal for computing professionals who are looking for information on new high-speed communications technologies, and information on the dynamics of ADSL communications in order to create compliant applications. Get calculation examples for all signal environments, and coverage of ADSL and a multitude of other xDSL technologies.

## Gigabit Ethernet Networking

by David Cunningham and Bill Lane
1st Edition
$50.00
ISBN: 1-57870-062-0

Gigabit Ethernet is the next step for speed on the majority of installed networks. Explore how this technology will allow high-bandwidth applications such as the integration of telephone and data services, real-time applications, thin client apps such as Windows NT Terminal Server, and corporate teleconferencing.

## Supporting Service Level Agreements on IP Networks

by Dinesh Verma
1st Edition
$50.00
ISBN: 1-57870-146-5

An essential resource for network engineers and architects, *Supporting Service Level Agreements on IP Networks* will help you build a core network capable of supporting a range of service. You'll also learn to create SLA solutions using off-the-shelf components in both best-effort and DiffServ/IntServ networks. See how to verify the performance of your SLA, as either a customer or network services provider, and use SLA's to support IPv6 networks.

## Directory Enabled Networks

by John Strassner
1st Edition
$55.00
ISBN: 1-57870-140-6

*Directory Enabled Networks* (DEN) is a completely new paradigm for leveraging the network. While networks are currently able to provide Class of Service and Quality of Service, these services currently have high associated cost of ownership. If these services can be centrally controlled and provisioned by simpler means, then they can support existing applications as well as new network-aware applications that require dynamic, yet guaranteed levels of service while reducing the Total Cost of Ownership.

## Understanding Public-Key Infrastructure

by Carlisle Adams
1st Edition
$50.00
ISBN: 1-57870-166-X

This book is a tutorial on, and a guide to the deployment of, Public-Key Infrastructures. It covers a broad range of material related to PKIs, including certification, operational considerations, and standardization efforts, as well as deployment issues and considerations. Emphasis is placed on explaining the interrelated fields within the topic area, to assist those who will be responsible for making deployment decisions and architecting a PKI within an organization.

## Intrusion Detection

by Rebecca Bace
1st Edition
$50.00
ISBN: 1-57870-185-6

Intrusion detection is a critical new area of technology within network security. This comprehensive guide to the field of intrusion detection covers the foundations of intrusion detection and system audit. *Intrusion Detection* provides a wealth of information, ranging from design considerations and how to evaluate and choose the optimal commercial intrusion detection products for a particular networking environment.

### Designing Addressing Architectures for Routing and Switching
by Howard Berkowitz
1st Edition
$45.00
ISBN: 1-57870-059-0

One of the greatest challenges for a network design professional is making visible the users, servers, files, printers and other resources on their network. This title equips the network engineer or architect with a systematic methodology for planning the wide area and local area network "streets" on which users and servers live.

### Understanding and Deploying LDAP Directory Services
by Tim Howes; Mark Smith; Gordon Good
1st Edition
$50.00
ISBN: 1-57870-070-1

This comprehensive tutorial provides the reader with a thorough treatment of LDAP directory services. Minimal knowledge of general networking and administration is assumed, making the material accessible to intermediate and advanced readers alike. The text is full of practical implementation advice and real-world deployment examples to help the reader choose the path that makes the most sense for the specific organization.

### Switched, Fast, and Gigabit Ethernet, Third Edition
by Sean Riley and Robert Breyer
3rd Edition
$39.99
ISBN: 1-57870-073-6

*Switched, Fast, and Gigabit Ethernet, Third Edition* is the one and only solution needed to understand and fully implement this entire range of Ethernet innovations. Acting as both an overview of current technologies and hardware requirements as well as a hands-on, comprehensive tutorial for deploying and managing switched, fast, and gigabit ethernet networks, this guide covers the most prominent present and future challenges network administrators face.

### Wireless LANs: Implementing Interoperable Networks
by Jim Geier
1st Edition
$40.00
ISBN: 1-57870-081-7

*Wireless LANs* covers how and why to migrate from proprietary solutions to the 802.11 standard, and explains how to realize significant cost savings through wireless LAN implementation for data collection systems.

### Wide Area High Speed Networks

by Dr. Sidnie Feit
1st Edition
$50.00
ISBN: 1-57870-114-7

Networking is in a transitional phase between long-standing conventional wide area services and new technologies and services. This book presents current and emerging wide area technologies and services, makes them understandable, and puts them into perspective so that their merits and disadvantages are clear.

### The DHCP Handbook

by Ralph Droms
and Ted Lemon
1st Edition
$50.00
ISBN: 1-57870-137-6

*The DHCP Handbook* is an authoritative overview and expert guide to the set up and management of a DHCP server. This title discusses how DHCP was developed and its interaction with other protocols. Also, learn how DHCP operates, its use in different environments, and the interaction between DHCP servers and clients. Network hardware, inter-server communication, security, SNMP, and IP mobility are also discussed. Included in the book are several appendices that provide a rich resource for networking professionals working with DHCP.

### Designing Routing and Switching Architectures for Enterprise Networks

by Howard Berkowitz
1st Edition
$55.00
ISBN: 1-57870-060-4

This title provides a fundamental understanding of how switches and routers operate, enabling the reader to effectively use them to build networks. The book walks the network designer through all aspects of requirements, analysis and deployment strategies, strengthens reader's professional abilities, and helps them develop skills necessary to advance in their profession.

# Software Architecture and Engineering

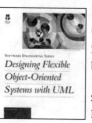

**Designing Flexible Object-Oriented Systems with UML**
by Charles Richter
1st Edition
$40.00
ISBN: 1-57870-098-1

*Designing Flexible Object-Oriented Systems with UML* details the UML, which is a notation system for designing object-oriented programs. The book follows the same sequence that a development project might employ, starting with requirements of the problem using UML use case diagrams and activity diagrams. The reader is shown ways to improve the design as the author moves through the transformation of the initial diagrams into class diagrams and interaction diagrams. The author continues offering tips and strategies for improving the design and ultimately incorporating concurrency, distribution, and persistence into the design example.

**A UML Pattern Language**
by Paul Evitts
1st Edition
$45.00, Winter 2000
ISBN: 1-57870-118-X

While other books focus only on the UML notation system, this book integrates key UML modeling concepts and illustrates their use through patterns. It provides an integrated, practical, step-by-step discussion of UML patterns, with real-world examples to illustrate proven software modeling techniques.

**Constructing Superior Software**
Paul Clements, et al.
1st Edition
$40.00
ISBN: 1-57870-147-3

This title presents a set of fundamental engineering strategies for achieving a successful software solution, with practical advice to ensure that the development project is moving in the right direction. Software designers and development managers can improve the development speed and quality of their software, and improve the processes used in development.

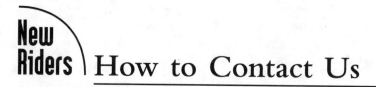 # How to Contact Us

## Visit Our Web Site

**www.newriders.com**

On our Web site, you'll find information about our other books, authors, tables of contents, indexes, and book errata. You can also place orders for books through our Web site.

## Email Us

Contact us at this address:
**newriders@mcp.com**

- If you have comments or questions about this book
- To report errors that you have found in this book
- If you have a book proposal to submit or are interested in writing for New Riders
- If you would like to have an author kit sent to you
- If you are an expert in a computer topic or technology and are interested in being a technical editor who reviews manuscripts for technical accuracy

**newriders@mcp.com**

- To find a distributor in your area, please contact our international department at the address above.

**nrmedia@mcp.com**

- For instructors from educational institutions who wish to preview New Riders books for classroom use. Email should include your name, title, school, department, address, phone number, office days/hours, text in use, and enrollment in the body of your text along with your request for desk/examination copies and/or additional information.

## Write to Us

New Riders Publishing
201 W. 103rd St.
Indianapolis, IN 46290-1097

## Call Us

Toll-free (800) 571-5840 + 9 + 4511
If outside U.S. (317) 581-3500. Ask for New Riders.

## Fax Us

(317) 581-4663

# We Want to Know What You Think

To better serve you, we would like your opinion on the content and quality of this book. Please complete this card and mail it to us or fax it to 317-581-4663.

Name_____

Address _____

City _____ State _____ Zip _____

Phone _____

Email Address _____

Occupation _____

Operating System(s) that you use _____

**What influenced your purchase of this book?**

❑ Recommendation ❑ Cover Design
❑ Table of Contents ❑ Index
❑ Magazine Review ❑ Advertisement
❑ New Riders' Reputation ❑ Author Name

**How would you rate the contents of this book?**

❑ Excellent ❑ Very Good
❑ Good ❑ Fair
❑ Below Average ❑ Poor

**How do you plan to use this book?**

❑ Quick reference ❑ Self-training
❑ Classroom ❑ Other

**What do you like most about this book?**
Check all that apply.

❑ Content ❑ Writing Style
❑ Accuracy ❑ Examples
❑ Listings ❑ Design
❑ Index ❑ Page Count
❑ Price ❑ Illustrations

**What do you like least about this book?**
Check all that apply.

❑ Content ❑ Writing Style
❑ Accuracy ❑ Examples
❑ Listings ❑ Design
❑ Index ❑ Page Count
❑ Price ❑ Illustrations

What would be a useful follow-up book to this one for you? _____

Where did you purchase this book? _____

Can you name a similar book that you like better than this one, or one that is as good? Why?

_____

_____

How many New Riders books do you own? _____

What are your favorite computer books? _____

_____

What other titles would you like to see us develop? _____

_____

Any comments for us? _____

_____

_____

_____

*DCE/RPC over SMB: Samba and Windows NT Domain Internals,* 1-57870-150-3

Fold here and tape to mail

----------------------------------------

New Riders Publishing
201 W. 103rd St.
Indianapolis, IN 46290